DATE DUE

DEMCO 38-296

Unity Temple: Frank Lloyd Wright and Architecture for Liberal Religion is the first comprehensive study of one of the seminal works of America's most renowned twentieth-century architect. In this study, Joseph Siry examines Unity Temple in light of Wright's earlier religious architecture, his methods of design, and his innovative construction techniques, particularly the use of reinforced concrete, which he here explored and expressively deployed for the first time. Siry also sets Unity Temple against the tradition of the liberal Unitarian and Univeralist religious culture, the institutional history of the Oak Park congregation that commissioned the building, and the social context in which the structure was conceived and built. Throughout, Unity Temple is treated as a work of art that embodies both Wright's theory of architecture and liberal religious ideals.

Unity Temple

Unity Temple

Frank Lloyd Wright and Architecture for Liberal Religion

Joseph M. Siry
Wesleyan University

CAMBRIDGE
UNIVERSITY PRESS

Published by the Press Syndicate of the University of Cambridge
The Pitt Building, Trumpington Street, Cambridge CB2 1RP
40 West 20th Street, New York, NY 10011-4211, USA
10 Stamford Road, Oakleigh, Melbourne 3166, Australia

First published 1996

Printed in the United States of America

Library of Congress Cataloging-in-Publication Data has been applied for.

A catalog record for this book is available from the British Library

ISBN 0-521-49542-3 Hardback

The longer quotations from Frank Lloyd Wright's *An Autobiography* are reproduced here by permission. Copyright © The Frank Lloyd Wright Foundation. Courtesy The Frank Lloyd Wright Archives.

Materials from Unity Temple's Historical Files and from the Unity Temple Collection, Oak Park Public Library, are used with permission of the Unitarian Universalist Church in Oak Park and Beacon Unitarian Church.

To my family

Contents

List of Illustrations

Acknowledgments

This project developed over eight years with the help, advice, and encouragement of many persons. Those who helped provide access to archival materials and photographs include Barbara Ballinger, former Head Librarian, Oak Park Public Library; former Rev. Frank Baldwin and Rev. Ed Bergstraesser, First United Church, Oak Park; Lorna Condon, Society for the Preservation of New England Antiquities, Boston; Rev. Thomas Chulak, First Unitarian Church of Chicago; former Rev. Scott Giles and Rev. F. Jay Deacon, The Unitarian Universalist Church in Oak Park; Rev. Neil Gerdes, Librarian, Meadville-Lombard Theological School, Chicago; Rev. Peter B. Godfrey, Minister Secretary, London District, Unitarian and Free Christian Churches, England; Elaine Harrington; Thomas Heinz, Evanston, Illinois; Michael Houlahan, Hedrich Blessing Photographers, Chicago; William Jerousek, Oak Park Public Library; Karl Kabelac, Manuscripts Librarian, Rush-Rhees Library, University of Rochester; Carol R. Kelm, Curator, The Historical Society of Oak Park and River Forest; Margaret Klinkow, Research Center Director, The Frank Lloyd Wright Home and Studio Foundation, Oak Park; Pat Kostopulos, Unity Temple Restoration Foundation, Oak Park; Daniel Meyer, Special Collections Department, The Joseph Regenstein Library, University of Chicago; Harold L. Miller, Reference Archivist, The State Historical Society of Wisconsin, Madison; Dreama Monty, formerly of the Unitarian Universalist Church in Oak Park; Oscar R. Muñoz, Administrator, and Bruce Brooks Pfeiffer, Director, The Frank Lloyd Wright Archives; Janet Parks, Curator of Drawings, Avery Architectural and Fine Arts Library, Columbia University; Franklin W. Porter, Richardson, Texas; Paul Rocheleau, Richmond, Massachusetts; Deborah J. Slaton, Project Architect/Historian, Wiss, Janney, Elstner Associates, Inc., Chicago; Philip A. Turner, Architectural Photography, Chicago; Wim de Wit, formerly Curator, Chicago Architectural Archive, Chicago Historical Society; Timothy N. Wittman, Commission on Chicago Landmarks; Mary Woolever, Architectural Archivist, Burnham Library, Art Institute of Chicago; and Linda Ziemer, Department of Prints and Photographs, Chicago Historical Society. Additional individuals and institutions are acknowledged in captions to photographs, and in the notes. If anyone who helped with this study does not see his or her name above, its omission is inadvertent, and their efforts are most appreciated.

The College Art Association granted permission for use of material from my earlier article on Unity Temple in the *Art Bulletin,* as did the Society of Architectural Historians for material from my article on the Abraham Lincoln Center in the society's journal.

Scholars and experts who have shared their knowledge and enthusiasm include Daniel M. Bluestone, University of Virginia; Robert J. Clark, Princeton University; Richard A. Etlin, University of Maryland; Robert A. Furhoff, Chicago; Rev. Thomas E. Graham, University of Winnipeg; John O. Holzhueter, State Historical Society of Wisconsin; Anthony Jones, Rector, Royal College of Art, London; John Quinan, State University of New York at Buffalo; Peter Reed, The Museum of Modern Art; Alan Seaburg, Curator of Manuscripts, Andover Harvard Theological Library, Harvard Divinity School; Lisa D. Schrenk, Department of Architecture, The University of Texas at Austin; Edgar J. Tafel, F.A.I.A., New York City; and the faculty and graduate students in the Program in History, Theory, and Criticism of Architecture, Massachusetts Institute of Technology.

My colleagues in the Program in History of Art, and throughout the Art Department, at Wesleyan University have been unfailingly and generously supportive of this project. Wesleyan provided a project grant and supplementary grants in support of scholarship to help defray costs of research and photographs. The late Stephen Lebergott, Head, and his colleagues at Interlibrary Loan, Olin Library, Wesleyan, were invaluably helpful at every stage. Also, my students over the last eleven years at Wesleyan have been a pleasure to teach and to learn from.

Dr. Beatrice Rehl, Fine Arts Editor, Mr. Alan Gold, Production Manager, and their colleagues at Cambridge University Press, have guided the book through to realization with reassuring dedication and skill.

Finally, my family has been deeply supportive beyond all measure throughout the long processes of research, writing, editing, and production. To them it is gratefully dedicated.

Introduction

UNITY Temple, which houses the Unitarian Universalist Church in Oak Park, Illinois, is among Frank Lloyd Wright's most renowned works of architecture. Its auditorium is one of the most distinctive rooms for worship in the United States, and architects from all over the world visit the building every year. Admired since its completion in 1909, Unity Temple's innovative form has made it a canonical work in the international history of modern architecture. This book analyzes the building both as a model of Wright's art and as a symbol of the liberal religious culture that the structure was to serve and signify. From these perspectives Unity Temple marks the intersection of Wright's philosophic and aesthetic agenda as an artist with those Unitarian and Universalist traditions of belief that his forms were meant to house and convey. Wright himself was raised in a liberal Unitarian spiritual and intellectual environment. Thus his creation of Unity Temple engaged his powers of synthesis and invention as an architect in the service of convictions and ideas that he had known from childhood. For these reasons, a historical account of this building must have a depth of facility in its treatment not only of the architecture, but also of the cultural context from which Unity Temple emerged and which its memorable form helped define, for both its creators and its audiences. In this way, the story of the building's creation connects both to Wright's other works in the period and to other narratives of regional and national liberal religion and its architectures around 1900. Unity Temple thus provides a point of entry into broader questions whose study enriches understanding of this singular work.[1]

* * *

Today a contemporary visitor encounters Unity Temple in an immediate context that is partially transformed from that at the time of the building's

FIGURE 1

Unity Temple, showing west front along Kenilworth Avenue, Oak Park, Ill., 1906–9. Frank Lloyd Wright, architect. Reprinted from *Ausgeführte Bauten von Frank Lloyd Wright* (Berlin: Ernst Wasmuth, 1911). © by Ernst Wasmuth Verlag GmbH & Co., Tübingen.

completion in 1909. The structure stands on the southeast corner of east–west Lake Street, Oak Park's axial main street, and north–south Kenilworth Avenue. Figure 1 shows the building's western flank along Kenilworth Avenue in 1909. At the time the suburban village of Oak Park was a community of about 18,000 residents, connected by streetcar and elevated railway to Chicago eight miles to the east. On Lake Street only the central roadway was paved for the streetcar line that ran at grade in front of Wright's site. Frame houses on ample lots flanked Wright's building to the east and west on the south side of Lake Street, as shown in a map from 1908 (see Fig. 58). One frame house stood on the southwest corner of the intersection across Kenilworth, where Oak Park's new post office was built in 1933. In 1909 nearby along Lake Street there were several larger mansions, including one on the northwest corner of Kenilworth owned by Edwin O. Gale, a prominent member of Unity Church who also owned the site on which Unity Temple would be built. Before the land was sold to Unity Church, the site was considered a prime location for Oak Park's village hall, in part because the land sloped down in three different directions.[2]

In 1909 the context for Wright's building was not only residential but institutional. North across Lake Street was the spired First Congregational Church, rebuilt after a fire of 1916; the structure can be seen there today

with a lawn to its west owned by the church. East of this church building was the original Scoville Institute, where the Oak Park Public Library now stands. Farther west on Lake Street stood the Grace Episcopal Church and the First Presbyterian Church, both of which still exist. These were the village's newest ecclesiastical structures when Wright designed Unity Temple, whose innovative forms were intended in part to stand in symbolic contrast to these neomedieval monuments.

Looking at Unity Temple from across Lake Street, one is confronted by the looming volume of Wright's auditorium – a room apprehensible but not directly accessible from outside. Walls of concrete, refaced for a second time in 1973–74, are unbroken above the two-stepped base as a visual and literal foundation that continues below ground. Atop the walls the auditorium's interior skylights are seen through clerestory windows screened by ornamental concrete columns beneath roofs shaped as slabs of concrete that cantilever 5 ft. beyond these columns. The instepped base of the wall below serves to accentuate by contrast the projection of the slabs above. Entry is not immediately visible, yet straight, level paths lead past the high, flanking walls to exterior steps set back from Unity Temple's front on its east and west sides. These steps, abutted by squared flower boxes of cast concrete, lead to the building's east and west entrance terraces.

Unity Temple's system of access is unusual for a church and was questioned when it was built. To approximate the convention of a front door, one observer recommended that the side walls to Unity Temple's west terrace be removed and that a flight of steps lead directly up to this terrace from Kenilworth Avenue. However, another local resident claimed that Unity Temple's chief attraction lay in its uniqueness: "Seeing it, one is curious. An open entrance tends to dispel curiosity. Much of the charm vanishes. But now one wonders what mysteries lie behind the wall. The fascination of the alluring days, when we reveled in fairy tales, returns. Our wondering selves are fairly drawn to the place beyond the wall. We are embarked on an adventure. And it impels us, sooner or later, to discover the coziness within. The mystery alone is enough to charm and win."[3]

Once on an entrance terrace, one is standing 60 ft. back from Lake Street, sheltered by the mass of Unity Temple and, across the rear of the site, the wider building of Unity House (used for social events and Sunday school). Above the doors to the foyer between Unity Temple and Unity House are words in bronze letters, designed by Wright, which convey the Unitarian ideal: "For the Worship of God and the Service of Man" (Fig. 2). Below, six doors with ornamental panels of clear glass framed in oak lead to the foyer. This room's 27-ft. width contrasts with its 9-ft. height to create a laterally expansive space. The carpet is set in a depression in the floor, sustaining its horizontal continuity. Surfaces are muted gray and yellow. On the south, through a clear panel of plate glass with flanking doors, one sees the skylit Unity House and its broad central fireplace (Fig. 3).

Inside Unity House, four hollow concrete columns denote its central

FIGURE 2

Wright, Unity
Temple, west en-
trance terrace
(Frank Lloyd
Wright Archives,
Photograph No.
0611.0019.
© The Frank
Lloyd Wright
Foundation).

volume of space flanked by balconies on the east and west (Fig. 4). Wright once envisioned inscriptions on these balconies, for which he designed folding screens of art glass that would partition them from the central space. The areas on the east and west sides of Unity House, on both the balcony level and the main floor, were to be used as Sunday school classrooms lit by continuous horizontal window bands. Wright had at first envisioned a mural over the fireplace on the south wall of this room. The capacious kitchen behind the south wall was designed to accommodate church suppers in Unity House (Fig. 5). In 1908 Wright organized one of the first events in this room, an evening gathering of Chicago's leading artists. If one turns to Unity House's north wall, stairs on either side rise behind the northern columns to the balconies (Fig. 6). Overhead, art glass windows of the pastor's study open into Unity House's central space. Above the concrete floors, the room's walls and ceilings are divided into fields of colored plaster by bands of oak, now stripped but originally stained a dark brown to complement yellow, green, and brown tones of the plaster and those of the art glass in the seven bays of the ceiling's skylight. Unseen above the ceiling plane are deep trusses that span the length and breadth of the room.

To enter the auditorium, one was originally meant to go through other interior doors that face west (left) or east (right) off the foyer's north side into spaces that Wright termed cloisters. Their floor is level with the foyer's. From these low, dark passages along the east and west sides of the auditorium, one was to mount the steps in the corners of the auditorium either to its main floor or to seating in its two levels of galleries (Fig. 7). Entry into the room for worship was thus elaborately indirect. As in many of Wright's residential designs of the period, in Unity Temple one ascends from a darker

FIGURE 3

Wright, Unity Temple, entrance foyer, interior looking southeast. Photograph by Thomas A. Heinz.

FIGURE **4**

Wright, Unity
House, interior
looking southeast.
Reprinted from
Cement World 2
(15 February
1909).

low entrance into a brighter high ceremonial room (Fig. 8). To go from Lake Street outside to a seat in Unity Temple's lower gallery, one makes no less than nine right-angled turns, as if the passage calls up the spatial experience of a labyrinth through different levels and conditions of light. The contrast between the wide, broad steps up to the terraces and the narrow, high steps between levels in the auditorium suggests the ancient and universal religious concept of the narrow path to salvation or a heavenly realm. Through changes in light, orientation, and level, the journey from street to sanctuary is made more complex and engaging than the conventional entrance sequence through a church's narthex directly into its nave. Wright may thus have intended to create an architectural metaphor for the difficult yet rewarding passage from the secular to the sacred. In this way, his proposed path of access to the auditorium has an archetypal quality.[4]

Once seated in a pew of the auditorium, one is removed from the world of the street outside, yet connected to light and air through the clerestory windows on all four sides. A brightness without direct sunlight pervades the auditorium, crowned by a skylit ceiling of twenty-five art glass panels. To one seated on the main floor, the auditorium appears cubic and vertically elevated in its proportions. Visual richness is concentrated at the front in the organ screen and pillars framing the central pulpit. As in Unity House, bands of oak delineate a complex visual system of colored planes. Yet in the auditorium, the colors are muted. Details finished in a cement plaster evoke the idea of the building as a monolith. Unity of spatial and material form signifies religious values.

If one is seated in an upper gallery, the compactness of Unity Temple's auditorium is apparent. By designing a space only 35 ft. wide between galleries on opposite sides, Wright created a room for worship that can seat 450 persons. Vertically tiered galleries on three sides enable worshipers to

FIGURE 5

Wright, Unity Temple, plan of entrance floor level (Frank Lloyd Wright Archives, Drawing No. 0611.064, © The Frank Lloyd Wright Foundation).

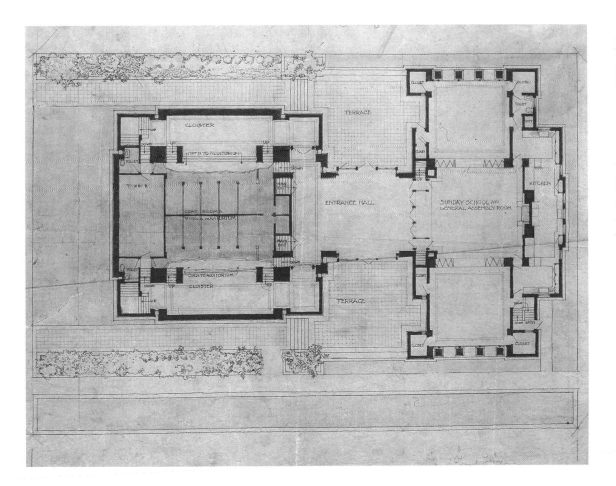

FIGURE 6

Wright, Unity
Temple, interior of
Unity House
looking north.
Photograph by
Philip Turner, for
Historic American
Buildings Survey,
HABS ILL, 16-
OAKPA, 3-5.

hear the voice of a speaker at the pulpit distinctly. Here the historic type of the meetinghouse has been reinterpreted in a modern structure and innovative aesthetic. One feels not only close to the pulpit, but part of a group of worshipers visually encountered on all sides. When congregants speak their voices are also easily heard. By virtue of the architecture, a worshiper in Unity Temple cannot be solely an observer but is spatially a participant.

Unity Temple's auditorium comes to life when its organ is played and hymns are sung. When Wright wrote of the room as "a good-time place," he perhaps alluded to the importance of music in this church's worship.[5] No feature of the auditorium preoccupied Wright's building committee more than the organ, whose every pipe and stop were detailed to insure a range and tonality that would enable music to provide the celebratory keynote of services. In this aim, Wright's idea paralleled precisely those of the church's leadership. Here his own experience of religious music, profound from early childhood, aligned with Unity Church's tradition of worship. Yet the music most often played on Unity Temple's organ was not Wright's favorite passages from Bach, but hymns written to convey liberal religious ideas equally well known to him.

To exit the auditorium, one was to descend the stairs on either side of the pulpit. At the bottom of these stairs the hinged panels of the foyer's north wall were to be swung open for egress into the foyer. The original description of the building noted that these panels were not to "be used as entrances at times of regular services."[6] When these panels were closed, they became part of the opaque wall separating the auditorium from the foyer (Fig. 9), unlike the clear plate glass panels and doors that join Unity House to the foyer on its south side (cf. Fig. 3). Wright thus made the room for worship distinct by contrasting its opaque walls and indirect access from the foyer with the glass walls and direct physical passage between the foyer and Unity House. Also, the foyer's plastered walls and ceiling, painted in an unaccented gray and yellow, are subdued relative to the more varied colors in Unity Temple and Unity House, thus marking the foyer as the room of arrival between these spaces.

* * *

Experiencing Unity Temple raises many questions about the building's origins, intentions, and reception. It is clearly a work of Wright, whose individual aesthetic is also found in his other buildings of the period. Yet here those forms serve the special purposes and character of a church. How was Unity Temple's architecture linked to Wright's other works as a developmental

FIGURE 7

Wright, Unity Temple, plan of auditorium floor level (Frank Lloyd Wright Archives, Drawing No. 0611.065, © The Frank Lloyd Wright Foundation).

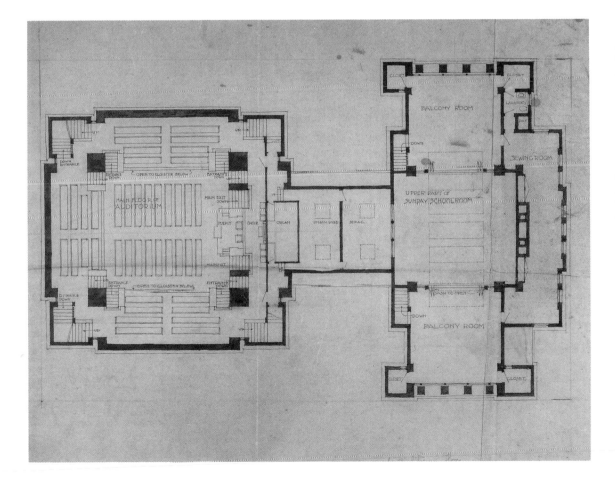

variation on his distinctive style? This structure was inventive and original to a high degree. Yet in its forms was Wright also assimilating a wide range of sources, both from historic architectural styles and from buildings of his own time, as resources for his creativity? When he was designing the build-ing in 1905, what architectures was he looking at, and how was he thinking of these in relation to his own artistic goals? How did Unity Temple relate to Wright's attitude toward modern expression in architecture? Specifically, how did his concept of its forms fit within a contemporaneous trend of experimentation with concrete as a new material, in his own and in Ameri-can architecture? How did Wright's building relate to his other buildings from this period associated with his family's liberal religious tradition? How was this tradition being defined by his Unitarian contemporaries, and how did views of what constituted a modern liberal religion shape expectations for and reactions to Unity Temple as architecture? Finally, how did Wright reshape perceptions of the building in his later life as part of his own historiography, and in relation to discussions in modern architectural cul-ture through the mid-twentieth century?

FIGURE 9

Wright, Unity
Temple, entrance
foyer looking
northeast. Photo-
graph by Thomas
A. Heinz.

The following chapters engage this range of questions in order to gener-
ate insight into Unity Temple from as many perspectives as possible. The
building marked a convergence of two dynamics: Wright's clarification and
elaboration of his style, and the theological and social ideals of regional
liberal religion in 1900. To reveal this process, one must critically reassess
Wright's own statements on Unity Temple in light of surviving documents,
drawings, and observation of the building itself. Such analysis does not
refute Wright's testimony, but offers a more complex and multifaceted story.
From such exploration, Unity Temple emerges as a synthesis of multiple
concerns. In its creation, stylistic, theoretical, programmatic, technical, environmental, and symbolic issues are all interrelated. Wright's early church
in Oak Park is inextricable from its historical contexts; yet, at the same time,
it is irreducible to those contexts. A close analysis of Unity Temple in
relation to Wright's thought and work illuminates this building as both an
intricately consistent, densely imaginative work of art and a focus for distinctive religious and cultural aspirations of its period.

1 Religious and Institutional Architecture of the Lloyd Jones Family

Lᴀᴛᴇ in his life, Wright maintained that he had always considered himself to be deeply religious. He often spoke generally of Nature and architecture in spiritual terms. In the late 1940s, however, while building the meetinghouse of the First Unitarian Society of Madison, Wisconsin, Wright stated more specifically: "I am a Unitarian, descended from Unitarian ministers on both my father's and mother's side of the family."[1] From his mother's family, the Lloyd Joneses, Wright had gained familiarity with their specifically Welsh tradition of Unitarian beliefs. This inherited faith was linked to a familial struggle for religious freedom going back to the early eighteenth century. Wright's first contact with the Unitarian tradition in the eastern United States dated from his father's brief pastorate at the First Baptist Church in Weymouth, near Boston, from 1874 to 1877, when Wright was in mid-childhood. As Wright later recalled, his "father had been a Baptist in that land consecrated to Unitarianism. But Unitarianism in the air and the mother's Unitarianism of a more colorful kind at home, must have had its effect, for the preacher resigned – a Unitarian."[2] From his resignation until his return to Wisconsin in April 1878, Wright's father began to give sermons and talks at Weymouth's Universalist Church. In that same year Wright began to live and work on the farmlands of the Lloyd Joneses during the summer months, a practice that continued until he entered the University of Wisconsin in 1885 at the age of eighteen, when his father was an active Unitarian in Madison.[3]

By the time Wright designed Unity Temple in 1905, his familial origins had led to his involvement in a series of experiments in new architecture for Unitarian churches. His maternal uncle, Rev. Jenkin Lloyd Jones, had been the patron of All Souls Church in Chicago, Unity Chapel in Wisconsin, and the Abraham Lincoln Center in Chicago. Wright was also the architect for the Hillside Home School in Wisconsin, commissioned by his maternal aunts, Jane and Ellen C. Lloyd Jones, who had founded the school. These projects developed from 1885 to 1905, the same period in which Wright had first apprenticed in architecture and developed his own practice. Wright's works for the Lloyd Joneses provided several points of reference for his design of Unity Temple, which similarly embodied the ideal of an architecture distinctly expressive of liberal religion.

All Souls Church and Unity Chapel

Jones advocated innovation in church building to serve his broad program for a radical reshaping of Unitarian life in the western United States. The distinction of Jones's ideas may be traced to his Welsh background. Born in Wales in 1843, Jones had been brought to the United States as an infant by his parents, Richard and Mary Lloyd Jones, who ultimately settled in the valley in southern Wisconsin where Wright later built his home, Taliesin. The Lloyd Joneses had a religious heritage anchored in the memory of their familial Unitarian chapel at Llwynrhydowen, Wales (Fig. 10), built in 1733 as a stronghold of dissent by Rev. Jenkin Jones, great-grandfather of Jenkin Lloyd Jones and founder of the Unitarian community in this region of Wales.[4] Settled in America, the Lloyd Joneses remained loyal to their religious ideals, whose Welsh origin made them distinct from Unitarian tradition in New England.

After military service in the Civil War, Jenkin Lloyd Jones studied for the Unitarian ministry. His wide-ranging early denominational service found its permanent pastoral focus in November 1882, when he founded All Souls Church in the Oakwood neighborhood on Chicago's South Side. In his inaugural sermon, entitled "The Ideal Church," Jones envisioned the new institution as "a free congress of independent souls," which would "stand upon a grand emphasis of the great word of the century, UNITY. . . . This church will seek to welcome high and low, rich and poor, better and worse, believer and unbeliever."[5] While remaining nominally Unitarian, All Souls Church would not ask its members to subscribe to a creed.

Wright's uncle imagined this new kind of church housed in an innovative type of building that signified its religious ideals. His church obtained a site on the southeast corner of Oakwood Boulevard and Langley Avenue (Fig. 11, B) and Jones presented his ideas on design in a sermon of May 1885 on "The New Problems in Church Architecture,"[6] when he unveiled plans made by Joseph L. Silsbee (1848–1913) for a new building for All Souls Church.[7] A Unitarian, Silsbee was related to Jones's colleague, Rev. William C. Gannett, who introduced Silsbee to Jones in 1885.[8] Though Silsbee became architect of All Souls Church, it was later reported that "the conception and plan of the building belong to the Rev. Jenkin Lloyd Jones."[9] While Wright's uncle admired the original medieval cathedrals, he asserted: "The modern church [built] after the conventional cathedral type is an obvious anachronism."[10] Jones believed that in American cities of his time,

FIGURE **10**

Unitarian Chapel,
Llwynrhydowen,
Wales, 1733. Re-
printed from
Chester Lloyd
Jones, *Youngest
Son* (Madison,
Wis., 1938).

the idea of church as cathedral was giving way "to the finer ideal of many smaller homes, where those of like mind and taste band themselves together with home-like ties. The individual will not allow himself to be lost in the crowd, not even a crowd of devotees. In the coming church the presence of each will be recognized, and the absence of any one will be felt."[11]

To Jones, a church building should be like a residence, for the congregation "is the larger family and its building must be made the larger home."[12] In this vein Jones asked rhetorically: "Would you build us a house of worship? O architect, build it low with humility, and make it warm with human tenderness." He commanded: "Build us, . . . O architect, a building whose very walls will be instinct with human fellowship and human needs. Flood it with sunlight and fill it with pure air."[13] Wright's uncle emphasized that he did not want the new type of church building to be less beautiful than the old, for "the line of beauty ever tends to the line of truth. The rational faith will only demand that the architect recognize the broad distinction between the conventional and the genuine in art."[14]

In June 1885 Jenkin Lloyd Jones published the sermon containing these ideas together with floor plans of the proposed building for All Souls and a perspective sketch of its exterior signed by Silsbee (Fig. 12).[15] Jones urged: "Let architects give us buildings so simple, earnest and ethical that they will present no external excrescence."[16] The building was begun in March 1886 and dedicated in October of that same year. Jones believed that the new home for All Souls would stand "for a religious faith broader than its walls, simpler than even its architecture."[17] Silsbee's final design for All Souls Church, like his earlier drawing, does not emphasize the auditorium on the exterior (Fig. 13). Instead, the visible street fronts on both levels convey the building's residential character. Wright later recalled his impression that Silsbee's design appeared "in no way like a church, more like a 'Queene Anne' dwelling. . . . I went along Oakwood Boulevard to look it over in perspective."[18] A view of the auditorium in 1890 shows a level hall for varied events generously lighted by windows on its side walls and by a large central skylight (Fig. 14). The room was like an expansive parlor, as if to express the motto carved on its foyer's mantel: "Here Let No Man Be Stranger."[19]

Frank Lloyd Wright's contact with All Souls Church may have begun in December 1884, when his father preached there.[20] The *All Souls Church Fourth Annual*, dated 6 January 1887, is the first to list Wright as a member, with a Chicago address a few doors away from that of Jenkin Lloyd Jones.[21] This implies that Wright came to Chicago sometime during 1886. Such a date for Wright's arrival in the city corresponds to his recollection that he first saw All Souls as a "nearly completed building,"[22] implying that he had first visited the church between its groundbreaking in March and its dedication in October 1886. That Wright began working with Silsbee while All Souls Church was being built is suggested by a drawing of All Souls Church signed by Wright (Fig. 15). This drawing resembles an unsigned sketch of the new church, published in the *All Souls Church Third Annual* in the winter of 1886, which has been attributed to Silsbee (Fig. 16).[23] Silsbee's drawing, appearing just before construction began, shows the exterior almost as built, differing in a number of details from his earlier perspective published in June 1885.

* * *

If Wright came to Chicago to begin working for Silsbee between March and October 1886, then his entry into architecture there coincided with his

FIGURE **11**

Environs of All Souls Church, Chicago, ca. 1900, showing (A) site of future Abraham Lincoln Center, (B) All Souls Church of 1886, (C) Holy Angels Church, (D) Oakland Methodist Church, and (E) Memorial Baptist Church. Rascher Fire Insurance Map of Chicago, originally prepared in 1896.

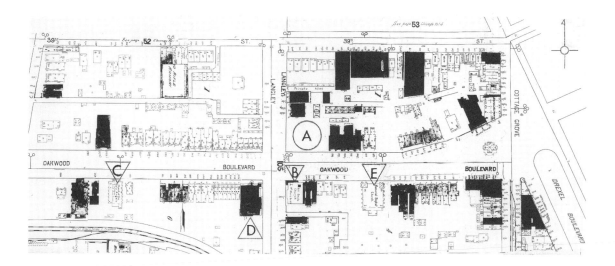

uncle's greatest influence with Silsbee, for Jenkin Lloyd Jones was then the client not only for All Souls Church (Silsbee's first commissioned church in Chicago),[24] but also for Unity Chapel in Helena Valley, Wisconsin, intended as a familial memorial and site for local worship. Jenkin Lloyd Jones's father, Richard, had dreamed of such a building in memory of the eighteenth-century chapel at Llwynrhydowen. In 1879 a new chapel was built near this one. On his first journey overseas to Europe in summer 1882, Jenkin Lloyd Jones made a pilgrimage to his homeland and preached in this new chapel, then famous as a regional landmark of Unitarian belief.[25]

While rooted in Jones's familial history, Unity Chapel was also intended to be a prototype for smaller, inexpensive rural church buildings for liberal congregations throughout the Western Unitarian Conference. Jones sought a simple but expressive type of building to house new congregations. His colleague, Rev. William Channing Gannett, wrote: "A thousand valleys are waiting for this type of churchlet to-day, – something homelike within, a grace without, and buyable with very humble means."[26] Wright's early unbuilt 1887 design for a chapel in Sioux City, Iowa, embodied this ideal for a congregation that had been founded with Jones's support in 1885. The rusticity and simplicity of such buildings were pragmatic and symbolic, so that, as one contemporary wrote, "our church buildings will speak truly of our aims."[27]

FIGURE 12

All Souls Church, Chicago, proposed design of 1885. Joseph L. Silsbee, architect. Reprinted from *Unity* 15 (20 June 1885).

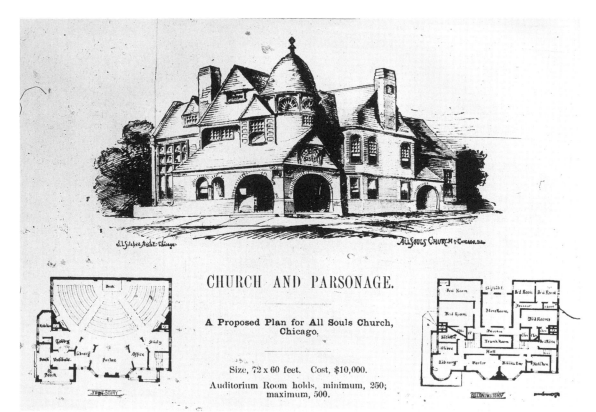

CHURCH AND PARSONAGE.

A Proposed Plan for All Souls Church, Chicago.

Size, 72 x 60 feet.   Cost, $10,000.

Auditorium Room holds, minimum, 250; maximum, 500.

In August 1885 Jenkin Lloyd Jones presided over a large annual grove meeting near the site of the future familial chapel in Wisconsin, announcing that $600 of its projected cost of $1,000 had been raised. He expressed the hope that the structure would be ready for dedication the following summer. On 22 August, within days of the grove meeting, Frank Lloyd Wright wrote to Jones, noting that "I have forwarded to you today my preliminary sketches for 'Unity Chapel.' I have simply made them in pencil on a piece of old paper but the idea is my own and I have copied from nothing. Any changes which you think proper or anything to be taken off if you will let me know I will make it to satisfy you. . . . Wise and I have figured it up and it can be built for 10 or 12 hundred."[28] The drawings to which Wright refers are not known, and as late as October 1885, it appears that the chapel's architect had not been selected, for Jones then wrote that "they are only waiting for the plans at Helena, Wis., before beginning work on that model, three-room country church. . . . Where is the architect who will show us how to do something in this line, prettier and more practical than anything yet embodied between the Atlantic and the Pacific?"[29]

Shortly afterward, Silsbee had developed a design for the chapel, which Jones published in *Unity* in December 1885 (Fig. 17). In Silsbee's sketch, the chapel's plan shows an audience room with a round-edged platform at its front. At the room's rear, a broad portal frames passage to a separate

FIGURE **13**

Silsbee, All Souls Church, Chicago, 1886, view from northwest. Reprinted from *Abraham Lincoln Centre [and] All Souls Church; Reports for 1912.* Photograph courtesy of Oak Park Public Library, Oak Park, Ill.

FIGURE 14

Silsbee, All Souls
Church, audi-
torium in 1891.
Reprinted from
*All Souls Church
Eighth Annual,*
1891. Courtesy
of Meadville-
Lombard Theo-
logical School
Library.

parlor equipped with a fireplace, to one side of which are a kitchen, porch, and vestibule. This arrangement recalls the axial continuity of auditorium and parlor in All Souls Church, an idea later developed in alignment of Unity House with Unity Temple. At Unity Chapel, "this convenience is intended to facilitate the holding of Sabbath schools and other literary exercises. Also to have a department serve as dining room during church festivals."[30] The sketch, which is signed "J. L. Silsbee Architect," resembles another perspective of Unity Chapel subsequently published in the *All Souls Church Fourth Annual* of January 1887, which Wright signed as delineator and which is cited as the earliest of his published drawings (Fig. 18).[31]

Construction of Unity Chapel proceeded simultaneously with that of All Souls Church, and the projects were related in Jones's view of his ministry. Later Jones's stationery letterhead depicted the two buildings, one at the edge of the city and the other in the valley, beneath a banner reading: "In the interest of Morality and Religion, and to promote Truth, Righteousness and Love in the World" (Fig. 19). In style Unity Chapel (Fig. 20) resembles All Souls Church, "built somewhat after the Queene Anne pattern."[32] For

FIGURE 15

Silsbee, All Souls Church, drawing signed by Frank Lloyd Wright in lower right. Reprinted from *Prairie School Review* 7 (Fourth Quarter 1970).

ALL SOULS CHURCH AND PARSONAGE, CHICAGO,
Cor. Oakwood Boulevard and Langley Ave.

FIGURE 16.

Silsbee, All Souls Church, drawing attributed to Silsbee. Reprinted from *All Souls Church Third Annual,* 1886. Courtesy of Meadville-Lombard Theological School Library.

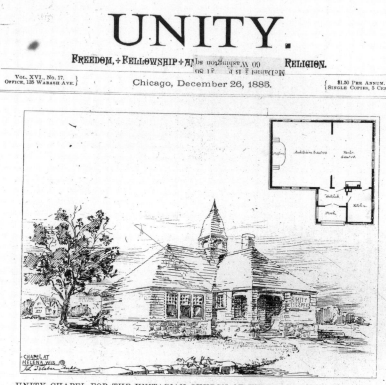

UNITY.

FREEDOM, + FELLOWSHIP + AND   RELIGION.

VOL. XVI., No. 17.   Chicago, December 26, 1885. $1.50 PER ANNUM.
OFFICE, 135 WABASH AVE.   SINGLE COPIES, 5 CENTS.

UNITY CHAPEL FOR THE UNITARIAN CHURCH OF HELENA VALLEY, WISCONSIN.

Above is a perspective sketch of the little chapel now in process of erection at the above place for the above society, of which mention was made in our last issue. This society was the first ever organized by the senior editor of this paper, and has been the object of his missionary care ever since. Now these walls are going up with a special memorial significance, for it will be consecrated to the memory of the parents from whom he received his religious faith. The building is 43 x 28, with porch and kitchen extension. The auditorium is to be 15 feet high in the clear. The underpinning to the level of the window-sill is of rock-faced broken ashlar, quarried in the neighborhood, and now completed. The roof and exterior walls above stone work are to be covered with stained shingles. The architect is J. L. Silsbee, of this city, the one who has planned the All-Souls church for the editor's other parish in this city, and we publish it as a suggestion to other societies. We are disposed to claim for it the greatest success yet attained in the way of an economical, rational, three-room church. It is all that most of our smaller and newer societies need to begin with. We hope it will be duplicated in other societies, or else surpassed. We know of no one better equipped for giving the rational combination of beauty and economy than the architect of this plan, and are glad to commend him, and recommend building committees to correspond with him.

FIGURE 17

Silsbee, Unity Chapel, in what was formerly the village of Helena, Wis. Reprinted from *Unity* 16 (26 December 1885).

about 3 ft. above its floor level, Unity Chapel's "underpinning to the level of the window sill is of rock-faced broken ashlar, quarried in the neighborhood," its "sides and roof being shingled with material soaked in oil. The exterior of the wooden part is stained a dark brown with creosote stain."[33] Shingled walls make Unity Chapel a taut-skinned volume above its base. The chapel has hipped roofs that converge beneath a belfry set near the hearth's chimney in Silsbee's picturesque residential style. Unity Chapel's shingled walls bring to mind Gannett's likening of it to a cottage or school-

UNITY CHAPEL, HELENA, WIS.

FIGURE 18

Silsbee, Unity
Chapel, 1886,
drawing signed by
Frank Lloyd
Wright below
chapel entrance.
Reprinted from
*All Souls Church
Fourth Annual*,
1887. Courtesy
of Meadville-
Lombard Theo-
logical School
Library.

house, types of buildings wherein the Lloyd Joneses and their neighbors had met before the chapel's completion. Its L-shaped asymmetrical massing may recall the T-shaped form of the eighteenth-century chapel at Llwyn-rhydowen. A Welsh-born mason, David Timothy, set the walls of the new Llwynrhydowen chapel of 1879 before he emigrated to the United States, where he set the foundations and walls of Unity Chapel seven years later.[34] These two buildings more than an ocean apart were crafted by the same man, underscoring the degree to which Unity Chapel signified the transplanting of familial religious traditions from the old world to the new.

Unity Chapel's architecture was presumably meant to be distinct from that of other churches in its region, such as the Congregational Church in nearby Spring Green, as shown in a photograph of 1909 (Fig. 21). This church's squared sanctuary was crowned by a gabled rather than a hipped roof as in Unity Chapel. The chapel's door had a covered porch, unlike the central pedimented door on the street front of the Congregational Church. The church featured horizontal clapboards, pilastered corners, and cornices where walls met roofs and gables. Walls were painted rather than stained, and there was no stone base to visually and symbolically tie the Congregational Church to the earth like Unity Chapel's. The Congregational Church's windows were evenly separated to mark the nave's volume within, whereas Unity Chapel's windows were grouped in threes to suggests a quasi-

FIGURE 19

All Souls Church
and Unity Chapel,
as depicted on
letterhead of
Jenkin Lloyd
Jones, 1899. Wil-
liam Channing
Gannett Papers,
Department of
Rare Books and
Special Collec-
tions, University
of Rochester
Library.

domestic interior. The ogival profile of Unity Chapel's belfry contrasted with the squared tower atop the Congregational Church's entrance. Clearly Silsbee's chapel was a building whose shapes, materials, and colors blended with the countryside in which it was situated and where its congregants lived their lives.

Unity Chapel is set in a grove of fir trees planted by Thomas Lloyd Jones, a brother of Jenkin. The grove shelters the south side of the chapel, east of which are the Lloyd Joneses' familial graves (Fig. 23, A). The chapel's interior is a simple, memorable space (Fig. 22), in part because even within its small auditorium, there is a pervasive sense of the land surrounding the building. Wherever one looks while inside the chapel, windows frame views of fields and hills in which it is set, just as its siting in the landscape was depicted on Jones's stationery. As completed, "the interior is finished with filling and oil-finish, giving the clear pine timber its naturally light color."[35] Wright later claimed to have designed the chapel's ceiling as a set of concentric squares of oak bands. His role in the making of Unity Chapel is suggested in Gannett's account of its dedication in August 1886, which noted that both the parlor and auditorium "are wood ceiled, with the pine in its own color; one is calcimined in terra cotta, one in olive green; – a boy architect belonging to the family looked after this interior."[36] Wright later recalled: "This family chapel was the simple wooden temple in which the valley-clan worshiped the images it had lovingly created and which in turn reacted upon the family in their own image."[37] Unity Chapel's siting and symbolism continued to hold significance for Wright throughout his life.[38]

The Hillside Home School

Wright's building most closely related to Unity Chapel was the Hillside Home School of 1887 (Fig. 23, B), sited to the northwest of the chapel on

February 27, 1899.

Religious and
Institutional
Architecture of
the Lloyd Jones
Family

FIGURE 20

Silsbee, Unity
Chapel, 1886,
from northeast.
Photograph by
Ernest Hailey.
Courtesy of Hai-
ley's Photography.

FIGURE 21

Congregational
Church, Spring
Green, Wis., as
seen in 1909.
Photograph by
Sherwin Gillet.
Courtesy of the
State Historical
Society of
Wisconsin,
WHi-(G5)-1897.

FIGURE 22

Unity Chapel, in-
terior looking
northeast (Photo:
author).

the Lloyd Joneses' farmlands. However, the structure whose binuclear plan
and massing most directly anticipated the concept of Unity Temple was the
second Hillside Home School, the main parts of which were built in 1901–
2 (Figs. 23, C and 24),[39] just west of the first school building. Both of these
structures responded to the intentions of the school's founders and its principal teachers, Ellen C. and Jane Lloyd Jones, Wright's maternal aunts. They
were sisters of Jenkin Lloyd Jones, who promoted the school's programs and
helped fund them. Jones's summer religious retreat, Tower Hill, was close
by. Like academies developed by Unitarians near their chapels in Wales,
the Hillside Home School, as Ellen Lloyd Jones wrote to William C. Gannett
in 1886, was to be "a permanent, good Unitarian school, for that is what it
must be in its essence whatever we may call it."[40]

As their parents' only unmarried daughters, Jane and Ellen Lloyd Jones
had inherited their parents' farm and house when Richard Lloyd Jones died
in 1884. This event drew them back to the familial lands from teaching
positions elsewhere and, in 1887, they opened their school "on the site and
in the original frame of [their] pioneer father's farmhouse,"[41] which became
the original residence for the school's pupils from beyond the valley. This
building stood on the parental farmlands surrounded by homesteads of
three of the founders' brothers, many of whose children attended the
school. At first, the Lloyd Jones sisters planned to use Unity Chapel for their
school's classes, yet by the spring of 1887 they had amassed sufficient funds
to build a new structure that would house both bedrooms and classrooms.
Their parents' farmhouse was moved across the road from its original site,
and, on this now vacant spot, Frank Lloyd Wright designed the school's first

new building in 1887 while he was working for Silsbee. As at Unity Chapel the year before, David Timothy set the stone for the school's foundations. Hillside Home School's architecture reflected its institutional philosophy, which emphasized a homelike environment in nature as a context for both academic studies and work, play, and worship in the surrounding country.[42]

After the school occupied this structure for fourteen years, increased attendance prompted the Lloyd Jones sisters to build a new school. In 1901 they commissioned Wright to design "a scheme where the efficiency of our work will be very much enhanced," and which was estimated to cost $8,000.[43] The new Hillside Home School's assembly room was named the Roberts Room, after Charles E. Roberts, a main supporter of the school and of Wright's Unity Temple. This room faced south, while the classrooms to its west extended to a rectangular gymnasium, which doubled as a theater (Fig. 25). Built of sandstone as a base for oak mullions and timbers originally upholding a roof of red tiles, the school from the exterior has a balanced asymmetry closely linked to the slope of its landscape. Wright later cited the

FIGURE 23

Taliesin and environs in the 1930s, showing (A) Lloyd Joneses' Unity Chapel and Hillside Home School buildings of (B) 1887 and (C) 1901–2. Drawing by John H. Howe. Courtesy of the Northwest Architectural Archives, St. Paul, Minn.

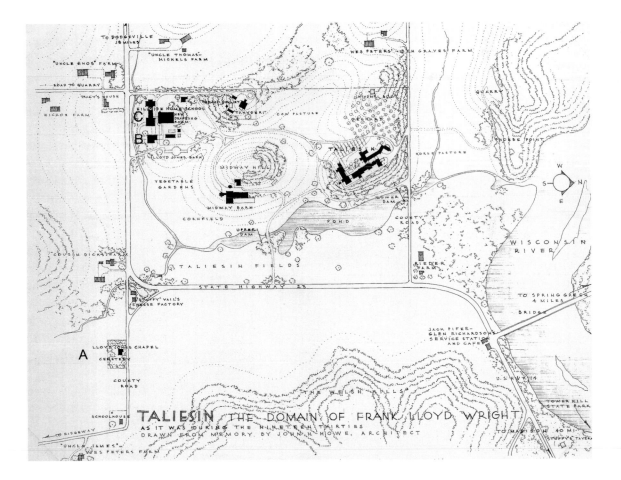

school's independently projecting forms of the assembly room and gymnasium as his early exercise in the distinct articulation of spatial parts as discrete masses.[44]

The school building not only was intended to effectively house the school's noted progressive educational program, but also was designed as a memorial to its founders' Welsh parents, Richard and Mary Lloyd Jones. Their sons contributed to the school's curricular and residential life. These Lloyd Jones brothers, together with neighbors whose children were also students, helped build the new building. The project had been initiated after Ellen and Jane Lloyd Jones, accompanied by Anna Lloyd Wright (Frank Lloyd Wright's mother), journeyed to Wales and visited the village of their parents in the summer of 1899.[45] When construction of Wright's new building for their school was nearing completion in November 1902, the sisters wrote that "The architect, Frank Lloyd-Wright, has given us a beautiful and ideal building, and something very much out of the ordinary. He, together with the principals, desired to make it in a way a memorial to his Welsh grandparents, and the whole building is suggestive of the old Celtic structures of Wales. The inside finish is of oak, sacred to the old Druids, and so with these beautiful associations and its delightful completeness it is a great joy to our principals."[46]

At the turn of the century Druidic monuments were seen as the most primitive kinds of religious building in English and Welsh cultural history. Druidic sites were thought to include Stonehenge, which was discussed and illustrated in Charles Knight's *Old England*, a book that Wright knew as a child. His younger sister Maginel recalled of their mother: "Sometimes in the evening she read to me from a great book called *Old England*. A lot of it

was over my head but I did love the parts about Stonehenge and the Druids."[47] Knight introduced Stonehenge as "the most remarkable monument of antiquity in our island," whose site in a plain of Salisbury "would seem to be the cradle of English civilisation."[48] While earlier observers thought that Stonehenge was Roman, by the 1840s "the belief now appears tolerably settled that Stonehenge was a temple of the Druids. It differs, however, from all other Druidical remains, in the circumstance that greater mechanical art was employed in its construction."[49] Knight's volume included a sheet of engraved reconstructions of Stonehenge contrasted with its extant state (Fig. 26).

Wright may also have known Emerson's later response to Stonehenge. In 1848, just before returning to America from a second journey to England, Emerson saw the site. Struck by the broad plain surrounding the ring of stones, he wrote: "It looked as if the wide margin given in this crowded isle to this primeval temple were accorded by the veneration of the British race to the old egg out of which all their ecclesiastical structures and history had proceeded. . . . It was pleasant to see that just this simplest of all simple structures – two upright stones and a lintel laid across – had long outstood all later churches and all history, and were like what is most permanent on the face of the planet."[50] Emerson viewed inquiry into antiquities like Stonehenge as a way of connecting the present to the thought of the past.[51]

Jenkin Lloyd Jones brought a similar perspective to his encounter with

FIGURE 25

Wright, Hillside Home School, main floor plan, and balcony floor plan of Roberts Room. From *Ausgeführte Bauten und Entwürfe von Frank Lloyd Wright* (Berlin: Ernst Wasmuth, 1910), Plate X(b) (Frank Lloyd Wright Archives, Drawing No. 0216.004. © The Frank Lloyd Wright Foundation 1994).

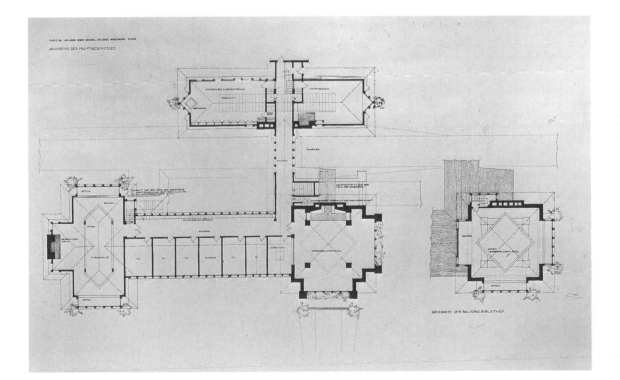

FIGURE 26

Stonehenge, Salisbury Plain, Wiltshire, England, ca. 2000 B.C. Reprinted from Charles Knight, *Old England* (London, 1846).

Stonehenge on his first visit to England in 1882. After pilgrimages to many cathedrals and ruined abbeys across the countryside, he noted that "from Stonehenge, the group of gray-stone giants clustered on the lonely plain, to Salsbury [sic] cathedral, the most perfect poem in stone, it seems to me, of all English cathedrals, is but a short distance of seven or eight miles in space, but it is a great, great distance in the history of religion and the growth of human thought and skill."[52] Yet Jones, perhaps following Emerson's famous views, wrote of a link between primitive and later religious monuments. Jones concluded that Stonehenge and Salisbury Cathedral "alike testify to the reality of religious sentiment and the inherent sincerity of the devout heart."[53]

On 31 December 1900 the only one of Stonehenge's monoliths to topple in over a hundred years was blown down in a gale. This event triggered a new wave of interest in the monument's origins. In April 1902, just as Wright's new Hillside Home School was being built, Jones's *Unity* announced that "Stonehenge is at last receiving the attention of archeologists, the absence of which was so lamented by Emerson in his day. It is said that in some recent handling of the fallen monoliths, that implements of the new stone age were discovered. This places the weird, inscrutable temple anterior to the bronze age. Earlier than 1500 B.C. is a ventured date."[54] The archaeological report of Sir William Gowland to which *Unity* referred concluded that Stonehenge's date was so remote as to preclude its having been created by the Druids. However, the myth of a Druidic presence at Stonehenge endured through the Edwardian period.[55]

Jones's interest in Stonehenge was linked to a familial preoccupation with its origins in Wales, where similar sites were thought to have been the settings for rituals of Druids in antiquity. The motto Wright ascribed to the Lloyd Jones family, "Truth against the World," believed to have been a phrase of Druidic origin, had been adopted by the Welsh poet Iolo Morganwg (1747 1826). He saw a direct link between the imagined pure Druidic religion and the rational religion of modern Welsh Unitarians.[56] The Lloyd Joneses had adopted this motto to signify their Unitarian religious ideas in the face of orthodox Anglicanism. In this spirit Jenkin Lloyd Jones cited the phrase in a sermon of 1879 to oppose what he called "The Religion of the Majority,"[57] much as Wright's usage of the motto signified his opposition to conventional developments in architecture.

In keeping with the Lloyd Joneses' familial legends, Wright's new building for the Hillside Home School was meant in part to convey Welsh and Druidic associations. As Jane Lloyd Jones later recalled, when she and her sister Ellen "determined to put up their school building, [they] would make a memorial Assembly Room which was also to serve as the chapel for the school, where the school would congregate during the vesper service of a Sunday evening. They told the architect that they wanted a Welsh feel about that room which the material, Druid oak and stone, would make possible."[58] The assembly room's outer sandstone walls and four internal piers support both a balcony and the roof (Fig. 27). The balcony's four inner sides form a square turned forty-five degrees off the orientation of the surrounding room, creating the image of a diamond set within this room's plan (Fig. 25). The balcony, originally to be the school's library, is supported by four stone piers. Each pier holds a pair of large oak beams that support one side of the floor of the balcony. These supporting beams project diagonally inward from near the room's corners. These beams are upheld by brackets on either side of each stone pier. The ends of the beams toward the center of the room are visible beneath the balcony fronts that the beams uphold (Fig. 28).

When the school's assembly room was built, the sisters expected that their nieces and nephews would continue the school to perpetuate the memory of their grandparents. On the great sandstone chimney breast in the assembly room's north wall there is carved a quotation from Gray's "Elegy in a Country Churchyard." It was selected "for the mother's sake," because this was the poem that Mary Lloyd Jones had learned in childhood and recited from memory almost in its entirety on the day of her death nearby, which Ellen and Jane Lloyd Jones and their siblings had witnessed in 1870:

FIGURE 27

Wright, Hillside Home School, Roberts Room, interior looking north. Courtesy of the State Historical Society of Wisconsin, WHi-(x3)-23644.

> Oft did the harvest to their sickle yield;
>   The furrow oft the stubborn glebe has broke;
> How jocund did they drive their team afield!
>   How bow'd the woods beneath their sturdy stroke.[59]

Inscribed above on the lowest fascia of the balcony are the first and last verses from Isaiah 40, a text recited by Richard Lloyd Jones at familial worship services.[60] This paternal immigrant is also recalled in the tall conical andirons, whose shape alludes to his trade as a hatter.[61] On the stone

above the fireplace was carved in Welsh a motto of the clan, which Jenkin Lloyd Jones and Wright both cited: "Truth against the World," a clear allusion to the familial religious stance and its Unitarian origins in south Wales. As in Unity Chapel, stone for the new Hillside Home School came from the Lloyd Joneses' nearby family quarry. The stone was set and the chimney mantel carved by David Timothy, who also carved a stone mantel for the hearth of the old school building.[62] Oak timbers in Wright's new school came from hills on the Lloyd Joneses' property.[63] An account of 1902 stated: "This plain but almost stately room is in reality a subtle memorial to them whom Druidic oak and enduring stone here typify, to them who, trusting, sailed forth to break the glebe of a new empire. Cenotaph, then, in spirit is this honest, beautiful room."[64]

Not only was the assembly room a memorial. It was also designed to be the central familial room of the school. The school met there for daily morning devotions, Sunday evening vespers, and special occasions.[65] On Sunday mornings, the school's faculty and students conducted religious services in Unity Chapel. In the assembly room, original casement windows had diamond-shaped leading framing colored glass. This complemented the light stone, the pink-red mortar, and the dark brown staining of the oak surfaces. Only 17 ft. wide between its four piers, this room's height, its light

FIGURE **28**

Wright, Hillside Home School, Roberts Room, interior looking west. Courtesy of the State Historical Society of Wisconsin, WHi-(x3)-23643.

and air from tall windows on three sides, its extraordinary structure, and its position on the slope combine to make it memorable, monumental, and of its place. Of all Wright's works to 1902, the room's form and character begin to approximate the later auditorium in Unity Temple. The later church's design brought together certain elements of Hillside Home School's assembly room with others from the larger more civic auditorium that Wright was designing for the Abraham Lincoln Center in these same years.

The Abraham Lincoln Center in Chicago

By the time the second Hillside Home School was completed in 1902, Wright had been at work on designs for Jenkin Lloyd Jones's Abraham Lincoln Center for five years. If the Hillside Home School represented an educational ideal in the country, Jones's center signified a social commitment to its city through an institutional transformation of All Souls Church. Though the smallest and youngest of Chicago's four Unitarian congregations, All Souls Church soon filled its residentially styled quarters with an expansive program of religious, educational, and social activities intended for the surrounding middle-class neighborhood of Oakwood. In the 1890s Jones's congregation was nationally recognized as a leader in the movement toward creation of institutional churches in major cities across the United States. This movement, which crossed denominational lines, minimized theological differences in favor of nonsectarian programs of civic reform and social action. To realize this vision of All Souls as a force for improving life in Chicago, Jones's colleagues were discussing plans for enlarging or replacing Silsbee's building only two years after it was built.[66]

By 1891 the trustees of All Souls decided to purchase 100 ft. of frontage across Oakwood Boulevard, opposite the church (Fig. 11, A).[67] In the fall of 1892 Jones chose the tenth anniversary of the church's founding to offer a first public statement about its future facility, which he thought "would really be the first of its kind in the world."[68] Instead of envisioning the new building as a house like the first, Jones initially proposed a multistory structure in which each level would house different activities. The first floor was to be "devoted to the development of the physical man." It would include baths, a gymnasium, and a bowling alley as facilities for an athletic club to be created within All Souls Church as a source of income. The second floor would be "set apart for man's spiritual and intellectual needs" and would thus contain an auditorium, a library, and reading rooms. The third story would be given over to the church's charitable work: its free kindergarten, a manual training school, and "domestic science" classes. The fourth through sixth floors would contain offices rented to doctors, dentists, and others serving the neighborhood, studios rented to artists, and rented apartments. The topmost seventh floor would be devoted to amusements. Its large hall and refectory could be rented for "amateur theatricals, concert purposes, lectures, and dancing parties."[69] Jones's church was to be the central tenant of this structure, envisioned as a familiar Chicago architectural type of an auditorium in a commercial block.

The new building's ideological character emerged more clearly over the next few years. In 1893 Jones helped organize the World's Parliament of Religions, as one among several conferences that focused on humanity's intellectual achievements since Columbus. The parliament's sessions met in the new Art Institute during the Columbian Exposition (Fig. 29). Jones and his colleagues negotiated with religious bodies from all over the world to schedule a meeting of their representatives to offer a comprehensive presentation of what all faiths believed. Held in September 1893, the parliament demonstrated to Jones "the essential unity of all religious faiths," with their universal emphasis on an ethical life, rooted in divine belief and focused on humane service.[70] The parliament prompted progressive religious leaders to work for the spiritual unification of humanity.

The following year marked a turning point for All Souls Church in response to the parliament's program, which related to ongoing debates among American Unitarian leaders. From the 1880s Jenkin Lloyd Jones and other western liberal Unitarians had opposed creedal tests for membership in the Unitarian denomination, while eastern Unitarians continued to support doctrinal affiliation with Christianity. In 1894, at the meeting of the National Unitarian Conference in Saratoga, New York, liberal and conservative Unitarians agreed that the conference should include in the preamble to its constitution a general statement of religious and ethical beliefs that its member churches accepted.[71]

Jones, who did not attend this meeting, did not accept the concept of a creedal test of belief. As an alternative he had founded the American Congress of Liberal Religious Societies, which convened for inaugural meetings

FIGURE 29

World's Parliament of Religions, Chicago, 1893, showing Jenkin Lloyd Jones (circled) on far right of platform. Reprinted from Rev. John H. Barrows, *The World's Parliament of Religions* (Chicago, 1893).

in May 1894 in Chicago's Sinai Temple. The congress sought to unite all who were "in sympathy with the movement toward undogmatic religion, to foster and encourage the organization of non-sectarian churches and kindred societies on the basis of absolute mental liberty."[72] On 13 May 1894, in a sermon on the congress that was to convene the following week, Jones called for the withdrawal of All Souls Church from the Unitarian denomination. In his view this step entailed the church's repayment of a total debt of $7,000 to the American Unitarian Association in Boston, which had stipulated that the building of 1886 be used as a Unitarian church. In order to free All Souls Church from this sectarian identity, Jones proposed to his congregation that they pay back these funds and then rewrite the church's bylaws, so that it would no longer be controlled by Unitarian denominational policies but, rather, "be a part of the fellowship of universal religion."[73]

Jones asked his church to leave the 1886 building, and build a new structure across Oakwood Boulevard that would be dissociated from All Souls' Unitarian origins. He stated that "we hope to build an institution that will appeal not to Unitarians alone, and whose work will not be distinctly Unitarian, but rather non-sectarian, humanitarian, a seven-day helper in the neighborhood, receiving support from many of differing faiths or denominational inheritances and helping many not affiliated with the Unitarian name or, necessarily, the Unitarian thought."[74]

Jones intended to house a newly independent All Souls Church in a much larger building, whose monumental scale would give its mission an architectural presence in its urban context comparable to that of medieval cathedrals.[75] In February 1902, after $100,000 had been pledged toward a new All Souls Building, Jones gave a sermon entitled "The New Cathedral: A Study of the Abraham Lincoln Centre," in which he set forth his vision of the new structure. For Wright's uncle, "the cathedral at its noblest is the best outward symbol of the spiritual nature of man, as it is also the most suggestive measure and prophecy of the corporate life of man. . . . It recognized, to an extent unrealized by any other building ever reared by the hands of man, the *com-unity*, the common life of those who dwell together."[76]

In his own time Jones observed the historic styles of religious architecture revived in smaller churches of varied denominations. Such a building was the Oakland Methodist Church (1886–87) on the south side of Oakwood Boulevard (Fig. 11, D) across Langley Avenue from Silsbee's All Souls Church and diagonally across the intersection from the site of Jones's Abraham Lincoln Center. This church, with its corner tower, is extant, as is Normand S. Patton's second building for the Memorial Baptist Church of 1899 (Fig. 11, E), which features a square tower above its large centrally planned auditorium. Also Romanesque in style, this building has varied brickwork framing its round-arched openings at all levels. The most elaborate new monument was the Roman Catholic Holy Angels Church to the west (Fig. 11, C), designed by James Egan in 1896–97. This nonextant work,

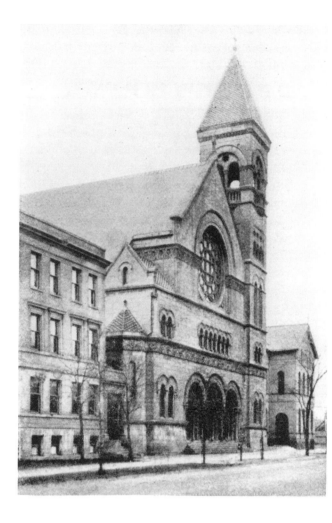

FIGURE 30

James J. Egan,
Holy Angels
Church, Chicago,
1896–97. Re-
printed from Rev.
J. E. McGavick,
*History of Holy
Angels Parish,
1880–1920.* Pho-
tograph courtesy
of the Arch-
diocese of Chi-
cago Archives
and Records
Center.

which Jones had admired as "very beautiful architecture," featured motifs of French Romanesque origin, from its triple-arched portico to the shaft of its tall bell tower. Walls of Bedford limestone had bands of intricately carved ornament (Fig. 30).[77]

To differentiate the new All Souls from the churches in its immediate urban context, Jones envisioned a building both modern in style and large in scale, as removed in its way from conventions of ecclesiastical architecture as had been Silsbee's All Souls Church of 1886. The new building's nonsectarian program was to encompass the concerns of its entire district; hence its avoidance of identification with styles of nearby churches would signify institutional outreach to all. Jones asserted that "in some new fashion, through fresh instrumentalities and up-to-date methods, religion and morals are yet to find cathedral expression. . . . Is there no need of some new corporate expression of the ethical sense of the community, of the religious life of the twentieth century? Is there not a new cathedral-building spirit to be born?"[78]

Modernity of style and novelty of type were to signify that the new All Souls would be engaged with the daily life of its city. Jones's building would be a participant in, not a sanctuary apart from, its community. The edifice would be a work "of modern architecture, gracious though not gorgeous, representing in its lines dignity, hospitality, and service, a building with four faces, each honest and clean, no pretense on the boulevard that is shamed by a slovenliness on the alley."[79] Its auditorium would be "not large but attractive, not sumptuous but artistic, refined and comfortable, with the maximum of light, the best of air; an auditorium that will be an open congress hall for everything that pertains to public weal, to civic advancement, as indeed the old cathedrals were, and on that account all the more a place for prayer, hymn and sermon in proper season."[80]

In early 1900 Jones had first proposed the Abraham Lincoln Center as the name for his new building. He set aside the name of All Souls because the new institution was to be legally separate from the parent All Souls Church. Jones proposed that it be called a center in order to suggest the centrality of divinity in the life of the institution, which in its acceptance of all people thus "has a center but no circumference."[81] In his view, this center would be a prototype for others that would be built in Chicago and elsewhere.[82] Jones chose to name the center after the president under whom he had served in the Union Army for most of the Civil War.[83]

The earliest dated document linking Wright to the new All Souls building is a letter from him to Jones of 15 May 1894, two days after Jones announced withdrawal of All Souls Church from the Unitarian denomination and his aspiration to build a new structure across Oakwood Boulevard from the 1886 church. By this time Wright had been practicing alone for about a year. He asked his uncle: "How about the plans for the new building? Am I to get a chance with the rest of the boys, or is it an open and shut walk away for Silsbee[?] . . . I do not want to let any architect walk off with a building with which an uncle of mine is concerned, without making some desperate effort to meet things half way."[84]

By January 1898 Wright and Dwight H. Perkins (1867–1941) were working informally as architects for Jones's new church building.[85] Wright and Perkins had not only known each other as members of All Souls, but the two architects had also shared office spaces on the top floor of Steinway Hall. This tall building, completed in 1897 as Perkins's first major independent commission, housed shops on its street floor, a theater seating 850 on a second and a third level, and eight stories of offices above.[86] Construction of Steinway Hall had given Perkins experience with a type of building not dissimilar to that which Jones envisioned for the new All Souls. Wright himself had yet to design such a multistory, structurally complex building on his own, though he had claimed for himself a role in the design of such projects while he had worked for Adler and Sullivan, including the firm's Schiller Building of 1892–93, which had a large theater below office floors.[87]

In January 1898 Perkins presented ideas at the church's annual meeting, but Wright claimed to be the main architect of the project. In February he wrote to his uncle: "If I can be of service to you in further promoting the interests of the 'Church scheme' let me know what I can do and it shall be done – Perkins has done nothing but the talking, so far all the expense has been borne by me. . . . I am glad and willing to do everything in my power to help you realize the 'church building,' both for your sake and my own too."[88] Wright and Perkins were publicly announced as architects for a new All Souls Church building in November 1898, and by February 1899, Jenkin Lloyd Jones wrote to his colleague, Rev. William Channing Gannett: "My big scheme is still of course a big one at which we are working as diligently as possible. . . . Dwight Perkins and Frank Wright have been at it now (on pay and under contract) for nearly two months. We have had two full meetings of the board on two full sets of plans and any number of minor ones have been splintered. The main features are very satisfactory, but there are so many things to avoid that it requires not only a great amount of creative genius but a great amount of patience to work it all out straight but they are at it heroically." Jones then added: "Frank is a boy of great artistic feeling and much power. He can hardly be said to be a 'success' yet although he has done some very fine things and is much complimented by the profession but he has not the hustle and the get-there of a successful man."[89]

Wright and Perkins exhibited a design for Jones's new building at the Chicago Architectural Club's annual exhibit of April 1900 (Fig. 31).[90] Plans show church offices and rooms around the main entrance hall at street level (Fig. 32). Stairways were to lead up from either side of the entrance foyer to the second floor, which was the main level of the auditorium. This main level included several tiers of seating with a continuous peripheral corridor at the level of the topmost tier. The auditorium's gallery, whose plan is not shown, formed the building's third floor. Above the third floor were to be six additional stories for varied tenants and church activities, including a large skylit hall on the top level behind the crowning parapet. The floor plans were based on a square module of 7 ft. 6 in. as the distance between pier centers along the outer walls.

The drawing of the exterior shows the nine-story block, apparently free from adjacent structures on all sides, with its front facing west on Langley Avenue. These elevations give almost no hint of the existence of the varied internal functions of successive floors – among them, the auditorium, the principal space in the plan. As Robert Spencer had written, the scheme is "characterized by an austere repression of decorative detail, and with its rifted outer walls of solid brick construction sprung from a broad stylobate, its powerfully stiffened corner piers and clean cornice reduced to a mere molded coping, it will stand like a great rock of progress in practical Christianity and art."[91]

Wright and Perkins's project of 1900 has been compared to Adler and

FIGURE 31

Wright and
Dwight Heald
Perkins, All Souls
Building, Chi-
cago, project of
1900. Reprinted
from *Chicago Ar-
chitectural Club
Annual,* 1900.

Sullivan's Wainwright Building in St. Louis of 1890–92, on which Wright claimed to have worked and which he considered to be an admirable prototype for design of the tall office building as a new architectural type.[92] That Wright and Perkins's design of 1900 resembled the Wainwright recalls Jones's initial proposal of rentable offices on the upper floors of the Abraham Lincoln Center. Yet, in the Lincoln Center's exterior, Wright proposed a monumental form derived in part from its distinctive system of construction. Walls of Wright and Perkins's project were to be of "buff-colored pressed brick and terra cotta moldings of the same color and texture."[93] The Wainwright's exteriors are carried by a steel frame that also supports its interior floors. Yet the Lincoln Center's outer walls were to be load-bearing piers of solid brick, with a skeleton of steel columns and beams inside the building to support the weight of its interior floor areas and brick partitions. Such a shell of masonry encasing a metal frame derived from Chicago commercial projects like Adler and Sullivan's Meyer Building of 1893, on whose design Wright claimed to have worked.[94]

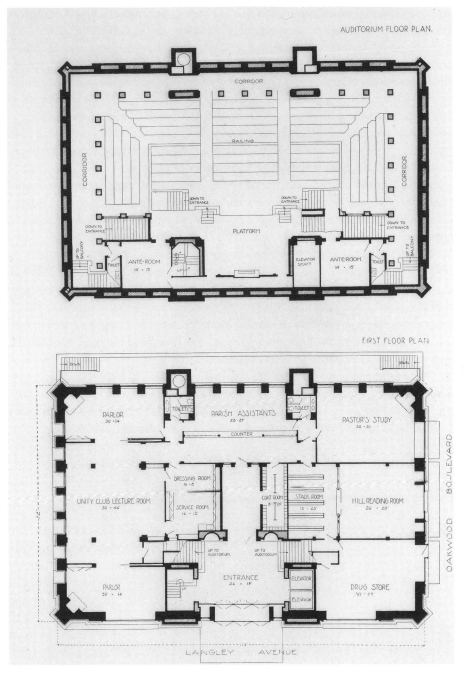

FIGURE 32

Wright and Per-
kins, All Souls
Building, project
of 1900, plans of
first and second
floors. Reprinted
from *Chicago Ar-
chitectural Club
Annual,* 1900.

As a brick edifice, the Abraham Lincoln Center would be more monolithic than the Wainwright in order to represent Jones's ideal of unity. This
concept underlay the choice of a nearly uniform brick for exteriors. Vertical
brick panels between the piers to either side of the central entrance bay
denote the location of a staircase and elevators inside (Fig. 31). An eighth-
story loggia is formed by the pier capitals in front of recessed glazing. The

resulting shadows accentuate the massiveness of the solid planar attic story above with its stepped flared cornice. Unlike the Wainwright, for which Sullivan had designed a program of ornamental terra cotta on its upper floors, the Abraham Lincoln Center was to have its plain brick exterior almost entirely devoid of ornament. In these ways, Wright inflected the model of the Wainwright to serve the ideological aim of his uncle, creating a new form for an All Souls now distanced from its Unitarian origins.

When Jones gave his programmatic sermon on "The New Cathedral" in February 1902, Wright and Perkins had revised their project of 1900. In March 1901, at Jones's request, they sent their plans for the building to architect Ernest Flagg in New York for his candid criticism, noting that it had been their intention to shape "a housing for a practical educational institution in this Machine Age," with a design that "tries to make something dignified of it honestly."[95] Flagg, educated at the Ecole des Beaux Arts and by then one of the most important and innovative eastern architects, had not built in Chicago. He had, however, made well-publicized Neo-Renaissance designs for the National Episcopal Cathedral of Saints Peter and Paul at Washington, D.C., in 1895, for which he was not ultimately selected as the architect. In his unbuilt design for this cathedral, Flagg had favored the centralized auditorium rather than the longitudinal nave as the optimal spatial form for modern Protestant churches, emphasizing the need for unobstructed visibility, better acoustics, and fireproof construction. Flagg tested these ideas in his realized plans for the Farmington Avenue Church in Hartford, Connecticut, of 1897–99, where the auditorium is clearly expressed on the exterior.[96]

In his reply to Wright and Perkins regarding the design for the Abraham Lincoln Center, Flagg found their plan to be "orderly, logical and convenient as far as I am able to judge except that I doubt if the large hall will be sufficiently light." He then offered this critique of the elevations:

> In regard to the decorative clothing of the plan, I think it might be improved. The exterior does not tell the story of the interior, there is nothing to indicate the presence of the great hall, and the general appearance is heavy and forbidding. . . .
>
> I must say that I am unable to place myself quite in what appears to have been your point of view. It seems to me that the design is too coldly logical, and that you have reasoned all the poetry out of it. You have stripped it of the time honored conventionalities of architecture and have given nothing to supply the void. I am an advocate of progress, but I do not think we should relinquish what we have without replacing it by something better.[97]

In May 1901 Jenkin Lloyd Jones wrote to Wright, urging him to give Flagg's suggestions "prayerful consideration," and adding that "I do believe that somehow the auditorium ought to shine on the outside. Can't you put an eyebrow over it and so arrange at least the upper tier of windows so that there will be a crystal belt of light horizontally emphasized, encircling the building, inviting the outsiders in and reassuring them, when once in, that they have not been trapped."[98] Jones encouraged his nephew not to be discouraged by his own and Flagg's suggestions, for he reminded Wright that he and Perkins were working on a novel kind of building, concluding that the center "is a mighty innovation and from the first my fundamental anxiety has been an architectural and not a financial one."[99]

Perhaps in response to Flagg's critique, Wright agreed to develop a new elevation, and from June through December 1901 Jones repeatedly requested that Wright send him such a drawing. By 2 January 1902 it was agreed to reduce the size of the building, though Jones advised Wright against radical change in the plans, urging his nephew to keep on perfecting the existing plans and concentrate on "improvement of the exterior."[100] Jones hoped to begin building in the spring of 1902, perhaps to show good faith to those who had donated funds,[101] and in January he pressed Wright for elevations incorporating his ideas. Jones wrote to his nephew: "May I ask you to put your constructive work on to it *for all* you are worth right away? Show us the best you can do in this direction. It is an *architectural problem* that will make or break your reputation, the chance of your lifetime."[102]

A revised design for the new Abraham Lincoln Center was exhibited with Wright's work at the Chicago Architectural Club in March 1902, though when published this design was credited to Wright and Perkins as associated architects.[103] The published watercolor rendering shows the proposed center with its longer main front still facing west onto Langley Avenue (Fig. 33). The auditorium occupied the tall second and third levels behind tall casement windows of ornamental glass. Wright's revised exterior of 1902 perhaps responded to Flagg's and Jones's concern that the auditorium be given a distinctive external identity. The main change evident in the plans of 1902 was a reduction in the number of stories above ground from nine to six. The reduced height of the 1902 design, which covered the same ground area as that of 1900, increased the visual importance of the exterior's horizontal lines.

Like the ornamental crowning cornice, the short squared columns on the upper loggia were to be of cast concrete.[104] Rows of columns screening bands of glass behind anticipated Wright's use of this motif in Unity Temple. Yet Jenkin Lloyd Jones was critical of this feature, writing to Wright that he should "throw away those short pillars, thirteen of them on the Langley Avenue side, that give the loggia effect to the upper story and bring the windows out flush. The fine belt of plain wall which you have given above and below will mean more when you get those meaningless pillars that hold nothing up, out of the way. Do not be fooled by your window gardening, for we are not in Italy. . . . In the wintertime those ledges will simply catch snow drifts and form icicles to stain the walls below and crack them." In general Jones concluded: "I believe you can scrape off several thousand

FIGURE **33**

Wright and Perkins, Abraham Lincoln Center, project of 1902. Reprinted from *Chicago Architectural Club Annual,* 1902. Photograph courtesy of The Art Institute of Chicago.

dollars worth of minor lines, counting the four sides, and still retain the major lines or something better."[105]

In an updated letter to his uncle, Wright responded to concerns like those Jones raised in his letter, including those regarding the loggia on the fifth floor. Wright tried to assure his uncle that "the loggia story is *anything but dark*[.] 13' – 0" of clear daylight on three sides of a room 24 × 60 is fierce without something to soften the glare." Wright claimed that "the loggia is essential to the life and character of the building, the feature calculated 'to lend verisimilitude to an otherwise bald and uninteresting narrative.' . . . I *know* and would *stake my life* that you will like it when you know it."[106]

*   *   *

After the building committee expressed serious doubts about the design, Jones had to intervene to keep Wright from being removed from the project. He persuaded the building committee to give Wright and Perkins until 12 August 1902 to present a much revised project, whose "cost must not exceed $110,000 including architects' fees."[107] Jones stressed that in order to abide by the committee's desire for a less costly design, the exterior was to be radically simplified: "So I beg of you to throw to the winds once and forever all thoughts about 'monumental' construction, effects, and the like.

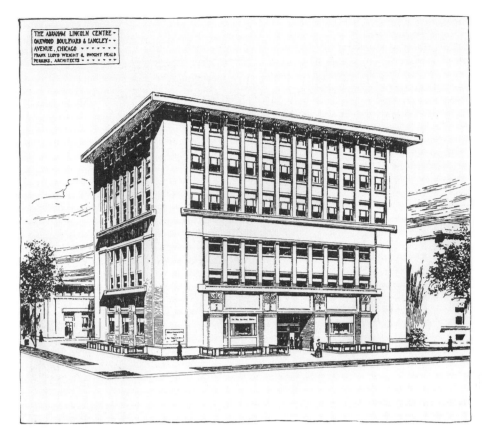

THE ABRAHAM LINCOLN CENTRE · OAKWOOD BOULEVARD & LANGLEY · AVENUE , CHICAGO · · · · · · · FRANK LLOYD WRIGHT & DWIGHT HEALD PERKINS . ARCHITECTS · · · · · ·

FIGURE 34

Wright and Per-
kins, Abraham
Lincoln Center,
project of 1903.
Reprinted from
*All Souls Church
Twentieth Annual,*
1903. Courtesy
of Meadville-
Lombard Theo-
logical School
Library.

My monument will not be built, I trust, in brick and mortar – certainly you have no commission of that kind. So throw away as much of the present exterior as you possibly can based on that idea. I have pled for simple lines, plain exterior, for artistic and ethical reasons as well as *economic*. If the first reasons do not carry with you the last must. . . . 'Schools,' orders and styles of architecture to the winds; the only radical architect is the architect who is free to use whatever serves his purpose in any way he can. . . . If any *one* person is building this Lincoln Centre it is Jenkin Lloyd Jones. . . . I want no more debating exercises over the history and philosophy of architecture. I want a building." Jones reminded Wright and Perkins that though they had made common cause in the face of the committee's threat to their continua-tion on the project, through August 1902, the plans for the Abraham Lincoln Center had "never represented but the judgment of one," meaning Wright. Before Wright and Perkins consulted outsiders, they had better consult with each other, because, for Jones's purposes, "the wisdom of two is better than the wit of one."[108]

Jones kept after his nephew through the autumn of 1902, yet Wright continued to demur over the matter of the façade. Finally, in February 1903, Jones approved another design for the new center, which was published by Easter (Fig. 34). This carried the names of Wright and Perkins as associated

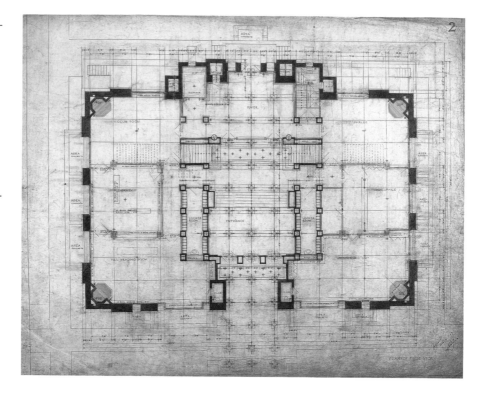

architects. The trustees noted that "from funds especially provided, 25 feet of additional land was purchased adjoining the lot on the east, which permits the building to be fronted on Oakwood Boulevard and assures good light on the east side."[109] The plans approved by Jones showed the entrance floor (Fig. 35) almost as it was later built, with a broad central lobby and long stairways on both sides that rise to the auditorium on the second floor (Fig. 36). The platform of the auditorium was now on the north side of the room, with tiered seating on the main level and galleries above on the east, south, and west. The east–west section (Fig. 37) shows the building to be a square, the total height from the basement floor to the skylight's crown being equal to the building's east–west breadth. The same ratio of 1:1 or unity pervaded Wright's later design for Unity Temple. The interior perspective of the auditorium (Fig. 38) shows this space extending across the full width of the building to permit daylight from windows all around. The seating on the main floor and in the galleries is arranged in stepped tiers. The interior shows plastered surfaces bordered with strips of dark oak around the room, except its outer walls and outer ring of square piers, which were envisioned in brick. The lowered parts of the central ceiling express the structural beams, which span from the front to the back of the room. The main brick piers on each side of the frontal platform were hollow to serve as risers for mechanical ventilation. In such features, the design of

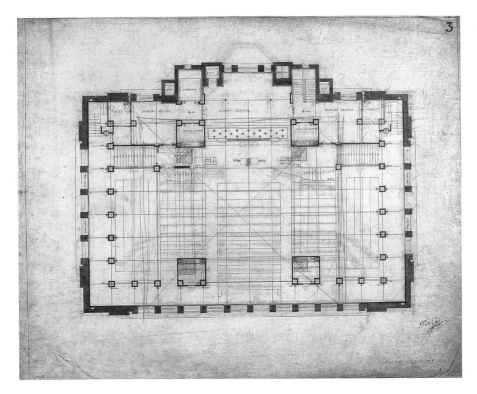

FIGURE 36

Wright and Per-
kins, Abraham
Lincoln Center,
project of 1903,
second-floor plan.
(Frank Lloyd
Wright Archives,
Drawing No.
0010.005, © The
Frank Lloyd
Wright Founda-
tion 1991).

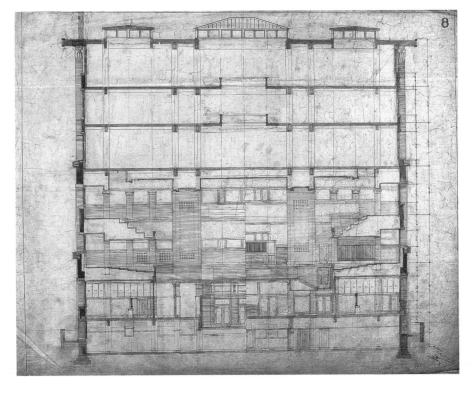

FIGURE 37

Wright and Per-
kins, Abraham
Lincoln Center,
project of 1903,
longitudinal east–
west section
(Frank Lloyd
Wright Archives,
Drawing No.
0010.011, © The
Frank Lloyd
Wright Founda-
tion 1991).

1903 for Lincoln Center's auditorium anticipated Wright's plans of 1905 for Unity Temple's auditorium.

The 1903 design did address Jones's concern for a clear expression of the auditorium, and the church's annual report noted that "in the opinion of the [Building] Committee the plans have been greatly improved."[110] Yet the design still did not satisfy Jones's desire for rigorous simplicity of exterior expression. In addition, Wright had yet to complete plans and specifications sufficiently detailed for potential builders to show to subcontractors in order to permit them to prepare definite bids. This final delay proved to be the breaking point in Wright's relationship with his uncle, for by the spring of 1903 Jones and his committee turned to Dwight Perkins as their "constructing architect" to prepare for building. Wright's sister later wrote of Wright and his uncle: "Those two were never meant to build together, they couldn't agree on anything. Neither would compromise. . . . Finally, despite his mother's pleadings to both of them, Frank withdrew."[111] In June, Perkins signed a new contract with the building committee "as architect succeeding Perkins and Wright" for superintendence of the construction, for details of iron and carpentry work, and for the design of an "elevation satisfactory to Jenkin Lloyd Jones with all constructive detail appurtinent thereto."[112] Perkins, too, soon became exasperated with Jones's involvement, yet he did stay on to fulfill his contract by supervising the center's construction from groundbreaking in June 1903 through its formal dedication in May 1905.[113]

In its urban context today, the Abraham Lincoln Center has a distinctly vertical appearance, notably tall compared with buildings in the district around it. As built, upper walls were deep red brick, with horizontal bands of chocolate brick between floors (Fig. 39). Jones approved this brick, so that in its surfaces the building would interpret "the spirit in which this

FIGURE **39**

Abraham Lincoln
Center, Chicago,
view from south-
west, with All
Souls Church of
1886 at right and
Jenkin Lloyd Jones
(circled) with
white beard and
light suit near
center, during
meeting of the
National Uni-
tarian Conference,
1909. Jenkin
Lloyd Jones Col-
lection. Courtesy
of Meadville-
Lombard Theo-
logical School
Library.

Centre is reared, – simple dignity and plain honesty, – for these constitute the first and indispensable elements of good art everywhere."[114] Jones had tried to erase typical differences between front and rear in a center "of fireproof construction, built 'four-square,' the same material and architectural honesty carried all around."[115] Wright later employed concrete for all the exterior surfaces of Unity Temple in Oak Park, perhaps to signify the same ideals of simplicity and honesty. Wright's solution for the north or rear wall of the Abraham Lincoln Center contains projecting brick towers that house an elevator, a staircase, and ventilation flues (Fig. 40). As architectural expressions of internal functions, the projecting masses in the rear of the Lincoln Center anticipate Wright's detached corner stair blocks in his later Larkin Building (Fig. 41) and Unity Temple (cf. Fig. 1).

The auditorium of the completed center was first opened for services on Easter 1905 (Fig. 42). Fifty years later Wright claimed that the interior as finished had been of his design, though the exterior "belonged to my uncle

FIGURE **40**

Abraham Lincoln Center, view from north. Photograph © Philip A. Turner.

FIGURE **41**

Wright, Larkin Company administration building, Buffalo, N.Y., 1904–6 (Frank Lloyd Wright Archives, Photograph No. 0403.030, © The Frank Lloyd Wright Foundation).

J[enkin] Ll[oyd] Jones and Dwight Perkins."[116] Wright's sister recalled: "I will never forget Frank's white, furious face the Sunday the church was dedicated, when he saw printed on the announcement, 'Architect, Frank Lloyd Wright.' Mother, who had had a difficult time to persuade him to come at all, had all she could do to keep him in his seat. I think Uncle Jenk thought he was doing Frank justice. After all, the original plans were his."[117]

When it opened, the auditorium was described as "unique in shape and if there had been fears in the minds of any for its acoustic properties these were speedily set at rest, for every word was distinctly audible in the farthest corners of the room. . . . If you have ever been half resentful of the darkening of the light of day as it filtered through stained glass windows into 'dim cathedral aisles,' you would have rejoiced in the yellow glass of these windows, distilling a flood of amber light and glorifying the very sunlight." The yellow color of the glass was keyed to that of the brick, which, "with the rich dark brown of the severely plain weathered oak trimmings, produced a harmony delightful to the eye and restful to the spirit."[118]

In scale, the auditorium for Abraham Lincoln Center was like a civic hall, whereas Unity Temple's smaller auditorium is distinctly a sanctuary for worship (see Fig. 8). Yet, like the center, Unity Temple has raised alcoves of tiered seats below galleries on three sides of its central floor of seats facing a frontal raised platform. Both rooms are visually and structurally anchored

by four main hollow columns, which are the sole internal supports for the beams in the ceiling. Light enters both spaces from clerestories on several sides, though Unity Temple's auditorium also had central skylights. While the temple's interior was of cement-finished concrete, its visual treatment with a linear system of dark oak bands outlining planar surfaces was anticipated in the Lincoln Center. The auditorium of the center may thus be understood as Wright's earlier essay in the kind of architectural space whose details he would further integrate in Unity Temple.

Unity Church in Oak Park to 1905

T HE same regional denominational culture provided the context for the creation of both the Abraham Lincoln Center and Unity Temple. In May 1905, when the center opened, the congregation of Unity Church in Oak Park was discussing the question of whether to build a new structure. Like Jones's Abraham Lincoln Center, Unity Church had been founded to provide a center for liberal religious life in a community dominated by more theologically and socially conservative churches. Wright would design Unity Temple not only as an exploration of his novel architectural aesthetic, but as a symbol of Unity Church's identity, both to itself and in the eyes of its community. Unity Temple would convey meanings for its congregation that derived from the church's role in Oak Park and were linked to earlier Unitarian architecture with which its minister had been familiar.

Unity Church and Earlier Unitarian Architecture

In January 1871 Universalist and Unitarian members of Oak Park's original Union Church formed a separate Church of the Liberal Christians in Oak Park, which was soon renamed Unity Church. From its origins, Unity Church was closely identified with Universalism. In 1884, when its membership numbered about 125 persons, three-fourths of these were Universalists and one-fourth were Unitarians.[1] Universalists, who traced their origin and growth to Massachusetts from the 1770s, historically held to belief in the idea of universal salvation, maintaining that after death all persons would eventually be reconciled with their Creator.[2] The chief precept of Unitarian thought was a belief in the oneness or unity of the Divinity. Both Universalist and Unitarian positions were at the liberal forefront of religious life in the early United States.[3] In Oak Park, this meant that Universalists and Unitarians sought the simplest possible statement of their beliefs in a single article of faith: "We believe in God, the Father Almighty, maker of heaven and earth, and desiring to erect and maintain a church to be devoted to His worship wherein each member shall be allowed every liberty of thought and opinion consistent with such belief, we do hereby unite and associate ourselves together for this purpose."[4]

Unity Church's first building (Fig. 43), dedicated in August 1872, was sited away from Oak Park's center, on the west side of Wisconsin Avenue south of Pleasant Street (Fig. 49, C). This structure featured a second-floor auditorium above a parish hall on ground level. Outside Gothic lancet windows alternated with pier buttresses along the sides of the church, while on the front, smaller pinnacles flanked a central spire 125 ft. tall. This first building for Unity Church had board-and-batten wooden walls above a stone base. The main structure was a simple rectangular volume, 40 ft. wide by 80 ft. long.[5] Wright's later Unity Temple was similarly controlled in scale, though square in shape.

Inside old Unity Church, the auditorium on the second floor seated about three hundred persons (Fig. 44). In 1905 one account recalled that this room, "while not up to date in any of its appointments, was yet a comfortable and homelike place of worship."[6] Against the far west wall stood a massive organ with its display of pipes above the altar. This instrument was added in 1897, when the building was "all overhauled, painted and repaired."[7] The organ in the new Unity Temple would have a prominent frontal screen. The old church's platform had a raised pulpit whose dark-stained wood finish contrasted with bright-colored floral displays, a regular feature of worship that "brought vividly to mind the Author of all good works."[8] A central aisle divided the pews, which appear to curve in toward the auditorium's center, like Chicago's auditorium churches of the period.[9] This was the Unity Church that Frank Lloyd Wright knew since coming to Oak Park with his mother, Anna, and his sisters, Jennie and Maginel, in 1887. Anna and her two daughters joined Unity Church in 1890. Wright and his wife Catherine also joined in that year, after their marriage in 1889.[10]

In the spring of 1892 the church invited Rev. Rodney Johonnot (1855–1932) to its pastorate.[11] Johonnot's paternal ancestors were Huguenot emigrés to Boston in the 1680s, while his mother's family were Quakers. Before the ministry, Johonnot had studied and practiced law briefly in Boston in the 1880s before enrolling in Harvard's Divinity School.[12] After ordination as both a Unitarian and a Universalist minister, Johonnot served churches in Massachusetts and his native Maine before going west. In vitality of spiritual life, membership, and finances, Rev. Johonnot's ministry in Oak Park was a success from the start.[13] As a speaker, "Dr. Johonnot's naturally clear and logical mind, reinforced perhaps by his legal training, made him an unusually careful and exact thinker. If such a distinction can be made, he was essentially a teacher rather than a preacher, always com-

FIGURE **43**

Old Unity
Church, Oak
Park, Ill., 1872.
Reprinted from
*Year Book and
Manual of Unity
Church 1904–
1905*. Unity Tem-
ple Historical
Files, Oak Park,
Ill. Courtesy of
Unitarian Univer-
salist Church in
Oak Park and
Beacon Unitarian
Church.

manding the thoughtful hearing of the best minds in his congregation and in his community."[14]

In his autobiography Wright characterized Rev. Johonnot as a minister who knew only one style of church building, "that of the little white New England church, lean spire pointing to heaven – 'back East.'"[15] This was not the case, however, because Johonnot had decided to begin study for the ministry while he was attending one of the most influential Unitarian centers in America, Rev. James Freeman Clarke's Church of the Disciples in Boston. Perhaps with Clarke's encouragement, Johonnot enrolled at Harvard, where Clarke then served as a professor of ecclesiastical history. Clarke had founded the Church of the Disciples a generation earlier in 1841. Although it was nominally Unitarian, the Church of the Disciples was so named to connote both belief in the teachings of Christ and the church's organization as a spiritual family in emulation of the first disciples.[16]

By the Civil War's end, Clarke's preaching attracted an average attendance of about five hundred persons at Sunday services. Clarke's innovative church was unusual in the Boston of its time for being a free church,

meaning that it was supported entirely by voluntary contributions of members and not by sale or rental of pews.[17] If a new building were to be built, it
had to be as inexpensive as possible in order to maintain the idea of a free
church with no purchased or rented pews. Control of costs meant selection
of a less expensive site and an economical architectural design.

In 1867 Clarke and his church commissioned the Boston architect Isaac
Samuels to plan their new building sited on the southeast corner of West
Brookline Street and Warren Avenue in the developing residential South
End (Fig. 45).[18] Samuels's building is 85 ft. square, with one large room
superimposed on another. On a lower level is the parish hall. From the
entrance vestibule one ascends corner stairways to the auditorium on the
second floor (Fig. 46), not unlike the path of entry into Unity Temple's
auditorium. This room has a wide main floor with a rear gallery. Above, the
ingenious timber- and iron-framed roof culminates in a crowning octagonal
clerestory. The construction enables the entire expanse of the sanctuary to
remain free of supports. Ceiling and roof are one, eliminating the expense of
a hung plastered ceiling below the roof structure, and evoking the visible
timber framing characteristic of old meetinghouses. The room seats 1,500,
with the pews curving around the width of the auditorium.

The front had a long, wide platform with a central bench and reading
chairs behind a pulpit fashioned as a reading desk. The pulpit was "made of
olive wood from the Holy Land."[19] A communion table stood in front of the
platform. On the front platform, there was no fixed altar of wood or stone

FIGURE 45

Isaac B. Samuels,
Church of the
Disciples, Boston,
1868–69. Courte-
sy of the Society
for the Preserva-
tion of New Eng-
land Antiquities
(15189-B).

and no sculpted crucifix. Wainscoating and pews were of brown ash. Clarke's favorite biblical mottoes were stenciled around the ceiling. Comparable features recurred in early designs for Unity Temple. The Church of the Disciples embodied Clarke's ideal of a church structure whose "auditorium is large, cheerful, perfectly easy to speak in, a pleasant room to look at."[20] Expense for land and building was $65,000, about Unity Temple's cost in 1908.

Clarke conceived of the new church as a meetinghouse that was socially functional in its plan and interiors, not monumentally ostentatious. Its square volume recalls that of meetinghouses like Hingham's, which Clarke admired.[21] Unlike larger neighboring spired churches, Clarke's compact Church of the Disciples did not stand out in its residential district, as if its architecture signified the institution's identification with its neighborhood. In the 1880s Johonnot worshiped in this structure, whose simplicity, ingenuity, and civility were as notable as the ministry it sheltered. If Clarke was Johonnot's pastoral model, then the Church of the Disciples would have been one source for Johonnot's ideas for a new Unity Temple in Oak Park twenty years later. Wright's building was similarly scaled more to nearby houses and thus contrasted with spired churches in its vicinity.

In defense of Wright's later design for Unity Temple, Rev. Johonnot mentioned one American building, King's Chapel in Boston, as an admirable example of religious architecture in a non-Gothic style (Fig. 47). He referred to the second King's Chapel, designed by Peter Harrison in 1749

FIGURE 46

Samuels, Church of the Disciples, auditorium, looking northeast. Alden Photo Co., 1908. Courtesy of the Society for the Preservation of New England Antiquities (45254-A).

and opened in 1754, which replaced the first chapel of 1686 on its site in Tremont Street.[22] Harrison's building contrasted with that of other churches in the city because King's Chapel had been founded to serve the British colonial garrison, and hence was the only Anglican church in Puritan Boston. King's Chapel was built of gray Quincy granite; its frontal Ionic portico was added between 1785 and 1787. This was the first church in the American colonies to be built of stone rather than of brick. In Johonnot's mind, the monolithic form of King's Chapel may have been associated with that of Wright's Unity Temple, whose massive concrete walls were likened to granite.[23] King's Chapel's sanctuary also had galleries along the sides of its longitudinal nave.

The chapel's importance in Unitarian history dated from the War of Independence. When the British evacuated Boston, a part of the church's congregation left. The remaining members revived King's Chapel, first as an Episcopal parish, inviting James Freeman to become a reader in 1782. Freeman became receptive to teachings of English Unitarians, brought to the new United States by thinkers like Joseph Priestley. Soon after becoming

minister to King's Chapel in 1787, Rev. Freeman omitted traditional references to the Trinity in his services. His action was later cited as the inauguration of Unitarian teaching in the United States.[24] This historic role of King's Chapel was stressed at the time of its 200th anniversary in 1886. The event had great meaning for the Unitarian leader James Freeman Clarke, grandson and namesake of James Freeman. At the chapel's bicentennial in 1886, Clarke, who recalled attending services there as a child to hear his grandfather's sermons, closed his address with a poem, one verse of which read:

> From that old-fashioned pulpit, in my youth,
> Came the calm voice of simple, honest truth, –
> Came from an honest man, who left the broad
> Highway of custom for a lonely road,
> Firm to resist each rude, opposing shock, –
> Like Hindu temple, cut in solid rock.[25]

When Clarke gave this address, he was then serving as mentor to Rodney Johonnot, who lived in Boston at that time, attending Clarke's church and beginning studies at Harvard Divinity School. Yet King's Chapel may have had a personal significance for Johonnot apart from its style, because his paternal forebears had escaped religious persecution of French Protestants that followed Louis XIV's revocation of the tolerant Edict of

FIGURE 47

Peter Harrison, King's Chapel, Boston, 1749–54, interior, at the congregation's 200th anniversary, 15 December 1886. Photograph of Baldwin Coolidge. Courtesy of the Society for the Preservation of New England Antiquities (9086-B).

Nantes. Many Huguenot emigrés became Anglicans, including the Johonnots, who were sustaining members of King's Chapel during the eighteenth century before its Unitarian period. The Johonnots were among the most prominent mercantile families in Boston, along with the Faneuil and Bowdoin families.[26]

* * *

FIGURE 48

Essex Church, London, 1774, interior, at 100th anniversary, 1874. Reprinted from Mortimer Rowe, *The Story of Essex Hall* (London, 1959), courtesy of the General Assembly of Unitarian and Free Christian Churches, England.

In the summer of 1903 Johonnot took his first trip abroad to Europe, touring parts of Belgium, France, Germany, and Italy. Johonnot's trip broadened his knowledge of architecture for churches in styles other than the Gothic.[27] He wrote in 1907 that "churches of other types had existed in Europe for more than a thousand years before the cathedral type was born."[28] Johonnot had high regard for English Unitarians, and during his visit to London in 1903, he was to preach, presumably at a Unitarian church.[29] He thus may have had contact with that city's tradition of smaller plain, square, galleried chapels for Unitarians, which had developed since the late eighteenth century.[30] The oldest, most prominent of these was Essex Chapel, built in 1778, where Unitarian teaching in England was first publicly professed and from which Unitarians organized as a force in English life.[31]

A view of Essex Chapel on its centenary in 1874 (Fig. 48) shows a square auditorium with galleries on three sides. This room, raised on a second floor, seated three hundred persons. Frontal boxed pews and open

rear pews on its main floor were arrayed around three sides of the raised pulpit. Unoccupied in this view, the pulpit was reached by stairs to its rear. Its height was meant to enable the speaker to effectively address the audience seated in the galleries around the room. Access to the galleries was by staircases outside of the auditorium itself, yet inside the chapel's building. Listeners sat close to one another on floor and galleries, within sight of each other and near the voice of the speaker as if to assert the solidarity of a dissenting congregation, whose convocations were technically illegal until the early nineteenth century. When Wright's Unity Temple was opened in 1908, its square, galleried auditorium was described as a similarly compact space for worship that provided for intimate visual and acoustic contact between a speaker and the surrounding congregation.[32]

Unity Church and Oak Park's Religious Architecture

When Rev. Johonnot traveled in Europe, he may have had a new building for Unity Church in mind. At its annual meeting in March 1901, his congregation, with Johonnot's support, resolved to start a fund for a new structure.[33] This act may have been prompted not only by the church's own needs, but also by its position among Oak Park's other major churches, all of which were engaging in major architectural projects. The suburb then had about ten thousand persons, 95 percent of whom belonged to local Protestant churches. In the village, between 1900 and 1906, six new congregations were founded and seven new church edifices were constructed, while others were remodeled. Though initiated by separate congregations, this wave of church building was perceived as a communal enterprise. In the spring of 1906, the season that building began on Unity Temple, it was reported that "half a million dollars have been expended in the last five years by the people of Oak Park, in erecting new houses of worship and remodelling and refurnishing old structures. Unstinted contribution and cooperation with pastors by congregations have built up an organization which preserves sectarian demarcations, yet puts all the churches on a basis of unified endeavor."[34]

The central axis for this newly monumental religious architecture was the east–west Lake Street, as shown in a bird's-eye view of 1873. This street's central civic focus was close to the future site of Unity Temple (Figs. 49, A and 58, A). In 1873 First Congregational Church built its large steepled stone edifice on the north side of Lake west of Grove Avenue (Figs. 49, B and 58, B). Designed by Chicago architects Burling and Adler, the church's plan and massing have been credited to Dankmar Adler based on similarities with other churches he had designed when in earlier partnerships.[35] The 175-ft. steeple flanking the church was the village's tallest, rising above walls of Lyons stone, a soft yellowish limestone. Its rusticated surfaces had ornamental details of carved stone, including a cinquefoil rose window above the south door (Fig. 50).

FIGURE 49

View of Oak Park
and River Forest,
Ill., 1873, show-
ing (A) site of
Unity Temple, (B)
First Congrega-
tional Church
(1873), (C) old
Unity Church
(1872), and (D)
site of Wright's
home and studio.
Historical Collec-
tion of Philander
W. Barclay. Pho-
tograph courtesy
of the Oak Park
Public Library,
Oak Park, Ill.

The building, which cost $47,000, was primarily a large auditorium seating 550 with pews arranged in curved rows around the frontal platform. Behind this platform a central niche framed a large organ, donated in 1881, when the church was first expanded and a rear gallery was added. Figure 51 shows the auditorium after it was enlarged again in 1886 and 1892. The architect for all these additions to Burling and Adler's original building was Normand S. Patton, a church member and village resident.[36] The First Congregational Church's building was "renovated, redecorated and materially improved during the summer of 1903."[37] At that time, the congregation's minister was Rev. William Barton, who was Johonnot's closest colleague in Oak Park. Rev. Barton had a strong scholarly interest in biblical history, making trips to both Europe and the Holy Land.[38] He had three symbols of early Christianity painted on the wood ceiling of his church's remodeled sanctuary,[39] whereas figurative symbols would be minimal in Unity Temple's auditorium for a liberal religion. Architectural and symbolic contrast between Unity Temple and nearby churches would thus be vivid to residents who met occasionally in the different local sanctuaries for civic events and communal religious services.[40] The form of Unity Temple was to convey alternative ideas, much as Wright's prairie houses in Oak Park presented his vision for a way of life in contrast to that of the suburb's Victorian houses.

First Congregational Church was also a civic center. A main benefactor,

James W. Scoville, sought to provide a free public library for the village, and in 1883, he commissioned Patton to design the new institute on the northwest corner of Lake Street and Grove Avenue (Figs. 52 and 58, E). Its corner tower, gabled roofline, asymmetrical massing, and Lyons limestone were "built to match the church."[41] Yet Patton's institute was not Gothic, but "designed in a style which may be termed the American Romanesque."[42] As Oak Park's civic centerpiece after its dedication in 1888, the Scoville Institute, with the First Congregational Church next door, presented a local model of two adjacent types – one public, one ecclesiastical – whose institutional purposes and architectural forms were interrelated. When Wright came to design Unity Temple, he, too, had to relate and distinguish its auditorium for worship from its building for less formal meetings (Unity House). As we will see, their architectural and symbolic linkage was central to his ideas.

Two blocks west of the First Congregational Church, on the south side of Lake Street, stood the First Presbyterian Church, a new edifice designed by William Williamson (1861–1922), begun in 1901 and dedicated in 1902 (Figs. 53 and 58, C).[43] This church was the suburb's third largest, with eight hundred members. Its exterior, in a Romanesque style of round-arched openings, featured a monumental tower over a portico and walls of polychrome boulders. This edifice was built at the same time as a new building for Oak Park's Episcopal Grace Church in 1901–6 (Figs. 54 and 58, D),

FIGURE 50

(left) Edward Burling and Dankmar Adler, First Congregational Church, 1873–74; and (right) Normand Patton, Scoville Institute, 1886–88, Oak Park, Ill. Courtesy of the Illinois State Historical Society Library (W-1434).

FIGURE 51

Burling and Adler,
First Congrega-
tional Church,
interior looking
toward altar, after
addition of tran-
septs, designed by
Normand Patton,
in 1892. Photo-
graph courtesy of
the First United
Church of Oak
Park, Ill.

sited on the north side of Lake Street almost directly opposite. As Oak Park's
largest congregation, Grace Church counted some one thousand communi-
cant members and three thousand total adherents in 1906.[44] The new
Grace Church's cornerstone was laid in May 1901 just after Unity Church
had initiated its rebuilding fund. John Sutcliffe (1853–1913), born and
trained in England, was the architect. Sutcliffe, a member of Grace Church
and resident of Oak Park, was nationally known for historic yet inventive
interpretations of English Gothic styles for churches.[45]

Costing over $124,000 upon completion in 1906, the new Grace
Church was the most expensive and elaborate building yet constructed in
Oak Park. The site for church and parish house behind had a frontage of
166 ft. on Lake Street and a depth of 320 ft., enabling the church to be set
far back.[46] The plot available to Sutcliffe in designing Grace Church was
over one and a half times as wide and nearly twice as deep as the site on
which Wright would design Unity Temple. Grace Church's outer walls and
interior piers are of Bedford limestone, dressed smooth with passages of
carved ornament. There is a square tower over the southwest entrance
flanking a window of seven lancets below a cinquefoil rose motif.[47] The
new Grace Church had a nave 186 ft. long (Fig. 55), lighted by sixty-three
windows filled with stained glass imported from England. Their program
was a complete series, including figures from the Old Testament, the apos-
tles, and various saints. Marble steps led to the chancel and the reredos of

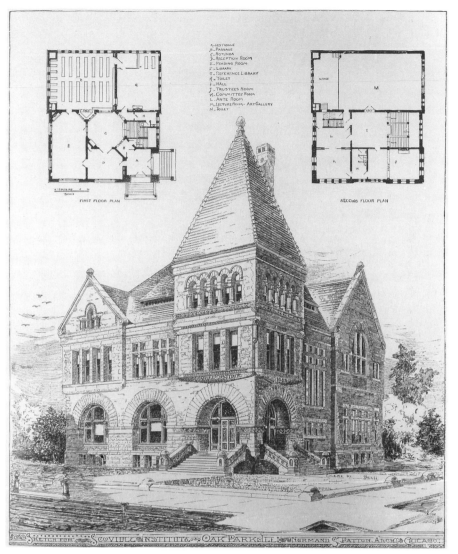

FIRST FLOOR PLAN   SECOND FLOOR PLAN

FIGURE 52

Patton, Scoville
Institute. Re-
printed from
*Inland Architect
and News Record*
5 (February
1885).

the altar was carved in marble in an English Decorated Gothic style of the fourteenth century. The building exemplified a literal architectural historicism and its association with religious orthodoxy to which Unity Temple was to be an alternative.

* * *

In 1905 Oak Park's central churches were engaged in an effort to control the village's central open spaces as the setting for its public architecture. Oak Park had just won its struggle for political autonomy in 1901, and successfully blocked Chicago's attempts to annex the suburb. Yet its residents feared that their community would be assimilated de facto into the

FIGURE 53

William G. Wil-
liamson, First
Presbyterian
Church, Oak,
Park, 1901–2.
Reprinted from
*Inland Architect
and News Record*
39 (May 1902).

larger city and lose its identity if the pattern of development in Oak Park included apartment buildings.[48] Whereas apartment construction was less resisted on the south side of the Chicago and Northwestern Railroad line, it was consistently and successfully opposed to the north of the tracks, within Oak Park's more exclusive residential area. One contested area between the north and south halves of the village was Lake Street, whose trolley lines to Chicago made it a logical location for apartments, yet whose identity as Oak Park's civic and commercial axis inspired opposition to this pattern of development. So reluctant was Oak Park to present an urban image that residents opposed an ordinance for the paving of Lake Street in order not to "destroy the rural simplicity of the village."[49]

Congregations built new churches on Lake Street around 1900 not only because of their own institutional interests, but as part of a broader effort to reclaim the village's arterial street as the place of its religious values, evoking the model of a Puritan village.[50] In this period, one editor noted that "among the serious architectural problems of this community is the question of what is to be the final disposition of the frontage on both sides of Lake Street between the Marion street and Oak Park avenue business districts. . . . We believe that in the working out of the future of a beautiful Oak Park every foot of this frontage should be occupied by public buildings and their surrounding grounds."[51] Partly for this reason Grace Church purchased additional frontage for its building in 1903, while First Congregational Church bought the large plot to the west of its house of worship in

FIGURE **54**

John Sutcliffe,
Grace Episcopal
Church, Oak
Park, 1901–6
(Photo: author).

1905. This plot remains as the open lawn across Lake Street from Unity Temple (see Fig. 50). This land was not needed by the church for immediate use, but the "purchase is recommended as an assurance that the land will not be put to any use inimical to the beauty of the architectural group formed by the church and Scoville Institute. This is recognized as the architectural center of the village, and the erection on the lot of something out of harmony with the rest would be a sad marring of the village."[52] In 1908 the First Presbyterian Church was among the churches urged to buy land adjacent to their sites to block apartment building. When Unity Church rebuilt on Lake Street, its new structure would respond in part to the question of shaping this street as the suburb's civic axis.

Rev. Johonnot's Concept of a New Building

In May 1904, on the twelfth anniversary of his ministry in Oak Park, Johonnot gave a sermon entitled "Building a Temple unto God," in which he

FIGURE 55

Sutcliffe, Grace
Episcopal Church,
interior looking
toward altar. Re-
printed from John
Moelmann, *Grace
Church, Oak
Park, 1879–1939*
(Oak Park, Ill.,
1939).

presented his ideas for the new edifice of Unity Church. In his statement he
presented certain programmatic and symbolic ideas that were embodied in
Wright's later design. Johonnot stated: "This temple when built must comply
with three conditions. It must be adapted to the community. In some places
an institutional church was needed, but in Oak Park it was the family
church that was called for. It must be durable and permanent, a type of the
stability of the work to be done, and it must be beautiful, a type of the high
character of the ideals for which it stood."[53] Praising the sacrifices that had
enabled construction of the original Unity Church thirty-three years earlier,
Johonnot concluded that "since that day there ha[s] been great development in church construction and new conceptions of art and architecture
which [can] not be ignored."[54]

If a new Unity Church were to convey its congregation's mission in the
community, then its architecture would have a civic as well as an ecclesiastical character. During his twelve years in Oak Park, Johonnot had
broadened Unity Church's public service, writing in 1899 that "it is only as

a church regards itself first of all as an agency for promoting the moral and religious welfare of society and not as an end [in itself] that it can succeed and become a real power in the community."[55] Unity Church's Fellowship Club "met in Unity parlors for years to discuss live topics of the day, and advanced thinkers in all recognized lines of public benevolence and progress appeared."[56] After Johonnot came, Unity Church was invited to participate in communal events such as the village's union services held every Thanksgiving. Within a year of his arrival, Johonnot organized charitable societies of the village into a single association. From 1905 to 1906 he led the effort to create and endow the Hephzibah Children's Home, of which Unity Church was a supporter.[57] In 1907 one local observer concluded that Unity Church had "taken an important part in the religious and social work of the village. A marked change has been brought about in the attitude of the other churches toward this society. The attitude of suspicion and mistrust which was more or less pronounced for many years has given way to one of complete fraternity."[58]

Unity Church's civic role paralleled Oak Park's program for construction of new public buildings following its achievement of autonomy in 1901. One leader in this effort was a trustee of Unity Church, John Lewis, whose wife served on the plans committee that selected Wright.[59] Lewis, who also authored a commemorative local history of Oak Park at the time of its independence, had been the leading advocate of the new village hall (1903–5) by architect Eben Roberts. This building, originally envisioned on the site where Unity Temple was later built, was instead sited two blocks to the east on Lake Street at Euclid Avenue (Figs. 56 and 58, F).[60] In these years, a new YMCA (by architects Allen B. and Irving K. Pond) and a new post office were built north of Lake Street on Oak Park Avenue (Figs. 57 and 58, G, H) east of what became Scoville Park (Fig. 58, I).[61] In 1905 Johonnot was an honored participant in the laying of the cornerstones of both the new post office and YMCA. By that spring "never before have so many public enterprises been begun and so many public institutions established."[62] All of these structures were communal initiatives. All were classical in style, symmetrically planned, and built of dark brick with stone or terra cotta trim in conventional motifs. All had simple cubic shapes with low hipped or flat roofs. They were thus clearly differentiated from the village's new medievally styled stone churches to the west on Lake Street. Wright's Unity Temple shared the cubic compactness of these civic works, yet not their explicitly classical style.

While stating that Unity Church's edifice should have a civic character, Johonnot noted that, unlike Abraham Lincoln Center, the building would not be an institutional church but a family church. Not only would his congregation be largely composed of suburban households, but also its new building's scale and character should harmonize with its residential environs. In this way Johonnot responded to Oak Park's communal ideal of preserving its identity as a suburb of individual homes. The new Unity

Temple's site was west of five houses on Lake Street, and Wright's design for the building adapted a style found in his local domestic architecture in the same period.

Johonnot's view of the new building as signifier of the permanence and stability of Unity Church's mission coincided with the fact that its wood building was then aging and in need of major repair.[63] An ideal of permanence also may have informed his usage of the word "temple," which he invoked here for the first time to refer to a future Unity Church. Well before Wright designed the new building, Johonnot's use of this term suggests that he envisioned a type of edifice that would differ architecturally from nearby churches built in conventional neomedieval styles. Johonnot explained the rationale for the name "Unity Temple": "While it is common to speak of our houses of worship as 'churches,' the use of the word 'temple' is better for many reasons. It allows us to keep the word 'church' to its distinctive meaning, namely, that of the body of Christian worshippers, and thus prevents much confusion resulting from the different meanings of the word. This usage also keeps us in line with the Biblical use of the terms; for in it the word 'temple' is always used to designate a house of worship, while the word 'church' always refers to the body of worshippers."[64] Johonnot here echoed a Puritan preference for differentiation between the terms "church" and "meetinghouse," to denote respectively a people and their edifice.[65]

For Johonnot, the term "temple" perhaps had special meaning because of his Huguenot ancestry. From the sixteenth century, Huguenot houses of worship were known in French as *temples protestants*, to distinguish them from consecrated Catholic edifices, described as *églises*.[66]

Johonnot's final condition, that the new church embody liberal religious ideals in beauty of form, prefigured his statements on the importance of an aesthetic revival in the emerging religious life of the new century. In 1909 he set forth these views in an essay on "The Modern Reformation," published just before the dedication of Unity Temple.[67] Like Jenkin Lloyd Jones, Johonnot felt that the art of the church before Luther's time had been a legitimate aid to the expression of devotion. To enable the church of 1900 to regain its central role in society as the primary source of spiritual well-being, Johonnot wrote: "A new Reformation is demanded whose characteristic is not so much that of protest against the old as of the creation of positive values."[68] He believed that "there will be a return to the recognition of the demand made by the emotions and the esthetic sentiments in the matter of worship. The services of public worship will take on more of dignity, order, and beauty. The places of worship will be so constructed as to make appeal to the emotions of reverence and aspiration."[69]

* * *

Just before Christmas 1904, Unity Church's trustees, at Johonnot's urging, renewed an appeal to the congregation for increased donations to the build-

FIGURE 57

(left) Allen B. and Irving K. Pond, YMCA building, 1905, and (right), post office, 1905, Oak Park, Ill., architect unknown. Courtesy of the Illinois State Historical Society Library (W-1427).

ing fund.[70] In a sermon of 7 May 1905, Johonnot again raised the question of a new building.[71] On 24 May the church unanimously resolved to build anew, if possible, and the trustees began to study the question.[72] Eleven days later, early on the morning of Sunday, 4 June, storms caused lightning to strike several church spires in Chicago and its region.[73] Lightning struck the steeple of the old Unity Church. Because the water pressure available to Oak Park's fire department was too low for its streams to reach the flames in the tower, fire spread quickly to the church's roof and upper auditorium.[74] The chair of the trustees, James Heald Jr., recalled how "the blazing steeple fell to the ground with a great crash, and fire seemed instantly to spread to all parts of the building. The stained glass windows melted and ran out of their frames and our dear old church building was a mass of flames. . . . Providence had decided we must have a new church building."[75]

The Choice of a Site and Wright's Selection as Architect

On 9 June 1905, five days after the destruction of old Unity Church, the congregation voted unanimously to build a new edifice, and the trustees

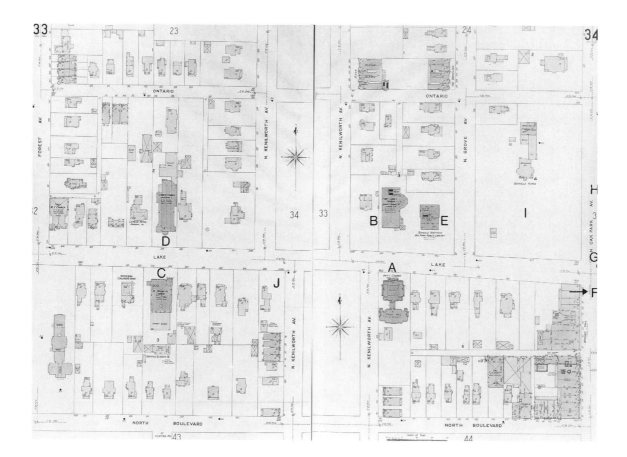

appointed four committees: a first on ways and means for raising funds; a second on site, to select a location for the new building; a third on plans, chaired by Rev. Johonnot, to engage an architect and decide on a plan; and a fourth on construction, initially chaired by Charles E. Roberts.[76] The appointment of the site committee reflected "the well nigh unanimous opinion of the membership that the new building ought not to be in the old location, but that it should be in some place more central and where it will add more to the architectural beauty and unity of the village."[77] With opinion heavily favoring a site on Lake Street, four such lots were studied, including both the southwest and southeast corners of Lake Street and Kenilworth Avenue (Fig. 58, J, A).[78] In 1905 the southwest corner, occupied by a residence, was "considered one of the most beautiful corners in Oak Park for a public building."[79] Yet the southeast corner, where Unity Temple was built, was then open. This site was owned by one of the wealthier parishioners of Unity Church, Edwin O. Gale.

The site stood on the south side of Lake Street almost directly opposite the First Congregational Church to the north, which adjoined the Scoville Institute to its east. Rev. Johonnot preferred this southeast corner, where Gale owned property 105 ft. wide on Lake Street and 250 ft. deep on Kenilworth Avenue. In August 1905 Unity Church acquired from Gale a part of this lot 100 ft. wide on Lake and 150 ft. deep on Kenilworth. The price was $10,000, or about $5,000 below the property's market value. Along with the First Congregational Church, the new Unity Church would "form a good balance for the two other churches standing in like relation to each other, the First Presbyterian and the new Grace Episcopal Church, directly opposite each other a little farther west on the same street."[80] Four churches forming a square recalled the medieval idea of many churches forming a geometric unit in a town plan.[81] Unity Church's new site signified Johonnot's aim of centering his liberal church in the village as an equal partner with these larger churches. Yet Unity Church's move was also consistent with these neighboring churches' attempts to buy land along the village's central axis in order to control its development.

On 30 August 1905 Rev. Johonnot was invited to give the trustees a first informal report on the plans committee's search for an architect. He stated that his committee

> had visited quite a number of churches and had talked with and had spent an evening with several architects namely Mr. E[mory] S. Hall, Mr. [William G.] Williamson, Mr. E. A. Mayer, Mr. [John] Sutcliff[e], Mr. [Henry P.] Harned, Mr. Dwight H. *Perkins*, Frank Lloyd *Wright*, William A[ugustus] *Otis*, and Mr. [Normand] S. *Patton*. When asked if the committee could reduce the number to three or four [Rev. Johonnot] said that the committee gave preference to the last four. Each one of these men was then discussed by Dr. Johonnot and the other members of the committee, enumerating points for and against each one showing the thorough and painstaking way in which the committee [had] gotten the situation in hand and giving the board of trustees a clear insight [in]to the situation.[82]

FIGURE **58**

(facing page)
Lake Street east and west of Kenilworth Avenue, showing (A) Unity Temple, (B) First Congregational Church, (C) First Presbyterian Church, (D) Grace Episcopal Church, (E) Scoville Institute, (F) municipal hall, one block to the east, on southeast corner of Euclid Avenue, (G) post office of 1905, (H) YMCA, (I) Scoville Park, and (J) alternative site for Unity Temple. (Sanborn Map Co., Insurance Map of Oak Park, Cook County, Ill., 1908, Atlas 57, Plates 33–34.)

Of the four architects preferred, Perkins, who was also a Unitarian, had worked with Wright on the Abraham Lincoln Center. In addition, Perkins's cousin was Marion Mahony, Wright's assistant, who had been the architect of All Souls Unitarian Church in Evanston, Illinois, completed in 1903.[83] William A. Otis (1855–1929), trained at the Ecole des Beaux Arts, designed the Hull Memorial Chapel in Hyde Park for the First Unitarian Society of Chicago in 1896–97.[84] Patton (1852–1915) had remodeled First Congregational Church, and, in 1905, he had designed Oak Park's new high school. He was also architect of Memorial Baptist Church in Chicago of 1899 sited across the street from the Abraham Lincoln Center.[85] By 1905 Wright had worked for years on the Abraham Lincoln Center with which Johonnot was familiar.

Rev. Johonnot later said that the chief criterion for the design of Unity Temple was "the desire to make a building expressive of the faith held by the worshipers."[86] He influenced the choice of a site, and, as head of the plans committee, was centrally responsible for the choice of an architect. As an articulate advocate of liberal views, Rev. Johonnot would presumably have sought a designer who would be knowledgeable of and sympathetic to Unity Church's ideals. Of the four candidates for whom his committee had reported a preference, three had designed Unitarian churches.

When the new Abraham Lincoln Center was completed and dedicated on Sunday, 29 May 1905, Johonnot congratulated Jones. Yet, by the time Jones replied, old Unity Church in Oak Park had burned down. Anticipating that the Oak Park church would rebuild, Jones's *Unity* advised Johonnot and his congregation against "slavish or reckless obedience to the conventional or the mere artistic without reference to the many-sided necessities and opportunities of the modern church."[87] On 14 June Jones replied to Johonnot:

> I am almost tempted to return the compliment by congratulating you over your smoke. I am sure this like most fires of the Almighty has a benignant side to it. You have a chance now to express yourself in a new building. I am more and more persuaded that my contention of the last fifteen years and more is a vital one – that new occasions teach new duties architecturally, and the coming church must find more adequate expression of its purpose and meaning in the brick and mortar and cement. Beware of architects but rejoice in their power and make them go in the right way.[88]

Of the architects interviewed, Wright was well known as an architect for Jones and as a congregational member. By 1905 he had also worked for other members of Unity Church. He had designed houses in Oak Park for Walter and Thomas Gale, whose father had provided the site for the new building. Wright had also designed a house in Oak Park for another church member, George W. Smith.[89] Wright had also been a friend and collaborator of Charles E. Roberts (1843–1934) since at least 1892. Of Welsh descent, Roberts, a mechanical inventor and founding head of the Chicago

Screw Company, was a key benefactor and trustee of Unity Church. He was also widely known as the innovative director of its Sunday school.[90] Though few were built, Wright's many projects for Roberts up to 1905 show that he was a patron of Wright's novel prairie house, just as Roberts would favor Wright's innovative aesthetic for Unity Temple. Clearly Roberts had extraordinary confidence in Wright, and their relationship grew more multi-faceted while Unity Temple was being built.[91] Wright's aunt, Ellen Lloyd Jones, wrote to Roberts: "You know Frank Lloyd Wright, his enthusiasms, his weaknesses, as I do – as his mother does – perhaps better."[92]

In his autobiography Wright recalled that in the wake of the fire "a competition was first thought of for Unity Temple, but the idea abandoned and the commission given to me after much debate among the committee. . . . In this case the committee was so 'run' by Charles E. Roberts – inventor. He was the strong man in this instance or Unity Temple would never have been built."[93] Earlier Wright affirmed: "The only way superior work in Architecture, (and superior work in Architecture is always individual), can ever happen is by virtue of some individual responsibility, sufficiently strong in faith and able to dictate, putting that faith and power behind the project and making that thing happen. . . . But wherever I have built a building, in every case there has been such individual force and authority back of the project as I have described, even in the case of Unity Temple built in Oak Park."[94]

When Unity Church searched for an architect, Roberts was chairing the building committee; hence his influence in Wright's favor may have been as decisive as Wright claimed. At the trustees meeting of 30 August 1905, where Johonnot reported on interviews with nine architects, "after all questions had been answered the [plans] committee asked that the Building committee be associated with them in some way in formulating the plans for the church."[95] If these two committees came together at that time, this would account for Wright's recollection that Roberts dominated a single committee to insure Wright's selection. However, on Sunday, 3 September, the trustees charged only Rev. Johonnot's plans committee "to employ an architect" and "to cause plans and specifications to be made for the new church edifice."[96] Within two weeks, on 16 September, it was announced that Unity Church had chosen Frank Lloyd Wright "to construct a church that will be dignified and devotional in aspect and also suited to the working needs of a modern church. The reputation of the architect assures the people of Oak Park of an artistic edifice in which all can take pride and which will be an ornament to the village."[97] Yet, at this time, perhaps neither Unity Church nor its suburb anticipated how unconventional Wright's response to these criteria would be.

3

Wright's Design for Unity Temple

W RIGHT first shared his plans for Unity Temple with the church's trustees in December 1905. He had high aspirations for the project that was both his first church and first work designed wholly in concrete. It was also his only public edifice in his own community. In Unity Temple, Wright reworked and combined ideas recurrent in his architecture of the previous ten years. Yet Unity Temple's design emerged in the context of Unity Church's demands, and Wright worked continually to persuade the congregation and its leaders that his unconventional building was appropriate for their spatial and symbolic needs. Unity Temple was thus a synthesis of ideas internal to the development of Wright's style, the church's function and meaning, its site, and its method of building. His plans show how Wright sustained his aesthetic agenda by transforming limitations into resources that were made to enhance the richness of his design. As he said in 1900: "The limitations within which an artist works do grind him and sometimes seem insurmountable. Yet without those very limitations there is no art. They are at once his problems and his best friends – his salvation in disguise."[1]

The Spire or the Auditorium

Unity Church wanted to build quickly, for when Wright was engaged, it was hoped that the new structure would be complete within a year and ready for worship by September 1906,[2] although three years would pass before Unity Temple opened in 1908. When the trustees authorized the selection of Wright as architect, they told the plans committee that the new church must contain a space for worship, another for the Sunday school, and another for a secular meeting room. Wright was to prepare designs "for the new church edifice to cost not exceeding $30,000 including decoration, the seating of the auditorium, and the equipment of the building for lighting and heating and excluding the organ and other furnishing."[3]

In *An Autobiography*, published in 1932, Wright recalled that, in designing Unity Temple, he had focused initially on what he called "the philosophy of the building."[4] As Wright had stated in his address of 1900 on "A Philosophy of Fine Art," he opposed what he had termed representational or literary symbolism in the fine arts. In architecture Wright opposed the adoption of conventionally inherited symbols, such as the spire of a church as a sign of aspiration to a heavenly salvation. In 1892 a Chicago Universalist, writing of the religious culture of New England a century earlier, affirmed that steeples were sometimes added to old meetinghouses at risk and expense in part to signify belief in the reality of heaven as the realm of the soul's salvation.[5] Wright rejected the spire for Unity Temple's architecture because it did not convey the ideals of liberal religion. In his account of the origins of his design, Wright recalled that, instead of adopting such a traditional ecclesiastical symbol, he had initially proposed to the building committee a rethinking of the purpose of a church as an institution:

> I told the committee a story. Did they not know the tale of the holy man who, yearning to see God, climbed up and up the highest mountain – up and up on [to] the highest relic of a tree there was on the mountain, too? Ragged and worn, there he lifted up his eager perspiring face to heaven and called on "God." A voice . . . bidding him to get down . . . go back!
>
> Would he really see God's face? Then he should go back, go down there in the valley below where his people were – there only could *he* look upon God's countenance.
>
> Was not that "finger," the church steeple, pointing on high like the man who climbed on high to see HIM? A misleading symbol perhaps. . . .
>
> Was not the time come now to be more simple, to have more faith in man on his Earth. . . .
>
> Why not, then, build a temple, not to God in that way – more sentimental than sense – but build a temple to man, appropriate to his uses as a meeting place, in which to study man for himself for his God's sake? A modern meeting-house and a good-time place.
>
> The pastor was a "liberal." His liberality was thus challenged, his reason piqued and the curiosity of all aroused.
>
> What would such a building be like? They said they could imagine no such thing.
>
> "That's what you came to me for," I ventured.
>
> "I can imagine it and I will help you create it."[6]

The story of the holy man that Wright paraphrased in this account was his variation on the story entitled "The Traveller and the Temple of Knowledge," by the English author Beatrice Harraden (1864–1936), found in a collection of her work entitled *Ships That Pass in the Night*, published in numerous editions, three of which appeared in Chicago in 1893 and 1894. In Harraden's version, the seeker is only a traveler, rather than a holy man, who vowed to climb the summit of a high mountain, the highest in a chain of peaks called "The Ideals." Atop this summit he knew was a temple, reached along a difficult road, on which the traveler had made a lifelong pilgrimage. Once at the gate of the temple, he was greeted by an old white-haired man, who said:

> This is not the Temple of Knowledge. And the Ideals are not a chain of mountains; they are a stretch of plains, and the Temple of Knowledge is in their centre. . . . Go back to the plains, and tell the dwellers in the plains that the Temple of True Knowledge is in their very midst; any one may enter it who chooses; the gates are not even closed. The Temple has always been in the plains, in the very heart of life, and work, and daily effort. The philosopher may enter, the stone-breaker may enter. You must have passed it every day of your life; a plain, venerable building, unlike our glorious cathedrals.[7]

With this story Jenkin Lloyd Jones had begun his sermon at All Souls Church on 13 May 1894, wherein he had described his plans for The American Congress of Liberal Religious Societies, which he founded at that time. Jones proposed: "Substitute the word 'religion' for 'knowledge' and you have in this parable of Beatrice Harraden's the message of the Spirit to the churches in this last decade of the nineteenth century. Nay, you have the message of the Spirit to the churches of all ages and in all countries."[8] In biblical terms, Jones interpreted the story to mean that "God dwells not remote in some high mountain of metaphysics or theology, but his kingdom is within you. . . . This is the divine temple with open doors, the temple of easy access."[9]

Wright's underlying philosophy for the design of Unity Temple was rooted in his uncle's view of liberal religion as a nondenominational movement that stressed the unity of humanity and the presence of divinity in the souls of human beings. In Chicago after 1900, a leading advocate of this view was Frank C. Doan, a follower of William James, whose *The Varieties of Religious Experience* (1902) was widely read as a comprehensive study of the philosophy and psychology of religion. In 1904–13 Doan taught philosophy and psychology of religion at the Unitarians' Meadville Theological School. His main work was a collection of essays, *Religion and the Modern Mind*, published in 1909. In that year Doan addressed the National Unitarian Conference gathered in Chicago at the Abraham Lincoln Center. He argued that "the modern soul of man requires an experience of God as human," adding: "All these years the expert seekers after God have been star-gazing, deducing God in celestial magnitudes of one sort or another. Do we do some earth-gazing! Mount we together to some mystic height and look down, down upon these habitations of men! See the great spirit of God settling upon people!"[10]

In accord with such ideals, Unity Temple would present its auditorium for worship as a symbol of divinity living naturally in humanity. In May

1905, in a sermon wherein he urged that Unity Church construct a new building, Johonnot stated that his congregation's liberal mission was based on "the freest and largest interpretation of religion; whose foundation is . . . the natural relationship of God to man."[11] The idea of Unity Temple as a humanistic symbol of liberal religion recurred in Johonnot's statement of 1906: "Without tower or spire it expresses the spirit of the ideal. By its form it expresses the thought, inherent in the liberal faith, that God should not be sought in the sky, but on earth among the children of men."[12] Johonnot's opposition to a spire recalled that of his Quaker maternal forebears, who considered spires to be symbolically inappropriate.

Wright's omission of a spire from Unity Temple was also consistent with ideas current in Chicago's architectural culture of the period. While tall spires had been almost synonymous with the church as architecture in the city from the 1850s to the 1870s,[13] they became much less popular in local Protestant churches from the 1880s, for both stylistic and practical reasons. In 1890, when Wright was working for Adler and Sullivan, Sullivan believed that the spire in an urban church was an anachronistic motif, because it had lost its earlier function as a belfry and had thus become solely ornamental. He stated: "It is a pity in some respects that the church spire is an idea going out. It was a pretty one, but in this utilitarian age the tendency is to the practical. . . . The church spire in the city is a thing of the past."[14] Sullivan maintained that building committees for modern churches preferred to spend funds on usable rooms, not on spires. In Oak Park of 1905 Wright's avoidance of the spire was pragmatically consistent with the need to protect church buildings from fire caused by lightning. Of the first seven church buildings constructed in the village to 1886, four were destroyed by fire. Of those so destroyed, Unity Church in 1905 and First Congregational Church in 1916 were struck by lightning. When local churches were rebuilt, square-topped towers usually replaced pointed spires in part to reduce the risk of fire[15] and thus ease cost of insurance.

By 1905 the spire as a conventional motif for churches had been called into question throughout the United States. In that year, New York's *Church Economist*, a journal devoted to the administration of parishes, estimated that within the preceding year, five thousand church buildings had been built around the country, meaning that, on average, twelve to fifteen were being completed each day.[16] From their array of data, the editors concluded that, in general, the architecture of these buildings was influenced by two recurrent factors: "one of economy of site, due to the rising value of land in central locations, where churches naturally are placed, and the other, the tendency to satisfy the demand for utility."[17] For both of these reasons, "we find a strong set against the continued use of Gothic. It is claimed to be wasteful of space, and ill-adapted for a complex social plant. . . . In our practical day, the lofty ceilings and the tapering spires are voted quite out of the question for the ordinary, everyday purposes of the modern church."[18] A third factor militating against the Gothic style, especially for urban churches, was their submergence among tall office buildings: "Such an environment dwarfs and makes trivial Gothic structures which, before the modern 'skyscraper' came to town, were the dominating features of the landscape."[19]

This modern symbolic condition was poignantly felt in Manhattan. In 1905 an editor wrote of New York's Trinity Church, whose spire of 284 ft. had been the city's tallest structure to 1875, yet whose context had been transformed by skyscrapers: "One looks at it through a kind of tunnel called Wall Street. Great, splendid boundless-looking buildings frown down upon it. Acres of men and women, in chairs, sit with their feet above its nave. . . . Time was when people used to climb up in the tower and feel the wonder and stillness and the looking-down-upon-the-world of God's church."[20]

In the case of the Madison Square Presbyterian Church, the Metropolitan Life Insurance Company bought its old site covered by a spired Gothic structure. The church responded in 1904 by asking McKim, Mead, and White to design an edifice nearby to be "of an early Christian type, in the form of a Greek cross surmounted by a dome."[21] This church regained a distinctive symbolic identity with a style that contrasted rather than competed with recent surrounding office towers (Fig. 59). In this period, Wright's decision to seek an alternative to the spire in Unity Temple was thus consistent not only with the denominational culture of Unitarians and Universalists, but also with a broad rethinking of symbolic forms in American church architecture of the new century.

In Unity Temple Wright may have rejected the convention of the spire for theological reasons as he claimed. Yet his avoidance of the spire's vertical form also corresponded to the horizontality of his new architectural style for houses. Wright viewed Victorian house styles as unsympathetic to the regional landscape, and thus decried them as spiritually unsettling. In his autobiography he later wrote: "Buildings standing around there on the Chicago prairies were all tall and all tight. Chimneys were lean and taller still – sooty fingers threatening the sky. And beside them, sticking up almost as high, were the dormers. These house walls were be-corniced or bracketed up at the top into the tall purposely profusely complicated roof, dormers plus." He added: "The whole exterior was bedeviled, that is to say, mixed to puzzle-pieces, with corner-boards, panel-boards, window-frames, corner blocks, plinth blocks, rosettes, fantails, ingenious and jigger work in general. This was the only way 'they' seemed to have, then, of 'putting on style.' "[22]

Wright's style related his house forms to the land. In 1908 he wrote: "We of the Middle West are living on the prairie. The prairie has a beauty of its own and we should recognize and accentuate this natural beauty, its quiet level. Hence, gently sloping roofs, low proportions, quiet sky lines, suppressed heavy-set chimneys and sheltering overhangs, low terraces and out-reaching walls sequestering private gardens."[23] He wrote of his works through 1909: "The horizontal line is the line of domesticity. The virtue of the horizontal lines is respectfully invoked in these buildings. The inches in

Vol. X. No. 5.   31 Union Square W., New York.   May, 1905.

WORKING OUT THE PROBLEM OF "CHURCH AND SKY-SCRAPER."

A Photographic "Object Lesson," showing the Conditions and the Proposed Remedy. The old and the new Madison Square Presbyterian Church, New York, with the towering business structures that surround both. A further discussion follows on the next page.

height gain tremendous force compared with any practicable spread upon the ground."[24] Finally, Wright wrote retrospectively in his autobiography: "I had an idea that the horizontal planes in buildings, those planes parallel to the earth, identify themselves with the ground – make the building belong to the ground. I began putting this idea to work."[25]

Wright's stylistic preferences for simplicity and horizontality recalled ideas of Jenkin Lloyd Jones, who had equated these qualities with ethical and spiritual values. In 1901, in a sermon on artists' roles in the new century, Jones observed: "Walk the avenues and boulevards of Chicago and you find plenty of expensive houses where there is a manifest outlay of skilled labor and valuable material but how few houses touch you with restfulness, give a sense of grace and lend harmony to the street. . . . The eye has been battered, the senses scattered and the soul distressed by a confusion of lines. . . . One longs for the power to wield some great architectural sad-iron to iron out the wrinkles, smooth out the ruffles and give us a little plain wall on the fronts of our mansions."[26] Earlier, in his sermon at All Souls Church's dedication in 1886, Jones alluded to the restfulness of the horizontal line as a metaphor for the biblical idea of an inner peace beyond understanding. Jones noted that "the most helpful view Chicago can offer is that indefinite line of vision far out in the lake where the water meets the sky. The finest view of every landscape is the horizon line. On the borderland of thought lie the reverences."[27]

Wright's Early Sketch for Unity Temple

Although the design for Unity Temple was related to its denominational culture, Wright wrote of the plan's emergence as a solitary exercise of his imagination. As he claimed to have done in other works, Wright recalled that he developed the entire scheme for Unity Temple in his mind, and that he only drew preliminary plans and a perspective before sharing the scheme with anyone. While he may have begun imagining a design in the summer of 1905, he probably developed Unity Temple between his selection as architect in early September and early December, by which time it was reported that Wright "and the building plans committee of the church are fast getting the plans for the new church into their final shape."[28] By 9 December Edwin Gale, who had sold Unity Church the site for Wright's new building, chose to donate an additional 20 ft. of land on the south side of the site fronting north–south Kenilworth Avenue, making the site 170 ft. in depth. He made this gift because "it was found advisable to set the church back farther from the walk than was at first contemplated."[29] At that time, Lake Street was still unpaved and trolley cars connecting Oak Park with Chicago ran along tracks down its center. For these reasons Wright may have proposed increasing Unity Temple's setback, just as he sought to screen the auditorium from Lake Street.

On 12 December Wright recorded that the building committee had finally accepted his plans for the church. On 17 December Johonnot's plans committee, "appointed by the Board to employ an architect and to prepare plans for the new church edifice, reported to the Board that they had employed Mr. Frank L. Wright as architect, and submitted to the Board plans for a new church edifice which had been prepared by Mr. Wright under the

direction of the Committee and recommended the adoption and acceptance of such plans."[30] Johonnot's committee may have had a role in the
development of Wright's scheme in the autumn of 1905. Yet Wright described his formulation of the design as independent of any input from the
church. He recalled that he focused first on locating the auditorium for
worship, known as Unity Temple proper:

> Then the Temple itself – still in my mind – began to take shape. The site
> was noisy, by the Lake Street car tracks. Therefore it seemed best to keep
> the building closed on the three front sides and enter it from a court at the
> center of the lot.
>
> Unity Temple itself with the thoughts in mind I have just expressed,
> arrived easily enough, but there was a secular side to Universalist church
> activities – entertainment – Sunday school, feasts, etc.
>
> To embody these latter within the temple would spoil the simplicity of
> the room – the noble ROOM – in the service of MAN for the worship of GOD.
>
> So finally I put the space as "Unity House," a long free space to the
> rear of the lot, as a separate building to be subdivided by moveable
> screens, on occasion. It thus became a separate building but harmonious
> with the Temple – the entrance to both to be the connecting link between
> them.[31]

The earliest known preliminary drawing for Unity Temple is a freehand
plan (Fig. 60) on the end page of John Lloyd Wright's personal copy of *The
House Beautiful*, designed by his father, Frank Lloyd Wright, as one of
several published versions of a sermon by Rev. William Channing Gannett.
This version was printed at William Winslow's Auvergne Press in River
Forest, Illinois, in the winter of 1896–97. John Lloyd Wright later wrote:
"This pencil sketch, in the hand of Frank Lloyd Wright, is Frank Lloyd
Wright's first drawing of his original conception for the plan of Unity Tem-
ple, Oak Park, Illinois, about 1903. The building was constructed about
1905 with no basic change from this concept."[32]

This sheet shows a preliminary plan above an elevation. The plan is
drawn on a lot whose size is noted as 100 ft. wide by 150 ft. deep. The
notation of the plot's depth as 150 ft. indicates that the plan predates Edwin
Gale's gift of additional land in December 1905. Unity Temple's rear as
built spans the lot's full width, yet this plan shows the building as less wide,
set inside its east and west property lines. The plan notes the church's front
to be 40 ft. back from Lake Street, and well forward from the rear of the lot.
The drawing thus shows a building less than 100 ft. deep, much smaller
than Unity Temple's built depth of about 144 ft. Its setback from Lake Street
appears to match that of the house that then stood to its east, whose front is
partially indicated on the drawing above that of Unity Temple. The church's
long north–south axis aligns with the midsection of the house on an adjacent lot to the south down Kenilworth Avenue. Unity Temple's initial scale
and siting were thus to respond closely to neighboring residences.[33]

Before Wright had developed his design, the trustees had asked for both

a meeting hall and Sunday school rooms. Yet Wright combined meeting hall and schoolrooms into Unity House as one architectural unit. As his assistant Charles White noted, Wright often fit utilitarian requirements of a program into the architectural order of his design, rather than permitting functional criteria to determine the logic of his architecture. White wrote: "I do not mean by this that he ignores the requirements, but rather he approaches his work in a broad minded architectural way, and never allows any of the petty wants of his client to interfere with the architectural expression of his design. The petty wishes are taken care of by a sort of absorption and suppression within the scope of the plan as a whole."[34]

In his autobiography, Wright recalled that his first drawings for Unity Temple were measured plans after he had thoroughly conceived the building in his mind. He wrote that in the case of Unity Temple, "there is no 'sketch' and there never has been one. There seldom is in a thought built building."[35] When Wright referred to sketches as a basis of design, he meant preliminary perspectives of the exteriors of buildings that would be made first and then used as a guide for developing the internal plan to conform with the predetermined exterior composition. He identified this prevalent method as the opposite of his own professed ideal of organic form.[36] This was an approach to design from the plan outward, considering the logic of the building internally before making an exterior drawing. This approach followed the methods of the French Ecole des Beaux Arts, and was characteristic of the work of H. H. Richardson and other American architects trained at the Ecole, who included Louis Sullivan.[37] Wright's adaptation of this idea of the plan as the generator of three-dimensional form is implicit in a drawing of his own studio included in the Wasmuth folio of 1910 (Fig. 61), where a plan is drawn below a frontal view of the building.[38] Wright wrote that his works to 1908 "were conceived in three dimensions as organic entities, let the picturesque perspective fall how it will. While a sense of the incidental perspective the design will develop is always present, I have great faith that if the thing is rightly put together in true organic sense with proportions actually right the picturesque will take care of itself."[39]

Wright's method of developing the plan as a basis for study of elevations may be visible in his early drawing for Unity Temple. The plan atop the sheet appears to depict the entrance in a connecting link between Unity Temple and Unity House. Yet it also indicates a small rectangular projecting volume at the central front of Unity Temple, which could be read as an entrance vestibule with steps leading directly up and into the auditorium from its north side on Lake Street. Columns and possibly steps are also drawn on the west front of Unity House, as if Wright perhaps contemplated a direct entrance to this part of the building. For Unity Temple, a small projecting block with a central door appears in the sketch at the bottom of the sheet, which may be a north or Lake Street elevation related to the plan drawn above. If so, the sheet departs from the convention of depicting the

FIGURE 60

(facing page) Wright, preliminary plan (above Lake Street elevation?) for Unity Temple, before December 1905, drawn on verso of rearmost flyleaf of copy of Rev. William C. Gannett, *The House Beautiful* (River Forest, Ill.: Auvergne, 1896–97), a book designed by Frank Lloyd Wright, in the John Lloyd Wright Collection, Avery Architectural and Fine Arts Library, Columbia University in the City of New York.

plan below an elevation. It presents a north elevation that does not correspond to the west side of the plan that is drawn just above it. Yet the elevation is similarly circled as if it were related to the plan above. In the elevation the church is set back from Lake Street among trees, while a rectangular block frames what appears to be the door. Above and around the portico, there is a wide band of arches drawn along the wall's upper face, framed in a rectilinear border that turns down the wall to anchor the elevation near both ends. Behind and above this frontal wall, there appears to be a high chimney breast atop the building's rear mass.[40]

If Wright did initially contemplate a front entrance to Unity Temple, his decision to move the doorways back between the two parts of the building may have been necessitated by the shortness of the lot. Wright also said that he recessed the entries to keep the auditorium closed off from the noise of the streetcars. While other churches on Lake Street had frontal entrances, they had plots much wider and deeper than Unity Church's eventual site of 100 ft. by 170 ft. If Wright's building were to grow no larger than that shown on the sketch plan, then its setback of 40 ft. from Lake Street would perhaps have made a front entrance reasonable. Yet once Wright worked out the required areas for both Unity Temple and Unity House, the building's total length of 144 feet, even on a lot of 170 ft., would mean any conventional front doors would be closer to the street and far from Unity House. Front doors would also have meant a changed plan for the auditorium. Thus, out

FIGURE 61

Wright, studio, Oak Park, Ill., 1898. From *Ausgeführte Bauten und Entwürfe*, Plate VI (Frank Lloyd Wright Archives, Drawing No. 9506.019, © The Frank Lloyd Wright Foundation 1994).

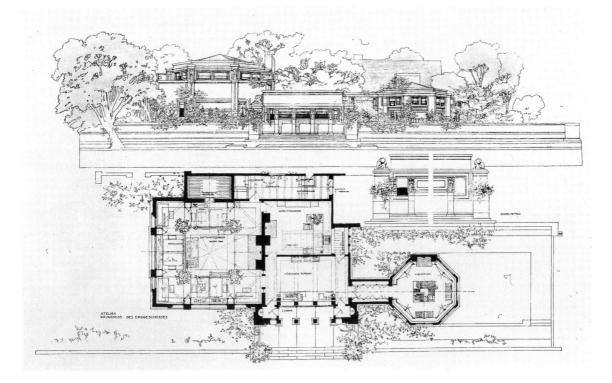

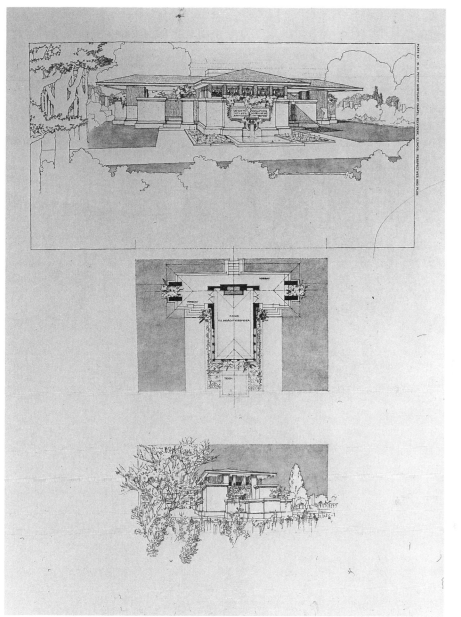

FIGURE 62

Wright, William
H. Pettit Memori-
al Chapel, Belvi-
dere, Ill., 1906.
From *Ausgeführte
Bauten und Ent-
würfe*, Plate XLI
(Frank Lloyd
Wright Archives,
Drawing No.
0619.019, ©
The Frank Lloyd
Wright Founda-
tion 1994).

of the apparent limitation of the site's dimensions, Wright created one of his most memorable schemes of entrance, one that heightens expectations about the auditorium seen, but not entered, from the street front.

Through 1906 Wright's other realized religious building of his own design was the W. H. Pettit Memorial Chapel, in a cemetery in Belvidere, Illinois (Fig. 62), which Wright described as a "simple, not unhomelike room for services, with shelter at rear and sides to accommodate people

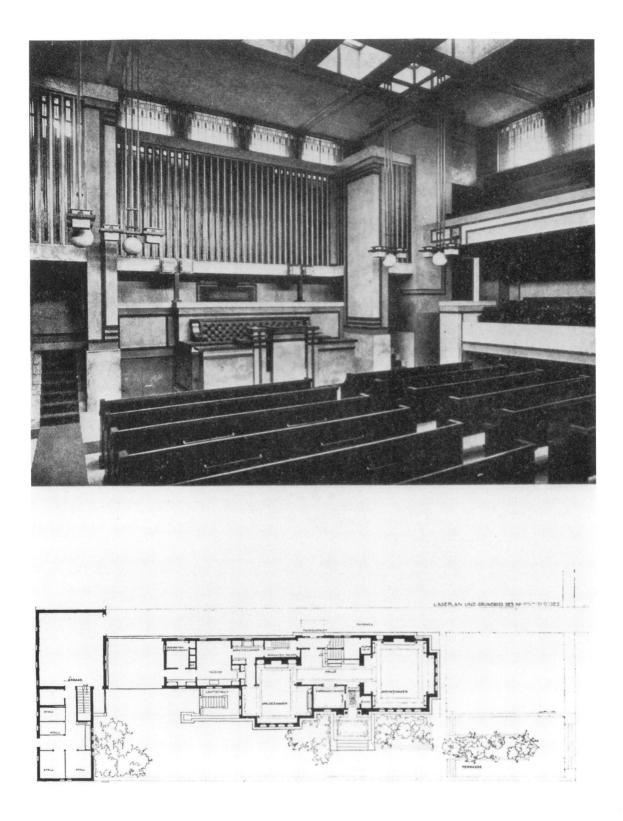

waiting for cars."[41] The building faces east onto a carriage way. As at Unity Temple, the chapel is approached along either of two paths on the flanks of its central projecting volume. Mounting steps to the portico, one then turns ninety degrees to enter the chapel on either side toward its rear. Steps at the rear of the portico are for egress to the street. As a wood-and-plaster chapel for occasional smaller groups, the Pettit Memorial is different from Unity Temple. Yet in both of these early religious designs, the process of arrival is purposefully and gracefully attenuated as if to prepare the mind for the service to be held within.

*   *   *

Wright's plan for Unity Temple (Fig. 60) shows several ideas for the building, one laid quickly over another. This gives the drawing a vividly immediate and decisive quality. The shaded square at left connecting to the shaded rectangle at right indicates Unity Temple and Unity House much as they were ultimately built. As Wright recalled, the pivotal idea of the plan was the articulation of Unity Temple and Unity House as independent yet connected volumes. This approach distinguished his attitude toward plans from that of other architects of the period, who condensed dissimilar spaces of a program into a single volumetric envelope, packing varied functions in one geometric form like a square or rectangle. Compacted plans were characteristic of Oak Park's public buildings nearby like Scoville Institute (Fig. 52), or Village Hall (Fig. 56) which contained meeting rooms and a fire station, both within a simple neoclassical envelope.

The idea of distinct volumetric expression of spatial parts apparent in Wright's early drawing of Unity Temple's plan appeared in his own work about a decade earlier in the form of his own studio as an addition to his Oak Park house. In the Wasmuth folio of 1910, Wright published the studio's plan below a drawing of its north front (see Fig. 61). There he described the studio as "an early study in articulation – the various functions featured, individualized, and grouped."[42] His assistant, Charles White, wrote of the plan for Unity Temple in 1906: "The motif . . . is an evolution of Wright's Studio. An entrance in a link connecting a dominant and subordinate mass."[43] As shown in the Wasmuth folio plate, each built volume of Wright's studio, entry, and library is a different geometric shape, whereas Unity Temple and Unity House are uniformly rectilinear in plan and closely related to each other in their three-dimensional form.

Wright had explored this idea of distinct yet connected volumes in the plan of the Isadore Heller House in Chicago of 1896, which resembles Unity Temple in its long narrow lot whose depth accommodates the aligned main rooms.[44] In the arrangement of photographs of Wright's built works published in his *Ausgeführte Bauten* (1911), the Heller House directly followed Unity Temple at the beginning of the book, with the house's plan published on the same page as an interior view of the church (Fig. 63). The

FIGURE 63

(facing page) Wright, (above) Unity Temple, interior, and (below) plan of Isadore Heller House, Chicago, 1896. Reprinted from *Ausgeführte Bauten von Frank Lloyd Wright.* (Berlin: Ernst Wasmuth, 1911). © by Ernst Wasmuth Verlag GmbH & Co., Tübingen.

page's layout suggests a link between these works that were separated by a decade in Wright's oeuvre. As noted earlier, his building whose binuclear plan and massing most closely anticipated Unity Temple was the Hillside Home School in Wisconsin, of 1901–2 (Fig. 25). In its plan, a square assembly room balances a rectangular gymnasium, much as Unity Temple's square balances Unity House's rectangle.

Wright's early design for Unity Temple displays a more consistent geometry than any of these early binuclear plans. Unity Temple's form has been understood as an exercise in composition inspired by Wright's childhood fascination with Froebelian geometric forms. The elemental, square shape of Unity Temple has also been linked to Wright's receptivity to the concept of pure or abstract design current in Chicago in 1900. As Wright wrote of the building's concept: " 'Design is abstraction of nature-elements in purely geometric terms' – that is what we ought to call pure design."[45] Unity Temple appears to fulfill this conceptual program, which had emphasized separate geometric shapes as the architectural expression of different interior spaces. However, Wright's plan for Unity Temple and Unity House may also represent his condensation of a range of other buildings known to him.

Sources and Preliminary Plans for Unity Temple's Auditorium

While Wright's extant sketch for Unity Temple's plan engaged a formal theme found in his earlier work and akin to pure design, his diagram recalls the plan of the Taiyu-in mausoleum at Nikko (Fig. 64), a historic city that Wright had visited in April 1905 shortly before his return to the United States.[46] Begun in 1653 for the Tokugawa shogun Iemitsu (whose posthumous name was Taiyu-in), this building was the second mausoleum built in Nikko in the seventeenth century. This well-known Japanese monument showed a spatial composition of separate but linked geometric forms like that which Wright had explored for a decade prior to his trip to Japan. The Taiyu-in mausoleum featured a square main hall with an altar. This most sacred room was separated from a rectangular worship hall by a recessed intermediary foyer or *ai-no-ma*. One entered the worship hall first, passing up a central staircase through paneled folding doors. A smaller set of steps led from the *ai-no-ma* into the main hall.

If Wright adapted this Japanese shrine's plan for that of Unity Temple, he retained certain ideas from this model while reworking others. In the Taiyu-in mausoleum, there is a clear spatial and symbolic distinction between the main hall, as a mortuary chapel identified with the deceased, and the worship hall. In Unity Temple's plan, the more sacred square auditorium is for worship, while the less sacred and rectangular Unity House is not primarily for worship. Yet in the Taiyu-in mausoleum, the path of access is internal from the worship hall, through the *ai-no-ma* to the main hall, while in Wright's plan the intermediary entrance hall provides access to both

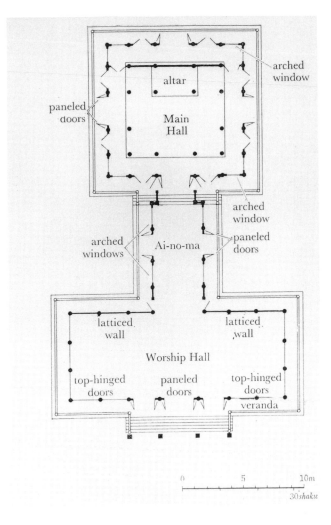

Labels within the plan:
- altar
- Main Hall
- paneled doors
- arched window
- arched window
- arched windows
- Ai-no-ma
- paneled doors
- latticed wall
- latticed wall
- Worship Hall
- top-hinged doors
- paneled doors
- top-hinged doors
- veranda

Scale: 0 — 5 — 10m / 30 shaku

FIGURE 64

Taiyu-in mauso-
leum, Nikko, Ja-
pan, 1653, main
floor plan. Plan
by Chuji
Hirayama. Re-
printed by per-
mission of the
publisher from
Naomi Okawa,
*Edo Architecture:
Katsura and Nik-
ko* (Tokyo and
New York:
Heibonsha and
Weatherhill,
1964).

Unity Temple and Unity House. In this way Wright's plan for Unity Temple and Unity House more closely resembles that of the earlier mausoleum at Nikko for Tosho-gu of 1634, where stairs rise to the *ai-no-ma* between the rectangular worship hall and the more square main hall (Fig. 65). Unity Temple's strictly symmetrical plan echoes observance of symmetry in such Japanese sacred architecture.

One approaches these mausolea from the end opposite the square main hall, whereas one approaches Unity Temple along the outside of its frontal auditorium. The altars of the Nikko mausolea are toward the wall opposite the entrance, while Unity Temple's pulpit is on the south side near the doors. Finally, in both of Nikko's shrines, doors open out from all interior spaces onto a peripheral exterior veranda that runs continuously around the buildings. This veranda, important as an intermediary platform for sacred spaces, has no close parallel in Wright's plan for Unity Temple. Thus,

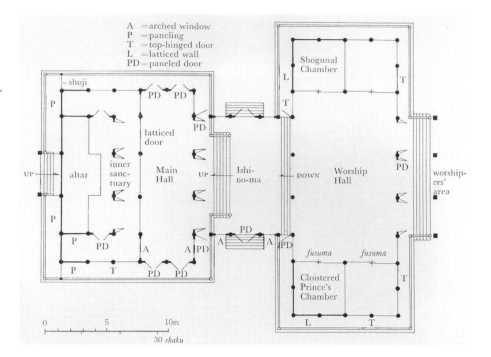

FIGURE 65

Tosho-gu mauso-
leum, Nikko, Ja-
pan, 1634, main
floor plan. Plan
by Chuji
Hirayama. Re-
printed by permis-
sion of the
publisher from
Naomi Okawa,
*Edo Architecture:
Katsura and Nik-
ko* (Tokyo and
New York:
Heibonsha and
Weatherhill,
1964).

Wright transformed the spatial logic of the Nikko mausolea to serve the programmatic needs and communal context of Unity Church.

Once the arrangement of Unity Temple and Unity House on the site had been decided, Wright implied that his next step was the planning of Unity Temple's main space. In his essay of 1908 Wright presented this auditorium as "a frank revival of the old temple form, as better suited to the requirements of a modern congregation than the nave and transept of the cathedral type. The speaker is placed well out in the auditorium, his audience gathered about him in the fashion of a friendly gathering, rather than as fixed in deep ranks, when it was imperative that the priest made himself the cynosure of all eyes."[47]

Wright's words resonated not only with the recent plans of Jenkin Lloyd Jones for the auditorium of the Abraham Lincoln Center, but also with a long tradition of ideas for the architecture of Protestant churches that had developed continuously since the sixteenth century. Even before new structures were built, the early architectural consequences of the Reformation included the transformation of basilican church buildings to accommodate changed belief and practice. A fundamental change was the inclusion of the congregation as a corporate participant in worship. This meant not only the audibility of the sermon, but also the theological ideal of all worshipers partaking in the liturgy and Communion. Such rethinking the conventions of worship led to a new type of Protestant architecture: the smaller, centrally planned auditorium with galleries, whose origins are identified with the Swiss and French congregations in the period of Calvin, when such a structure became known as the *temple protestant*. Wright's description of "the old temple form" corresponds to this early Protestant type, which had emerged as a symbolic and programmatic alternative to basilican churches.[48]

Jacques Perret had proposed a geometrically ideal type of small squared temple in a treatise, *Des fortifications et artifices. Architecture et perspective*, printed about 1601. Perret's publication was a statement of the architectural ideals of French Huguenot communities under Henry IV.[49] In this volume, after elaborate plans for fortified cities, the first design for an individual building was that for "un petit temple quarré," suitable for a seigneurial patron and a site outside city walls (Fig. 66). The design called for a structure some 12 *toises* or about 75 ft. on a side, exclusive of its attached belfry over the west door. At that time a bell tower was one of the few architectural elaborations of Huguenot temples legally permitted under the specific provisions for their form in the Edict of Nantes. The temple was to have its thick stone walls set on a four-step platform, with a single vault of stone for its ceiling arcing from the rear entrance to the frontal raised pulpit.

Perret's plan provided for fixed seating in the form of benches throughout the auditorium. Furnishing of churches with permanent seating for the congregation distinguished Protestant spaces for worship from churches antedating the Reformation, such as French cathedrals and Italian basilicas whose floors were often left open.[50] The compact ordering of Perret's plan around fixed seating, with its emphasis on access to and visibility from

FIGURE 66

Jacques Perret, project for "Un Petit Temple Quarré." Reprinted from Perret, *Des fortifications et artifices. Architecture et perspective* (Paris, ca. 1601).

ranks of pews on many levels, marks the design as a setting for preaching and corporate participation in a reformed liturgy. Around the room's four sides, three tiers of seating rise from a main floor to the outside walls "en manière de théâtre," with chairs at their base for leading seigneurial parishioners. On the main floor are rows of benches in four sections divided by centrally crossing aisles. These benches face the frontal raised pulpit. A continuous passage surrounds the benches on the main floor and connects to the three doorways on the three sides of the building. On the fourth side, behind the pulpit, a staircase leads to the galleries, which are not visible on the floor plan. The galleries were also accessible from staircases on either side of the tower over the main door on the side of the building opposite the frontal pulpit. As seen in the drawing of the building's exterior, tall windows on all the upper walls lit the room.

As both a spatial arrangement and ideogrammatic symbol, Perret's project appears like a distant ancestor of Unity Temple's auditorium. Yet Wright's room for worship also had precursors in earlier American and

Unitarian architecture. In his autobiography, Wright recalled that he imagined the auditorium as "a modern meeting house."[51] The only extant seventeenth-century meetinghouse in New England was the second one at Hingham, Massachusetts, built in 1680 (Fig. 67). Wright had lived close to this well-known work as a child in Weymouth, a few miles west of Hingham on the south side of Massachusetts Bay. Hingham's meetinghouse may have been in Wright's mind when he was composing his autobiography before its publication in 1932, because the building underwent its major modern and well-publicized restoration in 1930.[52]

In 1813 the First Unitarian Society in Philadelphia had dedicated its initial, octagonal building designed by Robert Mills (Fig. 68). As a noted advocate of a rational neoclassical architecture, Mills approached his art in a way that was consistent with the ideals of a congregation whose founders were English freethinkers. Among American churches of the period, this auditorium was one of the first to depart from the basilican halls adapted from London churches of Wren and Gibbs. Instead, a centrally planned

FIGURE 68

Robert Mills, First
Unitarian Church,
Philadelphia,
1813. From the
collections of the
South Carolina
Historical Society.

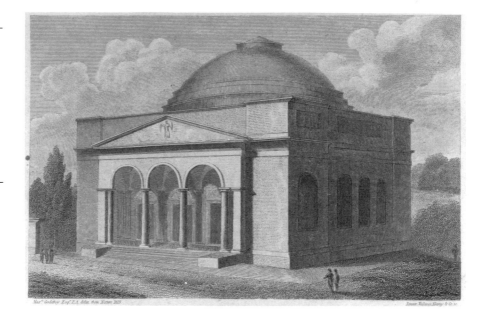

FIGURE **69**

Maximilian Gode-
froy, First Uni-
tarian Church,
Baltimore, 1817–
18. Collection of
the Maryland His-
torical Society,
Baltimore.

room was to optimize the audibility of preaching. This building served as the center of the early pastorate of Rev. William Henry Furness (father of architect Frank Furness) from 1824 to 1828, when it was replaced by a new edifice. Frank Furness then designed the third building for his father's former church on a different site in western central Philadelphia in 1885–86.[53]

Equally lucid as a convergence of Unitarian ideals and neoclassical aesthetics had been Maxmilian Godefroy's First Unitarian Church in Baltimore of 1817–18 (Fig. 69), whose square cubic mass housed an auditorium with a coffered domed ceiling. It was at the dedication of Godefroy's building in 1819 that Rev. William Ellery Channing, the chief Unitarian thinker of the period, delivered his sermon on "Unitarian Christianity," which was soon recognized as a definitive statement of liberal ideals. The compact central plan of Godefroy's church contrasted with Benjamin Latrobe's nave for Baltimore's nearby Roman Catholic Cathedral of St. Mary of the Assumption, begun in 1806 and completed in 1821.[54]

By 1905 there were other models for auditorium churches in Chicago that would have been familiar to Unity Church or to Wright. In 1887 St. Paul's Universalist Society, which had been the church of Edwin Gale's father, Abram, built a new edifice (Fig. 70) in the wealthy residential district of Prairie Avenue. Its octagonal lantern crowned a central auditorium planned in the amphitheatrical form developed in Chicago's churches of the 1860s and 1870s. When built, its form was "unlike anything else in Chicago or elsewhere in the line of churches."[55] As Chicago's major Universalist monument, St. Paul's exterior volumes exhibited the form of its auditorium as a distinctively shaped interior space.

While he worked in Adler and Sullivan's office, Wright participated in

FIGURE 70

St. Paul's Univer-
salist Church,
Chicago, 1887.
Courtesy of the
Chicago Histori-
cal Society
(ICHi-23699).

the design of a synagogue for Kehilath Anshe Ma'ariv of 1889–91 built on
the southeast corner of Indiana Avenue and Thirty-Third Street (Fig. 71).[56]
Its large second-floor galleried auditorium is clearly evident in its exterior
mass. Kehilath Anshe Ma'ariv's height is equal to its length of 116 ft.,
yielding the image of a monumental cubic form. Built as the home of a
Reform congregation and perceived as modern in style, this building may
also recall the hip and tiered roofs of certain synagogues in Europe.[57] Unity
Temple similarly would be intended to signify both the modernity and the
antiquity of liberal religious beliefs.[58]

The auditorium type recurred in Adler's late work, the Isaiah Temple,
built in 1898–99 on the southeast corner of Vincennes Avenue and Forty-
Fifth Street (Fig. 72).[59] As a center of liberal reform, this building also
departed from tradition in its exterior. Its auditorium's galleries are served by
frontal corner stairs. Adler placed rooms for the congregation's social activity in a block with its own entry behind the auditorium. This concept
anticipated Wright's decision to place Unity House behind Unity Temple,
although their separate masses contrast with Adler's compact design. Jenkin
Lloyd Jones, whose own All Souls Church was close by, praised Isaiah
Temple's auditorium, observing that "as the Christian churches are generally breaking away from the conventional parody of the great medieval
cathedrals, so this Jewish congregation have broken away from the low
domed Moorish type."[60]

Parallel spatial, stylistic, and symbolic ideals were then shaping the
architecture of early Christian Science churches in Chicago, where more
such churches were being built around the turn of the century than in any

FIGURE 71

Adler and Sullivan, synagogue for Kehilath Anshe Ma'ariv, Chicago, 1889–91. Photograph by Richard Nickel. Courtesy of the Richard Nickel Committee, Chicago, Ill.

other city in the United States. Between 1897 and 1911 six of these were designed by Solon S. Beman (1853–1914), a colleague of Adler and Sullivan. Built after the World's Columbian Exposition, Beman's Christian Science churches were all neoclassical, stone, cubic structures with square auditoria. Wright presumably knew of these buildings, especially because several of his most important clients of the time, including Darwin Martin, Susan Lawrence Dana, and Mrs. Avery Coonley, were Christian Scientists. Wright also worked with Hugh M. Garden, whose Third Church of Christ Scientist (1899–1901) stood on the southeast corner of Washington Boulevard and Leavitt Street on the city's West Side (Fig. 73). Its second-floor auditorium was served by stairs in each corner. The design thus anticipated Unity Temple's, which became the early meeting place for Oak Park's Christian Scientists.[61]

In Unity Temple Wright replaced the symbol of the spire with the level roof lines and cubic volume of an auditorium. Expression of the auditorium as a building's main space was a concept that Wright perhaps owed to Flagg's critique of the design of 1900 for Abraham Lincoln Center. In stress-

ing clear exterior expression of a major interior space, Flagg was recounting a time-honored Beaux-Arts principle of design that was consistently evident in his own church buildings. The idea appeared in Richardson's influential Trinity Church in Boston, whose cruciform space recalls a meetinghouse.[62] Thus, in Unity Temple, Wright did not invent a new type of room for worship, nor was he the first to emphasize exterior legibility of interior space as a guiding rationale. Rather, Wright's process of design at Unity Temple was to condense typological models known from historical and contemporaneous architectural culture into a formal synthesis that bears the stamp of the distinctive individual style found in Wright's other works of these years. His design was no less creative if it emerged from such a process; rather, its creativity was based less on pure inventiveness, as Wright implied, than on his integration of many ideas and forms in a personal idiom.

While Wright's choice of a square auditorium for a new Unity Church had numerous historical and recent precedents, it would be unique among Oak Park's church buildings, most of which had longitudinal naves entered from the rear. Unity Temple's auditorium, as Wright's explicit architectural rebuttal of the cathedral type, would effectively convey the idea that its congregation's liberal religious beliefs were distinct within its community. Wright's choice of plan for Unity Temple was thus not only functional, but iconographic, both historically and contextually. Also, because long naves

FIGURE 72

Dankmar Adler, Isaiah Temple, Chicago, 1898–99. Reprinted from *Reform Advocate* 16 (10 September 1898): 53.

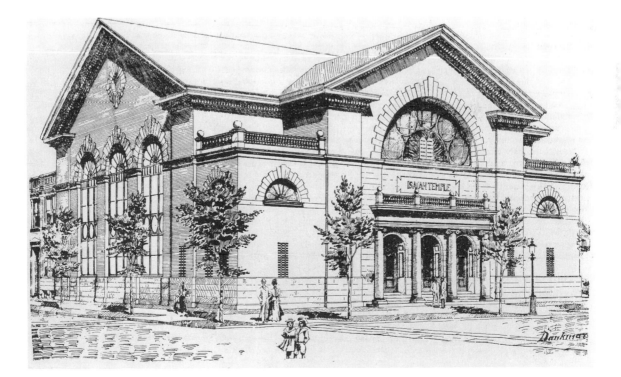

were associated with medieval churches, Wright's aversion to this spatial shape was consistent with his rejection of the neomedieval styles found in other churches in the village.

* * *

Given a square shape for the auditorium, there remained questions of orientation and movement within the room. In his autobiography, Wright wrote of the auditorium's plan:

> To go back to the Temple itself. What kind of "square room"? How effect the cube and best serve the purpose of audience room?
>
> Should the pulpit be put toward the street and let the congregation come in and go out at the rear in the usual disrespectful church fashion so the pastor missed contact with his flock? And the noise of the street cars on Lake Street come in?
>
> No. Why not put the pulpit at the entrance side at the rear of the square Temple entirely cut off from the street and bring the congregation into the room at the sides and on a lower level so those entering would be imperceptible to the audience? This would make the incomers as little a disturbance or challenge to curiosity as possible. This would preserve the quiet and the dignity of the room itself. Out of that thought came the depressed foyer or "cloister" corridor on either side leading from the main

entrance lobby at the center to the stairs in the near and far corners of the room. Those entering the room in this way could see into the big room but not be seen by those already seated within it.

And when the congregation rose to disperse here was opportunity to move forward toward their pastor and by swinging wide doors open beside the pulpit let the flock pass out by the minister and find themselves directly in the entrance loggia from which they had first come in. They had gone into the depressed entrances at the sides from this same entrance to enter the big room. But it seemed more respectful to let them go out thus toward the pulpit than turn their backs upon their minister to go out as is usual in most churches. This scheme gave the minister's flock to him to greet. Few could escape. The position of the pulpit in relation to the entrance made this reverse movement possible.[63]

Wright implied that the unusual scheme of entrance into Unity Temple's auditorium was his idea. Yet he subsequently noted that the scheme for leaving the room was "important to the pastor,"[64] suggesting Rev. Johonnot's concern for this feature of the plan. A comparable system of access and exit appeared in Wright's scheme for Abraham Lincoln Center. One of his plans of 1903 for this project shows the center's second floor containing the main level of the auditorium (Fig. 36). In this plan, the frontal platform is on the north side of the room facing a main floor of seats sloping down toward the platform; ramps lead down from the back to the front of the room. Raised tiers of seating are on the east and west sides. In the later Unity Temple, such raised tiers or alcoves of seating around the auditorium's rear and sides were to "serve as a practical substitute for the usual troublesome banked or sloping floor."[65]

The Lincoln Center's first-floor plan (Fig. 35) shows stairs leading to the second-floor auditorium behind each side of the room's frontal platform. Atop these stairs in the auditorium is a peripheral corridor at the level of the topmost rear tiers of seats around the east, south, and west sides. In the corridor's northeast and northwest corners, stairs lead to the galleries above on these three sides of the room, not shown on this plan. As in Unity Temple, the path of movement from the Lincoln Center's entrance to the auditorium involves passage inward and upward, turning from darkness into light. To exit Lincoln Center's auditorium, worshipers would proceed down the ramps on the second floor toward the frontal platform, then go out down staircases to the left and right of this platform to the first floor. As in Wright's plan for Unity Temple, worshipers leaving the Abraham Lincoln Center's auditorium could thus move forward to greet their minister, and leave this second-floor room by a different path than that of their arrival.

If, as Wright implied, Rev. Johonnot had asked him to include such a scheme of movement through Unity Temple, then the request may have been based on both minister's and architect's familiarity with the auditorium of the Abraham Lincoln Center. Rev. Johonnot's plans committee had probably included this building among the many that they had visited.

FIGURE 74

Wright, Unity
Temple, "Scheme
A," floor plan of
entrance level,
1906 (Frank Lloyd
Wright Archives,
Drawing No.
0611.047, © The
Frank Lloyd
Wright Founda-
tion 1994).

For Wright, Unity Temple and the Abraham Lincoln Center were presumably related as his only designs for auditoriums up to 1905. Suggestion of
their linkage in his mind may appear in the second-floor plan of the center's
auditorium (Fig. 36). This is an ink-on-linen drawing, yet penciled in freehand over the ruled inked lines is a large square with diagonal lines connecting its corners. Within this square are drawn four solid square columns,
inside or adjacent to the larger hollow piers around the room's center.
Between the sketched columns on the room's east and west sides, there are
pencil lines that may indicate rows of seats moved in from the side seats of
Abraham Lincoln Center. From the central front of the platform are sketched
radiating lines to the right that may represent the sound of a speaker's voice
projecting out to a curved line swung around the room's right side. These
added pencil lines may show a contemplated change in Lincoln Center's
auditorium. However, the freehand square is about 64 ft. on a side – almost
exactly the dimensions of Unity Temple. The four square columns are about
5 ft. on a side and 33 ft. apart, as in Unity Temple, hinting that Wright's

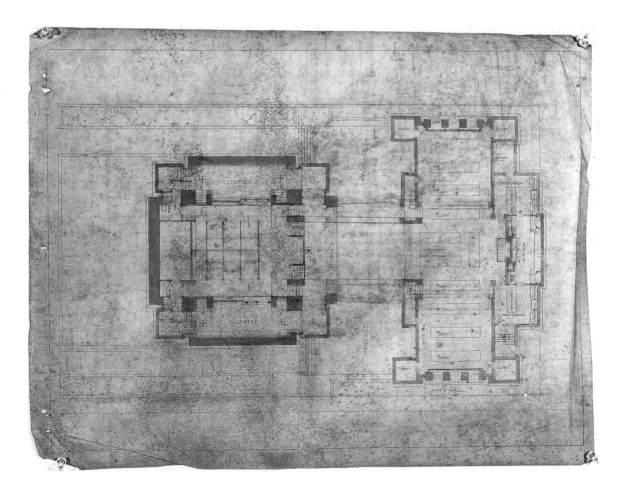

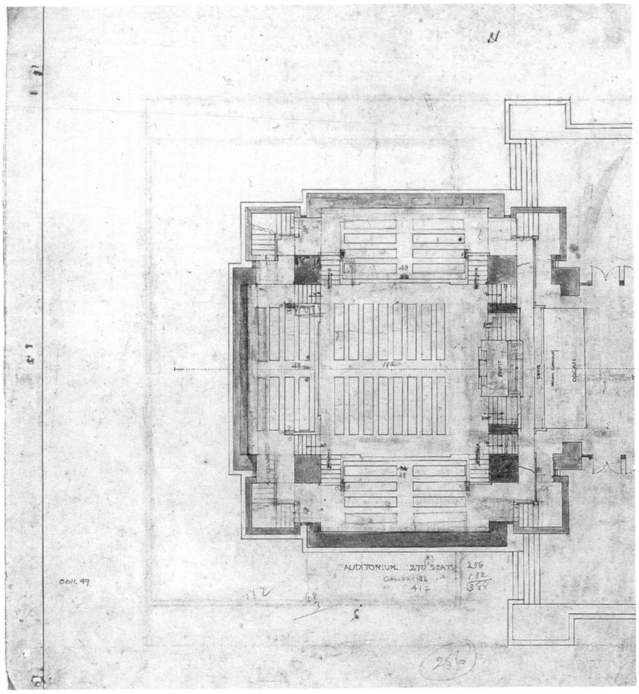

FIGURE 75

Wright, Unity
Temple, "Scheme
A," floor plan of
auditorium's main
level and lower
galleries, 1906
(Frank Lloyd
Wright Archives,
Drawing No.
0611.049, © The
Frank Lloyd
Wright Founda-
tion 1994).

design for the latter space was linked to his earlier studies for the Lincoln Center's auditorium.

*   *   *

Wright presumably prepared measured plans of Unity Temple for Rev. Jo-honnot's plans committee in time for their first presentation to the trustees on 17 December 1905. It is not known which, if any, of the surviving draw-ings for Unity Temple correspond to this early presentation of the design. Yet still extant are several preliminary plans for the building's interior spaces that Wright probably had made to present alternative schemes of seating to the trustees in February 1906. One of these, labeled Scheme A (Fig. 74), is a plan for movement and seats in the auditorium like that which Wright described in his autobiography and similar to the room as it was finally built. The lower galleries, which Wright termed "alcoves," are half a level above the main floor of the auditorium, as shown in a related plan of the building (Fig. 75). This drawing shows the pulpit on the room's south side, as built, with raised levels for a choir and organ behind the pulpit. Numbers on this drawing record the total number of seats found on the main floor and in the galleries.

Scheme A shows seating as fixed pews, like those in Unity Temple as built. Yet another set of plans documents a different scheme of movement and seating for the auditorium. These plans are the same size, medium, and

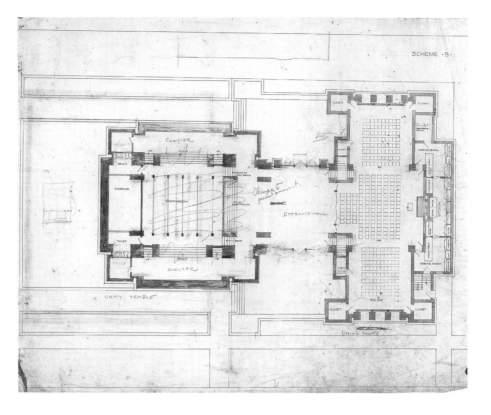

FIGURE 76

Wright, Unity Temple, "Scheme B," floor plan of entrance level, 1906 (Frank Lloyd Wright Archives, Drawing No. 0611.048, © The Frank Lloyd Wright Foundation 1994).

graphic style as those for Scheme A, as if made for comparison at the same time. One of these sheets, labeled "Scheme B" (Fig. 76), shows access to the auditorium's main floor from the entrance foyer up half a flight of wide steps all across the auditorium's south side. An upper-level plan for Scheme B (Fig. 77) shows the pulpit moved to the auditorium's north side and raised on a platform. Wright's Scheme B recalls the plan of the main hall or mortuary chapel of Taiyu-in (Fig. 64), also entered along a broad flight of steps at its rear, and whose altar is centrally placed on the side opposite the entrance. The auditorium as shown in Scheme B is also documented in a longitudinal or north–south section (Fig. 78), which shows an early design for the room's skylight and columnar detail.[66]

Scheme B was not adopted, as indicated by the hand-drawn lines forming a broad X through the section drawing. Similarly, on the lower-level plan (Fig. 76), a penciled note reads "Change to present arrangement." Scheme B's rejection corresponded with Wright's account that Johonnot wanted the auditorium to permit exit toward the pulpit, an idea that fixed its location on the room's south side. Thus Wright's evocation of the scheme of access into Taiyu-in's main hall in Scheme B for Unity Temple's auditorium was not built in the room, which was arranged as Johonnot preferred.

As noted in handwritten calculations on these drawings, Scheme A would seat 132 persons in the upper galleries, 144 persons in the lower

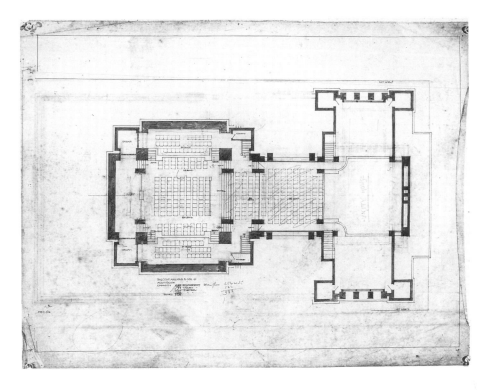

FIGURE 77

Wright, Unity
Temple, "Scheme
B," floor plan of
auditorium's main
level and lower
galleries, 1906
(Frank Lloyd
Wright Archives,
Drawing No.
0611.052, © The
Frank Lloyd
Wright Founda-
tion 1994).

galleries or alcoves, and 112 persons on the main floor of the auditorium, yielding a capacity of 388 seats, or just short of the 400 seats Wright recalled as part of the project's program. Scheme B could seat 478 persons, or 90 more than Scheme A, yet some seats in Scheme B appear to have a poor view of the pulpit. Such a capacity for the auditorium went beyond the size of the congregation itself, for in March 1909 Rev. Johonnot reported that the total membership of the church was about 144 families, while average attendance at Sunday services over the previous year had been about 130 – the largest in the time of his pastorate and an aberrantly high average because of several special occasions, such as the opening of Unity Temple in September 1908, when 350 persons were present.[67] By contrast, in 1907 the First Presbyterian Church had 798 members, First Congregational, some 861, and Grace Episcopal, 1,000. In 1906 Wright's assistant Charles White, who was then a member of Unity Church, wrote of its planning: "Of course, in plan, some room is wasted for architectural effect, but they have more seats than they really require."[68] Such an inflation of Unity Temple's seating capacity thus may have reflected either high expectations for the church's growth or anticipation of the auditorium's role as a civic meeting room for events drawing large audiences, thus resembling the auditorium of the Abraham Lincoln Center. Soon after their openings, Unity House and Unity Temple did host such local meetings on social, urbanistic, and political concerns, held under the auspices of the church's Fellowship Club.[69]

FIGURE 78

Wright, Unity
Temple, "Scheme
B," north–south
longitudinal sec-
tion, 1906 (Frank
Lloyd Wright Ar-
chives, Drawing
No. 0611.054,
© The Frank
Lloyd Wright
Foundation 1994).

The decision to avoid central access into the auditorium and to encourage movement at the room's edges also conformed to Wright's idea of an undivided major space. In his prairie houses of these same years, Wright often planned a sequence of access whereby one entered major rooms at their corners, so that one perceives the room's length and breadth at first sight. There is a clear distinction between entry into the building and arrival within a major space. Initial accounts of Unity Temple's auditorium noted that from its lowered side cloisters, "one looks directly into the auditorium and is in a sense within it, although they serve the purpose of sequestered aisles so that the congregation coming in finds seats directly without the distraction usual to the long, open, central aisle."[70] Wright's later apprentice, Edgar Tafel, wrote that Wright recalled how in Unity Temple he had been uncomfortable with the idea of passing into a church through a central rear door, then walking down the nave's length through a central aisle. Wright objected to this ecclesiastical convention because it perceptually split the building in two along its central axis. Thus, for Unity Temple, the scheme of peripheral movement around the square auditorium was to preserve the wholeness of this space for worship as an architectural affirmation of unity.[71]

Among preliminary drawings for Unity Temple, a similar arrangement of the auditorium with the pulpit on the south side is recorded in another plan (Fig. 79). This shows a platform and pulpit shaped differently than in Scheme A, and a different arrangement of piers and stairs on either side of the pulpit. It also depicts chairs instead of pews for seating. The earliest perspective of Unity Temple's interior (Fig. 80) corresponds to the plan in

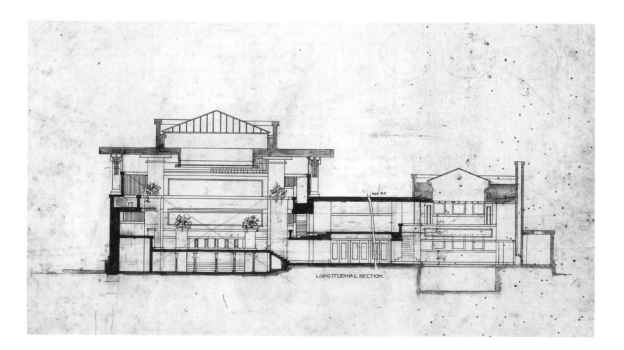

LONGITUDINAL SECTION.

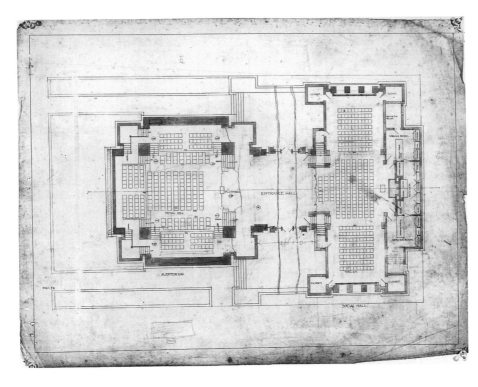

FIGURE 79

Wright, Unity
Temple, prelimi-
nary floor plan of
Unity House and
of main floor and
lower galleries of
Unity Temple,
1905–6 (Frank
Lloyd Wright Ar-
chives, Drawing
No. 0611.050,
© The Frank
Lloyd Wright
Foundation 1994).

Figure 79. This view, which was never published during Wright's lifetime, is from an imaginary position behind the platform's pulpit looking north into the auditorium filled with worshipers. The viewpoint selected for this drawing thus reverses the convention of depicting ecclesiastical interiors from the rear of a nave looking forward toward an altar. Instead, here the artist presents a tableau of the assembled congregation sitting around three sides of the room on the central main floor and on the two levels of galleries. The interior perspective is identified as a drawing of "Unity Temple" with a handwritten note in the sheet's lower right-hand corner, apparently in Wright's hand but perhaps added much later.

Foliate motifs on exterior columns match those seen in an exterior perspective of the design (Fig. 81), showing its west front. A version of this drawing was first published in February 1906.[72] Charles White then wrote: "Marion Mahoney [sic] has been doing great work (the Unity Perspectives are hers). I think she is one of the finest in the country at this class of rendering."[73] If, as White implied, Mahony drew the exterior perspective of Unity Temple's west front, then its graphic similarities to the interior view suggest that this depiction of the auditorium was also by Mahony.

As Wright later wrote in his autobiography: "The room itself – size determined by comfortable seats with leg-room for four hundred people – was built with four interior free-standing posts to carry the overhead structure. These concrete posts were hollow and became free-standing ducts to insure economic and uniform distribution of heat. The large supporting

FIGURE 80

Wright, Unity
Temple, prelimi-
nary perspective
of auditorium's in-
terior looking
north, 1905–6
(Frank Lloyd
Wright Archives,
Drawing No.
0611.021, © The
Frank Lloyd
Wright Founda-
tion 1986).

posts were so set in plan as to form a double tier of alcoves on four sides of the room."[74] The interior view (Fig. 80) shows designs for the auditorium's pulpit and platform that would be thoroughly transformed in Unity Temple as built. The perspective shows large urns for flowers in the four corners of the room at the level of the lower galleries, but such urns ultimately were not placed in the finished room. The drawing depicts a scheme of wood trim for the surfaces of the room that Wright developed much further in the final design. The completed Unity Temple would also feature a different treatment of the main interior columns and skylit ceiling. Wright also changed the art glass motifs in the clerestories and the ornament on the exterior columns, which would go from being literally foliate to geometrically abstract.[75]

The drawing shows a passage from Isaiah 40:8 inscribed along the lower edge of the upper galleries around the room. This passage is the one that Wright remembered his grandfather, Richard Lloyd Jones, quoting when he addressed gatherings of the Lloyd Jones family and its neighbors in his early church in Ixonia, Wisconsin. Wright recalled: "Grandfather preached as Isaiah preached. 'The flower fadeth, the grass withereth – but the word of the Lord, thy God, endureth forever.'"[76] This inscribed message plays against the literally natural foliage shown in urns below, as if the tangible flora evoked the idea of the biblical verse. The presence of flowers in the auditorium may also bring to mind Wright's view of Unity Temple's architecture as a formal system similar to nature: "Design is abstraction of

nature-elements in purely geometric terms."[77] This approach to form making appears in the motifs of the central skylight, the glass of the clerestories, and the linear pattern of wood in the ceiling, while more literally foliate ornamentation recurs on the columns outside the clerestory.

Together with the plans, this interior view conveys Wright's approach to architectural scale. He later wrote: "The human being is the logical norm because buildings are to be humanly inhabited and should be related to human proportions not only comfortably but agreeably. Human beings should look as well in the building or of it as flowers do. People should belong to the building just as it should belong to them."[78] As indicated by a depiction of every individual seat in the plan, Wright had designed the auditorium to be closely related in scale to the assembled congregation. Unlike the tall, long nave of a cathedral or basilican church of smaller size, Unity Temple's auditorium had no area or volume beyond the minimum needed by worshipers for seats and movement. The interior view conveys the volumetric compactness of Wright's room, whose galleries enabled about four hundred persons to be seated in a space less than 35 ft. wide between balcony fronts.

A fit between people and space recalls Wright's later assertion that his concept had been to "build a temple to man, appropriate to his uses as a meeting place."[79] As contemporaneous Unitarian humanistic theology emphasized the presence of divinity in man, this interior perspective suggests that for Wright the room was conceptually complete only when peopled by worshipers. Yet Wright's idea of a tiered space with optimal acoustics, in which an assembly was conscious of itself as a whole, also recalls the Chicago Auditorium, on whose design he had worked with Adler and Sullivan. As Wright viewed Unity Temple as a departure from conventional

FIGURE **81**

Wright, Unity Temple, rendering of west front, 1906 (Frank Lloyd Wright Archives, Drawing No. 0611.003, © The Frank Lloyd Wright Foundation 1994).

church interiors, so he later wrote of the Auditorium as "the first great room for audience to really depart from various and curious prevailing traditions."[80]

Unity Temple as Design in Concrete

The earliest announcement of Wright's intention for the new building appeared in Chicago's *Construction News* of 23 September 1905, which noted that Wright had already "prepared plans for a church to be built in Oak Park for the Unity Church. It will be one-story and basement of brick and stone, have probably a slate roof, hardwood finish, steam heat, electric wiring for light and cost $35,000."[81] Did Wright ever contemplate Unity Temple in brick? Figures 80 and 116 show surfaces with closely spaced horizontal lines, suggesting brick courses in walls and piers. However, brick is not recorded in other surviving drawings or accounts of the project. In his later autobiography, Wright stated that concrete had been the preferred material from the start:

> The first idea – to keep a noble ROOM in mind, and let the room shape the whole edifice, let the room inside be the architecture outside.
>
> What shape? Well, the answer lay, in what material? There was only one material to choose as the church funds were $45,000, to "church" 400 people in 1906. Concrete was cheap.
>
> Concrete alone could do it. But even concrete as it was in use at that time meant wood "forms" and some other material than concrete for outside facing. They were in the habit of covering the concrete with brick or stone, plastering and furring the inside of the walls. Plastering the walls would be cheaper than brick or stone but wouldn't stick to concrete in our climate. Why not make wooden boxes or forms so the concrete could be cast in them as separate blocks and masses, these separate blocks and masses grouped about an interior space in some such way as to preserve this desired sense of the interior space in the appearance of the whole building? And the block-masses be left as themselves with no "facing." That would be cheap and permanent. . . .
>
> There was no money to spend in working on the concrete mass outside or with it after it was once cast.
>
> Good reason, this, if no other, for getting away from any false facing. Couldn't the surface be qualified in the casting process so this whole matter of veneered "Facade" could be omitted with good effect? This was later the cause of much experiment, with what success may be seen.[82]

As Wright claimed, expense was perhaps decisive in his unusual choice of material. In 1906 Charles White wrote of Unity Temple: "The design is economical in the extreme. I do not know of a church of the same area that can be built in masonry for the same price."[83] Soon after, Rev. Johonnot wrote: "The financial resources of the church limited it to a building costing not more than $40,000. The location on the main street of the village in the midst of a group of many fine public buildings, none of which cost less than $65,000, and others from $75,000 to $100,000, imposed the civic obligation of creating a building worthy of its environment. Several of these edifices are churches forcing a competition in kind. . . . These conditions created a most difficult problem. It could not be solved upon the lines of traditional and customary church architecture, since a building of the same kind as those surrounding it, but cheaper, would suffer by comparison."[84]

As Johonnot observed, concrete was much less expensive than stone,[85] and, in 1905, it was also less costly than brick. In 1899 Boston's *Brick-builder* published designs for a prototypical modern "Village Church" costing $50,000.[86] These projects for smaller suburban churches featured brick arches, ornamental terra cotta, and richly profiled, spired towers – all prohibitively costly details given limited funds. If Wright's budget were restricted to Rev. Johonnot's figure, then even a new Unity Church of brick would indeed have had to be kept as a simple building, likely to look underfunded. Thus, as Johonnot wrote, a Unity Church in concrete "stands on its own merits and frees itself from any depreciatory contrasts with the other costlier churches."[87]

Before Unity Temple Wright had not designed a completed work whose structure and exterior were all of concrete. He was, however, clearly interested in the material's potential – an issue that also engaged other architects of the period. Wright's decision to design Unity Temple in concrete was in part related to the regional building industry, for Chicago in the years 1905–10 was a major center of innovation in this material. Nationally, American production of Portland cement had grown from 500,000 barrels per year in 1892 to 46,500,000 barrels in 1906, multiplying nearly a hundredfold in the fifteen years that corresponded closely to those of Wright's independent practice.[88] One account reported that, by 1895, reinforced concrete "had come to be firmly established and the increase of its employment was decidedly rapid. This advance movement was greatly stimulated by a shortage of steel which developed in 1897 and the year following. Deprived of steel at the time when sorely needed, the attention of architects was, almost per force, turned in the direction of concrete. European systems were adopted in this country, and the subject of reinforced concrete became a matter of practical and scientific study, to its decided development and advancement."[89] In April 1908 one representative of the Universal Portland Cement Company, which supplied cement for Unity Temple's concrete, wrote that Chicago's area had become "the distributing point of more barrels of Portland cement annually than any other city in the world. Clustering around Chicago lie more cement-producing mills than any other center in the country. The output of cement in Chicago and its contiguous territory is approximately 17,000,000 barrels per year, or about one third of the output of the whole country."[90] The account depicted Unity Temple, which was then nearing completion.

In the years 1905–9, when Wright was working on Unity Temple, his local architectural colleagues were working on varied types of buildings in which concrete was externally exposed rather than clad with other materials. In 1906–8 Schmidt, Garden, and Martin designed the Montgomery Ward warehouse along the north branch of the Chicago River. Its length of over 800 ft. and its area of 158,000 sq. ft. made it then the largest building in the world with a reinforced concrete frame. Schmidt, Garden, and Martin were also among the Chicago architects then designing pavilions in reinforced concrete for the city's park system. D. H. Burnham and Company designed a number of these structures from 1903 to 1906. For these municipally funded, open buildings, budgets were limited, and the cast concrete work was exposed as the finished surface in order to reduce expense, just as Wright proposed for Unity Temple.[91]

About 1905, in both national and regional architectural cultures, there was new enthusiasm for concrete's expressive and ornamental potential. In 1907 at the American Institute of Architects' convention in Chicago, Irving Pond, Wright's local colleague and chairman of the Committee on Applied Arts and Sciences, asserted that "the aesthetic possibilities of reinforced concrete, . . . can hardly be overestimated. Little beyond the introductory chapter has been written in the history of reinforced concrete, and every advance in the science of its manufacture and use will signal an advance along the line of artistic application."[92] Pond predicted that concrete's usage would grow beyond commercial buildings to become characteristic of monumental public architecture.

In a paper presented at this meeting on "The Artistic Expression of Concrete," architect Albert Elzner foresaw that concrete "will afford abundant opportunity for originality and individuality, and accordingly, bold excursions have been made into the new field with creditable results."[93] Yet at the turn of the century, concrete was typically used only for the internal structure of public buildings and churches, which were clad with brick or stone. In this era, those few places of worship whose structure and exterior were both of concrete included Carrere and Hastings's Presbyterian church, near the same firm's Ponce de León Hotel in St. Augustine, Florida; Ellicott and Emmart's St. David's Church in Rolland Park, outside Baltimore; Our Lady of Loretto Church in East New York, a suburb of Brooklyn; and the dome of Temple Adath Israel in Boston. Yet all of these buildings for worship were variations on classical styles, with concrete shaped in ornamental details as if it were stone. Given such works, Elzner claimed that "it is highly probable that our concrete architecture will carry with it for some time to come the practice of design in all current styles, or no style at all, and if we would ever expect it to assume a really artistic expression – that will have the true ring, and will endure for all times, it will be found only in isolated examples, produced now and then by some genius with the divine spark, as is the case with all true works of art."[94]

In this period of expectations for innovative forms in concrete, Wright saw in Unity Temple a timely opportunity to create a building that would be recognized as a new type of monumental architecture. A concrete church without overt historical forms would be a first. In 1902 Wright proposed to Jenkin Lloyd Jones that Abraham Lincoln Center be built entirely of concrete, as one way of meeting its budgetary limitations.[95] In this case, limited funds similarly may have provided Wright with a pretext for a highly innovative building, yet Jones and his committee had opted for a brick monolith. With Rev. Johonnot's church in Oak Park, Wright had found an institutional client who could be persuaded to support an experiment in a new architecture of concrete.

*   *   *

Wright's interest in concrete fit his broad theoretical agenda, which he had announced in his address of 1900 on "The Architect." In this address to fellow architects, he stressed new building types and materials, asserting that "the architect will know the capacities of modern methods, processes and machines and become their master. He will sense the significance to his art of the new materials that are his of which steel is but one. He will show in his work that he has been emancipated from the meagre unit established by the brick arch and the stone lintel, and his imagination will transfigure to new beauty his primitive art."[96] Wright developed this thesis in "The Art and Craft of the Machine," delivered to the Chicago Arts and Crafts Society at Hull House in 1901. There he envisioned architecture's renewal through its mastery of new means of construction. Wright asked: "And how fares the troop of old materials galvanized into new life by the Machine? Our modern materials are those old materials in more plastic guise, rendered so by the Machine. . . . Steel and iron, plastic cement and terra cotta."[97]

A guiding principle of Wright's program was his belief in the Ruskinian ideal of truthful expressions of materials. Wright claimed to have adopted this precept at the start of his practice in 1894 and to have realized it in his work to 1908, when he advised architects: "Bring out the nature of the materials, let their nature intimately into your scheme. . . . Reveal the nature of the wood, plaster, brick or stone in your designs; they are all by nature friendly and beautiful. No treatment can be really a matter of fine art when these natural characteristics are, or their nature is, outraged or neglected."[98] Yet Wright extended this ideal beyond the realm of surfaces and into his study of whole constructive systems, including the methods of fabricating and assembling structure. He thus expanded the idea of truth to materials to include the totality of the building process as a source of aesthetic expression in the visible architecture.

Wright recalled that when designing Unity Temple "the wooden forms or molds in which concrete buildings must at that time be cast were always the chief item of expense, so to repeat the use of a single one as often as possible was desirable, even necessary. Therefore a building all four sides alike, looked like the thing. This, in simplist terms, meant a building square in plan. That would make their temple a cube, a noble form."[99] As shown in the working drawing of the main auditorium level (Fig. 82), this meant that Unity Temple's large east, north, and west outer walls (each of which is 38 ft. wide above ground) would all be cast from the same wood formwork. There was no similar central wall on the south side, where the pulpit is located. The four corner stair towers (each of which was initially designed as 10 ft. 6 in. on a side) would all be cast from another set of molds. The temple's outer walls would thus be cast in only two different shapes of molds – one for the central outer walls and another for the corner stair towers.

Wright's design responded not only to the constructive logic of concrete, but also to his theory of organic form as the conceptual basis of his architecture. As he wrote in 1914: "I still believe that the ideal of an organic architecture forms the origin and source, the strength and, fundamentally, the significance of everything ever worthy the name of architecture," noting that "by organic I mean an architecture that *develops* from within outward in harmony with the conditions of its being as distinguished from one that is *applied* from without."[100] From this perspective, the plan is the primary expression of organic form because it registers the internal life of the build-

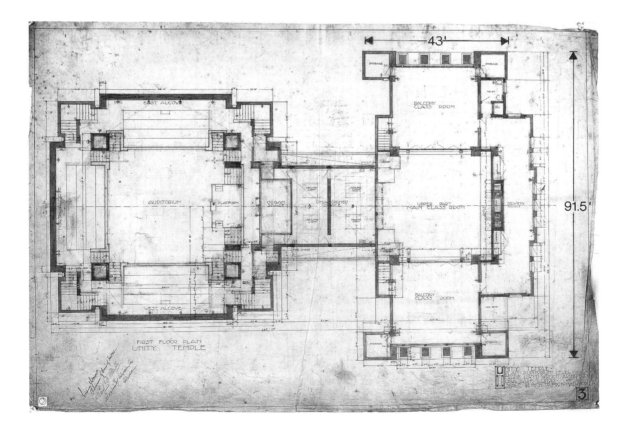

ing, as opposed to the elevation, which documents its external appearance. The plan holds within it implications for the architecture's outward, three-dimensional form. In 1928 Wright wrote that the plan was "the prophetic soul of the building – a building that can live only because of the prophecy that is the plan."[101] In his view, "every good plan is organic. That means that its development in all directions is inherent – inevitable. . . . There is more beauty in a fine ground plan than in almost any of its ultimate consequences. In itself it will have the rhythms, masses, and proportions of a good decoration if it is an organic plan for an organic building with individual style – consistent with materials."[102]

In Wright's view, an organic plan showed distinction of parts within the whole. The articulation of individual elements gave the plan its character. Wright wrote of his works to 1908: "The plans are as a rule much more articulate than is the school product of the Beaux Arts. All the forms are complete in themselves and frequently do duty at the same time from within and without as decorative attributes of the whole. This tendency to greater individuality of the parts emphasized by more and more complete articulation will be seen in the plans for Unity Church."[103] Wright later recalled that he had initially developed this idea in the Larkin Building, whose plan (Fig. 83) separates its larger atrium block from a flanking annex containing smaller rooms. Between these two elements was a connective entrance that led into the center of the larger office building's atrium. As in Unity Temple, the corner stair towers are distinctly detached from their central spaces, giving articulation to the plans. In the Larkin Building, the mechanical shafts next to each stair tower on the building's long sides are also separately articulated. In 1952 Wright recalled that

> When the Larkin Building model was first brought into the studio, that stair tower at the corner was part of the mass, part of the building. And I didn't know what was the matter. I was trying for something with some freedom that I hadn't got.
>
> Suddenly, the model was standing on the studio table in the center, I came in and I saw what was the matter. I took those four corners and I pulled them out away from the building, made them individual features, planted them. And there began the thing that I was trying to do. You see, I got features instead of walls. I followed that up with Unity Temple where there were not walls of any kind, only features; and the features were screens grouped about interior space. The thing that came to me by instinct in the Larkin Building began to come consciously in Unity Temple.[104]

Wright here described an approach to architectural form that could be developed in different buildings regardless of their variations in function or construction. While Unity Temple was a church made of reinforced concrete, the Larkin Building was an office building whose structure consisted of a steel frame inside, clad with brick. Along the Larkin Building's outer walls, load-bearing piers of brick carried steel beams that spanned between

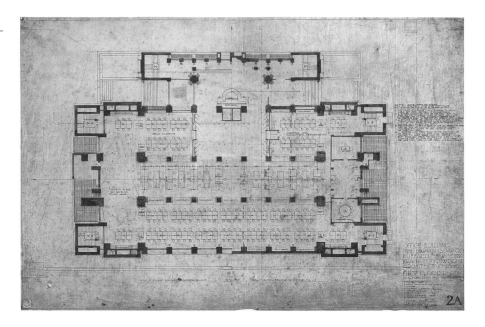

FIGURE **83**

Wright, Larkin
Company admin-
istration building,
Buffalo, N.Y.,
1904–6, entry
and upper floor
plans (Frank Lloyd
Wright Archives,
Drawings No.
0403.065 and
0403.069, © The
Frank Lloyd
Wright Founda-
tion 1994).

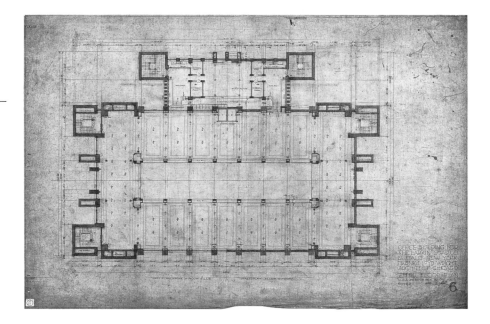

piers, while bearing walls of brick formed the corner stair towers and ventilation shafts. This construction is shown in the steel framing plan for the
Larkin Building's first floor (Fig. 84) and in a photograph of outer brick piers
flanking the central steel frame (Fig. 85). In this way, the Larkin Building's
structural system compares more closely to that of the Abraham Lincoln

Center, where brick piers and walls encased an internal steel frame. As noted earlier, Wright began to articulate distinct masses in the Abraham Lincoln Center. This idea was progressively developed in the Larkin Building and Unity Temple, even though these two works were quite different in social function and structural system.

Formal Integration of Unity Temple and Unity House

Wright recalled that after he pondered Unity Temple, he then had "penciled upon the sheet of paper, in the main, the plan, section and elevation . . . all except 'Unity House,' as the room for secular recreation came to be called. To establish harmony between these buildings of separate function proved difficult, utterly exasperating."[105] For Wright, the formal and symbolic problem of the exterior was "how to keep the noble scale of the temple in the design of the subordinate mass of the secular hall and not falsify the function of that noble mass? . . . Thirty-four studies were necessary to arrive at this as it is now seen. Unfortunately they are lost with thousands of others of other buildings. The fruit of similar struggles to coordinate and perfect them all as organic entities – I wish I had kept. Unity House looks easy enough now, for it is right enough."[106]

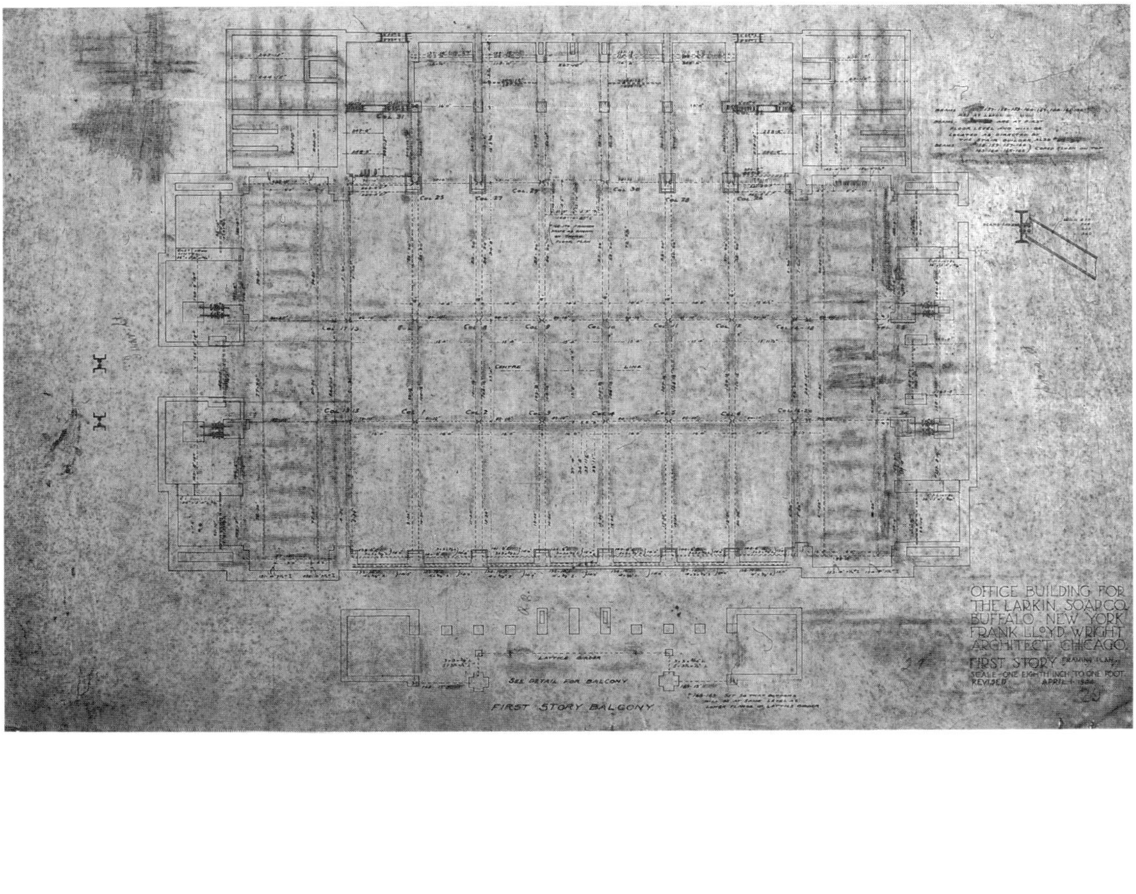

FIGURE **84**

Wright, Larkin Building, steel framing plan, first floor, 1 April 1904 (Frank Lloyd Wright Archives, Drawing No. 0403.120, © The Frank Lloyd Wright Foundation 1987).

FIGURE 85

Wright, Larkin
Building, con-
struction view
looking north, ca.
1904 (Frank Lloyd
Wright Archives,
Photograph No.
0403.0010,
© The Frank
Lloyd Wright
Foundation).

The relationship between Unity Temple and Unity House engaged a symbolic question central to American religious architecture of the period. In 1905 the *Church Economist* asked whether a modern religious center should be "a temple or social workshop." Recognizing that new church buildings included auditoriums and social halls, the editor concluded that a church's social functions are entirely subordinate to its main office, hence: "Let us not forget that the main and all-important object of any church is public worship. While it is desirable to provide a church with much that goes into the equipment of a modern club, there may be a danger lest, in our American habit of going to extremes, we put an emphasis on convenience and social interest that shall dim the spiritual office of the church. . . . In every church building the keynote should be that of reverence and holiness."[107] Rather than house social activities in the same building used for worship, "the parish building can be united architecturally with the church by cloisters, or in some other architectural treatment, bringing the whole into a symmetrical construction while keeping the social service somewhat distinct."[108]

Wright's approach to the relation of Unity Temple and Unity House had identified both as parts of a single church institution. The social hall was subordinated to the room for worship, which provided the keynote for the architecture of both spaces. The design thus embodied Rev. Johonnot's view that public worship was a church's primary function, and that its social life should be symbolically linked with its religious purpose.[109] He wrote of Wright's design:

A modern church building has a two-fold purpose: it is erected for the worship of God and for the service of man. These two functions demand a

different architectural treatment that each may be best served. In the design for Unity Church there were two distinct buildings, one designed for public worship and other suitable public meetings, and another for purposes of social service and religious meetings of a less formal character. They are, however, connected by a large Entrance Hall by which they are knitted together into a single integral and harmonious structure in outward appearance, thus giving unity to the two functions of a church.[110]

In distinguishing and connecting Unity Temple and Unity House, Wright's design contrasted with Jenkin Lloyd Jones's concept of an auditorium for services combined with other parish rooms in one architectural form, so that the room for worship in the Abraham Lincoln Center was not volumetrically distinct. In Unity Church's old building, the parish hall was below the auditorium for worship, thus raising the total built volume, which culminated in the spire. Yet Wright's new structure was to be a lower building with flat roofs, in which auditorium and parish hall were adjacent rather than superimposed volumes. In plan Unity Temple's ideal square contrasts with a rectangular Unity House at the site's rear. Yet both Unity Temple and Unity House share the plan's main axis as well as many similar motifs, so that the design is legible as variation within unity. The scheme's consistency derived from Wright's decision to limit its vocabulary of forms to squared elements. In 1910 he wrote that in each of his works, "the differentiation of a single, certain simple form characterizes the expression of one building. . . . From one basic idea all the formal elements of design are in each case derived and held together in scale and character."[111]

Among extant drawings there is one elevation in pencil on tracing paper of the west side facing Kenilworth Avenue (Fig. 86). This sheet's size

FIGURE 86

Wright, Unity Temple, drawing of west elevation, 1906 (Frank Lloyd Wright Archives, Drawing No. 0611.004, © The Frank Lloyd Wright Foundation 1962).

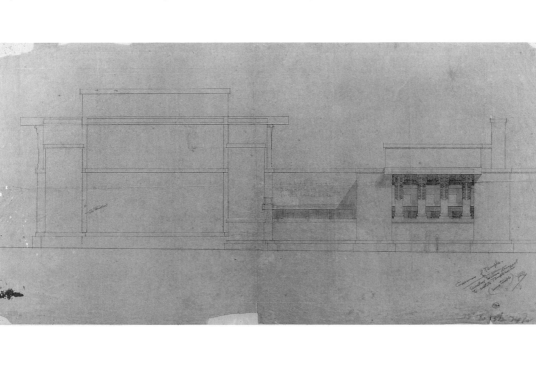

(41 in. × 21 in.) and its scale (1 in. = 4 ft.) are those of the working drawings. Barry Byrne recalled that this elevation "is by Wright himself and was for my guidance in developing the working drawings of this portion of the temple."[112] This sheet thus approximates the final design rather than one of Wright's earlier studies. Unity Temple's basic masses are here outlined, with the six ornamental columns in its upper clerestory not legible. A handwritten note calls attention to the "slot window" to the left. On the left side of the entrance terrace wall, there is a cubic lantern atop a pier to the right of the terrace wall's end block. Lanterns were later set in walls above steps to the terraces (see Fig. 100). Behind the terrace wall, above the six doors in shadow, a three-line inscription is shown. To the right, a diagonal shadow sets off the projecting mass of Unity House. Its central motif of four raised ornamental columns, with bands of glass running behind their base and crowns, and the cantilevered roof above, is the most intensively rendered part of the drawing. On the sidewalk sloping southward in front of Unity House stand two scale figures. At the lower right, a handwritten inscription, presumably added later, reads: "Grammar of Temple – Secular section designed to match Temple section (some trouble) FLlW."

This west elevation shows how Wright adapted a formal grammar first developed for Unity Temple at left to the end wall of Unity House at right. The horizontal ledge or sill on which Unity Temple's ornamental columns stand continues as the level of the roof of the entrance terrace and as the main cornice of Unity House. The top of Unity House's attic is level with the top of Unity Temple's stair towers. The low wall of the entrance terrace aligns with the low wall of Unity House. The end block of the entrance terrace wall is set in front of the southernmost stair tower of Unity Temple. The stair tower's height above the terrace's end block matches the full height of Unity House's corner blocks set to either side of its colonnade. Perhaps to prevent Unity Temple's size from overwhelming Unity House, Wright made the crown of Unity House's chimney level with the top of Unity Temple's projecting roof slabs. In these ways, Wright made the elevations of Unity Temple and Unity House visually interlock around the central entrance.

Unity Temple has six exterior columns on each of its four sides, while Unity House has four such columns on both its east and west sides. In form and height, the columns of Unity House match those of Unity Temple, yet those of Unity House are closer together. Other forms of Unity House that echo parts of Unity Temple (stepped base, corner blocks, flat projecting roof, and attic parapet) are all slightly smaller than the comparable features of Unity Temple. Yet differences in scale between parts of Unity House and Unity Temple are less noticeable to the eye because the two buildings are visually separated by the entrance between them. This distance between the masses of Unity Temple and Unity House thus functioned not only as a common entry, but also as a visual interval that enabled Wright to adjust the scalar differences between Unity Temple and Unity House almost imperceptibly.

The degree of formal integration between Unity Temple and Unity House is evident in a drawing showing the temple's north elevation, flanked by the ends of the north elevation of Unity House visible to the rear on either side of the temple's front (Fig. 87). This drawing corresponds closely to that published as Plate LXIII(b) of the Wasmuth folio, as if it were a definitive record of Wright's formal intention. Glass details are omitted to clarify arrangement of masses. No rendered shadows or changes in line weight indicate that the face of Unity Temple is far forward of Unity House, as if to emphasize the formal consistency between these two parts of the church. Unity Temple's central attic crowns the composition, stepping down on either side to the roof slabs. The sill level of Unity Temple's clerestory window continues as the coping level of the flanking stair towers. This in turn is level with the attic of Unity House behind. Similarly, the ledge below Unity Temple's central colonnade recurs on each side as the level of Unity House's flat roof. Unity Temple's stepped base aligns with that of

FIGURE 87

Wright, Unity
Temple, drawing
of north elevation,
n.d. (Frank Lloyd
Wright Archives,
Drawing No.
0611.059, © The
Frank Lloyd
Wright Founda-
tion 1994).

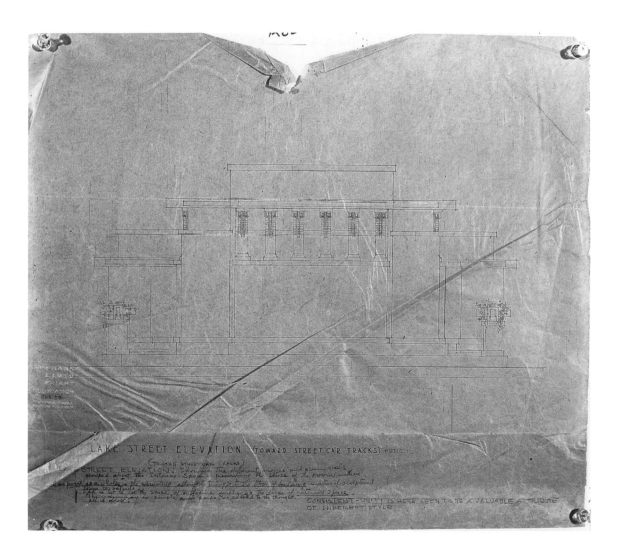

LAKE STREET ELEVATION (TOWARD STREET CAR TRACKS) PENCIL

Unity House on the entrance terraces to each side. The elevation shows the whole church raised on a massive base, which does not appear above ground in the built structure. An undated, hand-lettered caption at the bottom of the sheet conveys Wright's retrospective view of Unity Temple formed in the 1930s. Here he labeled the drawing as a "Lake street elevation (toward street car tracks): showing the different masses and screen walls grouped about the Interior-Space, preserving the sense of the room within as *point*, as a whole is the structure allowed to suggest the block of building material sculptured from the outside. All is set to let the sense of the enclosure emphasize the sense of *interior space*. The grammar is simple and perfectly adapted to the thought. All is[?] CONSISTENT – UNITY IS HERE SEEN TO BE A VALUABLE ATTRIBUTE OF INHERENT STYLE."

Wright's Unit System for Unity Temple

Wright's studies of the relations of Unity Temple and Unity House were guided by his unit system of design, which is the basis of the whole building's aesthetic integration. Wright's procedure for laying out a plan was described in a letter of May 1904 by his assistant Charles White:

> Wright's greatest contribution to Architecture, I think, is his unit system of design. All his plans are composed of units grouped in a symmetrical and systematic way. . . .
>
> The units are varied in size and number to suit each particular case, and the unit decided upon, is consistently carried through every portion of the plan. His process in getting up a new design is the reverse of that usually employed. Most men outline the strictly utilitarian requirements, choose their style, and then mold the design along those lines, whereas Wright develops his unit first, then fits the design to the requirements as much as possible, or rather, fits the requirements to the design.[113]

In his major article of March 1908, "In the Cause of Architecture," Wright similarly wrote of his work: "In laying out the ground plans for even the more insignificant of these buildings a simple axial law and order and the ordered spacing upon a system of certain structural units definitely established for each structure in accord with its scheme of practical construction and aesthetic proportion, is practiced as an expedient to simplify the technical difficulties of execution."[114] Wright could have drawn on a wide range of sources for his reliance on a unit system in design. In the 1870s Viollet-le-Duc, whose writings Wright admired, had stated that the principles of unity and harmony in architectural expression depended on neither symmetry nor uniformity. Instead, they demanded "in the first place, a strict regard for *scale*, that is, the proper relation of the various parts of a whole to a unit of measurement. This scale adopted by the Greeks in their temples was not an absolute but a relative unit, known as the *module*."[115]

Wright's reliance on modular design was perhaps rooted in his apprenticeship with Adler and Sullivan, who used unit dimensions to design steel-framed tall buildings. As Adler had written in 1897: "Under all conditions which may govern the subdivision of space, . . . there will be a regularity and symmetry which permits the introduction of a unit of subdivision. In determining this unit of subdivision the directing factors will be: – (a) the necessary dimensions of the room resulting from the proposed occupation; (b) the requirements of the framing of the skeleton of the building; and (c) the exigencies of the artistic expression of the proposed external presentation. The unit of subdivision will also be the unit of construction and the unit of design."[116]

Wright returned to this concept in his article of 1928 on plans, where he recommended that, in order to achieve consistent scale, a unit dimension should be adopted:

> This scale or unit-of-size of the various parts varies with the specific purpose of the building and the materials used to build it. The only sure way to hold all to scale is to adopt a unit-system, unit-lines crossing the paper both ways, spaced as pre-determined, say 4'-0" on centers – or 2'-8" or whatever seems to yield a proper scale for the proposed purpose. Divisions in spacing are thus brought into a certain texture as a result; ordered scale in detail is sure to follow.[117]

Regarding the relation of plan to materials, Wright wrote that "the more simple the materials used – the more the building tends toward a mono-material building – the more nearly will 'perfect style' reward an organic plan and ease of execution economize results. The more logical will the whole become." The choice of materials affects scale. Thus, a wood plan would be used on a different unit of size than a concrete plan. Wright described the plan for Unity Temple as "a cast-block and slab building,"[118] meaning that almost all its forms were concrete slabs set horizontally or vertically. For Wright, this method of building determined Unity Temple's architectural character and its unit of size: "Cast-slabs, set sidewise and lengthwise, and flatwise, making everything, as may be seen in the result. Planned on multiples of 7'-0"."[119]

To illustrate this point, Wright published a drawing of Unity Temple's plan on which different interior levels are shown overlaid with a grid of lines said to be marking horizontal divisions of 7 ft. (Fig. 88). This plan appeared below a drawing of the building's front on Lake Street, suggesting that a three-dimensional development of the design had proceeded from the logic of its ground plan. The implied relationship between plan and exterior is seen most clearly in the six columns fronting the clerestory of the auditorium. In plan, the grid's lines pass through the centers of these columns, indicating that they are spaced 7 ft. on centers. On the exterior, the spacing of the auditorium's columns visually marks the rhythm of this unit dimension that Wright claimed to have selected in order to control the scale of all parts of the building.

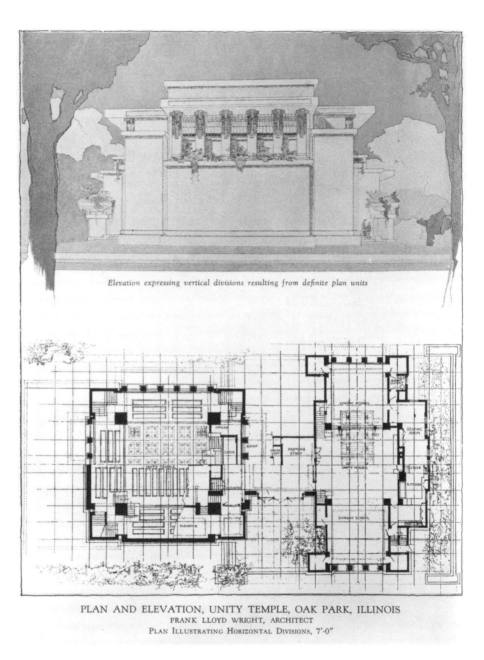

Elevation expressing vertical divisions resulting from definite plan units

PLAN AND ELEVATION, UNITY TEMPLE, OAK PARK, ILLINOIS
FRANK LLOYD WRIGHT, ARCHITECT
PLAN ILLUSTRATING HORIZONTAL DIVISIONS, 7'-0"

Wright's unit system is evident throughout the working drawings for Unity Temple prepared in his studio in March 1906.[120] Figure 89 shows the working drawing of Unity Temple's balcony and roof plan overlaid with a unit grid of 6 ft. 10 in., which is the spacing between column centers on all the sides of the auditorium. This dimension is slightly less than the unit of 7 ft. that Wright later recalled. The overlaid grid shows that the full square area of Unity Temple between the corners of the four stair towers was to be 61 ft. 8 in., or almost exactly 9 units (61 ft. 6 in.) on a side. Inside, the spatial core of the auditorium, as the square area between balcony fronts, is 34 ft. 5 in. wide or about 5 units (34 ft. 2 in.), as seen in the 5 × 5 grid of the skylight bays. Each balcony's depth, from the front of its railing to the cores of the columns outside the clerestories, is about 2 units (13 ft. 8 in.). Points on the grid also touch the inner corners of the auditorium's four main hollow structural columns; one such point is noted by the circle centered on the inner corner of the southeast column.

Analysis of the ground floor plan (Fig. 90) reveals that the dimensions of Unity House and the central entrance foyer also correspond to the unit grid. In Unity House the width of the central rectangular area including its north and south walls is 27 ft. 2 in. or 4 units (27 ft. 4 in.). Between the outer edges of its east and west structural columns, Unity House was designed to be about 11 units (75 ft. 2 in.) long. These are the dimensions of the major structural trusses that support the room's central roof, as shown on Unity House's roof plan on the right in Figure 89. This shows the skylight to be 17 ft. 2 in. or 2.5 units (17 ft. 1 in.) wide. The entrance foyer's doorways were to be 20 ft. 3 in. or about 3 units (20 ft. 6 in.) wide north–south between their flanking piers. The foyer was to be 27 ft. 9 in. or about 4 units (27 ft. 4 in.) across east–west between the inner faces of its door jambs. Thus the planned spatial dimensions of Unity Temple, Unity House, and the entrance

FIGURE **89**

Wright, Unity Temple, working plan of balcony and roof level, 1906, with author's notations showing multiples of unit dimension, a = 6 ft. 10 in. (Frank Lloyd Wright Archives, Drawing No. 0611.013, © The Frank Lloyd Wright Foundation 1986).

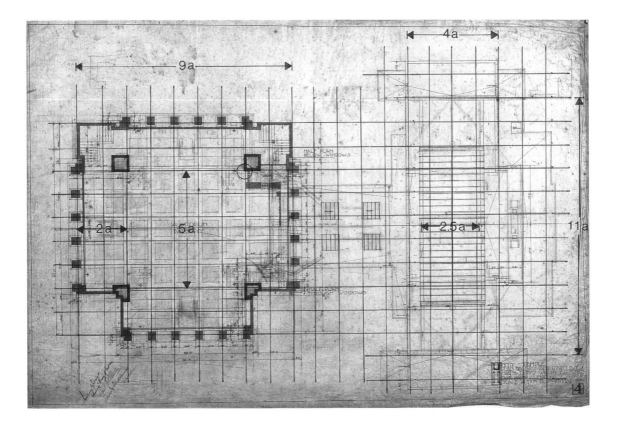

FIGURE **90**

Wright, Unity
Temple, working
plan of ground
floor, 1906, with
author's notations
showing multiples
of unit dimension,
a = 6 ft. 10 in.
(Frank Lloyd
Wright Archives,
Drawing No.
0611.011, © The
Frank Lloyd
Wright Founda-
tion 1986).

foyer between them corresponded closely to a single unit system, as Wright maintained.

Overlaying the same grid on the section through Unity Temple's auditorium (Fig. 91) reveals that the height of this main room from its floor to the bottom of the skylight coffers is 27 ft. or about 4 units (27 ft. 4 in.). The height from the auditorium's floor to the upper balcony's floor was planned as 13 ft. 6 in. or about 2 units (13 ft. 8 in.), as was the height from the upper balcony floor to the bottom of the skylight coffers (13 ft. 6 in.). Inside the entrance foyer's doors, the ceilings are 7 ft. 3 in. or just over 1 unit high above the floor. The unit system obtains not only in publicly visible spaces, but also in secondary areas, such as the coat room beneath Unity Temple, which was also about 1 unit high from floor to ceiling.

Overlaying the same grid onto Unity Temple's north or Lake Street elevation (Fig. 92) reveals that the width of its central wall, including the slot windows to either side, was to be 40 ft. 8 in., or about 6 units (41 ft. 0 in.). The temple's height from the top of its stepped base to the top of the central attic parapet is 41 ft. or exactly 6 units. The ratio of the temple's core width to core height is thus about 1:1, or unity. The building thus had a cubic central mass. The corner stair towers to either side of the central wall were to be 10 ft. 6 in. or about 1.5 units (10 ft. 3 in.) wide. The width of Unity Temple's flat roof between its outer fasciae on opposite sides was to

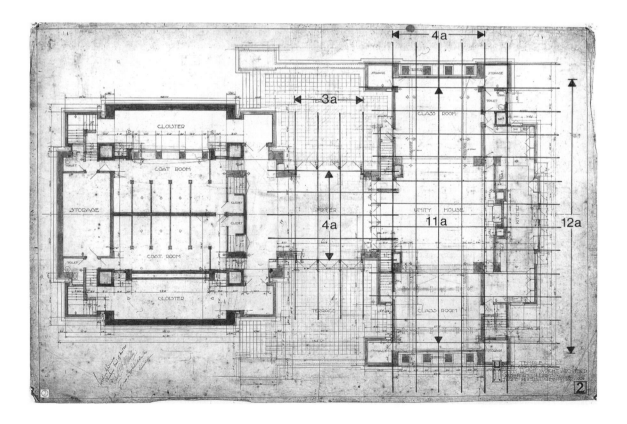

be 75 ft. 6 in. or about 11 units (75 ft. 2 in.). On the front of Unity Temple, the central wall's height from the top of its base to the bottom of the clerestory's sill is 17 ft. 6 in. or about 2.5 units (17 ft. 1 in.). The clerestory's height from the bottom of its sill to the top of its columns is 13 ft. 6 in. or about 2 units (13 ft. 8 in.), corresponding to the designed height of the upper balcony inside.

The south elevation of Unity House shows its width of 74 ft. 10 in. or about 11 units between its corner blocks. The chimney is 14 ft. or about 2 units (13 ft. 8 in.) high, and 34 ft. 10 in. or about 5 units (34 ft. 2 in.) wide, or about the width of Unity House's spatial core inside, and of Unity Temple's interior between balconies. The whole building's west elevation (Fig. 93) shows that the height of Unity House from the top of its stepped base to the top of its projecting flat roof is some 20 ft. 4 in. or about 3 units (20 ft. 6 in.) high. Its attic above the flat roof is about 1 unit (6 ft. 10 in.) high.

Using one unit in three dimensions, Wright brought all parts of the design into a single numerical order, not only to facilitate construction and control scale, but also to signify the concept of unity in mathematical terms, just as the building's construction in monolith concrete signified this idea in material terms. With this system Unity Temple also exemplified Wright's concept of organic architecture, where all parts are consistently related to each other and to the whole. The dimensions of the design are numerically

FIGURE **91**

Wright, Unity Temple, working drawing of longitudinal section, 1906, with author's notations showing multiples of unit dimension, a = 6 ft. 10 in. (Frank Lloyd Wright Archives, Drawing No. 0611.016, © The Frank Lloyd Wright Foundation 1983).

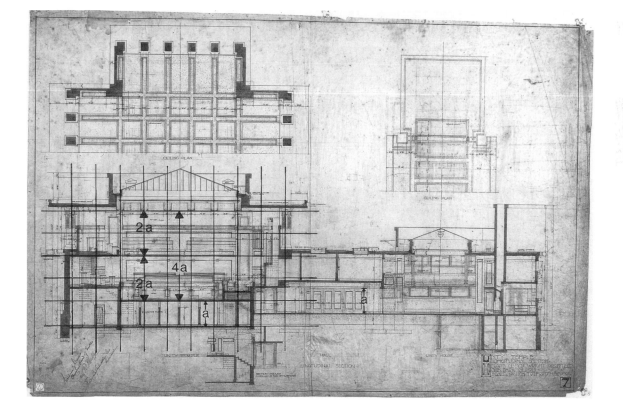

integrated, achieving the degree of formal consistency that Wright identified with nature. As Oak Park architect Robert Spencer wrote of Wright's work to 1900: "Nature, who knows the most rigid and subtle geometry, as well as the most voluptuous freedom of, and apparent confusion of form, is the source to which he has always gone for inspiration."[121] The design's usage of a square unit of size calls to mind Wright's association of that form with the idea of integrity. In Unity Temple the square as sign of integrity could imply both integration in a formal sense and honesty in an ethical sense, as if the design exhibited an ordering principle that conveyed both an aesthetic ideal and its associated moral meaning.[122]

Unity Church's Acceptance of Wright's Design

After Wright had made an initial presentation of his design to Unity Church's trustees on 17 December 1905, the church's leadership and the congregation debated its merits for about two months. Although the building's architectural logic and merit were clear to Wright, he had to convince the church that his design responded to its programmatic needs and symbolic ideals. On 2 January 1906 the trustees held a meeting at President Skillin's home to consider reports of both the plans and finance committees.

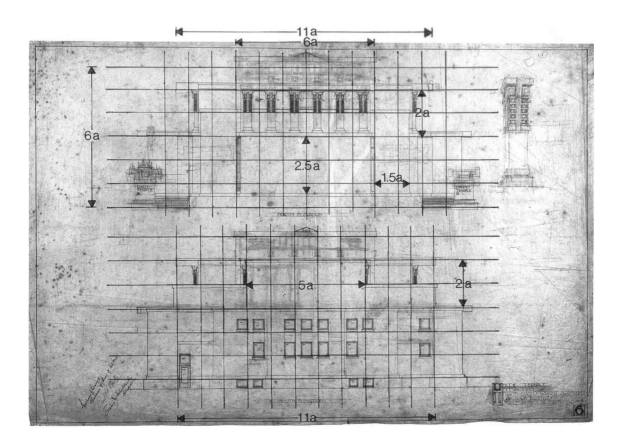

By that time one contractor had submitted estimates on Wright's designs, figuring that the cost of the new church would exceed the church's resources by $8,000 to $10,000. In spite of this, "the general opinion was that that amount should not stand in the way if it will get what we want."[123] Yet in terms of Wright's design, "there were some details not entirely clear to the Trustees and some question regarding lighting and ventilation of the first gallery in the auditorium and of the two rooms in Unity House. The seating capacity of the auditorium. Whether concrete construction would be satisfactory etc. etc.," so it was moved to adjourn to meet at Frank Lloyd Wright's.[124]

The trustees, without either Rev. Johonnot's plans committee or Roberts's building committee, did meet with Wright in his studio on the evening of 4 January. There "the plans for the new church were carefully examined, the members of the Board asking questions and Mr. Wright explaining."[125] Trustees did have "objections to details thought to be weak,"[126] and, as Wright later recalled, his chief critic was Mr. Skillin, who was "sure the room will be dark – sure the acoustics will be bad."[127] On 14 January the trustees met again, this time without Wright, but with the plans and building committees. Skillin had financial doubt, reporting total assets of $42,000 for the project and $11,000 of that total needed for purchasing the whole site.

FIGURE 93

Wright, Unity Temple, working drawing of west elevation, 1906, with author's notations showing unit dimension, a = 6 ft. 10 in. (Frank Lloyd Wright Archives, Drawing No. 0611.014, © The Frank Lloyd Wright Foundation 1986).

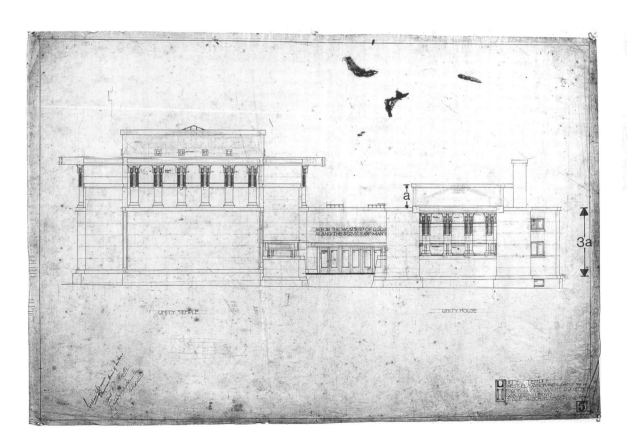

This left $31,000 in funds and pledges for construction. The plans committee estimated that the new edifice could be built for $40,000, yielding a debt of some $9,000. Skillin proposed that Unity House be built first, partly to conserve funds and partly to test the design's merits before going forward with the larger and more expensive auditorium. Yet others favored going ahead with the whole project, and "it was generally understood that the general scheme of the plans drawn by Mr. Wright and recommended by the Plans committee was satisfactory."[128]

On 18 January the trustees and committees met with Wright. After further explaining details of construction in concrete, Wright, perhaps in an effort to swing the board into a decisive mode, "offered to guarantee that the entire edifice, present plans unaltered, would be completed for $35,000, including architect's fee, seating of auditorium, tinting walls, movable screens, walks, grading, planting, shrubbery, everything complete. He thought $2,800 might be saved for the present by omitting the seating of the auditorium, tinting and finishing but promised to obtain more exact figures showing the cost of Unity House complete and the Auditorium complete on the exterior only."[129] On 21 January trustees met with the finance committee. John Lewis argued that "the entire edifice should be built complete [including] Unity House and omit for the present interior details of the Auditorium if necessary."[130] Yet Skillin "declared that the main floor of the auditorium was not large enough in the present plan and said that Mr. Wright had told him the distance between the columns could be increased. The Board asked Mr. Skillin and Dr. Johonnot to consult Mr. Wright regarding such changes in the plan of the auditorium."[131]

In his autobiography, Wright recalled that he had first invited Charles Roberts to his studio to see the drawings of Unity Temple and to hear Wright's explanation of the design. Wright claimed that Roberts understood the scheme and was delighted with it, suggesting that a model be made.[132] In Wright's recollection, he had such a model made to present the design to the church's leadership, including Roberts, Rev. Johonnot, and Skillin. Wright said that initially Johonnot was "impressed but cautious – very – and tactful. He has a glimpse of the new world." Whereas Skillin and others sustained their doubts about the design, Johonnot was soon "convinced" about Wright's plans and committed himself to work for their realization.[133] On the evening of 31 January the model and Wright's drawings were again presented to seventy-five men of Unity Church, who "met at the beautiful and commodious studio of Frank Lloyd Wright to inspect the plans of the new church. . . . Slides made from photographs of the drawings thrown on a screen gave a very good conception of the plans. A very pleasing and beautiful design has been produced, which was received with many expressions of favor and enthusiasm."[134] On 2 March church women met at the home of John Lewis, whose wife was on the plans committee. On this occasion "the plans and model of the new church were on exhibition, and

FIGURE **94**

Wright, Unity
Temple, photo-
graph of original
plaster model of
1906, showing
north front. Re-
printed from *Ar-
chitectural Record*
23 (March 1908).

Dr. Johonnot gave a very interesting talk, explaining the details of the church."[135]

As Wright suggested, the model helped others assess the capacity, light-ing, and spatial form of the auditorium, whose innovations may have been hard to visualize in plans. A photograph of the original plaster model of Unity Temple appeared in Wright's article "In the Cause of Architecture," of 1908 (Fig. 94). He later identified this as "The Model Made to 'Show' Mr. Skillin."[136] The photograph shows the temple's north front, with light from the upper left angled to clarify its masses, moldings, and ornamental motifs. The ornament on the column faces was changed when built. Angled light also reveals the auditorium's interior skylight, here transformed from the single central panel depicted in Figure 80 into the overall grid of square lights that were built. The auditorium's interior ceiling lights visible through the columns of plaster convey Wright's concept of the walls as a screen for the room within. As he wrote of the auditorium's galleries: "Flood these side-alcoves with light from above: get a sense of a happy cloudless day into the room. And with this feeling for light the center ceiling between the four great posts became skylight, daylight sifting through between the inter-sections of concrete beams, filtering through amber glass ceiling lights, thus the light would, rain or shine, have the warmth of sunlight. Artificial lighting took place there at night as well. This scheme of lighting was integral, gave diffusion and kept the room-space clear."[137]

Even with this model, Unity Church and its leadership evidently struggled first to understand all the implications of Wright's design, and then to accept its unconventional form. On 7 February Wright met again with the trustees and Rev. Johonnot to discuss "objections that had been [made] to the plans submitted by the Architect, and also in discussing the plans that

Mr. Wright had submitted for a different seating arrangement for the audi-torium."[138] Toward this meeting's close, the trustees finally moved to approve and adopt "the plans for the new church prepared by Mr. Frank Lloyd Wright, architect, and recommended by the Plans Committee . . . so far as their general plan and scheme and mode of construction are concerned," on condition that the whole project would cost no more than $36,200.[139] As Wright recalled, "Finally the commission to go ahead is formally given over [Skillin's] dissent and warnings."[140] Only at this point was Wright's project given assurance of realization. Soon after, his assistant Charles White wrote: "The chief thing at Wright's is of course Unity Church, the sketches of which are at last accepted, after endless fighting. We have all pleaded and argued with the committee, until we are well nigh worn out."[141]

*   *   *

On Saturday, 24 February 1906, exterior perspectives of Wright's design for Unity Temple, and a statement and description of the project "published by Dr. Johonnot" appeared in Oak Park's newspapers.[142] The next morning Rev. Johonnot delivered a sermon entitled "The New Spirit of Church Architecture," which was to be "descriptive of the new church and show the reasons for its design and the spirit which inspired it."[143] As chair of the committee that had approved Wright's project, Johonnot was presumably convinced of the merits of Wright's design, and now sought to build support for its realization, both within and beyond the congregation. Probably he had already encountered mixed responses. Sculptor Richard Bock, who modeled the columns for Unity Temple, recalled that "from the beginning it was a tug of war with the congregation, being so unlike any other church on earth."[144] Locally the project was seen as "the most radical departure in traditional church architecture ever attempted."[145] Anticipating such reactions, Johonnot in his published descriptions offered both a theological and contextual rationale for the new building's unusual form:

> Two reasons in the main have determined the style of architecture of Unity Church: First, the desire to make the building expressive of the faith held by the worshipers; second, the necessity imposed by local conditions of creating a building with a distinct character of its own.
>
> A recent writer on church architecture has raised the question whether a church building ought not to set forth by its form the character of the faith it represents. So far as possible this seems desirable. . . . It is in this spirit that Unity Church has been designed.[146]

The writer to whom Rev. Johonnot alluded was Charles De Kay, an editor of the *Architectural Record*, who authored an essay on "What Do Our Church Buildings Express?" published in December 1905.[147] Favoring change in church design, he wrote: "One of the cardinal doctrines of good architecture is this, – the building should express its purpose, and even indicate by its parts and members the use to which each one is put."[148] He thus advocated that "church buildings in the present day reflect or represent the religions, opinions or dogmas of the congregation,"[149] asking "how far our churches express in their exterior the main purpose for which they exist and the peculiar doctrines of their congregations."[150] For De Kay these symbolic priorities militated against a uniform style for religious buildings, like the Gothic Revival. Instead, he anticipated a "greater freedom from tradition than ever before, and a more perfect expression in the building of the ideas at the bottom of the sect, denomination, faith or religion to which the structure belongs."[151]

Rev. Johonnot was plausibly attracted to De Kay's ideas because they provided a rational basis for congregational and communal acceptance of Wright's unconventional design. As he stated elsewhere, for Unity Church to build similarly to neighboring churches would have misrepresented the ideals of the congregation. In addition, if it had chosen a more conventional design for its small site and meager budget, it would have also run the risk of creating a church home that suffered from close comparison with large nearby structures. Thus a conventional solution would have been questionable in both symbolic and contextual terms. Wright's forms appealed to Johonnot in part because they could be defended in terms of the time-honored Unitarian belief in rationality as a way of questioning convention in religion and its representation in architecture. Jenkin Lloyd Jones had similarly presented the unconventionality of All Souls Church and the Abraham Lincoln Center in terms of their symbolic and contextual, as well as their programmatic, rationality. As Johonnot wrote: "It is fitting that Unity Church, which represents a faith based upon reason and not upon tradition nor precedent, should depart from traditional forms of architecture . . . if there is good reason for so doing. True originality in architecture is as desirable and inspiring as in other forms of art, if its basis is rational and the result is beautiful."[152]

Renderings of Unity Temple and Wright's Concept of Conventionalization

The new Unity Temple's originality was apparent in the perspectives published with Johonnot's text, similar to the view of the building's west side on Kenilworth Avenue (see Fig. 81) and of its north front on Lake Street (see Fig. 88). These renderings differ from the church's built exterior in the ornament of the columns (drawn as different on Unity Temple and Unity House), the concrete urns atop the end blocks of the walls in front of the entrance terraces, and the foliage between columns. Unity Temple is shown as isolated in a stylized graphic setting of foliage, without indication of specifics of its built environment.[153] The crisp masses are set up on an indeterminately broad, blank foreground bounded by the curb line, which appears to become part of the building's base. The human figures are diminutive relative to the height of the building, enhancing the architecture's monumental scale. Floral beds overspilling the window ledges and terrace urns rhyme with the stylized trees in the foreground and behind, these rendered to show individual leaves. Light as depicted on the building reveals its masses and moldings, and creates the shadows cast by the roof slabs.

Among the most significant graphic conventions evident in the renderings for Unity Temple was the representation of shade trees all around the building. On one level these may refer literally to the environmental character of its suburb. Oak Park's name reflected local preoccupation with shade trees as one source of distinctive communal identity. In the period of Unity Temple's design, Oak Park's local Improvement Association was headed by Charles S. Woodard, an insurance agent, who was on Unity Church's ways and means committee for funding Wright's building.[154] Among this association's principal concerns was the care and extension of Oak Park's large stock of shade trees, especially in the older built-up and wealthier part of the suburb, where trees were equated with the highest land values and where the new Unity Temple was to be located. Located at the corner of Forest and Chicago avenues, Wright's own home and studio was then at the northern edge of this central section. In 1904 the association was reminded that "the presence of shade trees is the sine qua non of an ideal home site, second only to the consideration of sunshine and pure air."[155] Another editorial stressed: "It is the trees of Oak Park that have made the central portion what it is. . . . There can be no real beauty of landscape without trees, and there can be no real comfort of home without trees."[156]

In 1900 Wright conveyed to neighbors his concern that its shade trees not be uniformly trimmed, emphasizing that "if this town of Oak Park has one grace it is the profusion and simplicity of its foliage . . . a breathing spot where trees at least are in accord with a sweet and liberal domestic atmosphere; this wealth of drooping foliage, these masses of living green."[157] Wright's words convey the same point of view found in his style of architectural rendering, wherein arboreal masses of foliage surround Unity Temple, forming a backdrop for its massing and framing the building's profile. For Wright, however, in this period, the rendering of his works amid their natural settings conveyed his vision of architecture in which buildings were aesthetically conceived as part of their environs. Built form and natural form were to be unified and integrated. Of his work to 1910 he wrote: "It is quite impossible to consider the building as one thing, its furnishings another, its setting and environment still another. In the spirit in which these buildings are conceived, these are all one thing, to be foreseen and provided for in the nature of the structure."[158] Spacing of nearby trees as a complement to formal rhythms within the building, and shadows of foliage as a kind of ornament for its surfaces, appear in photographs of Unity Temple selected for Wright's *Ausgeführte Bauten* of 1911 (Figs. 1 and 99). Another view of Unity Temple published in 1930 shows its walls overlaid with ivy and other climbing plants (Fig. 95).

FIGURE 95

Wright, Unity
Temple, west
front. Reprinted
from Sheldon
Cheney, *The New
World Architec-
ture* (New York,
1930).

Wright also understood trees as models of organic form in themselves. Hence their depiction surrounding his work of architecture might suggest its conceptual sources in the study of nature. In late 1903 Wright's assistant, Charles White, wrote that Wright "tells me to stop reading books for a while, and do nothing but study nature and sketch. He says continually and eternally sketch the forms of trees – 'a man who can sketch from memory the different trees, with their characteristics faithfully portrayed, will be a good architect.'!"[159] Wright claimed: "A sense of the organic is indispensable to an architect. . . . A knowledge of the relations of form and function lies at the root of his practice; where else can he find the pertinent object lessons Nature so readily furnishes? Where can he study the differentiations of form that go to determine character as he can study them in trees?"[160] Wright claimed that "Japanese art knows this school more intimately than that of any people. In common use in their language there are many words like the word 'edaburi,' which, translated as near as may be, means the formative arrangement of the branches of a tree."[161]

*　*　*

The graphic composition of renderings of Unity Temple and of Wright's other projects in the same years was closely related to his enthusiasm for Japanese prints as models of aesthetic expression. In Wright's account of his drawings in the Wasmuth folio of 1910, which included those for Unity Temple, he wrote that "they merely aim to render the composition in outline and form, and suggest the sentiment of the environment. They are in no sense attempts to treat the subject pictorially. . . . Their debt to Japanese ideals, these renderings themselves sufficiently acknowledge."[162] When his drawings of Unity Temple appeared in February 1906, Wright was preparing the first exhibition of his collection of Hiroshige prints (acquired the year before in Japan) to open on 29 March at The Art Institute of Chicago, just after Unity Temple's working drawings were completed. In March 1908 Wright, together with Frederick Gookin and other local collectors of prints, organized the largest exhibition of Japanese prints then yet held in the United States. Wright designed the exhibition, shortly before he decided on final changes for the interior of Unity Temple's auditorium.[163]

Wright presented his ideas on the significance of the prints in his 1912 essay, "*The Japanese Print: An Interpretation.*" For Wright, the Japanese print embodied principles applicable to architecture, among which he highly valued the ideal of simplicity. For him, the print "has spread abroad the gospel of simplification as no other modern agency has ever preached it and has taught that organic integrity within the work of art itself is the fundamental law of beauty."[164] In his view, to artists, the Japanese print "must offer great encouragement, because it is so striking a proof of the fact readily overlooked – that to the true artist his limitations are always . . . his most faithful and serviceable friends."[165] Wright here referred not only to the techniques of a medium, but to the artist's self-imposed limitation of working only with pure geometric forms, such as the square, circle, and octagon. In 1909 he wrote that "there is quite room enough within these limitations for one artist to work I am sure."[166] Unity Temple was Wright's symphonic development of the form of the square, fulfilling this ideal; hence the propriety of its portrayal within the graphic conventions of Japanese prints which, Wright felt, exemplified similar formal richness within limitations. In this way, both the print and the building embodied an ideal of simplicity, which Wright then defined as "something with graceful sense of beauty in its utility from which discord and all that is meaningless has been eliminated."[167] For Wright, simplicity and repose were qualities that measured the true value of any work of art.

Wright's individual aesthetic and that of the Japanese print converged not only in the ideal of simplicity, but in what he saw as the related concept of conventionalization. Wright first articulated this idea in a 1900 paper on "A Philosophy of Fine Art." He described conventionalization as an artist's process of interpretive invention, as opposed to naturalistic imitation. In presenting this idea, Wright wrote that in portraiture, a painter as artist did not seek a photographic realism. Instead, "there was the conception first and then the revelation of that conception,"[168] meaning that the painter had first an interpretive vision of or insight into the subject, which was then expressed through the medium of painting, with respect for the possibilities and limitations of that medium. Like earlier theorists of ornament in the nineteenth century, Wright saw this concept at work continually in decorative art and architecture, where, for example, ancient Egyptian artists had conventionalized the form of the lotus flower to make a stone column capital. The result was not so much a realistic representation but a poetic invention. The artist put the lotus "through a rare and difficult process, wherein its natural character was really revealed and intensified in terms of building stone. . . . This is Conventionalization, and it is Poetry."[169] In Wright's view, Japanese printmakers had also conventionalized natural forms and human environs through the inventive pictorial geometry of their images.[170]

In his paper of 1900 and in subsequent writings, Wright expanded the concept of conventionalization from its origins in ornamental theory to apply to the whole of architecture, as both built form and social symbol. On one level he wrote of architecture as a conventionalization in the sense that buildings were geometric constructs of human invention, thus distinct from literally natural forms, just as ornament was a geometric conventionalization of nature. In renderings of Unity Temple, this idea may be inferred from the rectilinear geometry and hard material of the building as a complement to the leafage around it. In 1910 Wright wrote of his works up to that time: "In the conception of these structures they are regarded as severe conventions. . . . They are considered as foils for the foliage and bloom which they are arranged to carry, as well as a distinct chord or contrast, in their severely conventionalized nature, to the profusion of trees and foliage with which their sites abound."[171]

Wright also viewed architecture as conventionalization in the sense that it provided an interpretation for the life it housed. He wrote that "buildings are the background or framework for the human life within their walls and foil for the nature effloresence without. So architecture is the most complete of conventionalizations."[172] If buildings were to be settings for life inside as well as a foil for nature outside, then conventionalization in architecture implied that built form was derived from the study of its functions. As Wright had written in 1908, "I have endeavored in this work to establish a harmonious relationship between ground plan and elevation of these buildings, considering the one as a solution and the other as expression of the conditions of a problem of which the whole is a project. . . . What quality of style the buildings may possess is due to the artistry with which the conventionalization as a solution and an artistic expression of a specific problem within these limitations has been handled."[173]

Unity Temple's design illustrates Wright's concept of conventionalization in architecture as giving form to social ideals. In his 1912 essay on Japanese prints, he wrote: "As the Egyptian took the lotus, the Greek his acanthus, and the Japanese every natural thing on earth, as we may take any natural flower or thing, so civilization must take the natural man to fit him for his place in this great piece of architecture we call the social state. And today, as centuries ago, it is the prophetic artist eye that must reveal the idealized, conventionalized, this natural state harmoniously with his life principle."[174] Wright then concluded: "Our own art is the only light by which this conventionalizing process we call 'civilization' may eventually make its institutions harmonious with the fairest conditions of our individual and social life."[175]

By shaping the plan and the ornamental detail of Unity Temple as an essay on the motif of the square, Wright conventionalized this church's theological identity in its architectural geometry. A square served as the form for the plan of Unity Temple's auditorium and was repeated in such details as the interior skylights and the motifs of their art glass. Thus Wright's choice of the square as a motif was not compositionally arbitrary but rather institutionally symbolic. A quadrilateral whose sides were equal in length, the square presented a proportion of 1:1, or the geometric representation of Unity. This was the ideal central to both liberal religious thought and to Wright's concept of architecture as aesthetically harmonious. In this way Wright's process of conventionalization or geometric abstraction created an architectural symbol that characterized this church in the form of its room for worship. In his design for this space as built, Wright would seek to achieve Unity as an aesthetic ideal throughout the temple's language of form and material.

Construction of Unity Temple

$\mathbf{A}$LTHOUGH Wright produced the accepted design for Unity Temple by March 1906, the building he then envisioned was in important respects not the church completed in October 1908. His pursuit of innovation and consistency did not stop when construction began. Instead, each step prompted alterations, so that Unity Temple continued to develop beyond the grammar of style set forth in its working drawings. As the building rose, Wright rethought key issues of structure and surface throughout, weighing options to the last moment, and in some instances replacing partially completed work. The changes in Unity Temple exemplified an important yet elusive quality of Wright's architecture: that a work develops conceptually as it builds physically. He later wrote that, while a plan remains unbuilt, it "is a map, a chart, a mere diagram, a mathematical projection before the fact." Yet "the original plan may be thrown away as the work proceeds – probably most of those for the most wonderful buildings in the world were, because the concept grows and matures during realization, if the master-mind is continually with the work."[1]

In building Unity Temple, Wright sought to create a new grammar of expression in reinforced concrete. The degree of innovation in the design compelled him to find new methods for realization of his ideas in this material. Inside Unity Temple's shell of concrete, he developed a system of line and color through its interior surfaces as they were built. Wright thus made a structure that was both rational and lyrical. The church was rigorously consistent in its concrete exterior, yet its interior form exhibited a poetic invention that sprang from Wright's own imagination. Outside and inside, Unity Temple displayed a conceptual tension between built form and visual form; everywhere materiality and aesthetics were interwoven.

Creating a New Architecture of Concrete

In his autobiography Wright recalled that after the church authorized the construction of Unity Temple, it was hard to find a builder, for "after weeks of prospecting, no one can be found who wants to try it. Simple enough – yes – that's the trouble. So simple there is nothing at all to gauge it by. Requires too much imagination and initiative to be safe."[2] Wright implied that his church of concrete was so innovative that there were no works seen as standards of comparison for estimating its cost. Hence "the only bids available came in double, or more, our utmost limit. No one really wanted to touch it."[3] In 1905 most contractors whose habitual scale of operations was small enough so that they would be attracted to a suburban church did not have the special knowledge, equipment, and experience to build in the new material of concrete specified in the plans.[4]

Varied bids for Unity Temple might have been responses to the unusual forms of Wright's architecture. These were perhaps difficult for contractors to understand, especially in the case of a church wholly of concrete. Wright recalled that as the degree of innovation in his work increased from 1893, "contractors often failed to read the plans correctly. The plans were so radically 'different.'"[5] Wright's memory on this point is corroborated by other testimony from this period. In the summer of 1907 Johonnot solicited bids for an organ for the new auditorium. Organ builders were sent plans of the space Wright had allotted for the instrument in the auditorium's south wall. One organ company replied that it had "called on [Wright] with reference to the organ for the new Unity Church of Oak Park and we find the construction is so unusual that we think it necessary to send our draftsman to look over the church."[6] Another company wrote back to Rev. Johonnot: "We confess . . . our inability to clearly understand the drawings sent to us, though we have consulted with other Architects of our city. The drawings of the elevation are especially puzzling, though the floor plan indicates a room of ample area."[7]

Wright had consulted with Paul Mueller about building Unity Temple by January 1906.[8] His collaborations with Wright had included construction of the Larkin Building, Wright's first large steel-framed structure begun in 1904, and the construction of the E-Z Polish Factory in Chicago, Wright's first larger work primarily of reinforced concrete, built in 1905.[9] Both of these buildings were still being completed when Wright's plans for Unity Temple were approved in February 1906. Wright recalled that Mueller, unlike the other builders who submitted bids that spring, "reads the scheme like easy print. Will build it for only a little over appropriation – and does it."[10] Of the three recorded bids received, Mueller's figure of $32,221 for the complete edifice (presumably worked out in consultation with Wright) was by far the lowest, and the trustees accepted it at their meeting of 28 April 1906, when they approved the plans and specifications.[11] The board then moved to go ahead with the construction of both Unity House and

Unity Temple, and Mueller contracted to complete the entire building in a single season, from May to November 1906.[12] At that time, all parties based their expectations on the assumption that Wright's design was to be built unchanged from the working drawings. Yet, perhaps even then, Wright thought otherwise.

Ground was broken for Unity Temple on 15 May 1906.[13] After six weeks of work on the site, it was reported on 30 June that "work on the new Unity Church is being rushed, and the church lot at Lake street and Kenilworth avenue presents a scene of busy activity at all hours of the day. The massive concrete foundation is at present completed to the ground level, and work on the actual structure will soon be underway."[14] Wright's working drawing for these foundations (Fig. 96) shows the building's maximum width to be 100 ft., exactly the width of the lot. The building, from the front wall of Unity Temple to the rear wall of Unity House, is 144 ft. long, with its rear wall set 3 ft. inside the plot line.[15] The position of the church on the site thus permitted a setback of about 23 ft. from the north property line on Lake Street. The auditorium's side walls are set 18 ft. in from the east and west lot lines, providing the temple with an apron of narrow lawns. These give a spatial interlude between street and wall on these sides.

The continuous peripheral foundation walls support the church's upper

FIGURE **96**

Wright, Unity Temple, foundation plan, 1906 (Frank Lloyd Wright Archives, Drawing No. 0611.010, © The Frank Lloyd Wright Foundation 1986).

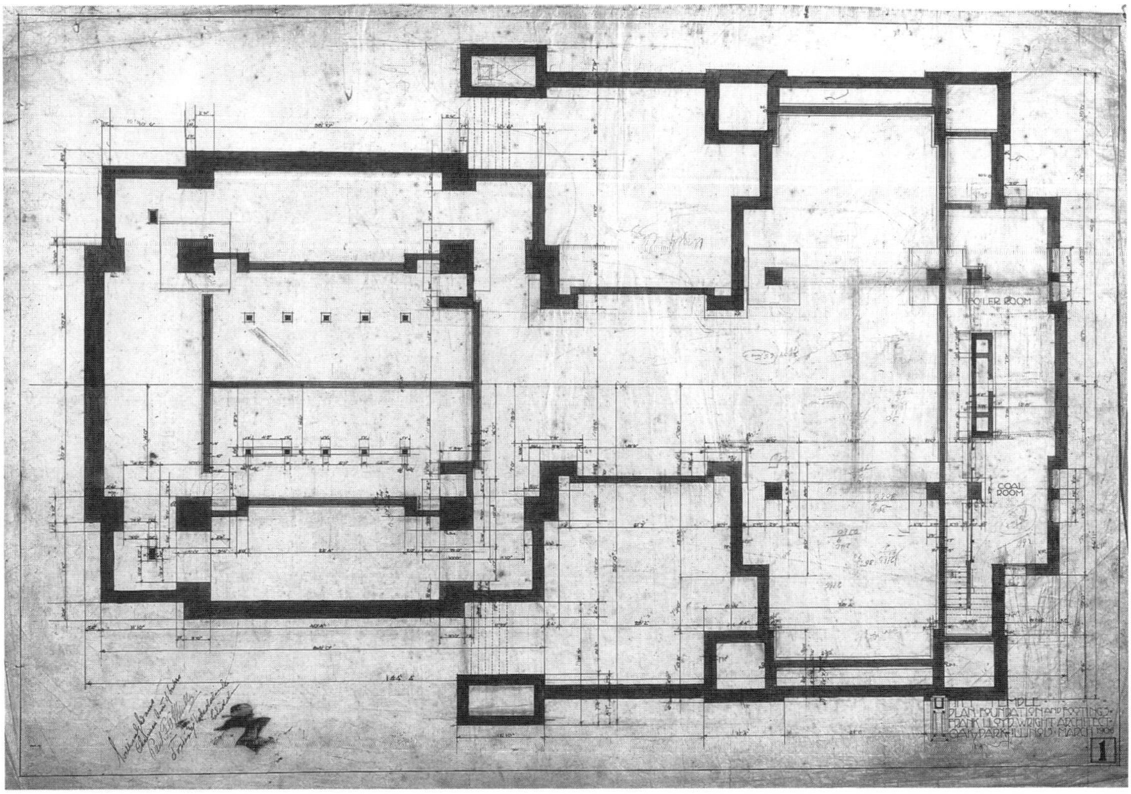

exterior walls above ground. Both foundation and upper walls were origi-nally designed to be unreinforced masses of concrete with an aggregate of crushed limestone. Both would thus be heavier than if they had been planned as reinforced walls. This may account for the 3-plus-ft. thickness of the peripheral foundation walls, a dimension that was increased further during building.[16] There were separate footings for the four columns of Unity Temple and the columns inside Unity House that support galleries and roofs. The footings were also to be concrete with a crushed limestone aggregate. The same concrete under both walls and piers would help to insure even settlement of the soil underneath the different parts of the building.[17]

The heavy concrete, with a crushed limestone aggregate, was specified for the upper walls and piers because these, like the bearing walls and column footings, were elements of the structure sustaining compressive stress. Concrete beams and floors that spanned horizontally between verti-cal supports, and which would thus experience bending stresses, were to be a light "cinder concrete," meaning an aggregate of soft coal cinders. Unlike the vertical walls, these spanning elements of concrete had to be reinforced with thin steel rods, whose high tensile strength would enable resistance to bending.[18] In addition, steel beams and roof trusses were used to span certain spaces, as over the entry doors, yet these elements are encased in concrete, so that such structural steel is not visible inside or outside Unity Temple or Unity House.

*   *   *

To save lumber and permit multiple reuse of wood forms into which the concrete would be poured, all formwork would be made from one size of wood boards assembled into standard units. Designing Unity Temple to fit such units also minimized joints so as to preserve the face of the walls unbroken. Thus Mueller "used a system of units mutually interchangeable and more closely fitted than would be necessary on less exacting work."[19] Wright recalled that "a unit suitable for timber construction was adopted as the false-work in which [Unity Temple] was cast was made of lumber. Mul-tiples of 16 inches, syncopated, was the scale adopted."[20] This unit for formwork was about one-fifth of the unit dimension (6 ft. 10 in.) that Wright used to plan the whole building.

Figure 97a shows the units of formwork for pouring one of the outer walls, as if looking down from above. Vertical 2 x 4 posts, spaced 16 in. apart, support the sides of boards that run horizontally. Figure 97b de-picts this same typical segment of formwork from the side, as if shown in a cross-section. This cross-section shows forms of horizontal boards, each 6 in. high and 1 in. thick. Each board is 12 ft. long, or 9 units of 16 in. On the inner side of the form toward the building, where the concrete's surface was to be refinished after it was poured, the horizontal boards of varied grain are simply stacked up the full height of the wall. On the outer face of the wood formwork toward the street, where the surface of the concrete as cast would approximate the finished surface, boards were matched together in panels that were 6 boards or 3 ft. 6 in. high, or about 2 units of 16 in. Thus, for Unity Temple's walls, Wright and Mueller developed a basic panel of formwork 12 ft. long and 3 ft. 6 in. high, or about one half the height of the unit dimension of 6 ft. 10 in. that was used for design.

The thorough integration of design and construction that Wright intended is visible in the working drawing for Unity Temple's Kenilworth Avenue or west elevation (Fig. 93). On this ink-on-linen drawing were penciled horizontal lines spaced 3 ft. 6 in. apart up the wall, or the height of 1 panel of wooden formwork. Unity Temple's lower central wall above its base and below its coping is 17 ft. 6 in. high, or about 2.5 units of 6 ft. 10 in. The temple's central wall was to be cast in 5 layers of wood formwork, each 3 ft. 6 in. high. The central wall is 38 ft. wide, or about 5.5. unit dimensions of 6 ft. 10 in. Each corner stair block of Unity Temple above its base and below its coping is 24 ft. 6 in. high, or about 3.5 units of 6 ft. 10 in. Thus, each stair block was to be cast in 7 layers of formwork, each 3 ft. 6 in. high. Each stair block's designed width of 10 ft. 6 in. equaled 1.5 unit dimensions of 6 ft. 10 in. or 8 16-in. units of formwork. The unit dimension of 16 in. also

FIGURE 97

Wright, Unity Temple, (A) left, horizontal plan of wall formwork and (B) right, vertical section through wall formwork. Reprinted from *Concrete Engineering* 2 (September 1907).

a

b

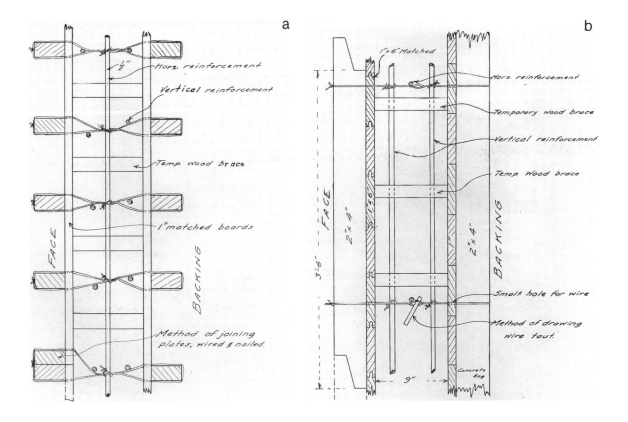

recurs in Unity Temple's elevation as the width of the slotlike vertical windows between the main walls and the corner stair blocks.

Structurally, larger masses of concrete sustained loads more effectively than smaller sections. As one of Wright's contemporaries wrote: "Reinforced concrete is a unit. . . . The fewer the number of units the more efficient and durable is the whole."[21] Yet the size of the walls was nevertheless limited by concrete's capacity to expand and contract during seasonal changes in temperature without cracking. Wright's dimensions for Unity Temple's walls, slabs, and corner stair blocks acknowledge this limiting condition. He wrote: "Here is a building, a monolith in monomaterial . . . left complete as it came from the moulds – permanent architecture. The whole is a great casting articulated in sections according to the masses of concrete that could safely be made to withstand changes of temperature in a severe climate."[22] To insure the thermal independence of each section, the slot windows between the central walls and corner stair blocks of Unity Temple's auditorium replaced conventional expansion joints between these large masses of monolithic concrete. Wright thus integrated the economic, structural, and thermal characteristics of concrete into his forms of architecture.

A photograph of Unity Temple under construction (Fig. 98), first published in May 1907 near the start of a second season of building,[23] shows panels of its wood formwork in place on the north Lake Street wall and on the upper parts of the corner stair blocks. Long diagonal braces of lumber hold the north wall's formwork in place. The east wall has already been cast and its formwork removed, although its scaffolding remains in place. This scaffolding would serve to facilitate pouring the roof slab above the east wall and finishing this wall's surface. The lower parts of the stair blocks have already been cast, and their formwork has been raised to cast the towers' upper sections. Atop the east wall the columns of the clerestory have been placed, whereas those atop the north wall have not. Roof slabs have yet to be poured, although the auditorium's four main structural columns appear to have been cast as the supports for the box of formwork visible above the center of the temple building.

Wright's design was conceptually inextricable from its way of building, yet dimensions sometimes had to be modified during construction. Of the stair blocks at the corners of Unity Temple's auditorium, Mueller recorded that they had to be enlarged from their designed width of 10 ft. 6 in. to their built width of 11 ft. 8 in. "to increase the width of stairs and platforms" inside each corner block, so that the interior steps and landings would be acceptably wide.[24] This increase in width meant that the formwork for casting the stair blocks had to be widened from the eight 16-in. units to the nine such units seen in the photograph in the nearest corner's top formwork. Since Wright integrated all forms of his building, this change entailed another. As seen in Figure 86, the pedestals for the flower boxes were the same width as the corner stair blocks. When the stair blocks were expanded to 11 ft. 8 in., Wright asked Mueller to widen the pedestals for the flower boxes in front of the stair blocks to the same dimension of 11 ft. 8 in.[25]

* * *

Wright had carefully considered the relations between Unity Temple's design and its means of realization, yet he was also concerned about the visual texture of its surfaces. Other American architects were then seeking ways to cast and finish concrete that would not imitate the details of carved stone or molded brick.[26] Wright emphasized exposing the aggregate to express the composite nature of concrete as a unique material. As he later wrote: "Ordinarily in itself [concrete] has no texture unless the mould leaves it on the surface. It is, however, possible to use fine colored-gravel or crushed-marble or granite in the mixture so the superficial cement (retarded in setting by some substance like soap applied to the interior surfaces of the 'forms') may be easily washed away, leaving the gleaming aggregate exposed in almost any color or texture."[27]

To achieve this effect in Unity Temple, Wright at first specified that wall cores be treated differently than outer wall surfaces. Before the main wall

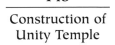

FIGURE **98**

Wright, Unity Temple, under construction, view from northeast. Reprinted from *Cement World* 1 (15 May 1907).

cores were poured as masses of stone concrete, the outer finishing mortar was to be applied with a trowel directly to the inner side of the wood forms and thoroughly tamped into place. This finishing mortar coating the cores of stone concrete was to be no less than 1.5 in. thick. The mortar was to bond with the concrete core when it was poured. Yet in order to insure a clean separation between the wood forms and the finishing mortar, wood forms were smoothed on their inner faces toward the mortar "and oiled in order that the surface might be smooth and even, without unsightly seams."[28] After a wall had been cast and its formwork removed, the finishing mortar would be exposed to sight.

Wright at first specified procedures to insure that the visible mortar contributed to the architectural ideal of unity. First, all the mortar was to be made with one kind of cement "to give all work same color and appearance. All possible precautions shall be used to insure complete uniformity of material."[29] To prevent a varied exterior surface, the Portland cement was to be purchased in large quantity from the same source before construction began. Once pouring started, each course or layer of concrete was to be "continuous throughout each face or panel, as directed, such course to be completed same day as started to give all uniform set and appearance."[30] After a section of wall was poured, it was to be protected with temporary coverings to allow the concrete to "dry out slowly and uniformly leaving surfaces of uniform color and general appearance."[31] Finally, Wright wrote: "Should courses show marked variety in color or texture when completed they shall be cut out and replaced to the satisfaction of the Architect."[32]

Throughout the project Wright sought to make a uniform surface, yet he changed his mind as to what the aggregate and finish of the concrete should be. As to aggregate, Wright at first specified that the mixture for surfacing mortar was to be "one part Portland Cement to three parts crushed red granite screenings."[33] If granite had been the aggregate ultimately used, the white of the Portland cement and the red of the granite would have given the visible surfaces of Unity Temple a rose color. As to the finish, Wright initially stated that "the plank forms shall be removed immediately after initial set and the surface gently floated with carpet float to sand finish."[34] To finish concrete in this way, wood formwork would be removed between twelve and twenty-four hours after the concrete's pouring, that is, after its initial but before its final set. In that interval of time, the concrete is sufficiently soft so that a "carpet float," probably a carpet-faced wood trowel, could be used with sand and water as a mild abrasive to clean the concrete and bring it to a uniform surface with the edge marks and grain of the wood forms removed. Disadvantages of this technique were that it took time, it had to be done by one skilled in the work, and it did not achieve good results when done in winter.[35]

On 10 July 1906, as pouring of concrete above ground was about to begin, Wright wrote to Unity Church's trustees to call their attention to experimental exhibits of finishes that he had had set up on the site.[36]

Mueller later wrote of "experimenting, screening different sizes and kinds of gravel and making 20 samples of 2' 6" x 2' 6" concrete for deciding the exterior wanted for the Unity House & Temple."[37] Of those displayed in July 1906, the first (called exhibit 01 because it conformed to the specification) was displayed among finishes like it. Apart from this set were displayed other finishes that Wright thought were superior to those like the one he had specified. The others had an aggregate of finely screened bird's-eye gravel of neutral color, instead of the red granite.

Instead of floating the surface to reveal the aggregate Wright now proposed to have it "treated with a preparation bringing the gravel into relief."[38] For this preparation, Wright was probably thinking of a solution of hydrochloric acid that would eat away the dried cement on and around the outer surface of the gravel aggregate, leaving a finish of glistening smooth pebbles.[39] Among the advantages of this technique were that it brought out the aggregate's color, brightened the surface, and could be delayed four or five days after the concrete was poured.[40] Wright warned that such a washing "will consume rather more time than floting [sic] but the Contractor prefers [this] method because the risk in obtaining a uniform result will be less than in the method originally specified. The chemically treated surface being a more dependable quality than the floted [sic] in the hands of indifferent or even in the hands of careful workmen, as no two men produce surfaces entirely alike."[41]

Although this chemically treated surface was adopted, one trustee wrote that he could not "understand why [Wright] has thrown out 01, not making a sample till the last thing and then not attempting to finish it as he has the others.[42] Wright undoubtedly had aesthetic reasons for his final choice of a surface, yet there may also have been pragmatic concerns. While Unity Temple was rising, it was reported that "Instead of the perfectly smooth concrete, a rougher surface will be on the outside. The idea is that the uneven craggy outside will not be so susceptible to the markings which the younger generation of Oak Parkers might make."[43]

Whether their impetus had been aesthetic or pragmatic, Wright's late changes in the surface's aggregate (granite to gravel) and in method of finishing (floating to acidic wash) prompted him to rethink the whole construction of the walls. As noted, Wright had initially specified concrete wall cores with limestone aggregate, and separate finish mortar applied to insides of the formwork. At first Wright specified that the wall cores be unreinforced. Yet he changed his mind, directing Mueller to make the cores of walls in Unity Temple and Unity House above their foundation courses from the same concrete with bird's-eye gravel aggregate used for their outer surfaces. Wall surfaces and cores could thus be poured as a monolithic whole. Wall cores would no longer contain heavy limestone aggregate like the foundations. To compensate for their lighter aggregate, the walls were now to be reinforced with steel rods, increasing their cost by over $4,000.[44] Walls were now to be reinforced masses of uniform aggregate, not unrein-

FIGURE 99

Wright, Unity
Temple, from
northeast, before
September 1909
(Frank Lloyd
Wright Archives,
Photograph No.
0611.009, © The
Frank Lloyd
Wright
Foundation).

forced masses with cores different from surfaces. Thus Wright's search for new visual and textural qualities led to a major change in the way Unity Temple was built, one that heightened its uniform character as a construction.

The original exterior surfaces of Unity Temple appeared in an exterior view (Fig. 99) prior to September 1909.[45] To insure evenness and solidity, concrete was to be poured and tamped in layers of 6 in. To avoid overstressing formwork, in parts of the wall, no more than 18 in. were to be poured in twenty-four hours.[46] This may explain undulating strata in the auditorium walls and stair blocks, so the nature of the casting process is seen. Wright wanted the aggregate of pebble-smooth gravel to evoke the image of hard stone. As Unity Temple neared completion in 1908, he wrote that its "exterior surfaces are washed clean to expose the small gravel aggregate, the finished result in texture and effect being not unlike a coarse granite."[47]

A view of Unity Temple's west front (Fig. 100), prior to a first resurfacing of the concrete in 1961, accentuates the degree to which the original exterior surfaces exhibited the horizontal linear marks of the formwork. Wright wished concrete to emerge crisply from the molds, perhaps to convey its nature as cast masses. He specified that "all edges and corners shall be left sharp and true and surfaces even and granular . . . as approved by the

Architect."[48] One observer wrote of Unity Temple: "The face of the building is a good example of what can be done with concrete. Birdseye gravel of approximately ½ in. diameter is used and by careful form work presents an appearance superior to brick and equal at least to stone. The work has been carefully done and there are no unsightly voids or cracks to mar the broad faces."[49] In Unity Temple, Wright had thus pioneered a treatment of concrete characteristic of modern architecture generations later, when surfaces that exhibited the patterns of their wood formwork became known by the Corbusian term *béton brut* from their prevalence in Le Corbusier's works after 1945.

All base moldings below and copings atop Unity Temple's concrete walls have squared profiles, echoing the rectilinear forms of the walls. The simple projection of Wright's mural details differs from intricate, curved profiles of classical moldings in carved marble. Rectilinear moldings were thus a means of distinguishing concrete from stone, as square edges conformed to the process of casting the moldings in boxlike wood forms.[50]

Wright further explored the nature of an architecture in concrete in his

FIGURE 100

Wright, Unity Temple, from southwest, before first resurfacing in 1961. Photograph by Hedrich Blessing. Courtesy of the Chicago Historical Society, HB 19311-B.

FIGURE 101

Wright, Unity
Temple, drawing
of concrete flower
boxes, with lan-
terns and bronze
plates (Frank
Lloyd Wright Ar-
chives, Drawing
No. 0611.079,
© The Frank
Lloyd Wright
Foundation 1994).

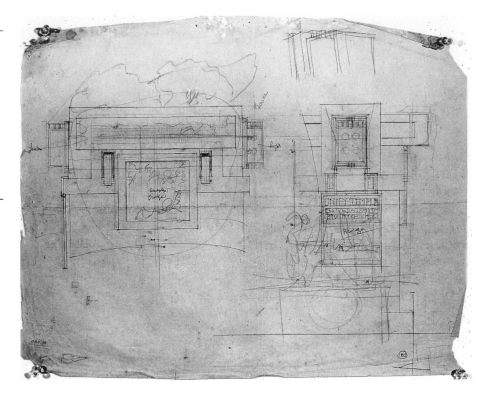

flower boxes for Unity Temple. A small drawing for these (Fig. 101) may be
compared with the boxes as rebuilt in 1973 (Fig. 102). As freestanding
sculptures of large scale, Unity Temple's flower boxes recall the stone urns
in front of Wright's houses of the period, from the Winslow house of 1893 to
the Robie house of 1909. Like such residential urns, Unity Temple's flower
boxes were intended to hold overspilling plants. The drawing atop Figure
88 shows that Wright contemplated rounded urns for plants atop the end
blocks of Unity Temple's terrace walls. Yet in the final design, he transformed the urns into flower boxes as a new type of sculpture in concrete
whose monumental scale and squared shape are more consistent with the
architecture.[51] Like the moldings of Unity Temple behind, the flower boxes
had rectilinear profiles for casting within forms of wood boards. Wright
designed each flower box as two interlocked rectangular masses of concrete, one set vertically and the other horizontally, partly cantilevered atop
small piers.

The motifs of the flower boxes are carefully related to the forms of all
three sections of the building behind them. Wright's drawing (Fig. 101)
notes that the top plane of the horizontal mass is level with the top of the
lintels above the main doors into Unity Temple from the entrance terraces.
The thickness of the horizontal mass is noted to be the same as that of the
projecting cornice at the end of Unity House. The end block of the entrance
terrace wall is a massive base for the small piers upholding the flower box,

FIGURE 102

Wright, Unity
Temple, detail of
west front and
flower box. Pho-
tograph by Hed-
rich Blessing.
Courtesy of the
Chicago Histori-
cal Society, HB
19311-0.

just as the main walls of Unity Temple support the colonnade upholding the temple's cantilevered roofs (Fig. 102). Thus, however one views the flower boxes in relation to the building, the eye can detect formal consistencies between the boxes in the foreground and the church's walls in the background.

On his trip to Japan in 1905, Wright became familiar with the traditional Shinto shrine as the other principal religious building usually found with the Buddhist temple in Japanese towns and villages. These Shinto shrines were less monumental and less ornate than Buddhist temples. The shrines served as both ceremonial and social centers of daily life. Wright similarly envisioned Unity Temple and Unity House as buildings that would occasionally function as a communal center. A Shinto shrine building was often in a small compound amid a thick grove of trees.[52] Such a type may have suggested analogies with Unity Temple, which was depicted in an arboreal setting.

Familiar with Japanese art since the 1880s, Wright had included square lanterns like those in Japanese architecture in his prairie houses from before 1905. One of Wright's photographs of a Shinto shrine, taken during his trip to Japan in 1905, shows stone lanterns lining this building's outer precincts.[53] As seen in the side and end elevations in Figure 101, Wright

FIGURE **103**

Wright, Unity
Temple, exterior
lantern near en-
trance. Photo-
graph by Brad
Bellows,
Tektonica.

designed square lanterns (each with four bulbs) for the front and rear of the
flower box above a bronze nameplate. In Unity Temple as built, he affixed
similar lanterns to the temple's walls at the entrance terraces to light the
steps. These lanterns are singular and prominent as one ascends the steps to
the terraces (Fig. 103). Japanese in inspiration, the lanterns' metal housing
echoes the geometry of the building, while their height matches the top of
its entrance doors.

* * *

Wright and Mueller worked out a special procedure for casting the ornamental exterior columns of both Unity Temple and Unity House. In early
stages of design, the columns on these two parts of the building were
different, yet as built all columns are identical, being cast from the same
molds. Sculptor Richard Bock recalled making one model for all the columns,[54] twenty-four of which screen four clerestories of the temple, while
Unity House has four columns on each of its two sides. Wright shaped the
columns as experiments in the decorative possibilities of concrete. Several
of his extant drawings suggest his development of their motifs. Of these, one
study (Fig. 104), drafted in pencil on tracing paper, depicts two preliminary

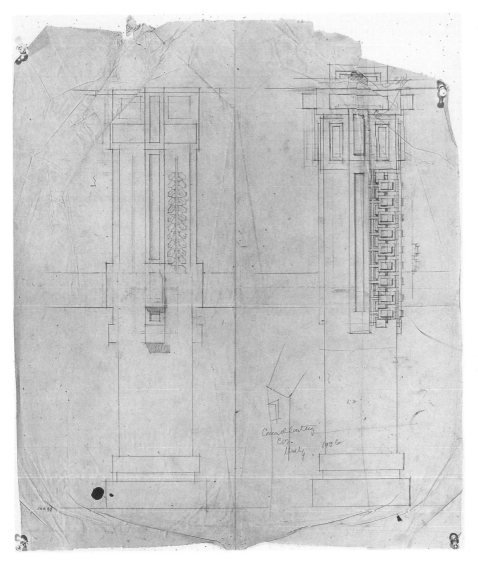

FIGURE **104**

Wright, Unity
Temple, prelimi-
nary drawing of
exterior ornamen-
tal columns of
cast concrete
(Frank Lloyd
Wright Archives,
Drawing No.
0611.083, © The
Frank Lloyd
Wright Founda-
tion 1994).

designs for their casting. Each drawing shows the column's molded base on a ledge. The columns' lower shafts, up to the window sill behind the columns, are unornamented. Each upper column shaft has cast ornamental relief on each side of the simpler vertical strip in the shaft's center. The upper shaft is then crowned by a capital-like block of rectilinear geometric shapes. On the drawing's left column, the upper shaft's ornament appears as literally foliate designs. On each side is a vertical stem with twelve pairs of leaves. Below the leaves, blocklike masses project from the shaft's center. On the right column the motif of projecting blocklike masses is now shifted up to the capital, leaving the shaft's midsection unaccented. The twelve pairs of leaves have become nine miniature blocks with stemlike links to an elongated central vertical strip.

These studies clearly illustrate Wright's approach to architectural ornament as the geometric conventionalization of natural forms. In an address in Oak Park in 1909 on the "Ethics of Ornament," he stated: "Flowers and other natural objects should not be used as ornaments, but conventional representations founded upon them. . . . This conventional representation must always be worked out in harmony with the nature of the materials used, to develop, if possible, some beauty peculiar to this material. Hence one must know materials and apprehend their nature before one can judge an ornament."[55] As Wright wrote of designing Unity Temple: "Nature-pattern and nature-texture in materials themselves often approach conventionalization, or the abstract, to such a degree as to be superlative means ready to the designer's hand to qualify, stimulate and enrich his own efforts. . . . Realism, the subgeometric, is however the abuse of this fine thing. Keep the straight lines clean and significant, the flat plane expressive and clean cut. But let texture of material come into them."[56]

Wright's concern for combining a conventionalization of foliate motifs with the nature of concrete as a cast surface appears in another study for the columns (Fig. 105). This is labeled in Wright's handwriting as "Slicing technique of Unity/Concrete shaft Unity Temple/slicing wood blocks forming the casting." This drawing shows the design of the upper shaft's ornamental motif and of the capital as built. The motif would be cast in molds of rectangular wood blocks. Penciled shading along the column's right side clarifies the degree of projection or recession of each cement surface as it was to be cast in wooden molds. Wright later recalled the process of making formwork for the building's ornament: "Unity Temple at Oak Park was entirely cast in wooden boxes, ornamentation and all. The ornament was formed in the mass by taking blocks of wood of various shapes and sizes, combining them with strips of wood, and, where wanted, tacking them in position to the inside faces of the boxes. The ornament partakes therefore of the nature of the whole, belongs to it. So the block and box is characteristic of the forms of this temple."[57]

The height of each column is over 12 ft.; thus it was impractical to make each in one piece. The unornamented lower shaft of each column with its molded base was poured separately on top of the wall. Each ornamental upper shaft was over 5 ft. tall; thus its weight made it necessary to cast it in four quarter-sections (like splitting a log down its length into four quarters). Division into quarters is the "slicing technique" that Wright noted in his drawing. The four quarters of each upper shaft were cast separately in molds before being brought to the building for assembly. There the quarters were set atop the plain lower shaft, as in Figure 106, which shows an upper shaft's plan and elevation. In the middle of each face there was a wood form marked "a" wherein vertical strips or pilasters were cast. These wood forms were lined with facing cement between the ornamental quarters.

Assembly of an upper shaft is shown in Figure 107a. Upper quarters were attached to the plain lower shaft, with care taken to set the quarters

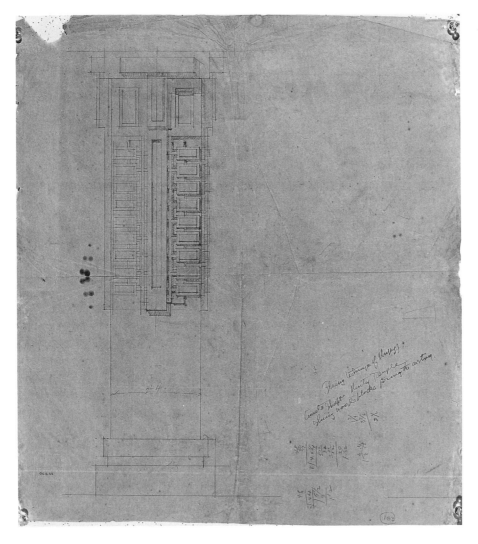

FIGURE 105

Wright, Unity
Temple, final de-
sign for exterior
ornamental col-
umns (Frank
Lloyd Wright Ar-
chives, Drawing
No. 0611.022,
© The Frank
Lloyd Wright
Foundation 1994).

parallel to each other and plumb with the lower shaft. After the quarters
were set up, wood forms for the vertical cement strips at the center of each
face were removed, as shown in Figure 107b. Once the quarters of the
upper shaft were thus assembled, a stone concrete was poured in to fill the
shaft's core. To complete each column, a crowning block was set atop the
lower part of each capital (Fig. 107c). Like the upper shaft, the capital
block's squared forms facilitated casting.

The range of techniques that Wright and Mueller devised for treating
concrete is evident in Figure 99, which shows Unity Temple's north front,
including its planar surfaces, squared moldings, and cast columnar ornament. As on Unity House, the decorative relief of the columns set in the
dark loggia serves as a textural foil for the smooth wall planes. The severe
surfaces are in keeping with the nature of cast concrete as a material not

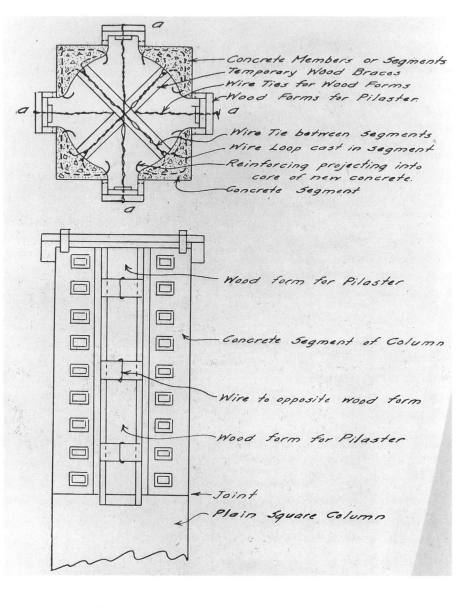

Concrete Members or Segments
Temporary Wood Braces
Wire Ties for Wood Forms
Wood Forms for Pilaster

Wire Tie between Segments
Wire Loop cast in segment
Reinforcing projecting into core of new concrete.
Concrete Segment

Wood form for Pilaster

Concrete Segment of Column

Wire to opposite wood form

Wood form for Pilaster

Joint
Plain Square Column

FIGURE **106**

Wright, Unity Temple, plan and elevation showing construction technique for exterior ornamental columns. Reprinted from *Concrete Engineering* 2 (15 February 1909).

given to precisely carved detail. In 1907 an observer wrote that "the design by Frank Lloyd Wright, architect, is exceedingly effective and will find many imitators. The execution is apparently faultless, as those columns put in early in the work have shown no signs of defects and are today a credit to those who conceived them."[58] Mueller was credited for devising the techniques to realize Wright's designs. Recalling their collaboration on Unity Temple, Wright wrote of Mueller: "It is exciting to him to rescue ideas, to participate in creation. . . . Together we overcame difficulty after difficulty in the field, where an architect's education is never finished."[59]

* * *

The crowning motifs of Unity Temple's exterior are its cantilevered slab roofs. As Wright wrote of the design, the building's profile followed from the nature of the material: "What had concrete to offer as a cover shelter? The slab – of course. The reinforced slab. Nothing else if the building was to be thoroughbred, meaning built in character out of one material. . . . The flat slab was direct. It would be 'nobly simple.' "[60] Perhaps referring to Wright's slabs, Rev. Johonnot wrote earlier that "the style of architecture eliminates the cost of spire, tower, and expensive roof and lends itself to the material and construction used."[61] In Wright's work of this period, he used different roof shapes, yet the flat slab was the only one consistent with concrete structure, as hip or gable roofs would demand other framing.

The cantilevered slabs project 5 ft. in front of the columns (see Fig. 99). As viewed from the street, the outer edges or fasciae of the slabs are about twice as high as the actual slabs behind the fasciae. This difference is seen in Unity Temple's section (see Fig. 91), yet the slabs' thinness is not visible from the street. The cantilevered roofs thus look more weighty from outside

FIGURE **107**

Wright, Unity Temple, (A) assembly of quarters for upper column shaft, (B) vertical cement strip joining upper column shaft quarters, and (C) crowning blocks set atop upper column shafts. Reprinted from *Concrete Engineering* 2 (15 February 1909).

than they really are. Wright thereby created an architecturally dramatic image of massive slabs projecting far out over the ornamental columns. This accentuated contrast of horizontal slab on columnar supports heightens the image of Unity Temple as elemental built form. The columns visibly up-holding the roof perhaps alluded to an archetypal concept of the temple type as a pillared edifice, thereby conveying both biblical and classical associations.

Unity Temple's cantilevered roofs visually complement its massive base. Wright wrote of his buildings to 1908: "It will be noticed that all the structures stand upon their foundations to the eye as well as physically. There is good substantial preparation at the ground for all the buildings and it is first grammatical expression of all the types."[62] Unity Temple's visible base above ground is an extension of the foundation walls below, whose thickness may derive from the fact that they were poured without steel reinforcing below ground. In Unity Temple, the base steps inward at two levels above the ground. Above this stepped base, the wall planes rise unbroken to projecting sills below the columns. The columns' bases then step inward twice. Their shafts culminate in outward-stepping squared capitals that meet the undersides of the slabs in shadow. The inward-stepping walls below and the visible recession of the columnar bases contrast with the outward projection of the horizontal roofs above. This enables the cantilevers to look more extended in space beyond the columns. Wright thus shaped the whole profile of Unity Temple from base to roof to achieve an expressive silhouette.

The width and projection of the cantilevered roof slabs follow Wright's unit system of proportion found elsewhere in the building. The slabs' relationship to other dimensions is seen in Figure 108. Each slab is 40 ft. 8 in. wide, or about 6 units of 6 ft. 10 in. The auditorium's height above its two-stepped base to the top of its attic is 41 ft., or 6 such units. Thus the width of the cantilevered roof slab virtually matches Unity Temple's height above its base, making the building's central mass appear to be a perfect cube. Each slab projects out about 2.5 units or 17 ft. 6 in. from the temple attic's square core. This projection of the cantilever matches the height of the temple's central solid wall above its base, to the sill underneath the columns. In this way Wright built into Unity Temple a consistency of 1:1 proportions in order to create an overall visual impression of unity. As he later recalled:

> Such architectural forms as there are, each to each as all in all, are cubical in form, to be cast solid in wooden boxes. But *one* motif may be seen, the "inside" becoming "outside." The groups of monoliths in their changing phases, square in character, do not depart from that single IDEA. Here we have something of the organic integrity in structure out of which issues character as an aura. The consequence is style. A stylish development of the square becoming a cube.[63]

FIGURE **108**

Wright, Unity Temple, view from northeast, before September 1909, with author's notations showing multiples of unit dimension, a = 6 ft. 10 in. (Frank Lloyd Wright Archives, Photograph No. 0611.009, © The Frank Lloyd Wright Foundation).

Structure and Form in Unity House

In the summer of 1906 the first phase of the work focused on the less prominent Unity House, where flaws in the concrete would be less visible. Its experimental construction proved slower and more costly than expected. By September, when it was clear that even this part would not be ready by the contracted date of 15 November, it was reported that "the walls of the new church are rising, but slowly."[64] Soon concrete pouring ceased for the winter. On 30 January 1907 Edwin Ehrman, who had replaced Charles Roberts as head of the building committee, expressed concern to Mueller over the pace of work: "The truth of the matter is that not a few of our people are discouraged and finding the payments on subscriptions very slow. The people want to see where the money is going and what they are going to get in return, and the committee has never been able to give them any satisfactory information as to when any part of the Church would be completed."[65]

Wright gave assurance that Unity Temple itself would be ready by September 1907, yet this estimate proved to be overly optimistic by a full year.[66] Instead, Unity House alone opened at that time.[67] Wright's concept for this room appears in a sectional perspective (Fig. 109), showing its south wall with a fireplace below a scenic mural, never made. Johonnot wrote to his congregation that Unity House, "while not designed primarily as a place of public worship, . . . will serve for this purpose fairly well and will give us fitting accommodations for all other church activities."[68] The first service

157

FIGURE **109**

Wright, Unity Temple, sectional perspective through Unity House, looking southwest, 1906, published in Rev. Rodney F. Johonnot, *The New Edifice of Unity Church* (Oak Park, Ill., 1906) (Frank Lloyd Wright Archives, Drawing No. 0611.001, © The Frank Lloyd Wright Foundation 1994).

was held in Unity House on 15 September. Its main room, which could seat about 250 people, was then filled to capacity, with a temporary platform for the minister placed in front of the south wall's fireplace.[69] When the whole of the hall was not used for church meetings, both the lower sides and balconies could serve as rooms for Sunday school. As Wright later recalled, the room "was tall enough to have galleries at each side of the central space – convertible into class-room space."[70] He also noted that Unity House was "to be subdivided by moveable screens, on occasion."[71] Above the balcony fronts, this perspective shows curtains for partitions, yet the working drawings show folding screens of glass. Folding screens of art glass were also originally intended as partitions for the east and west side areas of Unity House's main floor.[72]

As its name implied, Unity House was to have a distinct domestic character with a fireplace, furniture, and carpets. Unity House's cross-section, with its high central hall and fireplace flanked by low areas below balconies on each side, may be compared with Wright's sectional perspective through the main rooms of "A Home in a Prairie Town," published in the *Ladies' Home Journal* in February 1901 (Fig. 110).[73] In this design, a central living room two stories tall with a fireplace is flanked on either side by a library and dining room, each with a low ceiling and windows at its sides. The drawing shows interior windows of an upstairs hall opening onto the living room, just as the casement windows of the pastor's study high in

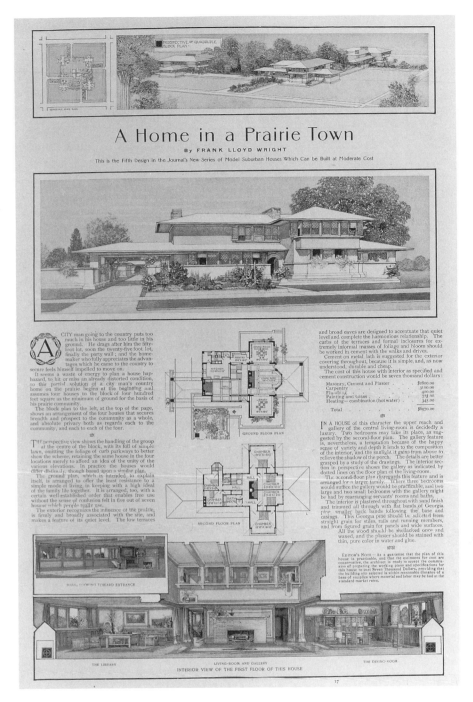

FIGURE 110

Wright, Project for
"A Home in a
Prairie Town,"
showing Quadru-
ple Block Plan at
top and sectional
view of interior at
bottom, from
*Ladies' Home
Journal* 18 (Febru-
ary 1901) (Frank
Lloyd Wright Ar-
chives, Drawing
No. 0007.009,
© The Frank
Lloyd Wright
Foundation 1994).

Unity House's north wall open into the room's central space (see Fig. 6). As Wright recalled, "the study thus looked down through swinging windows into the secular hall – while it was just a step behind the pulpit."[74]

Both Unity House and Wright's prairie house have cross-sections that recall that of a conventional basilican church with a central nave flanked by lower side aisles, evoking a cultural memory of this ecclesiastical spatial type. In the prairie house, such a churchlike form connotes a spiritual ideal of domestic life, like that described in Gannett's *The House Beautiful,* as if a spatial shape had ethical meaning. The basilican section would also be appropriate for Unity House as occasional setting for informal religious meetings. The room's elements of four columns, central skylights, and balconies on each side correspond to forms in Unity Temple. This correspondence gives Unity House a religious character to complement its domesticity, just as the prairie house of 1901 appeared to convey both residential and ecclesiastical associations. In both instances richness of meaning derives from the architecture's multiple associations. Interiors of Wright's houses can recall churches, while, in Unity House, the room is simultaneously like a parlor and a sanctuary.[75] An account of Unity House's opening noted that the space was "not designed as a room for public worship, yet the whole atmosphere of the place is restful and dignified and lends itself with ease to the higher sentiments, so that the effect of being in a place of worship is very marked."[76]

Unity House conveys religious associations in part because its forms share the system of unit dimensions found in Unity Temple. As seen in Figure 90, Unity House's east–west, wall-to-wall length is 82 ft. 10 in., or about 12 unit dimensions of 6 ft. 10 in., while its north–south width in its side areas including wall thicknesses is 27 ft. 2 in. or about 4 unit dimensions. Each corner storage closet is 1 unit square inside. The room's high central space is a square just under 5 units on a side (33 ft. 11 in. from its north to its south wall; 33 ft. 10 in. between folding glass screens on east and west balconies), about the size of the square central space in Unity Temple (33 ft. between the inner corners of the four main columns). The width of the recess framing the fireplace in Unity House's south wall (13 ft.) corresponds to the width of Unity Temple's pulpit as built (13 ft. 2 in.). Thus Unity House's interior was proportionally keyed to Unity Temple's, just as Unity House's exterior adapted motifs from Unity Temple's.

*   *   *

Wright's original interior of Unity House appears in Figure 4, published in 1909, which compares with another view, also looking southeast, taken in 1994 (Fig. 113). The richness of the interior's aesthetic derives from Wright's architectural treatment of the room's structure. The major supporting elements are eight columns circled in the room's floor plan (A), including the four central columns (Fig. 111). The columns support four short roof trusses spanning north–south (B), and two long east–west roof trusses (B'), marked as dashed lines on the room's roof plan (Fig. 112). These trusses are invisible from inside Unity House because they are above its high ceiling, whose flat planar surface gives the room its expansive, open feeling.

Within this larger main structure of Unity House, there is a system of smaller elements that support its east and west balconies. Each balcony is undergirded by two 15-in. steel I-beams (C) spanning east–west under the floors of the balconies (Fig. 111). Each pair of beams is carried by another beam (D) running north–south beneath the balcony front between two inner main columns. As with the larger roof trusses above, these beams are not visually pronounced. Yet where the I-beams under the balcony floors (C) join the beams under the balcony front (D), Wright marked these connections with two square motifs along the bottom of the balcony front (Figs. 4 and 113).

The smaller structural system supporting Unity House's balconies nests within the larger system upholding the roof. The scale of the room's four central columns contrasts with that of the inset small columns on the horizontals of the balconies (Fig. 113). These small columns on the balcony fronts were intended to serve as mullions for folding glass screens, which were never added.[77] Visible diminution of scale continues into small projecting wood arms for lights extending from the balcony columns into the central space (see Fig. 4). These arms support smaller wood crosspieces, from which chains descend to the glass lighting globes. On the upper rear of the small columns, short wood arms uphold pairs of smaller globes to light

FIGURE **111**

Wright, Unity Temple, working plan of ground floor, 1906, with author's notations showing in Unity House (A) principal structural columns, (C) steel I-beams under balcony floors, and (D) beams under balcony fronts (Frank Lloyd Wright Archives, Drawing No. 0611.011, © The Frank Lloyd Wright Foundation 1986).

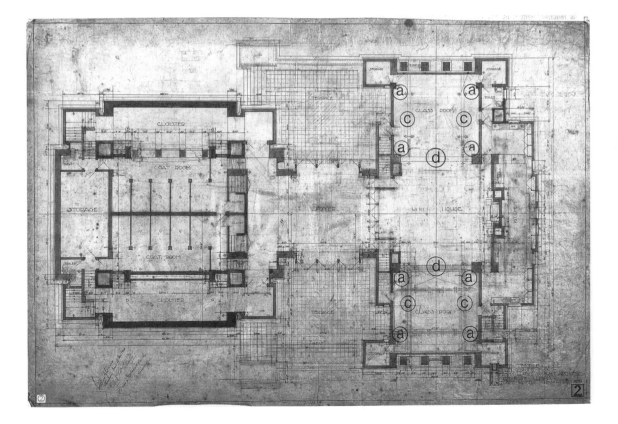

the balconies. Six pairs of similarly spherical lights originally illumined the room underneath each balcony. Early views show natural foliage completing the interior. Thus Wright developed an architecture within Unity House as a series of interrelated horizontal and vertical elements, from larger components of structure to smaller details of ornament.

As in Wright's prairie houses, woodwork in Unity House embodied a program set forth in his address of 1901 on "The Art and Craft of the Machine." Through this period Wright claimed to have studied concurrent industrial conditions in order to develop an architectural grammar simplified to fit modern processes of machines, and to use their capacities to the greatest aesthetic advantage.[78] He wrote of wood as both the oldest and most human of materials, one that was prepared by modern machines in ways that enabled architects to rediscover its intrinsically artistic qualities of grain, texture, and color. Wright advised: "Now let us learn from the machine. It teaches us that the beauty of wood lies first in its qualities as wood. No treatment that does not bring out these qualities all the time can be plastic or appropriate or beautiful. The machine teaches us that certain simple forms and handling are suitable to bring out the beauty of wood and certain forms are not; that all wood-carving is apt to be a forcing of the material, an insult to its finer possibilities as material."[79]

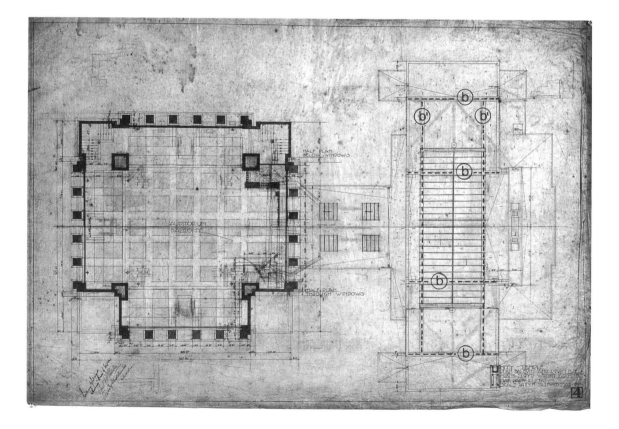

Wright, Unity
Temple, interior
view of Unity
House looking
southeast. Photo-
graph by Thomas
A. Heinz.

Unity House's aesthetic emerged from an interweaving of wood bands
over its surfaces. Because the building was made of concrete, its interior
woodwork was "not used structurally, but as an inlay to assist in the decoration."[80] The wood strips were not to be nailed directly into concrete. Rather

Wright specified that "the contractor shall furnish and with especial care shall locate and set into the underside of the floors and into the wall surfaces and structure members porous terra cotta blocks wherever directed to provide proper nailing for wood finishing strips."[81] For these interior strips, "all work is to be thoroughly seasoned straight sawed red oak, kiln dried, clear wood, prepared by careful sand papering for stain and oil finish."[82] Wright chose two widths of oak bands, 2.5 in. and 1.5 in., for the interior trim of Unity Temple and Unity House. Together with wider moldings of concrete, varied band widths enhance the effect of a graded scale of linear elements. Yet these wood bands are not purely ornamental; many of them serve to clad wiring for the interior electric lights. Such wiring runs along the surfaces of the concrete plaster, under the wood bands, rather than being wholly set in the plastered walls. Wright thus turned the difficulty of wiring a monolithic concrete building into an architectural advantage. Referring to the wood bands, he said: "Here electric lighting took visible form in wiring and became a decorative feature of the structure."[83]

In Unity House, linear wood bands embody Wright's ideal plasticity as an indispensable principle for successful use of the machine. In works of this period, he made wood trim "'plastic,' that is to say, light and continuously flowing instead of the prevailing heavy 'cut and butt' carpenter work."[84] In Unity House, wood bands serve as an agent of plasticity, leading the eye from one surface to another. On the ceiling, flat strips outline the room's edges and the seven rectangular bays of the skylight. Above the balcony fronts, these pairs of strips extend to the main columns, differentiating the central hall from the side balconies and perhaps alluding to the trusses above the ceiling there. Around the top of each column, other strips form a square to create a flattened "capital" at the plane of the ceiling. The bottoms of the main columns have bases below "pedestals" marked by horizontal strips about 4 ft. above the floor, as if the wood strips here suggest such a classical element.

Wood bands define necks for the smaller columns set in the balcony fronts, while their shafts are divided in two by vertical bands. Presumably these bands clad wiring for the electric lights. Wide and narrow wood bands complement the concrete moldings along the balconies, creating a depth and variety of profile within a unified system of linear relief. Only some of these bands appeared on drawings of March 1906. Before Unity House's completion in September 1907, Wright had asked Mueller to add wood bands to the balcony faces, to the ceilings and beams underneath the balconies, to the main ceiling, to the central north and south walls and pilasters, and to the east and west end walls of the classrooms. These numerous changes "were not shown on the original plans,"[85] as if Wright rethought the room's details as its walls rose. He sought a visual unity that sometimes superseded truth to materials, as some details of concrete and plaster, different in natural color, were apparently painted the same color.[86]

For wall and ceiling surfaces in Unity House and other interiors, Wright specified several layers of plaster, the visible finish coat of which was composed of a cement, lime putty, and sand.[87] The sand used was a washed mason's sand whose crystals had a smooth, rounded profile rather than the sharp edges of the quartz silica sand Wright had first specified.[88] The finish plaster was floated to remove excess cement and reveal the sand aggregate,[89] like the originally specified process of carpet-floating the building's exterior cement to reveal its stone aggregate. Then a thin translucent sealant was applied to the plaster as a nearly uniform undercoating before colors were added. The sealant had a white tint with a semigloss finish, creating a brighter underlay for colors than that provided by the plaster alone.[90]

Wright at first specified that colored plaster surfaces "shall be washed with water colors and glue, applied as directed. . . . Color to be selected by the architect."[91] All the original finishes were a water-based paint known as casein, applied in extremely thin coatings. Colors were not applied in opaque coats of paint, but laid on as a translucent glaze that allowed the plaster's sand texture to show through as a substrate.[92] Six colors were first applied to Unity House's interior walls and ceiling. The three main surface tones were grayish yellow, yellow green, and medium brown. Accenting colors were dark brown, yellow brown, and olive green.[93] Unity House's ceiling was first overlaid with a glaze of grayish yellow. This color also appeared on the east and west balcony faces. The ceiling's north and south edges were in a yellow green. Main columns were edged in grayish yellow, and their central shafts and pedestals were medium brown. On the south wall, the main plane around the fireplace was medium brown, with flanking pilaster-like panels of grayish brown. Above, the rectangular panels were originally all yellow green. The opposite north wall (see Fig. 6) was mostly medium brown, as were the small high horizontal panels to the outsides of the doors, along the sides of the staircases to the balconies. Base and sill moldings throughout the room were dark brown, while yellow brown and olive green accented small areas, such as the vertical bands flanking the fireplace or the square panels just beneath the necks of the main columns.[94]

Color was to activate relations between line and plane, so that all surfaces of the room participated in a geometric mural composition. The earliest description of Unity House noted how "the surfaces of the room are broken by paneling, thus affording opportunity for using different colors in the tinting of the walls which is taken advantage of by the use of browns, light greens and yellows. The woodwork is of unpolished oak which blends finely with the prevailing tone of the brown tinting."[95] The dark-stained lines of wood were the constant by which the varied planes of color were defined and integrated. In a later essay, Wright wrote that "the flat-strip came so easily into our hands, by way of the machine. . . . We may have plaster-covered walls banded into significant color-surfaces by plain woodstrips, thick or thin, or cubical insertion, wide or narrow in surface. We may have ceilings rib-banded in rhythmical arrangements of line to give the charm of timbering without the waste. We may use flat wood-strips with silken surfaces contrasting as ribbons might be contrasted with stuffs, to show what we meant in arranging our surfaces, marking them by bands of sympathetic flat-wood."[96] In his view, such treatment was "a most proper use of wood . . . using marking-bands or plastic-ribbons, defining, explaining, indicating, dividing, and relating plaster surfaces. It is economy in the material, while keeping the feeling of its beauty. Architectural-articulation is assisted and sometimes had alone by means of these dividing lines of wood."[97]

*   *   *

The colors of Unity House are seen underneath the light passing through the art glass of the skylights (Fig. 114), the rectangular coffers of which are painted grayish yellow like the high ceiling. No structural beams span north–south between the skylights except over the balcony fronts. Those beamlike elements running north–south between the skylights are hollow oblong boxes covered with plaster. They do not support the roof, but only frame the art glass. The sides of these boxes are like the deep reveals of windows whose surfaces reflect daylight passing through the art glass down into Unity House. One 15 ft. coffer holds four panes of art glass, each 4.5 ft. wide and framed with steel bars. Subdivision of glass skylights into panes of moderate size eased fabrication and reduced structural stresses.[98]

The art glass in Unity House and Unity Temple was made by the Temple Art Glass Company of Chicago, which fashioned glass for a number of Wright's works of the period.[99] The chromatic material is fused into the molten glass rather than applied to the finished glass by enameling or other modes of painting.[100] In this way, colored glass used by Wright returned to the methods of medieval glassmakers as advocated by William Morris, whose ideas influenced Wright's own. To hold the pieces of colored glass together, most American manufacturers in 1900 still used relatively thick, hand-soldered cames of lead.[101] Yet, by then, a new means of making stained glass had led certain firms to abandon the heavy lead lines and assemble the glass with thin strips of sheet copper. The assembled art glass would be subjected to a chemical bath, wherein galvanic action would fuse the copper strips to the glass edges, with "a little shoulder of copper sufficient to unite the composition into practically a solid pane without at the same time making the copper bands sufficiently conspicuous to mar the beauty of the design."[102]

Wright advocated and used a version of this process for fabrication of his art glass. In "The Art and Craft of the Machine," he had asserted that "multitudes of processes are expectantly awaiting the sympathetic interpretation of the master mind. . . . Electro-glazing, a machine shunned because too cleanly and delicate for the clumsy hand of the traditional designer, who depends upon the mass and blur of leading to conceal his lack

FIGURE **114**

Wright, Unity
Temple, interior
view of Unity
House looking
up at skylights.
Photograph by
Thomas A. Heinz.

of touch."[103] In the glass of the skylights in Unity House and Unity Temple, cames of thin zinc strips are galvanically bonded to the glass pieces,[104] thus creating an elegant linear pattern of metal as a frame for the squares and rectangles of colored glass. In this way, Wright modified a medievally inspired technique to turn skylights into light screens whose modern means of fabrication illustrated his ideal of an art and craft of the machine. In this period Wright said of his buildings: "The windows are provided with characteristic straight line patterns absolutely in the flat and usually severe. The nature of the glass is taken into account in these designs as is also the metal bar used in their construction. . . . The aim is that the designs shall make the best of the technical contrivances that produce them."[105]

Much glass in Unity House's skylights is opaque white, with motifs in green, brown, and yellow near the edges. Like wall surfaces, glass pieces in skylights are rectangular and square motifs that were likely seen as conventionalizations of natural forms, like patterns of leaves against sky. As Wright wrote of his work: "What architectural decoration the buildings carry is . . . conventionalized to the point where it is quiet and stays as a sure foil for the nature forms from which it is derived."[106] George Dean, one of his colleagues in Chicago, explained that conventionalization of natural forms meant that the original form's general pattern, rather than its literal shape, remains in the architect's design; hence leaves may be conventionalized as repeated rectangles. In Dean's view, such geometric abstraction was particularly appropriate in colored glass because "the extremely brittle, crystal character of the material cries out against naturalism and leads one to sharp and severe outline."[107] Thus, Wright's geometric patterns in Unity House's skylights embodied his principle of design in the nature of materials.

In each corner of each pane in Unity House's skylights, there are two motifs whose colors continue those of surfaces below. The motifs are a rectangle with a yellow-green core and yellow outer corners, and a square with a yellow-green core, brown corners, and yellow sides (Fig. 114). These two motifs are like small plans of Unity House and Unity Temple. Wright thus reiterated the plan's large forms at the tiniest scale of the art glass in the skylights, as if to convey the idea of organic architecture, where the visual logic of each detail unfolds consistently from shapes evident in the whole plan. Wright wrote that "the ornamentation of a building should be constitutional, a matter of the nature of the structure beginning with the ground plan."[108] There was a conceptual as well as formal continuity between plan and ornament. Not only the motifs but the process of design at one scale was analogous to that at the other. Thus a work's overall ground plan could have an ornamental form, while its smallest ornamental details echo the building's *parti.* For Wright, both plan and ornament were studies in geometric abstraction, meaning compositions of line and rhythm.[109]

Wright's point of departure for the creation of rooms like Unity House may have been interiors designed by Adler and Sullivan like the Chicago Stock Exchange trading room of 1893–94 (Fig. 115), reconstructed in The Art Institute of Chicago.[110] Like Unity House, the architecture of this space began with its structural system of trusses overhead resting on four main columns, although in the trading room, the depth of the trusses and of the girders spanning between them is visible. Skylights were placed only at the room's sides, because upper floors surmounted its center. Sullivan designed ornamental patterns for the skylights' colored art glass, for the elaborate polychrome stenciling on the room's ceilings and walls, and for the gilded plaster capitals of the columns, whose steel shafts were encased in surfaces of scagliola. In the reconstructed trading room, one can see Sullivan's concern for a consistent architectural treatment of every visible surface enriched in ornamental color. As in Wright's later rooms like Unity House, Sullivan made all the elements participate in a chromatically unified scheme. In both Sullivan's and Wright's interiors, it is their idea for the whole of the room that orchestrates details of color and motif. In both rooms the polychromy is inspired by form in nature, although Sullivan's motifs are literally foliate while Wright's are geometrically rectilinear. Thus one sees how Wright was conceptually indebted to Sullivan's models, but went beyond those models to anticipate the abstract aesthetic characteristic of later modern movements.

Wright not only designed the interior of Unity House, but also inaugurated a program of events to be held there. In February 1908 he organized and hosted an evening in Unity House entitled "A Symposium of Art," as a special meeting of Unity Church's Fellowship Club that was to be open to the whole local community. Never before had so many artists, each noted in a different field, been brought to Oak Park at one time.[111] Wright had invited the sculptor Lorado Taft; the poet William Guthrie; the conductor of the Chicago Symphony Orchestra, Frederic W. Stock; the actor Donald Robertson; the newspaper editor Wallace Rice; the German musician Ferdinand Steindel; the painter Charles Francis Brown; the director of the choral Chicago Musical Art Society, Clarence Dickinson; and the author Hamlin Garland.[112] The evening conveyed Chicago's role as a regional center for the arts, and Oak Park's patronage of them as one mark of its identity as a progressive suburb. Wright was described as "himself an artist, whose own reputation is not only becoming greater every day, but who is in close sympathy with all other forms of art and whose dearest wish is to have a hand in the promotion of artistic ideals in the community wherein he dwells."[113] Unity House was thus presented as part of a cultural program for which it was both symbol and setting.

Unity Temple's Foyer and Auditorium

When Unity House opened in 1907, Unity Temple was under roof but its interior was unfinished. Work had begun on the terraces, though the foyer's

FIGURE 115

Adler and Sullivan, Chicago Stock Exchange building, trading room, 1893–94, as reconstructed at the Art Institute of Chicago. Photograph by Bob Thall. Courtesy of the Office of John Vinci, A.I.A., Chicago.

floor was not poured.[114] Unity Temple's foyer as built (see Figs. 3 and 9) may be contrasted with one of Wright's drawings for the room (Fig. 116). This drawing in part follows the plan in Scheme A (see Figs. 74 and 75). In this plan, stairways with curtains in front of them led down from the entrance hall's north side into coat rooms.[115] The stairs leading down from the level of the auditorium into the foyer had exits that on the drawings were termed "removable slabs." These slabs have no frames, hardware, or other details that mark them as doors. Rather they are hinged as panels or sections of the entrance hall's north wall. Wright reinforced this reading of these elements in the foyer as built, where these movable panels are overlaid with the same wood bands that run across the foyer's entire north wall (see Fig. 9).

Wright's idea of the foyer as experiential prelude to Unity Temple's auditorium is apparent in their contrasting spatial proportions, light, and color. Though 27 ft. wide, the foyer is just over 9 ft. high from floor to ceiling.[116] The room has a broad, low proportion like that of the interiors in many of Wright's prairie houses of this period. The foyer's low breadth and its floor level with outer terraces contrast with the auditorium's higher cen- tral floor and vertical rise of 27 ft. from this main floor to the soffit of its skylit ceiling. Unlike Unity Temple and Unity House, the foyer has no skylights. Rather panels of clear art glass in six doors extend 20 ft. to admit light on both east and west sides. The foyer was first painted in broad areas of gray

* * *

Work on Unity Temple stopped again in the second winter of construction (1907–8). In late November 1907 Edwin H. Ehrman, the chairman of Unity Church's building committee, had written to Mueller that "I understand as well as anyone else that the building is costing you much more than you are going to get out of it."[118] By March 1908 Wright informed the church that Mueller had "already put into this structure nearly eleven thousand dollars over and above the sum he is finally to receive from you when it is completed."[119] The church wanted the auditorium finished and reimbursed Mueller for certain expenses beyond his contract so that by 7 April, a trustee informed Wright "that in all probability [Mueller] will shortly resume work on the building."[120] By then art glass was being placed in Unity Temple, and Johonnot's plans committee had chosen a pew design.[121] The trustees urged Wright to complete designs for lighting fixtures.[122] On 5 July they asked Mueller "to finish the plastering inside Unity Temple, which has long been delayed."[123] By 16 July "the plasterers [were] finishing up their work and the carpenters [were] about to begin on the wood trim."[124] Pews were being crafted in September, less than a month before the opening service in Unity Temple in October 1908.[125]

During this period, Wright used the delays in building to rethink the auditorium's interior architecture. He later recalled that after the first plans, he continued to make

> many subsequent studies in refinement – correction of correlation, scale tests for integration. Overcoming difficulties in detail, in the effort to keep all clean and simple as a whole, is continued during the whole process of planning and building.
>
> Many studies in detail yet remain to be made, to determine what further may be left out to protect the design. These studies never seem to end, and in this sense, no organic building may ever be "finished." The complete goal of the idea of organic architecture is never reached. Nor need be. What worth while ideal is ever reached?[126]

Partial understanding of Wright's creative work emerges from comparison of the earlier perspective of Unity Temple's interior (see Fig. 80), datable to before February 1906, with a view of the room as detailed in working drawings of March 1906 (Fig. 117). This perspective reverses the viewpoint of the earlier image. In the later study, instead of a central skylight descending below the ceiling, the motif overhead is now a grid of twenty-five coffer-like square skylights above the ceiling plane between crisscrossed beams, almost as the interior was built. The ceiling's center and sides are now

FIGURE 117

Wright, Unity
Temple, prelimi-
nary perspective
of auditorium,
corresponding to
working drawings
of March 1906
(Frank Lloyd
Wright Archives,
Drawing No.
0611.002, © The
Frank Lloyd
Wright Founda-
tion 1962).

integrated into one continuous horizontal plane. Wood bands extend out from the central coffering across the peripheral ceilings to the clerestories. These high windows resemble transparent screens, suggesting continuity from inside to outside, or what Wright termed "the unlimited overhead."[127]

Wright's concern for visual continuity and integration of structural and ornamental form is evident in the design of Unity Temple's central ceiling as built. In the cross-section published in the Wasmuth folio (Fig. 118), the beams running north–south between the coffered skylights of the central ceiling are hollow U-shaped concrete beams. As seen in a recent photo-graph of the roof area above the ceiling looking northeast (Fig. 119), the hollow north–south beams span between solid concrete beams running east–west. These primary solid east–west beams support the grid of vertical posts that uphold the auditorium's central sloped glass roof that sustains loads of snow and wind. The network of beams crisscrossing the audi-torium's ceiling helps provide lateral stiffness for the room's structure be-tween its four columns. Figure 118 also shows that between the four main columns, there span four deep box beams (marked 'A') set above the galleries' ceilings. These beams support the outer edges of the skylight's sloped glass and its upper parapet walls. Yet these major structural beams are not visible from inside the auditorium, much as Wright set Unity House's trusses above its ceiling.

Inside the auditorium (Fig. 120), beams running in both directions across the ceiling create the grid of twenty-five deep coffer-like square bays

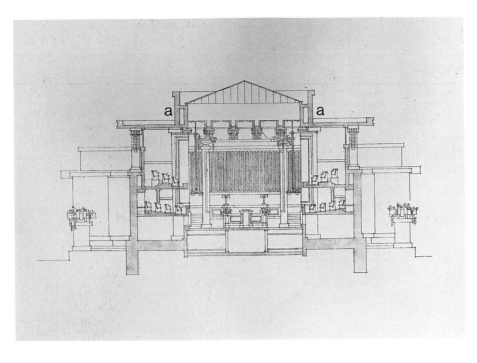

a a

FIGURE 118

Wright, Unity Temple, east–west cross-section through auditorium, looking south. From *Ausgeführte Bauten und Entwürfe,* Plate LXIII(b) (Frank Lloyd Wright Archives, Drawing No. 0611.090, © The Frank Lloyd Wright Foundation 1994).

N

W

E

S

FIGURE 119

Wright, Unity Temple, roof space above art glass ceiling and below skylight, looking northeast. Photograph courtesy of Wiss, Janney, Elstner Associates, Inc., Chicago.

N

W   E

S

FIGURE **120**

Wright, Unity
Temple, audi-
torium's skylights
seen from below.
Photograph by
Paul Rocheleau.

for the art glass. This is the one surface in the building where one sees a crystallization of the grid of 6 ft. 10. in. on which the design was based. Viewed from below, there appears to be no difference between the primary east–west and secondary north–south beams of the ceiling. Yet their structural distinction may be evident in the ornamental motifs of the skylight's panels of art glass. A drawing of these motifs in a reflected ceiling plan of the auditorium (Fig. 121) shows that the design of every panel is identical, but each panel is oriented differently. Each panel has a motif like the wide

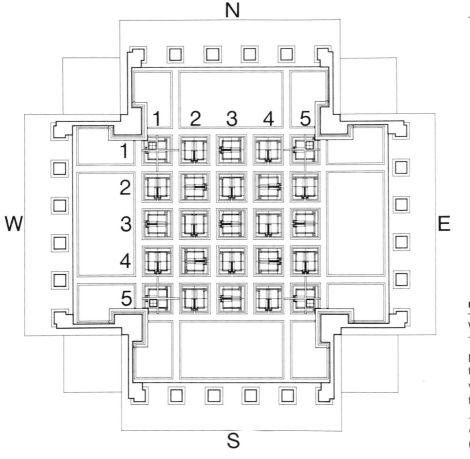

N

1 2 3 4 5

W

E

S

FIGURE 121

Wright, Unity
Temple, ceiling
plan of audi-
torium. Reprinted
with permission
from *Perspecta
22: The Yale Ar-
chitectural Journal*
(1984).

end of a fork on one side. Each such forklike motif joins the upper end of a vertical wood band rising up an inner side of each coffer, as seen in Figure 120. These vertical bands were among those added to Wright's design in construction. They were perhaps meant to encase wiring for electric lights above the art glass.[128]

The ceiling plan shows the skylight's twenty-five bays labeled as five east–west rows and five north–south ranks. In thirteen of these twenty-five ceiling bays, the wider forklike motifs in the art glass face either east or west. Of these bays, in east–west rows 1, 3, and 5, the forklike motifs in north–south ranks 1, 3, and 5 point west. In east–west rows 2 and 4, this motif in north–south ranks 2 and 4 points east. Thus, the forklike motifs that align with the primary east–west beams are oriented in both directions. The ceiling's twelve other glass panels have their forklike motifs pointing only to the south. In north–south ranks 1, 3, and 5, the forklike motifs in east–west rows 2 and 4 point south. In north–south ranks 2 and 4, the forklike motifs in east–west rows 1, 3, and 5 also point south. Thus, those forklike motifs that align with the secondary north–south beams point in only one direction.

The pattern of motifs in the ceiling glass suggests the metaphor of weaving, whereby secondary north–south beams are like a secondary woof crossing the primary east–west beams, as if these were the primary warp. This interweaving of the ornamental motifs through the ranks and rows of the ceiling coffers is difficult to see when standing in the temple, yet it is seen in the plan of the room's ceiling in Figure 121. The metaphor of weaving recurs in Wright's accounts of his architecture as an exploration of the concept of plasticity, wherein elements of different scale in his buildings are all integrated into a continuous three-dimensional fabric of its spatial and material form.[129] As Wright wrote of his work to 1908: "In the main the ornamentation is wrought in the warp and woof of the structure. It is constitutional in the best sense and is felt in the conception of the ground plan. . . . To me it is the most fascinating phase of the work, involving the true poetry of conception."[130]

*   *   *

Wright's development of the design through the stage of working drawings included changes in the auditorium's wood details. In the preliminary perspective (Fig. 80), the four main columns are bare plaster up to their squared capitals. In the perspective documenting the design at the time of the working drawings (Fig. 117), the columns' upper shafts have been enriched with three vertically superimposed ornamental motifs above the level of the upper balconies. These motifs were to be of stained wood surrounding central rectangles of plaster. Their closest precedents were the column capitals high atop the Larkin Building's five-story atrium, seen from a distance below. Yet Unity Temple's capitals were to begin at the level of the upper balcony railing, so as to visually divide each column about halfway up its shaft, thus serving to obscure the column's full height and control its scale.

Figure 117 depicts the south wall above the pulpit as a blank plaster panel below an upper screen, which has alternating square and vertical slots framed in wood. These emit sounds of the organ behind. The plaster panel and organ screen above are flanked by slender vertical piers. Projecting forward from the south wall on either side are larger freestanding piers rising from the main floor and carrying flanking sections of the slotted wood organ screen. These side sections of screen are suspended above stairs leading up from the main floor to lower galleries. The freestanding piers have wood verticals that rise up their faces to meet multiple horizontal bands below their capitals, shown holding flower urns. The piers frame the frontal area of the pulpit, serving as transitions from the south wall to the main columns, as if Wright were subsuming adjacent elements within one architectural system.

His effort to integrate motifs appears in comparison of the lower and upper balcony fronts in the early perspective (Fig. 80) with these surfaces shown in the later perspective keyed to the working drawings (Fig. 117). While the earlier study shows these surfaces as simple planes of plaster with wood bases and copings, a later study shows balcony fronts reduced in height and faced with wood bands. On the faces of the upper balconies, these bands frame pairs of globe-shaped electric lights toward each end, while other wood bands also return beneath the balconies' soffits. Again, the appearance of the wood bands in the later drawing corresponds to the introduction of electric lights on the railing fronts, suggesting that the bands may have been conceived as encasement for wiring. In both the earlier and later perspectives, the railings are flanked by piers as pedestals for urns, yet the later study shows these piers more developed and coordinated in detail.

While Unity Temple was being built, Wright decided to steeply bank the pews in the balconies. Mueller made higher concrete bases for these tiers of pews from revised plans prepared by Wright.[131] Figure 118 shows these bases with small steps of concrete to each level of pews. The elevated banks of seating in the balconies as built are quite high, enhancing both acoustic and visual access to the pulpit and frontal platform below. This effect is marked for pews in upper balconies, which are raised more steeply than those in the lower balconies. Tiered pews accommodated the fact that women of that time wore hats when seated in church, as shown in the earlier perspective view of the auditorium (Fig. 80). The custom of hats was a concern in old Unity Church's long navelike auditorium (see Fig. 44), where pews had all been on one level floor. In 1897 the women of Unity Church adopted a then novel custom of removing their hats as "a courtesy . . . particularly in auditoriums with level floors, that would be greatly appreciated by their neighbors."[132] In the new Unity Temple, the raised pews in the surrounding balconies heighten the image of a compact and intimate meetinghouse, as if the room was meant to evoke this cultural memory.

The pews in the auditorium were not designed by Wright. Figure 117 shows his design for pews with straight backs and sides, consistent with surrounding rectilinear architecture and with Wright's furniture in his other buildings of this period. Also shown are individual chairs behind the pulpit, presumably of Wright's design, though these were never made. In March 1908 Johonnot's plans committee recommended that the forward part of the pews' ends be cut down "at least 8" or 9" to allow enough space for people to comfortably enter the pews."[133] The plans committee also advised that the pews be plain paneled wood, without plaster panels, hinting that Wright had earlier envisioned pews with plaster backs and sides bordered in wood, perhaps to match the surrounding walls.[134] This early idea would have been consistent with Wright's view that interiors were optimal if the "furniture is built in as a part of the original scheme."[135] Wright, however, would continue to transform the temple's interior.

Wright's Final Changes in the Auditorium

A later drawing (Fig. 122) shows the auditorium almost as built. This study, in pencil on tracing paper, is about the same size as the earlier perspective from this viewpoint (Fig. 117), suggesting that it may have been a revision of this drawing. The later perspective shows the arms of the pews as curved, indicating that this drawing postdates Rev. Johonnot's recommendation of March 1908 on the pews' design. On ceilings above the balconies, bands of oak outline broad rectangular areas of the plaster. Pairs of these bands near the corners of the balcony ceilings extend the linear motifs of the coffers out to the clerestories. This ceiling design restores the skylight's centrality within the room. Mueller noted that Wright asked him to change "the main ceiling bands under the roof in the Temple, after same were practically completed, from a continuous beam effect as per original detail and architect's instructions, to a panel effect combined with column cap, faces and soffits as per final detail."[136] It was thus in the course of seeing the auditorium realized that Wright made crucial changes in expression. Reducing lines extended to the ceiling's edges returned visual weight to the space's core, so that the built ceiling's wood bands strengthen the room's distinction between central floor and side galleries.

As Mueller indicated, Wright also revised the ornamental bands for the main columns. Figure 123 shows the main southeast column's faces over-

FIGURE 122

Wright, Unity Temple, interior perspective of auditorium as built in 1908, looking south (Frank Lloyd Wright Archives, Drawing No. 0611.057, © The Frank Lloyd Wright Foundation 1985).

FIGURE 123

Wright, Unity
Temple, interior of
auditorium show-
ing southeast
main column
(Photo: author).

laid with double wood bands framing tall rectangles that extend from above
the column's base upward to just under its capital. No vertical strip marks
the juncture of planes along the inner corner of the columns. Thus the wood
bands frame a single color field of light yellow that flows around the two
right-angled faces of the column. These are thereby made to look almost

like a folded sheet of paper rather than a squared mass of concrete, as if Wright made the columns to join in the visual rhythms of the surrounding room. In the earlier design seen in Figure 117, the totemic pile of wood motifs through the upper shafts recalls the classic concept of a column as superimposed stones beneath a crowning block. Wright was here creating a variation on conventions familiar from architecture's history. By contrast, the built column, as delineated in Figure 122, has ribbon-like vertical bands articulating its shaft's planar face. Horizontal bands near the shaft's top appear like cantilevers turned inward toward the room's center, echoing the projection of the column caps above, as these spread outward to meet the ceiling.

At this juncture Wright had the ceiling bands flow into and around the column's capital (Fig. 124). Joints along these ribbons of trim are almost invisible where the bands meet at right angles, so their returns read clearly as fluid dark lines set in light planes. They have a visual presence that belies their diminutive widths and simple square edges. The wood bands are made to turn a variety of corners in all three dimensions. Single, double, and triple bands converge, disperse, and pass one another to tie together or distinguish between different planes of color surrounding a capital. In Unity Temple, the design of wood bands is more gymnastic and lyrical than those in Unity House, a difference attributable to the auditorium's special character as a room for worship, and perhaps to the fact that Wright developed Unity Temple's final design after Unity House's interior had been finished.

Wright's fusion of column and ceiling contradicts the classical distinction between supporting columns and their supported loads. Instead Wright's column and ceiling merge, losing their identity as individual elements to become part of the whole room's language of surfaces. Here he created continuities as the new convention of a modern architecture. Though decoratively poetic, Wright's columnar details were also structurally rational as an expression of the nature of construction in reinforced concrete. The old conventions of load and support in classical architecture presumed lintels and columns made of discrete blocks of stone. Yet concrete was a monolithic material wherein steel reinforcing fused columns and beams into one structural mass. Thus, as one of Wright's contemporaries wrote, "the meaning of many of the members of the conventional order, which has maintained its integrity from the days of Athens to our own, disappears in monolithic construction."[137]

As circled in Figure 89, the columns' inner corners, where ceiling bands meet capitals, mark points on the grid of 6 ft. 10 in. used to plan the building. Wright's choice of wood detail merging column and ceiling at these points in the room helps recall the design's ideal geometric order, as if the bands flowing around the capital in physical space correspond to intersecting lines of the grid in mathematical space. Wright's detail illustrates the architectural ideal that he termed plasticity. As he later wrote:

FIGURE **124**

Wright, Unity
Temple, interior of
auditorium show-
ing juncture of
ceiling and south-
east column (Pho-
to: author).

If form really followed function – it did by means of this ideal of plasticity –
why not throw away the implications of post or upright and beam or
horizontal entirely? Have no beams or columns piling up as "joinery." Nor
any cornices. Nor any "features" as *fixtures*. No. Have no appliances of
any kind at all, such as pilasters, entablatures and cornices. Nor put into
the building any fixtures whatsoever as "fixtures." Eliminate the separa-
tions and separate joints. Classic architecture was fixation-of-the-fixture.
Entirely so. Now why not let walls, ceilings, floors become *seen* as component parts of each other, their surfaces flowing into each other to get
continuity in the whole, eliminating all constructed features just as Louis
Sullivan had eliminated background in his ornament in favor of an integral
sense of the whole. Here an ideal began to have consequences.[138]

Wright explored this concept in his works of the period like the Mrs.
Thomas H. Gale house at 6 Elizabeth Court, Oak Park, built in 1909, which
Wright later saw as anticipating a modernistic style.[139] One drawing of this
residence (Fig. 125) is dated 1904, suggesting that it was conceived five
years before it was built.[140] Yet the house may have been designed for Mrs.
Gale and her children after the death of her husband in March 1907.[141] The
Gales were members of Unity Church, and Wright's design for Mrs. Gale's
house, if 1907 or 1908, coincided with Unity Temple's final design. In this
house Wright explored plasticity of the whole built form. The central chimney and frontal pier serve visually as vertical anchors for multiple horizontal
cantilevers that extend out on different levels and in different directions.

As in Unity Temple, Wright enriched his final design of the Gale house

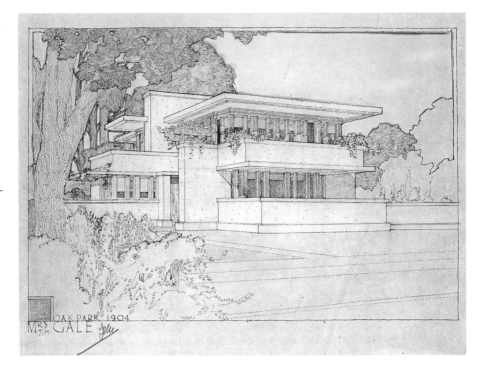

FIGURE 125

Wright, drawing
of Mrs. Thomas
H. Gale house,
Oak Park, Ill.,
built 1909 (Frank
Lloyd Wright Ar-
chives, Drawing
No. 0905.001,
© The Frank
Lloyd Wright
Foundation 1962).

by adding bands that pass around corners of the vertical frontal pier and
high rear chimney (Fig. 126). With corners crossed by horizontal bands,
these elements are less like masses upholding loads and more like planes
folded at right angles. As in Unity Temple, ornament for the Gale house
served to clarify Wright's broader aesthetic agenda of architecture as the
embodiment of a principle of continuity. Wright's depiction of the Gale
house adjacent to a tree with spreading branches suggests that he imagined
the building's plasticity as analogous to that of living natural forms. As he
later wrote: "Conceive now that an entire building might grow up out of
conditions as a plant grows up out of soil, as free to be itself, to 'live its own
life according to Nature' as is the tree. Dignified as a tree in the midst of
nature."[142]

Wright's final design for the frontal interior in Unity Temple included a
largely altered organ screen (Fig. 127). So extensive was this change that the
organ screen was built according to a supplemental contract.[143] This screen
was made as a uniform surface of vertical wood slots between the piers
flanking the pulpit area. The screen's new height and projection responded
in part to the specifications of the new auditorium's original organ installed
early in 1909.[144] In the earlier Unity Church, organ pipes were an elaborate
architectural backdrop for the frontal platform (see Fig. 44). In that period
the range and richness of tone in a church's organ were perceived as a mark
of the congregation's wealth. Yet Jenkin Lloyd Jones objected to instrumental display in the auditorium of the Abraham Lincoln Center. Its organ was

FIGURE 126

Wright, Mrs.
Thomas H. Gale
house (Photo:
author).

"hid behind the spindle work" above the auditorium's frontal platform (see Fig. 42).[145] Wright claimed to have designed this interior, and its organ screen met the criteria that an instrument be centrally and highly placed, and that it also be freestanding in a generous allotment of space so that its tones would not be dampened by a tight encasement.[146]

Chicago's architects were then advised that ornamental wood screens for organs would ideally be as high and as wide as the whole instrument behind. Screens should be designed "so that they do not interfere to any undesirable extent with the free egress of sound from the enclosed stops. [The architect] should in all cases strive to impart a refined and delicate character to the fronts, consistent with the nature of the instrument and the style of the architecture of the building."[147] Unity Temple's organ screen as built was moved forward from the south wall in order to deepen the chamber for the instrument behind. The screen thus projects partially over the choir loft, so that it looms right above the organist's console there. Advancing the screen required "changing the rail between the Pulpit and Choir loft, moving the partition forward over the Speaker's platform."[148]

The tall organ screen (Fig. 127) made the auditorium's south wall into a series of layered planes receding from the bottom to the top: first the pulpit, in front of the railing for the choir loft; then, above, the organ screen, which was surmounted by the crowning clerestory. Many surfaces render the room's visual limits more elusive. The same layering of planes appears in Wright's domestic interiors of the period, notably in the balconies on the west wall of the playroom he added to his Oak Park home in 1895 (Fig. 128). There the rising tiers with small railings were to serve as miniature galleries for viewing performances in the playroom. Wright then claimed to have "gotten more education in experimenting with his own premises, than in any other way."[149]

Figure 122 shows Wright's built version of the balcony railings. These had been "changed to trussed beams to carry the balcony floors"[150] between the main corner columns. Wood band motifs on the fronts of the balconies were altered to visually weight the far ends of their plastered faces. Atop the piers flanking the lower galleries, Wright designed urns for flowers, which appear in all his views of the room. Presumably the urns would hold living forms both as a visual complement to the rectilinear architecture around them and as signs of the natural creation that had inspired its form. Wright had eight such urns cast and delivered to the church two days before its opening. However, the trustees refused to accept them. The chair of the building committee wrote that the urns "would not only hide and obstruct the view of at least forty persons (and every particle of the seating capacity of the Church must be available as it now falls far below what we were assured of), but they would overhang the balcony

FIGURE 128

Wright, playroom
in Wright house,
Oak Park, Ill.,
1895, looking
west. Photograph
by Jon Miller,
Hedrich Blessing,
47560-H.

pews and the steps leading to the balconies to such an extent as to mate-
rially and seriously interfere with the head room. They are absolutely im-
practicable and must be taken away at once."[151]

If Wright's urns did not survive, his lighting fixtures did. Figure 123
shows a pair of these hanging from a wood cross suspended from a rod
hanging from the center of the southeasternmost coffer. Affixed to the
cross's outermost quadrant is a small lantern whose face repeats the cruciform motif (Fig. 124). Two of the arms of the cross each uphold three
vertical slats that connect to globes and cubic lanterns of amber glass at a

level even with the base of the organ screen. The cubic lanterns' shape is a miniature replica of the room's cubic form. The elongated vertical slats echo lines of the organ screen and columns. Thus the auditorium's fixtures extend the formal grammar of the surrounding surfaces. Barry Byrne, who made the working drawings for Unity Temple, stressed the ideal of aesthetic consistency throughout a building: "In Frank Lloyd Wright's designing of architecture, the matter of right relationship was of infinite importance; his insistence upon such relationship and his achievement of it link his architecture with the great architectures of the past."[152]

* * *

Unity Temple's pulpit shows how Wright could transform an isolated, conventional element into a component of his architecture. In the early perspective for the auditorium (Fig. 80), the pulpit is a central freestanding lectern of wood with a cloth draped over its top beneath an open Bible. This idea of the pulpit as frontal lectern on a platform had precedents in earlier Unity Church (see Fig. 44) and in Jenkin Lloyd Jones's Abraham Lincoln Center (see Fig. 42). In the perspective corresponding to Unity Temple's working drawings (Fig. 117) and in the cross-section (Fig. 118), the pulpit becomes a vertical block of concrete centrally anchored to its horizontal platform. This recalls the ancient idea of an altar as an immovable block of stone more than the modern convention of the pulpit as an elevated wooden box.[153] A hieratic character for the pulpit is reinforced by flanking chairs of Wright's design. In Figure 117 the pulpit is the vanishing point, where the perspectival lines from floor, ceiling, and balconies converge. In the section, the pulpit is also presented as the room's center of gravity, as there is no separate altar in Unity Temple's auditorium.

Wright's final design for the pulpit (Fig. 129) was so different from earlier studies that Mueller built it from a separate contract.[154] Open slots separate the pulpit from side railings, yet both are joined along their tops by wood copings that tier upward toward the raised central lectern. Paired lights for reading stand behind to either side of the pulpit on the organist's railing. The platform's seating is a continuous bench rather than individual sedile, a system that recalled Clarke's Church of the Disciples in Boston. Horizontal wood bands run across the railings' faces, while the vertical blocks astride the pulpit are faced with bands whose forms resemble an elongated Latin cross. The pulpit and its platform are set well out into the room as the focal point of worship. Wright thus reshaped an ecclesiastical furnishing into the auditorium's architectural centerpiece. The pulpit's design condenses motifs of surrounding surfaces, thereby participating in the temple's unified aesthetic.

Wright's pulpit for Unity Temple illustrates a process of design characteristic of his work before 1910. In his domestic architecture of this period, Wright often developed conventional elements of roof, porch, or chimney into motifs that were consistent with his own style. In this way, he could create houses that looked simultaneously traditional and innovative, because he acknowledged and assimilated the conventions of residential architecture, yet reworked these according to new formal ideals. This process underlay Unity Temple's design at many levels. Wright created a radically new church that nevertheless echoed numerous conventions at different scales, from its overall plan to its built pulpit. Like Wright's prairie houses, Unity Temple could function symbolically both at the level of cultural memory and as an exercise in an architectural vocabulary then unprecedented.

While the pulpit focused attention on the auditorium's frontal center, Unity Temple's scheme of colors draws the eye through the whole room up to its crown. In general, colors are muted on the auditorium's lower and peripheral surfaces, becoming lighter toward the room's central space and skylit ceiling. The depressed cloisters below the east and west galleries are darkly shadowed. Above, the back walls of the lower and upper balconies are a yellowish gray, while their side walls have panels of pale green, perhaps alluding to natural foliage. Atop the room's periphery, clerestories are largely colorless glass (Fig. 130), although the upper panels have a rapid rhythm of squares in white glass above paired green rectangles. This glass

187

Construction of
Unity Temple

FIGURE 129

Wright, Unity
Temple, interior of
auditorium looking toward pulpit
(Photo: author).

FIGURE 130

Wright, Unity
Temple, interior of
auditorium look-
ing northwest,
showing cleresto-
ries. Photograph
courtesy of Wiss,
Janney, Elstner
Associates, Inc.,
Chicago.

pattern is similar to that in the entrance foyer's doors. Above the auditorium's south wall, the 9-in. width of the clerestory's glass motifs matches
that of wood slots in the organ screen below (Fig. 127). Wright's glass
designs in the clerestories also recall the rectilinear cast concrete ornament
of the columns just outside seen through the glass. The motifs in both the
glass and the columns in turn read as conventionalizations of the foliate tree
branches seen outside the clerestories, intimating architecture's link to its
natural environs.[155]

Inside the auditorium, the dark and medium brown colors found in
Unity House were omitted. Instead, Unity Temple's baseboards, frontal pier
bases, and the copings of the lower galleries' end blocks are unpainted
finish concrete (Fig. 127). The muted tones of the monolithic construction
heighten the dignity of the room for worship. For inner faces of frontal piers
and main columns, Wright chose a pale yellow, bordered in the pale green
and yellow gray of the galleries' walls behind the columns. The pale yellow
recurs on the gallery fronts, though their central faces within bands are
yellowish white. The same pale yellow overlays the galleries' ceiling panels
and the skylights' coffers. The coffers' sides slant inward from bottom to top,
reflecting the light that passes through their crowning panels of art glass.
These panels repeat and interlace the room's motifs of square and rectangle
at ever smaller scales. The varicolored yellow-amber glass recalls the
warmth and brightness of sunlight, yet the light changes with the weather
outside (Fig. 120). The art glass's colors are also keyed to that of the incan-
descent electric lights that illuminate the panels from above for evening
services.

Wood bands on railings flanking the pulpit may resemble crosses, yet the auditorium is largely devoid of explicit religious images or symbols. The spiritual significance of the room had to be conveyed through the totality of its form. As a whole, the balance and richness of its colors create a room that is both restrained and joyous. No literally historical forms appear, yet the auditorium's range and integration of motifs call to mind the classical ideal of beauty as variety in unity. Wright presumably intended that Unity Temple's auditorium be an optimal room for music as well as for preaching. His building committee was much concerned about the mechanical features of the original organ, all of whose pipes and stops were precisely specified.[156] The finished architecture's visual system has a complexity of expression that may serve as a built metaphor for the polyphony of the organ music emanating through its massive frontal screen.

Unity Temple and the Larkin Building

Unity Temple has been compared with Wright's preceding Larkin Building in Buffalo, New York, which was completed in 1906 (see Fig. 41).[157] As noted earlier, both were shaped as systems of rectilinear masses. In both, major central rooms are flanked by partially detached closed corner stair towers. Also, in both buildings, Wright linked the primary spatial volumes to smaller built volumes housing secondary functions, with the main entrances between the two volumes. Upon entering each structure, one turns to arrive in the major space, although in Unity Temple the entrance to the auditorium is indirect and its main floor is raised half a level up from that of the entrance foyer.

In the Larkin Building's hall (Fig. 131), as in Unity Temple's auditorium, tiers of seating surround that on the main floor. In both rooms, light enters from both skylights above and peripheral clerestories on all four sides. As Hendrik Berlage wrote after having visited both buildings in 1911, in the Larkin, "the interior hall has excellent light in spite of the masses of brick which surround the exterior corner towers. The effect is similar to that of Unity Temple."[158] In each building's central room, the vertical lines of the major structural columns are countered by the horizontal lines of the upper floors or seating galleries surrounding the central space. The Larkin interior provided one point of reference for Wright's early designs for Unity Temple, whose interior column capitals were at first modeled on those of the Larkin Building's central atrium.[159]

In each structure the primary spatial volume serves as a setting for a group whose collective self-awareness was heightened by Wright's design. In this way the Larkin Building's hall for work corresponds to Unity Temple's room for worship. In the Larkin atrium head managerial personnel worked visibly on the main floor, while workers on the upper floors could see one another through the building. Unity Temple's galleries have pews focused on the center, so the auditorium enables mutual visual contact among

FIGURE 131

Wright, Larkin
Building, view of
light court looking
north from third-
floor balcony.
Photograph cour-
tesy of Buffalo
and Erie County
Historical Society,
Larkin Collection
(C25,012).

worshipers. A comparable effect was realized most intensively on special
occasions in the central atrium of the Larkin Building.

While both structures exhibit a rectilinear geometry and communal
solidarity, the Larkin Building's atrium and Unity Temple's auditorium were

distinct as expressions of different purposes. Each building had a character keyed in part to its context. The Larkin Building was in an urban district amid factories and railroads, whereas Unity Temple was in a suburban setting of churches and civic structures. As a church, Unity Temple's auditorium recalled the older type of the meetinghouse, whereas the Larkin Building's more navelike atrium had sources in the immediately preceding generation of skylit atria in commercial buildings. In scale and spatial shape, the rooms were quite unlike each other. Whereas Unity Temple's auditorium is nearly cubic in proportion, the Larkin Building's atrium was a rectangle three times as long as Unity Temple's volume of central open space. The Larkin atrium was similarly nearly three times the height of Unity Temple's interior, yet the width across the Larkin's atrium was actually less than that between the galleries on opposite sides of Unity Temple.

Differences in scale and proportion between the Larkin atrium and Unity Temple derive not only from their different purposes, but also from their different structural systems. While Wright selected a square module of 6 ft. 10 in. in the design of Unity Temple to shape its concrete's formwork, the Larkin Building's central steel frame has rectangular bays 16 ft. wide by 32 ft. deep. The rectangular shape of the atrium is consistent with Wright's selection of a rectangular bay, just as Unity Temple's square shape is a multiple of its square unit dimension. Different systems of construction created different visual rhythms in the two interiors. In the Larkin Building, the fundamental cadence is the 16 ft. spacing between steel columns. This rhythm continued above in the spacing between the beams that spanned the atrium. In Unity Temple, the coffers of the ceiling mark the unit of design. This unit dimension of 6 ft. 10 in. repeats in the spacing of the ornamental cast concrete columns outside the clerestory windows.

Differences in construction underlie different aesthetic emphases. Unity Temple's concrete mass is monolithic, with columns and beams integrally connected. Wood bands tie together surfaces in three dimensions. In this way, the interior becomes an architectural metaphor for the religious ideals it serves, as well as an expression of the nature of the construction. In the Larkin Building, the glazed brick cladding of the frame was a material with utilitarian connotations in a building for commercial labor. The individual vertical columns and horizontal lintels cross each other, yet they remain distinctly articulated elements. Each upper floor is marked by projecting copings and bases of the horizontal brick lintels slightly recessed between columns, and each vertical column is crowned by story-high capitals. Distinct expression of column and lintel would be consistent with the nature of the steel frame as a system of structure.

Inside the Larkin Building, an organ at the north end crowned the fourth floor. Its literal singular presentation contrasts with Unity Temple's organ screen as a surface integral with the wood detailing of the room's south front. In the church the focal point is the pulpit rather than the organ behind. The mural below the Larkin's organ has no parallel in Unity Temple, whose auditorium lacks explicit figurative imagery. The famed inscriptions of inspirational words and biblical verses in the Larkin atrium contrast with the absence of any textual inscriptions inside Unity Temple as built. There the central symbolic ideal of Unity was inscribed in the proportional and decorative systems of the architecture itself.

Similarities and differences between the Larkin atrium and Unity Temple's auditorium reveal that Wright developed an individual style sufficiently broad in its principles to create interiors of different types. While these spaces may be seen as variations on similar formal and communal themes, their differences reveal Wright's commitment to architecture that expressed an individuality of function unique to each of his buildings. The primacy of this idea in his thinking provided the logic behind his solutions for these interiors. Moreover, the degree of integration and formal poetry within the later Unity Temple demonstrate Wright's aesthetic ideal of plasticity in a way distinct from that found in the Larkin Building.

Initial Responses to the Completed Unity Temple

Unity Temple's auditorium drew praise from the time of its opening service in October 1908. Wright recalled that he did not attend, but that church members, including the doubtful Skillin, telephoned their congratulations on the design, admiring its lighting and acoustics.[160] As if to address lingering concern over these issues, one assessment of the opening noted that "all who were present, and many visitors who came in after the service, were impressed by its beauty of form, the simple dignity of its lines, the soft and harmonious colors of the walls and the ceiling lights, and the general feeling of restfulness and reverence befitting a place of worship. Though the day was dark, the light was ample without any aid from the electric lamps, and the acoustic properties proved to be of the most satisfactory character, the lowest tones being distinctly heard in every part of the room."[161] By shaping a compact auditorium rather than an expansive nave, Wright transformed constraints of site and funds into an architectural space that contrasted effectively with its local neighbors. The room's distinction was evident at its opening service, when 350 persons filled its auditorium. On that occasion, "the grouping of the people about the pulpit brought all within easy reach and gave to all a sense of nearness to preacher and choir, and of intimate and even family relations with one another."[162]

Perhaps because of its departure from convention, Unity Temple's qualities were not immediately apprehensible from Wright's drawings and model before it was built. His scheme would be appreciated when complete, after Wright's final set of interior details was realized. Yet, if the congregation had struggled with their commitment to his unusual design, they delighted in their occupancy of the finished building. Unity Temple's reputation developed quickly from the fall of 1908, when the new church grew "in popular esteem as well as with the people of the parish."[163] In December a view of the auditorium appeared in Chicago's *Inland Architect and News Record,* with an extended description.[164] In January 1909 Wright was identified to Oak Park as "one of the most famous architects in the world."[165] By April, "hundreds of visitors from all over the country [were] coming to study [Unity Temple's] architecture and construction."[166]

The sudden fame of their edifice may have surprised the congregation, yet Unity Temple's immediate renown would help sustain the congregation's collective effort to fund the work's completion. In 1906 the church contracted with Mueller to build Wright's design for $32,661. By the time work ceased toward the end of 1908, the cost of construction had reached $60,344.55, nearly twice the contracted amount. This figure did not include the costs of the site ($10,000), the organ ($3,500), the heating, ventilating, plumbing, and electrical systems ($3,400), and Wright's fee of $1,776, or 5% of $35,520, the earlier estimated cost of building.[167] These expenses yielded a total cost of over $79,000 for the entire project. To meet these costs, the church had $1,000 from the building fund before the fire, $9,500 in insurance for their old building, and $6,500 available from the sale of the old buildling's site, yielding a total of $17,000 in funds before the new project began. Unity Church borrowed $6,500 during construction and an additional $8,000 after the building was finished, leaving approximately $47,500 in expenses to be paid. By the end of 1908 the church's membership had subscribed to pledges of $32,199.50 for the new building. Of this amount, the Ladies Social Union had given $4,331, and other groups within the church had pledged $1,541.51, providing 18% of the total pledges. Another 18% or $5,900 came from five donors who each pledged from $1,000 to $1,350.[168] The remaining 64% of the pledges, amounting to $20,426.99, came from 150 persons in pledges ranging from $1 to $750. Fundraising for Unity Temple would continue for several years. Thus the entire congregation committed its resources to realize an experimental building, whose excellence they soon recognized. On 9 March 1909, at the church's first annual meeting after the auditorium's opening, the following resolution was adopted, and a copy sent to Wright:

> The members of Unity Church Society, in annual meeting assembled, desire to place on record their appreciation of the new church edifice.
>
> The new building is a noble, dignified, beautiful, and inspiring example of architecture and most admirably adapted to the various needs and activities of the church.
>
> Because of its uniqueness in style and construction, it is set apart as a thing by itself, at once honoring and distinguishing its designer and its possessors.
>
> Because of its simplicity, beauty and artistic effects it cannot but exert a refining and elevating influence upon all who frequent its portals.
>
> We believe the new structure will grow in honor and favor both with the parish and with the community.
>
> We extend to the architect, Mr. Frank Lloyd Wright, our most hearty

congratulations upon the wonderful achievement embodied in the new edifice and further extend to him our most sincere thanks for the great service which, through the building, he has rendered to the parish and to the community.

We believe the building will long endure as a monument to his artistic genius and that, so long as it endures, it will stand forth as a masterpiece in art and architecture.[169]

Religious and Architectural Interpretations of Unity Temple

INITIAL critical reception of Unity Temple had linked its innovative aesthetic to its denominational culture. The building was at first seen as both a work of Wright and a symbol of Unitarian and Universalist ideals. These readings of Unity Temple imply that Wright's artistic program in this case was not purely an individual credo, but was enmeshed in a system of thought and belief that he shared with liberal religious contemporaries who were close to the project. For Johonnot, Jones, and Gannett, Wright's building crystallized a vision of what the Unitarian movement in the western United States stood for and what role it might play in the broader spiritual course of the new century, which they believed would see the growth of liberal ideals into a universal religion. Their views, in turn, may have informed Wright's approach to Unity Temple as a work linked to both non-Western and ancient temples.

Rev. Johonnot's Defense of Wright's Design

If his congregation had praised the aesthetic merit of Unity Temple, then Rev. Johonnot had earlier championed the building's architecture in terms of its religious meaning. The design's symbolism was the central theme of the booklet, *The New Edifice of Unity Church, Oak Park, Illinois. Frank Lloyd Wright, Architect. Descriptive and Historical Matter by Dr. Rodney F. Johonnot, Pastor. Published by the New Unity Church Club, June, Nineteen Hundred and Six*.[1] This publication, prepared by a committee made up of Charles Woodard, Johonnot, and Wright, included theological and architectural ideas found in the project's announcements of February. Yet the booklet's text was credited to Johonnot as author, thus enhancing the credibility of the design in the eyes of Oak Park and Unity Church, which sent the booklet to members.[2]

Rev. Johonnot wrote that "the attempt has been made not merely to create a religious structure, but one that fitly embodies the principles of liberal Christianity for which this church stands."[3] In his view, Unity Temple's design conveyed ideas that his denominational cultures associated with the inclusive concept of unity. Wright's forms were to stand for the unity of divinity central to Unitarian thought and the Universalist view of the unity of humanity. Both liberal movements thought that these twin themes implied the coming unity of diverse religions in the modern period of the world's history. Wright's building was called a temple in part because this term had a broad intercultural as well as biblical usage. Johonnot wrote that "This building which is to be dedicated to the worship of the one true and living God in the spirit of Christian faith may then very properly be called a 'temple.'"[4] As a symbol of unity,

> The building is a harmonious unit; the style fitting the material and the material the form. While the structure is adapted to the various function [sic] of a church, the purposes of worship and services are clearly integrated, while separately set forth.
>
> Informed by the same spirit which characterized the ancient temples, this structure typifies the thought "while religions are many, religion is one." . . . The past and the present forms of religion are thus brought together in a spirit of unity. The temple form is especially fitted to a liberal church whose faith is that all religions are of God, are the attempts of man to feel after and find Him "in whom we live and move and have our being."[5]

While Unity Temple could be linked to earlier Unitarian churches, the edifice was unique among Universalist churches and Johonnot had to defend the design in this denomination's press. His justification of Wright's project emphasized its symbolic, as well as spatial and constructive, rationality. In October 1907, a month after Unity House was opened, the All Souls Universalist Church in Watertown, New York, was dedicated (Fig. 132).[6] This building's architect was Hobart B. Upjohn (1876–1949), a grandson of Richard Upjohn, the English-born architect who had done much to initiate the Gothic Revival in the United States with the design of such influential works as Trinity Church in New York City.[7] In the church for a Universalist congregation, Upjohn planned a nave with large hammer-beam trusses supporting its roof. Behind the church was a Sunday school building accessible from the street by a path along the nave's east flank. Clad in brownstone, the church featured exterior buttresses along its walls, pointed arch windows, and a square frontal tower.

Upjohn wrote that the "style adopted is the decorated English Gothic, a style originated by the Church for the church, the exact time at which this style having appeared being about the year 1272. . . . It has been the sincere desire of the architect to design a building which will impress those entering that they are in God's House, and there has been no desire on his

FIGURE **132**

Hobart B. Up-
john, All Souls
Universalist
Church, Water-
town, N.Y., 1907.
Reprinted from
*Universalist Lead-
er* 10 (19 October
1907).

part to surprise with novelties. Everything has been done in strict accord-
ance with the style adopted."[8] One clergyman of a neighboring church had
commended Upjohn's design at its dedication, stating: "I am glad to be here
because since it has been started it has looked like a church."[9]

The implication that a building had to be Gothic in style in order to be
typologically legible as a church drew a spirited response from Rev. Johonnot, who countered with a statement of ideas underlying Unity Temple.
Johonnot was fully in sympathy with the idea that a building for worship
should convey dignity and reverence. Yet, in his view, the idea that a
building had to be modeled on a Gothic cathedral in order to look like a
church "will not stand the test of rational criticism. . . . In fact to model
modern churches after this type of architecture is to my mind unjustifiable
by any canon of art."[10] For Johonnot a style of architecture for a great
cathedral was wholly unfitting for a smaller church. Yet, more important, he
believed that Gothic architecture did not fit modern functions of worship,
being born out of a time wholly unlike the modern period. Johonnot
claimed that Gothic cathedrals had not been designed for preaching. In his
view "our modern democratic ideals of worship" proposed a religion that
was, in theory at least, "of the people and by the people, as well as for the

people."[11] Johonnot asked why only the Gothic was regarded as the style suitable for new churches, speculating that

> It is not because it is by its nature more religious, nor because it is better fitted to our church uses, but merely because we are more accustomed to it. . . .
>
> To my mind it is time for us Protestants, and especially for us who are protestants of the Protestants, to cease from harking back to ancient forms simply because they have the stamp of custom, and to begin to put thought into our church buildings, to make them embody the ideas for which we stand. . . .
>
> Unity Church of Oak Park is trying to embody these feelings in a new type of church architecture. How well it will succeed must be left to the judgment of the time when its new edifice is completed; but it is at least making a rational effort along the lines indicated.[12]

Johonnot cited King's Chapel in Boston as an admirable example of non-Gothic religious architecture. At this time Boston's Church of the Disciples had started a new building, whose architecture was closely modeled on King's Chapel.[13] In Paris, Johonnot had admired the neoclassical Church of the Madeleine. Thus, he did not oppose historically derived architecture per se. Rather, like Jenkin Lloyd Jones at All Souls Church, Johonnot disavowed medievalism as antithetical to the Unitarian ideal of rationality. For liberal churches to prefer exclusively the Gothic style was "to take a very limited historical view of church architecture."[14]

Liberal religious emphasis on the theological rationale for Unity Temple's innovative design accompanied its opening in October 1908. The head of American Universalist churches viewed it "as symbolical of unity, joining many stones into one; of durability as befits the truth; as comprehensive, like universalism; as spiritual, taking its light from above; in its massiveness indicative of a place of refuge such as we need in God."[15] Unitarian and Universalist publications called Unity Temple "a most radical departure from traditional church architecture," yet "each feature has been adopted for a good reason. . . . The building has an individuality characteristic of the faith it represents, while the simplicity of line and structure within and without is also symbolic of a simple gospel."[16]

Such ideals of reason and simplicity underlie the words that Johonnot had helped choose for placement over Unity Temple's entrances: "For the Worship of God and the Service of Man" (see Fig. 2). This was the chief explicitly religious insignia of any kind outside or inside the building. In May 1906, just before building began, the trustees moved that "the matter of inscription and lettering on the exterior of the church be left to a special committee consisting of the President of the Board as chairman, Dr. Johonnot and the Building Committee."[17] Rendered in bronze letters selected by Wright, the carefully designed inscription set directly over the doors identifies the building's dual purpose, which was expressed in its binuclear plan with the auditorium for worship to the north of the doors and Unity House to the south. Yet this same phrase had also been included in the covenant of

Rev. Jenkin Lloyd Jones's All Souls Church and others of the Western Unitarian Conference since the 1880s. These proclaimed that "we unite for the worship of God and the service of man."[18] In Rev. Johonnot's view, the words affixed to Unity Temple conveyed a permanent and universal religious ideal consistent with the building's architecture. Observers in Oak Park had seen its style as severe, yet, to Johonnot, the simplicity of Wright's forms would signify the church's commitment to the most elemental purposes.

The formal dedication of Unity Temple in September 1909 coincided with the National Unitarian Conference's annual meeting, held that year in Chicago at Jenkin Lloyd Jones's Abraham Lincoln Center. The Unitarians praised Unity Temple as "perhaps the most strikingly original of any church in America."[19] Among other guests at Unity Temple, Jenkin Lloyd Jones was an honored speaker at the dedication's evening service. He was "introduced as representing the whole liberal fellowship of Chicago and the west, and as one who had on many occasions given his time and service in the interest of Unity church."[20] Of Wright's building, Jones's *Unity* stated: "It is a study in architecture as well as church history, probably the most deliberate, elaborate and successful attempt yet made to apply the 'new construction' to church architecture. The building is entirely constructed of reinforced concrete so that now in its completed state it is one solid monolith. It is not only built on the rock but it is a rock-built church."[21] One Oak Park observer viewed Unity Temple's concrete mass as an allusion to the biblical metaphor of the rock of Abraham as one origin of humankind described in the poetic prophecy of Isaiah. By analogy this observer associated Wright's monolithic Unity Temple with the modern Abraham – Lincoln – whose monument in Chicago was the foursquare rocklike edifice of Jenkin Lloyd Jones's Abraham Lincoln Center.[22]

The permanence and simplicity of concrete effectively signified the church's liberal credo. Views of the interior were first published in Chicago's *Cement World* in 1909 (see Fig. 4). Its editors concluded that Wright's building exhibited "concrete work that stands in a class of its own, for there is nothing else like it in the world." They describe how

> Unity church, from foundation to roof, with all its floors, pillars, beams and galleries, including the pulpit, is one piece of concrete – just like a great building hewn out of a cliff of granite. As you stand in the auditorium, beholding the wonderful work, you feel the impressiveness of this fact, and something of the unity spirit, the Oneness spirit, steals into your soul. When a style of church architecture is so pronounced in character as to impress one with the very creed taught within its walls there need be no question or even discussion of its propriety, for it is a masterpiece.[23]

Western Unitarian Perspectives on Emerson around 1900

Liberal emphasis on the ideal of Unity, which observers saw embodied in the monolithic form of Unity Temple, drew in part on a selective interpretation of Emerson's thought. By highlighting certain facets of Emerson that corresponded to their own convictions, Wright's Unitarian contemporaries had appropriated his reputation to support the liberal program they believed Unity Temple signified. Emerson began his career as a Unitarian minister and, even though his key essays postdated his leaving this role, his ideas remained influential for both eastern and western Unitarian culture. In 1879, in an attempt to characterize Emerson's relevance, Jones had presented him as one of "the liberal preachers of America out of the pulpit."[24] For many, Emerson had been the major prophet of transcendentalism. Yet Wright's uncle regarded Emerson's contribution to this intellectual and spiritual movement as impermanent relative to those truths found in Emerson's writings that would inform the future of human religious unity. Of Emerson, Jones emphasized that "back of the 'transcendentalism' in his thought," we discover "his undogmatic and non-evangelical religion."[25]

Jones placed the study of Emerson's writings at the end of his year's course on Western religious thought that began with the beliefs of Luther. For Wright's uncle, the arc of ideas that extended from the Reformation in the sixteenth century to transcendentalism in the nineteenth century could be clearly understood as "the flowering of Christianity into Universal Religion." From this perspective, both Luther and Emerson, together with the scores of thinkers between their periods that Jones proposed to consider in his course, were studied as prophets of Jones's own central idea, that "the hunger of the human heart at all times and all places is for unity."[26] Human unity would be the highest achievement of the coming universal religion, whose most recent prophet had been Emerson. For Jones, this was the line of development that had its local continuation in the life of his All Souls Church and the Abraham Lincoln Center.

Unitarian responses to Emerson in Unity Temple's period crested with the centennial of his birth in 1903, an event that coincided with publication of the definitive edition of Emerson's writings. Jones's colleague, William C. Gannett, who had known Emerson in Boston, portrayed him as a prophet of unity in nature. On the one hundredth anniversary of Emerson's birth, in a sermon on "Emerson's Vision of Unity," Gannett maintained:

> Emerson was no systematic philosopher. He neither borrowed formulas from philosophic idealism, nor cared to formulate a system of his own. He simply affirmed and re-affirmed certain insights of his own mind into Nature. What was his *central* insight? What idea more than others stands as equivalent and synonym for "Emerson"? . . . First and last, he beheld UNITY – UNITY as few have seen it.[27]

Wright's own formation had drawn on this Unitarian view of Emerson's significance. This process had begun under the tutelage of his mother's family, whose enthusiasm for Emerson had informed Wright's own. He recalled: "The Unitarianism of the Lloyd-Joneses . . . was an attempt to amplify in the confusion of the creeds of their day, the idea of life as a gift from a Divine Source, one God omnipotent, all things at one with Him. UNITY was their watchword, the sign and symbol that thrilled them, the UNITY of all things! This mother sought it continually."[28] When Wright's family lived in Weymouth, Massachusetts, in the 1870s, his mother "often wrote to her sisters and sent them the books she had discovered with delight; the works of Emerson, Channing, Theodore Parker, and Thoreau."[29] Of Wright's family's return to Wisconsin soon after, he recalled: "Now there was come back to the Valley from the East by way of Sister Anna and her 'preacher' the Unitarianism that had been worked out in the transcendentalism of the sentimental group at Concord: Whittier, Lowell, Longfellow, yes, and Emerson, too."[30]

Thirty years later, early in 1908, Anna Lloyd Wright was thanked by the Ladies Social Union of Unity Church for the papers she delivered on Emerson in the newly completed Unity House.[31] In Oak Park, study of Emerson also revived following Unity Temple's dedication in 1909. During January and February of 1910 two courses of lectures were offered at Unity House, focusing on what was then considered to be Emerson's greatest essay, "The Over-Soul," of 1841. In this text, he had asserted that "the only prophet of that which must be, is that great nature in which we rest as the earth lies in the soft arms of the atmosphere; that Unity, that Over-Soul, within which every man's particular being is contained and made one with all other. . . . Within man is the soul of the whole; the wise silence; the universal beauty, to which every part and particle is equally related; the eternal ONE."[32]

Emerson's vision of human unity across space and time, and of man's unity with divinity, paralleled Unitarian ideas in the lectures of Charles Everett, professor of theology at Harvard's Divinity School and a teacher of Rodney Johonnot. Everett also served as dean of the school from 1878 to 1900. His annual course of lectures studied philosophical sources for Unitarian beliefs, exploring different meanings of the ideal of Unity. The highest of these he termed "the unity which consists in the interpenetration of the finite by the infinite spirit."[33] While this concept echoed Emerson's idea of the Over-Soul, Everett claimed that the doctrine had found expression in the words of Paul: "for in Him we live, and move, and have our being." Johonnot had cited this same biblical phrase in his booklet on Unity Temple. Earlier, in 1907, he had emphasized that the contemporaneous movement toward a universal religion was based in part "upon [man's] longings after union with the infinite."[34]

If Wright, after Emerson, saw unity as the fundamental principle of nature, then its most visible manifestation in architecture was a continuity of material or a plasticity of form, wherein all parts appear to flow into each other or to be geometrically interrelated. Unity Temple embodied this concept in its monolithic concrete construction, the linear plasticity of its ornamental wood, and the unit system that ordered its form and fabrication. As in Wright's other work of the period, the church exhibited a consistency of motifs that conveyed to the eye an impression of Unity. On another level, the building signified human unity in its arrangement of space, whereby all worshipers would see one another in a cubic volume focused on the central pulpit. Thus, in Unity Temple's auditorium, Wright shaped a room that held a unified congregation, as a metaphor for the unity of man, within a formally integrated architecture.

Unity Temple and Non-Western Religious Architectures

For Emerson, the idea of unity was apparent not only in phenomena of nature, but also in human experience over time. In his essay of 1841 on "History," Emerson wrote that study of the past enabled modern man to reexperience the thought and feeling of earlier peoples. Emerson acknowledged that there were historical differences in social and technical conditions, yet he believed that later minds could empathize with those of the past. This view underlay his appreciation of earlier styles of northern European architecture, and of the most ancient monuments, like Stonehenge.[35] It was in this spirit that Johonnot and Gannett asserted that Unity Temple, while addressing the symbolic concerns of a modern liberal religion, was also a building that had the aura of an ancient temple. Its architecture was thus to convey the unity of human religious experience across time, as well as across cultures.

Since the early nineteenth century, American Unitarian thinkers had honored and investigated non-Western religions, and compared them with Christianity. Among such comparative studies was that of Charles Goodrich, whose book, *Religious Ceremonies and Customs, or The Forms of Worship Practiced by the Several Nations of the Known World,* was published in Hartford in 1834. In his library, Wright kept his father's copy of this book, while his mother owned a copy of William James's *The Varieties of Religious Experience* (1902).[36] Works such as Clarke's *Ten Great Religions* (1871, 1883) and Jenkin Lloyd Jones's *Religions of the World* (1893)[37] helped create the intellectual background for the World's Parliament of Religions. This event's focus on comparative appreciation of human religions was documented in the record of its proceedings, including transcripts of statements by religious leaders from both East and West, and photographs of temples and church buildings in Siam, India, Japan, Burma, Jerusalem, England, Italy, China, Norway, Turkey, Spain, Greece, Russia, Scotland, Germany, Ceylon, France, Armenia, Nepal, Tibet, and the United States. The editor and parliament's chairman, Rev. John Henry Barrows, wrote that "religion is the great fact of History. . . . These volumes are enriched with views of Eastern Temples, painted and tiled Pagodas, superb and stately Mosques, humble meeting-houses, and all the beautiful forms of Christian architecture in Europe and America. How these efforts of Man to embody his thoughts of God and of worship give a celestial gleam and glory to his struggling and sorrowing life!"[38] Such a statement echoed earlier studies of non-Western architecture by Victorian scholars like James Fergusson in his accounts of India. Fergusson's writings were referred to by James Freeman Clarke, who wrote of regional styles of Buddhist shrines as they developed in India and Japan: "As soon as the religion was well established, its peculiar architecture sprang up. Every great religion had produced its own special type of architecture."[39]

Unitarian thinkers were often drawn to the study of Eastern religions, whose temples evinced great traditions of belief.[40] Among the architectures associated with Eastern religions, Wright repeatedly praised the Shinto tradition of belief and art in Japan. Those qualities of simplicity, honesty, and purity that Wright identified as instructive virtues of Japanese building were consistent with many other contemporaneous American assessments of that country's architecture.[41] Yet, unlike that of many Western artists, Wright's appreciation of Japan developed in the context of liberal religious attitudes toward that country. From 1890 Japan had been the focus of missionary efforts by both American Unitarians and Universalists, as well as by representatives of other Christian churches.[42] In 1890 Rev. Augusta Chapin, the predecessor of Rev. Johonnot and a friend of Wright's mother, advocated support of Universalist efforts in Japan in her sermons at Unity Church.[43]

The Japanese buildings at the Columbian Exposition of 1893 are often cited as an important source for Wright's early understanding of traditional Japanese architecture.[44] Yet the Japanese delegates to the World's Parliament of Religions also made a strong impression on Jenkin Lloyd Jones, who described the Shinto Bishop Shibata's address to the parliament. Shibata spoke of his thirst for that "fraternity that would put an end to war, that fearlessness in investigating the truth of the universe that would be instrumental in uniting all religions of the world, bringing hostile nations into peaceful relations by way of perfect justice."[45] Jones wrote that "the representatives of the Orient . . . came as prophets and not as priests. They came to proclaim the universals, the things we hold in common."[46]

A comparable view of the imminent fusion of Eastern and Western civilizations informed the writings of Ernest Fenollosa (1853–1908), the scholar of Japanese prints whom Wright cited as his mentor in appreciating these works of art.[47] A first cousin of Joseph Silsbee as Wright's first employer in Chicago, Fenollosa had studied philosophy at Harvard, graduating in 1874, and briefly continued studies of religion and philosophy at Harvard Divinity School. Fenollosa's (as well as Johonnot's) mentor there was Charles C. Everett, whose annual course of lectures on philosophy, psychology, and history of religious thought was known for both serious attention to and wide knowledge of non-Christian religions.

After studying art, Fenollosa was appointed in 1878 as the first professor of Western philosophy at the University of Tokyo. He soon began a close study of Japanese art, and devoted the rest of his life in Japan and the United States to the preservation of Japanese artistic traditions. He was in Chicago repeatedly from the mid-1880s and became a friend of Frederick Gookin, the city's chief collector of Japanese prints, who also worked with Wright.

Fenollosa's student, Kakuzo Okakura, organized the Japanese government's exhibit at the World's Columbian Exposition. A prolific lecturer, Fenollosa gave a course of lectures at the University of Chicago in 1903 on the development of Eastern cultures.[48]

For Fenollosa, the most momentous historical process of his time was the convergence of European and American with East Asian civilization. A devotee of Hegel, Fenollosa saw the possibility of a global cultural future that would meld the most valuable traditions of both East and West. He wrote of his vision in an essay of 1898 entitled "The Coming Fusion of East and West," published just after the Spanish-American War. Fenollosa asserted that, for Americans, contact with Japan was "primarily a test of *ourselves,* whether we are capable of expanding local Western sympathy and culture to the area of humanity."[49] Fenollosa also believed that the Japanese faced a reciprocal test. In this moment, he hoped that the West would exhibit "a sympathy that shall thrill to amalgamate with everything human, aspiring, and constructive in that wonderful Eastern world."[50]

Fenollosa's vision focused most intensively on the art of Japan as one proof of that country's spiritual resources. His views on art paralleled Unitarian appreciation for the architecture of traditional Japanese Buddhist temples. In 1899 *Unity* published an account of old Japanese shrines, entitled "Thoughts in a Buddhist Temple," which concluded: "In Japan it would be an easy matter to become a Buddhist. Their temples are as full of the religious spirit as an English Cathedral. The Japanese have a genius for creating a religious atmosphere. They select the calmest possible natural scenery for their shrines of which there are 170,000 in the Kingdom." This observer praised "the great Honwagii temple in Kyoto, Japan, erected within in the last dozen years at a cost of $10,000,000. . . . The shrines of rural Japan are exceedingly beautiful, invariably surrounded with trees and in the loveliest possible scenery. Now upon a level mountain top commanding a view of rising and setting suns and a lovely sea and cape. These country temples are always beautifully clean and perfumed with incense."[51] The writer, an American minister, concluded: "I do not say these words because I am about to become a Buddhist, but simply because actual and visual examination convinces me that we have undervalued the merits of a very great religion."[52] Such Japanese Buddhist monuments as the Rokkakudo Temple in Kyoto were depicted in the record of the World's Parliament of Religions (Fig. 133).

These liberal religious accounts formed the distinctive background for Wright's admiration for Japanese architecture, which Wright saw on his first trip abroad to Japan from February to May 1905.[53] It had been on this journey, in April, that Wright first saw the Taiyu-in mausoleum at Nikko whose plan informed Unity Temple's, his chief project after returning to Oak Park. In 1904 Rev. Johonnot asserted that the new building for Unity Church should represent its congregation's liberal ideals in its community. Given the liberal thinking that Unity Temple was to convey, Wright's plan

FIGURE 133

Buddhist Rok-
kakudo Temple,
Kyoto. Reprinted
from Barrows,
*World's Parlia-
ment of Religions.*

for the building was an intentional symbolic contrast to the traditional ecclesiastical plans of the neighboring Congregational, Episcopalian, Presbyterian, and other church buildings on Lake Street.

Wright and his wife sought to educate their neighbors about the Japanese tradition. In February 1906 Wright gave a talk on "The Art of Japan" to the River Forest Women's Club. In March, the same month in which his studio was preparing working drawings for Unity Temple, Wright mounted an exhibition of his Hiroshige prints at The Art Institute of Chicago, for which he wrote the catalogue.[54] Also in March Wright and his wife hosted a Japanese social as the inaugural event of the Unity Club of Unity Church, the group that financed publication of the booklet on Unity Temple that appeared three months later. On that evening in March, Wright used lantern slides to illustrate "a very interesting trip through Japan."[55] In April, Wright's wife Catherine, accompanied by a model of a traditional Japanese house, gave a lecture to Oak Park's Nineteenth Century Club on the architectures of China, India, and especially Japan as the country that had "at last touched hands with America and thus completed the circle of the world."[56]

Among many photographs of buildings and landscapes that Wright took in Japan, there survive several views of religious complexes. Among these were photographs of the Great Hall or large Founder's Hall consecrated to the memory of the founder of the Shin sect, as part of the temple complex of Higashi Hongan-ji Betsuin in Nagoya (Fig. 134). As a center of pilgrimage for a popular Buddhist sect, the Hongan-ji complex at Nagoya had two main buildings, the Founder's Hall and the temple, set side by side and connected by an open, roofed corridor. Unity Temple's plan would be comparable. At Nagoya the temple proper was devoted to worship of Buddha, while the other larger though simpler building was devoted to the sect's founder, Shinran-shonin.[57] Wright's own frontal view of this Founder's Hall captured the building's monumental presence and flared roofs beyond its open forecourt, where worshipers had turned toward Wright and his camera. Wright took this photograph less than a year before his studio created the rendering of Unity Temple's north front on Lake Street, a view later redrawn for the Wasmuth folio (Fig. 135). This drawing presented a similar frontal view of Unity Temple across an open space. The drawing's viewpoint emphasizes the building's cantilevered roofs on each side, as if to evoke the silhouette of a Japanese temple.

* * *

Religious liberals believed that styles of building for worship the world over testified to humankind's religious aspirations. In February 1906, when the

drawings of Unity Temple were first published, Rev. Johonnot wrote of the design: "While departing widely from traditional forms of a church architecture, the building is distinctly reverential in feeling and spirit. . . . It impresses the beholder with a sense of dignity and permanence befitting a house of worship and it has a chaste, simple spirit of beauty uplifting to the emotions." He concluded that Wright's project "thus becomes associated with that spirit of worship which has caused men in all ages to rear temples unto God."[58] Such ideals were voiced again at Unity Temple's dedication in September 1909. Then Rev. William C. Gannett, the longtime colleague of Jenkin Lloyd Jones and a friend of Frank Lloyd Wright, authored the responsive reading between pastor and people that served as the Act of Dedication at the service. At one point in this ceremony, the minister, Rev. Johonnot, was to say: "In all times and places the children of God have acknowledged their dependence upon him, and have sought communion with him by ways of the holy life and the religious spirit. To this end they have builded houses of worship and have consecrated altars of prayer. In sympathy with these universal aspirations we have reared this house."[59]

FIGURE 135

Wright, Unity Temple, drawing of north front on Lake Street. From *Ausgeführte Bauten und Entwürfe,* Plate LXIV(b) (Frank Lloyd Wright Archives, Drawing No. 0611.005, © The Frank Lloyd Wright Foundation).

The elemental and universal idea of the temple embodied in Wright's building signified the liberal goal of religious unification of humanity, as pursued in several international meetings from 1893 to 1907.[60] In Oak Park, Johonnot spoke of this ongoing program in his sermon entitled "The Movement toward a Universal Religion," which he delivered on 13 October 1907 in Wright's newly built Unity House, four weeks after it opened.[61] In this sermon, published in Jones's *Unity,* Rev. Johonnot maintained that "there is a movement going on in the Christian world and also in other religions toward the development of a universal type of religion true for all times and peoples, based, on the one hand, upon the moral and religious nature of man and, on the other, upon his longings after union with the infinite."[62] In his view, "modern culture, founded upon scientific methods, is reaching a unity of religious thought which is tending to the establishment of a universal religion, casting off that which is merely traditional, racial or national in its characteristics, and emphasizing that which is universally human."[63] From this perspective, Johonnot defended Wright's architecture as signifying a simplicity of doctrine whose universality was both historically derived and modernistically prophetic.

Unity Temple and Temples of Antiquity

Unity Temple was to convey not only the universality of religious ideals but also the supposed antiquity of liberal Unitarian and Universalist views. These denominations had emerged in the later eighteenth century. Yet in 1903–4, before Unity Temple's design, Johonnot wrote of Unitarianism as "an ancient faith, much older than Christianity," while he had described Universalism as "one of the most ancient phases of Christianity."[64] Later Johonnot asserted that Wright's building was appropriately named because it "has the feeling and to some extent the form of an ancient temple."[65] Avoiding conventional use of the Gothic style of the Middle Ages, in Unity Temple Wright had achieved the character of a house of worship "by a frank return to the simpler and more ancient forms of religious architecture."[66] Wright's building was an original form that apparently did not recall any one style of ancient temple. Instead, Unity Temple condensed allusions to varied types of temples. Wright probably brought to the project a multifaceted view of human antiquity that included knowledge of very different traditions of ancient religious architecture. This breadth of view was implicit in the choice of the term "temple," which simultaneously conveyed biblical, primitive, and classical associations. The high walls as an enclosing shell around the exterior of the church may allude to biblical concepts of the temple. On Lake Street these walls rise 22 ft. from the ground (Fig. 99). Their mass, and the indirect means of entry, create an elevated and removed impression of the auditorium. One has a glimpse through the clerestories, but the room's architecture and the nature of its ritual are only known once inside. From outside, the high walls screen this space with a veil of authority and mystery.

In his *Ten Great Religions,* Johonnot's mentor, James Freeman Clarke, described the ancient Hebrew temple as a type whose form stressed the interior sanctity of worship set within the walls of the temple precinct.[67] In Unity Temple there are suggestions of the biblical prototype of Solomon's temple. One enters on a lower story and climbs to higher ones; the auditorium is an inner sanctuary apart from the building's environs; and the room's ceiling is an array of visible beams. Also, the foliate ornament initially designed on the exterior columns recalls that described on the exterior of Solomon's temple. The booklet of 1906 on Unity Temple closed with a Solomonic reference, claiming: "This building conveys the sense of dignity and permanence befitting a house of religion. It has the feeling of reverence and seems to say 'The Lord is in his holy temple; let all the earth keep silence before him.' It is informed by that spirit of beauty which led the Psalmist to say, 'Worship the Lord in the beauty of holiness.'"[68] The first of these biblical verses was also found in James Freeman Clarke's introductory sentences for morning worship at the Church of the Disciples in Boston.[69]

Below Johonnot's text is a plan that shows both the temple's upper galleries and the ceiling above them (Fig. 136). He described the temple as "a house of worship with cruciform plan," whose sides "form the arms of a Greek cross."[70] This plan exhibits such a symmetry, as if to signify the perfection of divinity. Such an ideal underlay theories of centrally planned churches in the Renaissance from the fifteenth century, to whose plans Unity Temple's has been compared. In Johonnot's booklet, the juxtaposition of holy words with symbolic form suggested that Unity Temple's shape was not only functionally derived, but also intended to be architecturally iconographic.

*   *   *

If Solomon's temple signified biblical antiquity, then the ruined Mayan cities of the Yucatán represented ancient religious life in the Americas. Mayan antiquities were a centerpiece of the ethnological exhibits devoted to non-European peoples at the World's Columbian Exposition in Chicago of 1893. There were assembled full-size plaster casts of parts of Mayan monuments, including the portal of the central structure within the ruins at Labna, and three sections of the Nunnery at Uxmal, including its central portal (Fig. 137). As freestanding architectural replicas exhibited outside the Anthropological Building, these ornate casts were "a great achievement in archaeology as nothing of the kind had been done before on anything like so grand a scale."[71]

The Mayan exhibit was curated by William Henry Holmes (1846–1933), who became Curator of Anthropology at the Field Columbian Muse-

FIGURE 136

Wright, Unity
Temple, ceiling
plan combined
with floor plan of
auditorium at lev-
el of upper galler-
ies. Reprinted
from Johonnot,
*New Edifice of
Unity Church.*
Courtesy of Uni-
tarian Universalist
Church in Oak
Park and Beacon
Unitarian Church.

um where the casts were placed following the exposition.[72] Once a topo-
graphical artist and engraver, Holmes had first traveled through Mexico in
1884, and again to the Yucatán in 1894–95, where he made detailed
studies of Mayan architecture, sculpture, and ceramic art. In 1895–97 the
museum published Holmes's *Archaeological Studies among the Ancient
Cities of Mexico,* for which he made the plans and drawings, including
panoramic views of such major ruined Mayan sites in the Yucatán as
Chichén-Itzá (Fig. 138). As a topographic image, this detailed drawing recalls Holmes's portrayals of geologic landscapes, such as his panoramic
views of the Grand Canyon for the U.S. Geological Survey.[73]

Writing on Mayan architecture, Holmes stressed the link between its
limestone forms and its regional geology. His accounts included photographs of partly ruined temples and religious complexes, such as the structures around the court then called the Nunnery at Chichén-Itzá, dating from
A.D. 1100 (Fig. 139). Their thick cubic walls were made from massive
limestone blocks, precisely fitted, with intricately carved ornament, also of
cut stone. All staircases lay outside the buildings. Yet Holmes stressed the

These qualities are present in this edifice in a marked degree. Without tower or spire it expresses the spirit of the ideal. By its form it expresses the thought, inherent in the liberal faith, that
God should not be sought in the sky, but on earth among the children of men. His word is not in the
heavens that we should say "who shall go up for us to heaven and bring it unto us that we may hear it
and do it," but his word is very nigh unto us in our hearts. This building conveys the sense of dignity
and permanence befitting a house of religion. It has the feeling of reverence and seems to say "The
Lord is in his holy temple: let all the earth keep silence before him." It is informed by that spirit
of beauty which led the Psalmist to say, "Worship the Lord in the beauty of holiness."

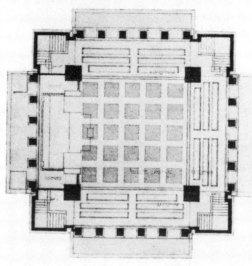

PLAN OF GALLERY

aesthetic and symbolic, rather than the tectonic, complexity of Mayan architecture. Its varied geometric forms were thought to have a cosmic and religious meaning. Hence Holmes concluded of the Mayans that "their status may be compared with that of the Greeks and Egyptians immediately preceding the dawn of history."[74]

Although recognized as a source for Wright's aesthetic after 1910, Mayan-inspired motifs first appeared in capitals of his screen fronting the fireplace of his Winslow house in River Forest built in the summer of 1894,[75] shortly after Holmes's exhibit of Mayan casts at the Columbian Exposition. Of his early interest in pre-Columbian architecture, Wright wrote toward the end of his life:

> I remember how as a boy, primitive American architecture – Toltec, Aztec, Mayan, Inca – stirred my wonder, excited my wishful admiration. I wished I might someday have money enough to go to Mexico, Guatemala and Peru to join in excavating those long slumbering remains of lost cultures; mighty, primitive abstractions of man's nature. . . . Those great American abstractions were all earth-architectures: gigantic masses of masonry raised up on great stone-paved terrain, all planned as one mountain, one vast plateau lying there or made into the great mountain ranges themselves; those vast areas of paved earth walled in by stone construction. These were human creations, cosmic as sun, moon, and stars! Nature? Yes, but the nature of the human being as he was, then.[76]

Wright's emphasis on the geologic setting and earthen character of pre-Columbian monuments recalls Holmes's views. Yet Wright sought an architecture of his own time and place. Thus, in a letter attributable to him late in

FIGURE **137**

Plaster casts of
Mayan ruins from
Uxmal, as exhib-
ited outside
Anthropology
Building, World's
Columbian Expo-
sition, Chicago,
1893. Reprinted
from Hubert H.
Bancroft, *The
Book of the Fair*
(Chicago, 1895).

his life, he restated his admiration for pre-Columbian architecture. Yet Wright asked, "of all ancient buildings, wherever they may stand or whatever their time, is there one of them suitable to stand here and now in the midst of our time, our America, our machine-age technique? Not one."[77]

Wright expressed a tension between his architecture's kinship with and distance from those of the past, much as Emerson had maintained that each mind is both at one with those of the past, yet also distinctly of its own place and period. Such a duality would logically have informed the design of Unity Temple as both like an ancient temple and yet a project for modern liberal religion built with a then technically novel material. Seen from their west side Unity Temple and Unity House (see Figs. 1 and 100) exhibit cubic forms, monolithic construction, thick squared moldings, and relation of masses that recall ruins of Mayan sites like the Nunnery at Chichén-Itzá, as shown in Holmes's study. The geometric ornament characteristic of Mayan architecture had its analog in ornamental motifs on Unity Temple's outer columns. While Wright may have derived the basic binuclear plan of Unity Temple and Unity House from the mausolea at Nikko in Japan, he also admired Mayan capacity for geometric abstraction. Thus his choice of purely rectilinear masses for his church in Oak Park is closer in form to Mayan monuments. However, as Wright's modern period differed immeasurably from Mayan society, a more explicit imitation of its forms would have been inappropriate. Thus Unity Temple exhibited a resonance with primitive types, yet transcended such models to signify its cultural present. Its design can be read not so much as a reference to one earlier tradition of temple building, but as an original synthesis, intended to be a contemporary statement that condensed formal and symbolic ideas from multiple pasts.

* * *

FIGURE 138

William Henry Holmes, panoramic drawing of Chichén-Itzá. Reprinted from Holmes, *Archaeological Studies among the Ancient Cities of Mexico* (Chicago, 1899).

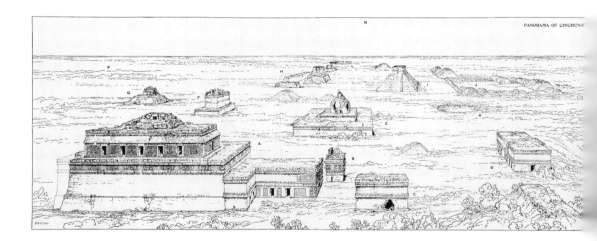

While the exhibit of Mayan ruins and works of Japanese architecture at the Columbian Exposition made these models locally accessible to Wright, the fair of 1893 was primarily a display of a new monumental classicism, which Wright also assimilated into his work before 1900.[78] Though he later contrasted Greek architecture with his own organic ideal, in his introduction to the Wasmuth folio in 1910, Wright cited the Greek, along with the Japanese and Gothic, as one of the aesthetically perfected styles of traditional architecture. In conventional accounts of the early development of Western architecture, Greek antiquity was seen as one starting point for the classical tradition. Yet Wright identified Greek architecture with older styles associated with a primitive ideal, such as the Egyptian, Mayan, and Japanese.[79] Thus, for him, a monument like the Parthenon was much closer in character to other ancient traditions than it was to later Western classicism such as the Renaissance.

In the Wasmuth folio Wright implied that in his work to 1910 he sought to realize anew that quality of style that he admired in Greek and other primitive models. This view of Greek antiquities as primitive art was consistent with the presentation of Greek sculpture at the Columbian Exposition. There copies of ancient Greek statuary were exhibited not in the Palace of Fine Arts, which featured mainly modern painting and sculpture, but in the

FIGURE 139

The "Nunnery,"
Chichén-Itzá, ca.
A.D. 1100. Reprinted from
Holmes, *Archaeological Studies
among the Ancient Cities of
Mexico* (Chicago,
1899).

Anthropology Building, where reproductions of statues like the *Winged Victory of Samothrace* were set at the center of a main aisle, surrounded with primitive fine and applied arts from around the world.[80] Wright posed miniature replicas of this statue in photographs of the interiors of his houses and public architecture before 1910, as in one view of Unity House (see Fig. 4). As he had written in 1900: "All the classics which are living in our hearts today are truly 'Sculpture' – the Venus, the Winged Victory, and a long list."[81] Among these, the *Winged Victory* had been a modern discovery, first reassembled in Paris in 1867, the year of Wright's birth.[82] Thus its inclusion in views of his early works was perhaps a statement of his identification with aesthetic ideals of Greek art.

Greek architecture held a special place in the thought of Jenkin Lloyd Jones. Of all the buildings at the Columbian Exposition, Jones had taken great interest in the Palace of Fine Arts, designed by Charles Atwood of D. H. Burnham and Company and considered the most successful academically neoclassical monument at the fair. Wright must have been drawn to the same edifice, because, as is well known, he based his design of 1893 for the Milwaukee Public Library and Museum on Atwood's front.[83] In 1897 Jones praised the full-scale replica of the Parthenon built as the Fine Arts Building for the Tennessee Centennial Exposition at Nashville.[84] Jones then cited the Parthenon as a model of aesthetic purity and perfection, writing that "in old Greek life it stood at the highest point of greatness, for its building was significant of the fullest attainment in art, in literature, in politics, in philosophy, that antiquity ever knew."[85] For Wright's uncle, classic Greece was "the matchless attraction of the antique world. It justifies more superlatives than any other spot on the globe."[86]

Ancient Greek intellectual ideals held a high place in American Unitarian thought. Jones identified the Athenian Parthenon with Greek rationality as an ideal personified by Socrates, whom Jones called "the prophet of reason,"[87] associating Socrates with Unitarian emphasis on the primacy of reason. Thus, at the Columbian Exposition of 1893 the pavilion of Jones's Western Unitarian Conference, as one of the exhibits of religious groups inside the Manufactures and Liberal Arts Building, was a small replica of a Greek Ionic temple. This housed a display of Unitarian literature amid busts of Emerson, William Ellery Channing, Theodore Parker, and other worthies in the liberal pantheon.[88]

In 1908 Wright described his motif of a stepped base in buildings like Unity Temple (see Fig. 99): "This preparation, or watertable, is to these buildings what the stylobate was to the ancient Greek temple."[89] As the basic rectangle of an ancient Greek temple's ground plan, the stylobate's ratio of length to width was a keynote for geometric proportions throughout the building. Unity Temple's foundational stylobate is an articulated square, the geometric shape that recurs in the building above. The square contrasts with the rectangle of Unity House, whose overall area was described initially as 90 ft. long by 40 ft. wide, slightly different from Unity House's area

as built (see Fig. 82). This initially proposed proportion of length to width in
plan of 9:4 is the ratio of length to width in the stylobate of the Parthenon.

215

Religious and
Architectural
Interpretations
of Unity Temple

Unity Temple's motif of six freestanding exterior columns upholding a
roof slab on each side suggests the prototypical trabeated rhythm of ancient
Greek hexastyle temples. In his *Ten Great Religions,* Clarke had contrasted
the ancient Greek temple's emphasis on exterior ornament as the backdrop
for festive ritual and visual display, with the ancient Hebrew temple's emphasis on an interior sanctity.[90] Unity Temple calls to mind both these
canonical ancient types of pillared Hellenic edifice and walled Hebrew
sanctuary, as if it were to evoke multiple cultural memories simultaneously.

The Dutch architect Berlage wrote: "Although Wright's talent developed in building houses, the opportunity was given him to reveal his extraordinary art in the building of a church (Unity Church near Chicago). . . .
For in that church – a rectangular building – something of the classical
temple is revived."[91] In 1906 Wright's assistant, Charles White, who was a
member of Unity Church, wrote of its new edifice:

> My personal feeling is that for a liberal church we at last have a design that
> is beautiful and consistent. The Unitarian idea calls for an institution rather
> than a church, and this leaves Wright free to follow out his natural inclina-
> tions. It seems to me that his design marks an epoch in the architecture of
> the entire country. It has all the chaste beauty of a Greek temple, and much
> of the sublimity of your favorite Taj Mahal. As a designer of an Orthodox
> church, he would, I am convinced, be a failure; indeed, I do not think he
> would take a commission for such, but as a designer of a liberal church, he
> is simply great. How I wish you could see the plaster model which has
> been made. The scale is tremendous, and the proportions ideal. . . . This
> building, I prophesy, will be admired for generations to come, as a beauti-
> ful and fitting memorial to the service of God, and the betterment of
> mankind. It will probably be adversely criticized from one end of the land
> to the other, but I think it will be one of the things that will live on. It has a
> virile quality that cannot die.[92]

The project of reviving the spirit of an ancient temple perhaps had
considerable significance for Wright, given his strong response to Victor
Hugo's well-known chapter "Ceci Tuera Cela," or "This Will Kill That,"
meaning the printed book will kill the building, from Hugo's novel *Nôtre-
Dame de Paris*.[93] In this text Hugo described how architecture's preemi-
nence as the chief medium of human expression in ancient and medieval
societies had since been superseded by printed books since invention of the
printing press in the fifteenth century. Hugo focused his analysis on the
temple as it developed in varied civilizations. Examples of this architectural
type had been the great symbols of religious thought before the age of the
Renaissance. Hugo believed "that architecture had been up to the fifteenth
century the principal register of humanity." To the time of Gutenberg, "humankind has had no idea of importance that it did not inscribe in stone."[94]

In his autobiography, Wright recalled that he borrowed Hugo's *Nôtre-*

Dame de Paris from the library of his uncle's All Souls Church in Chicago shortly after his arrival there to begin his career in architecture.[95] In 1886–87 Jones was leading an evening class at his church on Hugo, in whose events Wright had participated.[96] In his uncle's building Wright had first seen an attempt to revive the significance of architecture in the service of new ideals. In Wright's address of 1901 on "The Art and Craft of the Machine," he included parts of Hugo's argument from "Ceci Tuera Cela." Later Wright, paraphrasing Hugo, maintained that "for the first six thousand years of the world, from the pagodas of Hindustan to the Cathedral of Cologne, architecture was the great writing of mankind."[97] He recalled that "when sixteen years old, I used to read the great 'modern' of his day – Victor Hugo. Reading his discursive novel, *Notre-Dame,* I came upon the chapter, 'CECI TUERA CELA.' That story of the decline of architecture made a lasting impression upon me. . . . I saw the life-blood of beloved architecture slowly ebbing, inevitably to be taken entirely away from the building by the book." Wright lamented that "I saw that architecture, in its great antique form, was going to die. Ghastly tragedy – I could hardly bear the thought of the consequences."[98]

Hugo had maintained that, because of the pervasiveness of the printed word, "architecture will never again be the social art, the collective art, the dominant art."[99] Yet Wright's lifework was an individual attempt to restore architecture's central symbolic function and cultural primacy. In Unity Temple Wright may have sought to further his program for the renewal of his art by creating a design that called to mind the idea of the temple as the general type in architecture that had conveyed religious sentiment the world over. In this aim Wright's desire to revive architecture's importance in modern times thus coincided in the design of this church building with the distinctive religious ideals of Johonnot. In the process of conceiving and realizing this major work, both architect and minister were carrying forward a program of Jenkin Lloyd Jones, who had pioneered a new relationship between liberal religion and its expression in built form.

In seeking to create in Unity Temple a building that characterized a particular system of religious thought, Wright realized a concept that Hugo presented in "Ceci Tuera Cela." There Hugo, in the tradition of French architectural theorists like Quatremère de Quincy, wrote of the temples of antiquity as books in whose stone form ideas were inscribed. He compared their assembly of stones to the act of writing, describing columns as letters, arches as syllables, and pyramids as words. For Hugo religious thought had not only inspired temples, but conditioned their form as well: "The Temple of Solomon, for example, was not merely the outer binding of the sacred book, it was the sacred book itself. . . . Thus the Word was concealed within the edifice, but the Word's image was imprinted upon the building's outer envelope."[100] As noted earlier, the form of Unity Temple conveyed the leading idea of its religion, Unity, in its square and cubic geometry, in its monolithic construction, and in its three-dimensional integration of line and color inside its interiors. Thus, in this temple for liberal faith, where few literal images or figurative symbols stood, Wright inscribed religious meaning in the form of architecture itself, just as Hugo described the most meaningful temples of antiquity as registers of the thought of their makers and worshipers.

Principle in Wrightian Theory and Liberal Religion

In his accounts of Unity Temple and his other works of its time, Wright invoked a distinction between the principle of style formation and specific historical styles. In 1908 he argued that his works, while they did not imitate older particular styles, did aspire to a quality of style found in all great past architectures. Such a distinction between a general aesthetic ideal of style and particular past styles preoccupied theorists and historians of architecture in the late nineteenth century. Yet, in Wright's thought, it would have paralleled theological debates of the Western Unitarian Conference in the 1880s on the distinction between principle and belief in the history of human religions.

The leading voices in this debate had been Jenkin Lloyd Jones and William Channing Gannett. Like eastern Unitarians the western conference had examined the question of whether a creed or affirmation of specific religious beliefs should be required as a test of an individual's membership in any of its churches. Conservatives maintained that any such creed should contain clear reference to the Christian tradition, while liberals like Jones and Gannett felt that any such references were too limiting a characterization of Unitarian ideals. In defending this position, Gannett had equated the conservative view with the concept of belief, while he identified the liberal position with the broader idea of principle. In a sermon of 1883 entitled "What Is Unitarianism?" Gannett had stated that "the *principles,* intellectual, spiritual and moral, underlying the Unitarian movement are much more its soul, its very self, than *any* doctrines in which at any given moment these principles are formulated."[101] In Unitarian history, beliefs emerged in historically specific circumstances from constant principles that were unchanging and essential. Yet always, principle had meant methodology and attitude, while belief was seen as local manifestation of principle, to which it was ancillary.

Gannett attempted to characterize Unitarian belief in his time in a famous statement drafted for and approved by the Western Unitarian Conference meeting in Chicago in 1887, the first major event held in Silsbee's All Souls Church. This statement was entitled "Things Most Commonly Believed among Us."[102] As a statement to set Unitarian fellowship on as broad a theological foundation as possible, Gannett wrote that "All names that divide 'religion' are to us of little consequence compared with religion itself."[103] For Gannett, religion's essentials were conveyed in language similar to the inscription above Unity Temple's doors. He wrote: "Unitarianism is a religion of love to God and love to man."[104]

Jenkin Lloyd Jones emphasized a comparable distinction between principle and belief in his accounts of the World's Parliament of Religions. In his view, differences between the world's religions represented distinctions of belief in varied cultural situations. Yet all religions were based on the same principles of divine belief and humane service, on the principle of a divine or supreme being on the one hand and a devotion to the ethical life on the other. Wright's uncle maintained that "the message of all the great teachers of religion is essentially the same."[105] For Jones the task of the modern church was to proclaim these universals. In his first sermon in Unity Temple in 1908, Johonnot also affirmed one common source of all human religious beliefs, claiming that "out of this great fountain of faith in God as our Father, issue streams of many religious faiths and truths."[106] It was this western Unitarian viewpoint to which Johonnot alluded earlier when he first described Unity Temple. Because the church's form evoked a universal type of temple, Johonnot claimed: "It thus bears witness to the great truth of the unity of all religions."[107]

Johonnot's concept of Unity Temple as a symbol of the broadest principles of religion corresponded to Wright's view of Unity Temple as a demonstration of the principle of style in architecture. For both, the new church represented freedom from specifics of tradition, whether spiritual or aesthetic. In 1898 the Architectural League of America, which was then centered in Chicago, adopted the motto "Progress before Precedent."[108] The phrase conveyed the league's rejection of conventional historicism as a basis for design of modern buildings. It was to the league, at its second annual meeting in 1900, that Wright delivered his self-definitive address entitled "The Architect."

While Wright, too, sought to go beyond imitation of older styles, he advocated forms "based upon Principle instead of Precedent," as he later distanced his position from that of the league.[109] Wright identified the concept of principle with a quality of style found both in nature and in those past architectures that he admired, such as the Greek, Gothic, and Japanese. In 1908 he wrote: "From the beginning of my practice the question uppermost in my mind has been not 'what style' but 'what is style?' . . . If in the face of our present day conditions any given type may be treated independently and imbued with the quality of style, then a truly noble architecture is a definite possibility."[110] In a later autobiographical account of Unity Temple, Wright similarly presented the design as "the process of building on principle to insure character and achieve style."[111]

Wright's Response to Monroe's Criticism of Unity Temple

Wright's concern for his work's relation to tradition appeared in his reply to Harriet Monroe's critique of his work at the annual exhibition of the Chicago Architectural Club, held at The Art Institute in April 1907 (Fig. 140). Among objects displayed were a plaster model of Wright and Perkins's design of 1902 for the Abraham Lincoln Center, a plaster model of Unity Temple, and a miniature model of one of its columns, set next to a model of the Larkin Building. This was Wright's first exhibition of his works since 1902, and the first presentation of Unity Temple beyond Oak Park.

In her review, Monroe concluded that Wright "has cut loose from the schools and elaborated his own system of design. Like the art-nouveau enthusiasts abroad, he believes that the three Greek orders have done their utmost in the service of man, until in modern hands their true meaning is distorted and lost. Therefore he thinks it is time to discard them and all their renaissance derivatives, and begin afresh from the beginning. At least he believes such a rebirth to be the only course for him."[112] While Monroe commented favorably on Wright's residences, of his larger public works she concluded: "His limitations are obvious enough. We pass by the more ambitious buildings – the plaster models for Unity Church at Oak Park, for the Larkin Company administration building at Buffalo, and for a huge, square nameless structure, all of which look too much like fantastic block-houses, full of corners and angles and squat, square columns, massive and weighty, without grace or ease or monumental beauty. Manifestly his imagination halts here; it labors and does not yet achieve beautiful and expressive buildings for public worship and business."[113]

FIGURE **140**

View of Wright's exhibition with the Chicago Architectural Club, at The Art Institute of Chicago, April 1907 (Photograph courtesy of the Frank Lloyd Wright Archives. © The Frank Lloyd Wright Foundation).

Monroe's critique came at a difficult juncture for Wright, because at that time, only Unity House was near completion, and Unity Church's congregation was reaching a low point in its financial support for the project. He may have feared that such negative opinions of the design from a leading Chicago critic would reinforce congregational doubts and slow the work, possibly compromising the auditorium's form. Undoubtedly, he did not want to be perceived as an exclusively domestic architect, nor did he wish to lose possible future opportunities to design public or commercial buildings. Charles White wrote that Wright's practice had suffered from the timing of his trip to Japan, implying that Wright in 1906 was being partly sustained by fees from the Larkin commission, sequels to which he may have sought.[114]

Days after Monroe's article appeared, Wright wrote to her that her critique "has no power to harm the inherent virtue of good work but it does serve to hamper the man and confuse and hinder a practical issue that deserves all the help and strength that, grudgingly enough in any case, may come to it from a public in these matters diffident or indifferent."[115] He claimed that Monroe had inaccurately characterized his position. He asserted that the aim of his work was not a complete rejection of tradition, but rather an attempt to revive the spirit of classic periods and not to copy their outward forms. He wrote: "Need I say that it is the very spirit that gave life to the old forms that this work courts? That it is the true inspiration that made of the time honored precedent in its own time a living thing that it craves? Venerable traditional forms are held by this work still too sacred to be paraded as a meretricious mask for the indecencies and iniquities of the marketplace!"[116] He added that, someday, even educated critics like herself "will understand that the classic is no matter of the dead letter of former glory and will know that the old spirit which was so vital then is vital now and living in forms the newspapers pronounce eccentric."[117] Wright noted that European critics were then responding positively to similar experiments in geometrically simplified forms. He foresaw that "American Architecture is a possibility and will be a definite probability when conscientious efforts of this nature, wherever they may be found, receive the encouragement on their native heath that they already have received in conservative old England or in France where these square, squat experiments with boxes have been accorded the rare virtue of originality without eccentricity."[118]

Wright developed these ideas in his essay "In the Cause of Architecture," published in *Architectural Record* in March 1908 to coincide with another exhibition of his work at the Chicago Architectural Club that spring. The text's opening paragraph perhaps reflected Wright's desire to guard against perceptions of his work like those Monroe had voiced a year before. He thus began: "Radical though it be, the work here illustrated is dedicated to a cause conservative in the best sense of the word. At no point does it involve denial of the elemental law and order inherent in all great architecture; rather it is a declaration of love for the spirit of that law and order, and a reverential recognition of the elements that made its ancient letter in its time vital and beautiful."[119] When Unity Temple's auditorium opened seven months later, in October 1908, Wright expected that it would be perceived as distinct from any particular style of earlier religious architecture. Yet Unity Temple was nevertheless to be a building whose aesthetic qualities rendered it comparable to canonical works in his art's past.

Wright's Unity Temple and Olbrich's Secession Building

Wright's Unity Temple has been compared to Joseph Maria Olbrich's Secession Building in Vienna of 1898, a poster of whose façade was published in 1899 for an English readership in *The Studio,* where the building's interiors for exhibits were later illustrated. Wright's son Lloyd recalled that his father knew this periodical, which also published other work of Olbrich, in both Vienna and Darmstadt, in 1899 and 1901. Wright probably also knew the modernist program of Olbrich's mentor, the Viennese architect Otto Wagner, parts of whose major text, *Modern Architektur,* had been translated for the *Brickbuilder* in 1901, the year after Wright's own address on "The Architect" had appeared in the same periodical.[120] Wright saw the exhibit of works by Olbrich and native Germans at the Louisiana Purchase Exposition in St. Louis in the summer of 1904. One of the exhibiting German designers, architect Bruno Möhring, then visited Wright's studio in Oak Park. Another German architect apparently knew Wright's work from its publication in the *Chicago Architectural Club Annual* of 1902.[121]

In 1901–4 the German architectural publisher, Ernst Wasmuth, had issued a two-volume folio monograph on Olbrich's built works in Darmstadt. Wasmuth also published monographs on other individual German architects of the period before Wasmuth's folio on Wright of 1910. Yet Wright recalled that when he first went to Germany in 1909–10, Olbrich had been the only architect who had then interested him, because of Olbrich's work in Darmstadt.[122] Wright remembered being received in Germany as "the Olbrich of America."[123] Later, in his autobiography of 1932, Wright wrote that before this first visit to Europe, among its major cities, "Vienna had always appealed to my imagination."[124] Wright's awareness of the Viennese Secession and Olbrich's building before 1910 may be inferred from these facts and recollections. Wright recalled that he did not then know German, and thus would not have read of Olbrich's Viennese works in that city's professional journal, *Der Architekt.* This was the publication where Olbrich's preliminary scheme for the Secession Building was first presented in January 1898, and where the final design of the completed building was featured in January 1899.[125]

The Secession Building was different from Unity Temple in many important ways, yet their similarities are perhaps equally significant. Designed as an art gallery on the west edge of Vienna's Karlsplatz, Olbrich's structure was a major architectural statement of the Secessionists' aims to turn away from academic convention and historicism in the visual arts (Fig. 141). In its cultural ideology, Olbrich's work thus partially anticipated Wright's modernist agenda after 1900. Olbrich described how the Secession Building's design fulfilled the multiple requirements of an art gallery.[126] Both the logistics and ritual of art exhibition informed his plan for the main floor as a ceremonial hall (Fig. 142), whose cruciform shape resembles that of Wright's auditorium.

Although far removed from art and politics in Vienna, Wright conceived that Unity Temple might occasionally house cultural events. In the period after its opening, Wright's building served as a communal gallery for modern art. In the autumn of 1908 a Fine Arts Society was formed in Oak Park, with architect Charles White, then independent of Wright, as its president.[127] On 17 November, just over three weeks after the opening service held in Unity Temple's auditorium, the society held an inaugural exhibit in Unity House of the work of locally produced fine and applied art, accompanied by a lecture in the temple. Seven hundred people reportedly attended the lecture, the first civic gathering held in the auditorium, and a thousand came to the exhibit's opening. One account noted that "the temple, itself one of the most striking works of art on exhibition, made the ideal rendezvous for the occasion."[128] A larger reception was held almost one

FIGURE 141

Joseph M. Olbrich, Secession Building, Vienna, 1898. Photograph by Saskia, Ltd., Cultural Documentation.

year later on 2 October 1909, the Saturday evening after Unity Temple's dedication, when art on exhibit included not only local works but also reproductions of recent salon paintings from Paris and Munich.[129]

The Secession Building was to provide refuge or asylum for the contemplation of art; thus its gallery has windows for light only on its north wall. In Olbrich's interior, all the opaque walls meet the ceiling directly, unlike the glazed clerestories on all four sides of Unity Temple, which link the auditorium's interior with sky and trees outside. Olbrich set four major skylights above his galleries, to permit their subdivision for varied exhibits. Unity Temple and Unity House each have a central skylit roof above their coffered ceilings. Olbrich's interior has four minimal columns unlike the four architecturally prominent columns in Unity Temple's auditorium. Wright's fixed seating, balconies, and permanent elements convey his room's singularity of purpose, whereas Olbrich's interior permitted repeated rearrangement. Above its ceiling, Olbrich's hall has invisible roof trusses that span its exhibition spaces and support their skylights, not unlike Wright's roof trusses in Unity House or the beams above the ceiling in Unity Temple. The pitched crowns of Olbrich's skylights atop the building's roof are clearly visible from the outside, while the pitched skylights of Unity Temple's auditorium are screened from view by its crowning attic.[130] Olbrich's outer walls insulate the exhibition space raised up from the sidewalk outside, just as Unity Temple's outer walls insulate the elevated auditorium from noises of the street.

Olbrich's frontal portal contrasts with Wright's dual secluded side en-

FIGURE 142

Olbrich, Secession Building, floor plans of basement and main level. Reprinted from *Der Architekt* 5 (January 1899). Courtesy of Special Collections Department, Northwestern University Library.

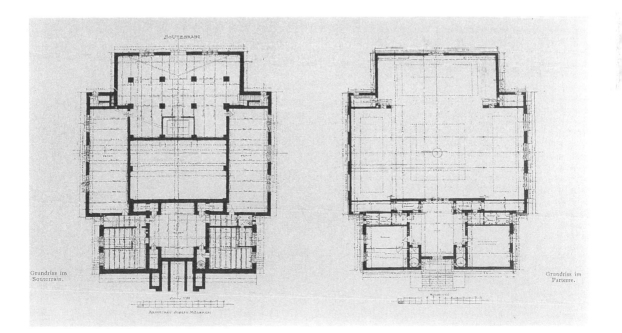

trances on terraces set well back from Lake Street. The Secession Building's doors are of cast bronze while Unity Temple's are of glass. Olbrich articulated his building's frontal corners, but did not detach them from the central mass. At the back he did reveal his cruciform plan in the building's inset rear corners (Fig. 143). In Unity Temple detached corner stair blocks reveal the auditorium's shape as a Greek cross. Olbrich and Wright thus developed a self-consciously modern architectural aesthetic through an emphasis on clear expression of volumetric space in exterior massing, and on a predominance of surfaces without ornament. In both works, the severe blocks and planar walls announce architecture's renewal through negation of historic details.

The stylistic comparability of Wright's work to that of early European modernists was one theme of Hendrik Berlage's lecture of 1912 in Zurich on American architecture. Berlage wrote of Wright as "an architect of very special importance" who "has nothing in his design-forms that reminds us of historical styles; his is an absolutely independent architecture."[131] Yet Berlage noted that "Wright leans on modern European architects more than Sullivan did, and like the modern Europeans, Wright struggles to simplify architectural masses and to treat ornament only as an aside; but his grouping of masses is so original that in the final analysis no European tendency is evident in his work."[132]

The originality of Wright's massing relative to early modern European works like Olbrich's Secession Building followed in part from Wright's exploration of innovative methods of construction. Olbrich's reliance on *Putzbau* or roughcast plaster applied over conventional brick bearing walls was unlike Wright's monolithic concrete masses for Unity Temple. As noted earlier, Wright's massing derived from the constructive efficiency of repeated usage of the wood formwork. His consequent repetition of forms on

all four sides of Unity Temple thus contrasts with Olbrich's distinct front, differentiated sides, and rear, whose varied walls are of brick. Individuated windows set in the wall planes of the Secession Building are unlike Unity Temple's continuous clerestories and slotlike windows between masses. The outer walls of both buildings rise monolithically from base to cornice, creating a quasi-Egyptian silhouette, and thus an aura of archaicism, as noted by contemporaries.[133] Unity Temple's moldings of cast concrete are simply squared, whereas Olbrich's moldings are less severe, with more varied profiles. Although the Secession Building's moldings create deep shadows atop its walls, these overhangs project less than Wright's massive cantilevered slabs.

Olbrich's ornament of tendrils and foliate relief near corners is lyrical and varied, while Wright's rectilinear motifs on Unity Temple's columns are severe and repetitive. They are not literal images of plants, but rather geometric conventionalizations of nature, realized in cast concrete. Olbrich's emblematic ornament conveys ideas and older myths related to his building's cultural purpose. For example, the bronze foliate dome signifies the Secession's ideal of artistic renewal as like the rebirth of spring. In Unity Temple, however, there are few individually symbolic forms. Instead, the whole building's form conveys the Unitarian ideal of Unity. Olbrich's dome of open metalwork contrasts in shape and material with the body of his building below, while Unity Temple's squared attic continues the form and material of the building's lower masses. Both buildings have dedicatory phrases over their doors rendered in two lines of thirty-six capital letters.

FIGURE **144**

Wright, Unity
Temple, view
along west front
with First Congre-
gational Church,
as rebuilt 1917–
18, at left in
background (Pho-
to: author).

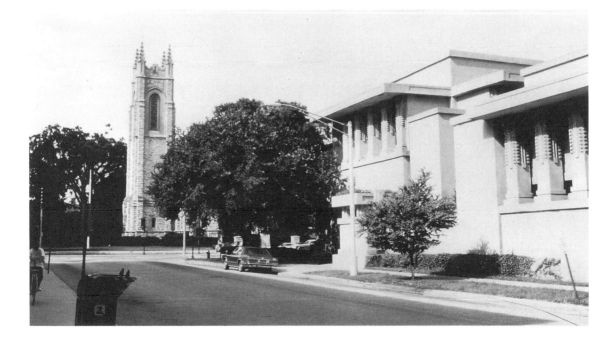

The Secession Building proclaims "DER ZEIT IHRE KUNST, DER KUNST IHRE FREIHEIT" ("To the Age Its Art, To Art Its Freedom"); Unity Temple, "FOR THE WORSHIP OF GOD AND THE SERVICE OF MAN."

Wright perhaps adapted the Secession Building's stance toward its context. Olbrich's monument and Unity Temple are oppositionally related to nearby traditional architectures. As seen in a photograph of 1900 (Fig. 143), the Secession Building's polemically charged design was set across from the baroque Karlskirche, the domed imperial church visible in the distance across Vienna's Karlsplatz. The horizontal cubic masses of Unity Temple were to contrast with nearby churches in neomedieval styles such as the towered First Congregational Church directly opposite across Lake Street, shown after its reconstruction following a fire in 1916 (Fig. 144). Unity Temple's simple monumental repose is intentionally different, making it a vivid symbol of denominational ideology. Looking at Unity Temple, one might not think that Unitarian and Universalist movements had emerged as recently as the eighteenth century, hence postdating the medieval Christianity to which nearby church buildings alluded. Instead, Wright's building appears to identify its congregation's liberal beliefs as antedating those of the other denominations housed around it. Thus both the Secession Building and Unity Temple were at once archaic in their reminiscence of ancient temples and avant-garde in their repudiation of conventional historicism.

Conclusion:
Unity Temple
and Later Modern
Architecture

UNITY Temple always held a pivotal position in Wright's view of his own achievement. He chose to place the building as the last work illustrated in drawings in the definitive publication of his architecture, the *Ausgeführte Bauten und Entwürfe* (1910) and as the first building illustrated in photographs in the companion publication of his *Ausgeführte Bauten* (1911), also published in Germany by Ernst Wasmuth. Since the period of Unity Temple's creation, much of what is known, or thought to be known, about this and other early works of Wright has been shaped by his own later writings. So successful was Wright in fixing the terms of discussion about his own architecture that the shifts in his accounts over time have often been left unexamined. His utterances, however, reveal levels of significance when they are studied in light of the architectural culture that they were meant to address at different times in Wright's career. His views of his work, and of Unity Temple in particular, changed in ways that have since shaped perceptions of Wright's position within the broader spectrum of modern architecture.

Unity Temple and the Prairie School

Unity Temple had immediate influence on architects who were Wright's contemporaries in both the United States and Europe. In some cases Wright's church exercised a stylistic influence. Yet, in other instances, Unity Temple may have provided a theoretical point of reference for the design of buildings whose forms were different from Wright's own. The design for Unity Temple and Unity House has been compared to William Drummond's First Congregational Church in nearby Austin, Illinois, built in 1908 (Figs. 145 and 146).[1] Drummond (1876–1948) was Wright's assistant from 1899 to 1909. He prepared the working drawings for the Larkin Building,

FIRST CONGREGATIONAL CHURCH, AUSTIN, ILLINOIS

AUDITORIUM OF FIRST CONGREGATIONAL CHURCH, AUSTIN, ILLINOIS

FIGURE 145

William E. Drummond, First Congregational Church, Austin (now Chicago), Ill., 1908. Reprinted from *Western Architect* 21 (February 1915).

and supervised construction of Unity Temple. Drummond had produced a design for the church in Austin by August 1905, when a building permit for it was issued. Yet the structure was not built until 1908, when Drummond was still working with Wright on completing Unity Temple.[2]

In plan and construction, Drummond's church is distinct from Unity Temple. Built for a Congregational rather than a Unitarian membership, Drummond's plan of two stories placed an entrance and narthex facing the street on the building's frontal north end. From this entry, one can pass ahead into the church's social room, descending several steps from the narthex. To reach the sanctuary one climbs stairs on either side of the narthex that lead to the rear of the nave on the upper level. Thus Drummond's frontal entrance leads to both major spaces superimposed on two levels, whereas Wright's recessed entrance leads to Unity Temple and Unity House as separate volumes.

Drummond's church, planned for no central aisle, had pews across its nave, side aisles, and flanking rows of pews in low-ceilinged spaces to either side of the nave. The open aisles lead to steps on either side of the frontal raised platform. Like Unity Temple, Drummond's platform has a central pulpit with no altar behind. On each side, steps lead up to a higher platform behind for a choir and organist. Also, like Unity Temple, a screen for the organ crowns the nave's south wall above its frontal platform. To the sides of the platform are a pastor's study and a choir room.

Unlike Unity Temple, Drummond's First Congregational Church in Austin was not built of reinforced concrete, but of exterior brick bearing walls and interior brick piers supporting a heavy timber frame. Its system of

FIGURE **146**

Drummond, First Congregational Church, ground and main floor plans. Historic American Buildings Survey, Survey No. ILL-1067.

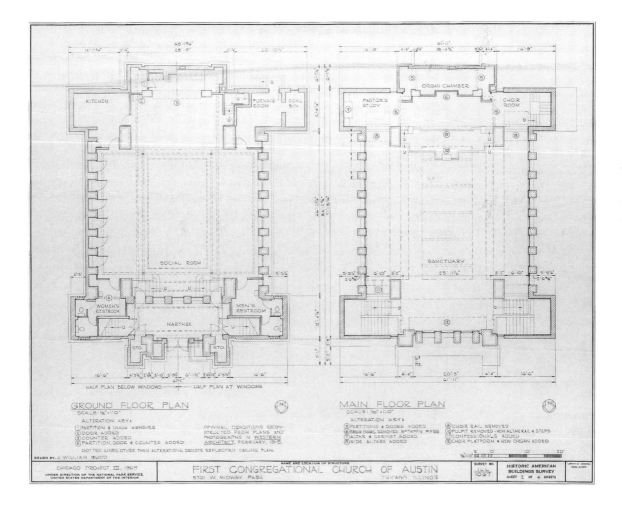

construction underlies its spatial character and method of lighting. On the nave's east and west walls, eight art glass windows are between the square brick piers. Unlike Unity Temple, there are no high clerestory windows, yet there is a skylight with panels of art glass over the length of the nave subdivided by cross-beams that span the nave's 26-ft. width. The rectangular bays of Drummond's skylight recall those of Unity House, unlike the square bays of Unity Temple's skylight.

Drummond supported the ceiling of his nave with deep timber trusses, encased within the nave's upper side walls, which span the 40-ft. length between front and rear brick piers. The result is a space unlike Unity Temple's auditorium, where Wright had set the major structural beams above the plane of the ceiling. The underside of Unity Temple's main ceiling is thus continuous with the ceiling plane above the surrounding galleries. This, together with the clerestory windows all around the room, gives Wright's auditorium its openness and continuity. By contrast, Drummond's interior appears massive. Its high nave is separate from the side aisles with lower ceilings. The unbroken sweep of the nave's upper side walls accentuates the longitudinal proportion of the nave. Its frontal orientation and seating only on the main floor similarly contrast with Unity Temple as a square auditorium with two levels of galleries on three sides. Details of Drummond's surfaces and lighting fixtures clearly followed Wright's stylistic model, yet the Austin sanctuary was a different kind of room for worship.

Externally, Drummond's frontal entranceway is set below the nave's north pillared wall. Urns atop piers flanking the entrance recall Wright's urns found in his houses of the period, but not in Unity Temple. Drummond's high attic may be compared with the crowning central attic of Unity Temple. On either side of Drummond's entrance, large unornamented blocks contain the stairways, not unlike Unity Temple's corners. However, the overall massing of Drummond's church has been effectively compared with that of the Larkin Building (see Fig. 41) with its longitudinal shape and lines of engaged piers along its flanks abutted by the massive corners. Drummond's exterior also borrowed the Larkin's material vocabulary of simple squared masses of brick trimmed with copings of stone atop the walls. Unlike Unity Temple, Drummond's church does not have cantilevered roof slabs, whose projections were key elements in Unity Temple's exterior form. The ornament cast in concrete on Wright's outer columns has no parallel in the unornamented brick piers and walls of Drummond's exterior. Thus, the Austin church, while clearly designed under the influence of Wright's works, shows Drummond's style in the service of a different institutional client.[3]

Unity Temple and Dutch Responses to Wright

From 1910 to 1925 Wright's work influenced architecture in the Netherlands, where Unity Temple was repeatedly at the center of discussion. The critical perspectives that Dutch modernists brought to Wright's architecture perhaps informed his own reassessment of his work from the 1920s. Different Dutch architects emphasized different qualities in Wright's work, depending on their particular ideas of modern architecture. Hendrik Berlage laid a foundation for his compatriots' views of Wright after his trip to the United States in 1911, when he visited Wright's works in Buffalo and Chicago, including Unity Temple. His trip followed Ernst Wasmuth's publication of Wright's *Ausgeführte Bauten* (1910), which featured Unity Temple as the initial project in a collection of photographs and plans of Wright's executed buildings. Berlage presented a lecture on "The New American Architecture" in March 1912 to the Zurich Association of Engineers and Architects, and, in the following year, he published a book, *Amerikaansche reisherinneringen* [American Travel Reminiscences].

In his lecture Berlage's thesis was that the work of Sullivan and Wright revealed "the real modern architecture of America – that architecture which is not fashioned in terms of historical style motifs."[4] Berlage saw Wright's work as an American counterpart of his own search for a Dutch architecture that was not historically derivative. He viewed both his own and Wright's work as part of an emergent international modern architecture of simple, judiciously arranged masses.[5] In 1912 he noted that in Unity Temple Wright had "built a church, actually a sort of meeting hall, which again reflects the great originality of his art. . . . The 'plasticity' of this building is imposing in the generosity of its scale, reminiscent of the scale of an Egyptian temple."[6] Noting Johonnot's booklet of 1906 on Unity Temple, Berlage stated: "I have heard that the elders of the church were extreme in their opposition to this building. I can understand this because the elders must have had . . . an entirely different image of a Protestant church."[7]

Berlage's admiration was the impetus for publication of Wright's early work in several Dutch architectural journals, in which articles referred to the book, *Ausgeführte Bauten.* Among Berlage's younger colleagues, the architect Robert van't Hoff had actually visited Wright in 1914 during a trip to the United States. Although Dutch by birth and early training, van't Hoff studied in London from 1911 to 1914. There he was drawn to the English Arts and Crafts Movement, whose leaders then included Charles Ashbee, who had known of Wright's work from his first visit to Chicago in 1900.[8] In 1913 van't Hoff's father sent him a German book devoted to Wright, the *Ausgeführte Bauten,* which included a German translation of a foreword by Ashbee, "Frank Lloyd Wright: Eine Studie zu seiner Wurdigung" [Frank Lloyd Wright: A Study in Appreciation]. In this essay, as in other writings on Wright, Ashbee underscored Wright's focus on the machine as the normal tool of modern civilization that architecture could employ as a resource for art.

This idea underlay Ashbee's other essay of 1910 wherein he compared English and American architecture. There Ashbee wrote that the discriminating use of machines was "essentially the question which the architect of the twentieth century has to study."[9] Ashbee had seen Unity Temple just after its completion in late 1908 on a second visit to the United States. He considered this church to be a fine example of discriminating use of machinery, stating that "this building seemed to me in every respect, sound and wholesome and truthful. . . . As it was of concrete there was no pretense to treat it as other than shaped from the mould, and as the architect had a fine sense of proportion, the result was one of the most interesting of the newer architectural creations in America."[10] For Ashbee, Unity Temple's leading virtue was that it exemplified the chief principle of the English Arts and Crafts Movement, "that truthfulness in structure is the first requisite."[11]

Ashbee's view informed that of van't Hoff, who traveled to the United States in June 1914 and visited Wright and his works in Chicago. Upon returning to Holland, van't Hoff was the architect for two villas, both of which echoed Wright's style. The second of these, the villa originally designed for A. B. Henny in Huis ter Heide, was built in reinforced concrete (Fig. 147). Created over four years, from 1916 to 1919, van't Hoff's Henny villa exhibited a repeated modular dimension in its window widths, like Unity Temple.[12] The Henny villa also featured concrete mullions between windows that recalled the columns on Wright's Unity Temple. Van't Hoff's design was almost square in plan. There is a balance of purely vertical and horizontal lines on its exterior, also like Unity Temple. Both buildings were also crowned by flat cantilevered roof slabs of reinforced concrete.

Robert van't Hoff's Henny villa was the first European building to reflect the influence of Unity Temple. Van't Hoff's analysis of Wright's building appeared in an article by van't Hoff for *De stijl* in 1919, just after the Henny villa was built. In van't Hoff's view, the modern task of architecture was to create a logical, comprehensible, and pure language of form based on technical perfection. In this light, he praised Unity Temple for its consistent use and expression of concrete. For van't Hoff, the church's logical design fulfilled Wright's ideal of architecture as the design of both a building's three-dimensional form and its nearby paths and steps.[13] Van't Hoff quoted Wright's own description of Unity Temple as "a concrete monolith, cast in wooden molds or forms. . . . The roofs are simple reinforced concrete slabs waterproofed."[14]

Van't Hoff's contributions to *De stijl* in 1918 and 1919 coincided with the influence of Wright's designs on Johannes Oud, another architectural participant in *De Stijl*. Although he had not visited the United States, Oud had known of Wright's work since 1910, when Oud began his friendship with Berlage. In his first contacts with Oud in 1917, van't Hoff brought numerous publications on Wright.[15] For Oud, as for van't Hoff, Wright's chief importance was not so much his removal from historical styles as his prophecy of a new aesthetic of the machine. This ideal informed Oud's article on Wright that appeared in the first volume of *De stijl* in 1918. As did other contributors to *De stijl*, Oud emphasized the radical renewal of art through the modern concept of a neoplastic aesthetic, meaning a continuity of form in three-dimensional space. For Oud, this idea superseded ornamental treatment of surfaces characteristic of the Amsterdam School in this period.

Oud devoted his article on Wright to an analysis of the Robie house of 1909, which Oud described as "a new departure from architectural design as we have previously known it. The embellishment of the building (which here in Holland is nearly always attempted by secondary means of detail – ornament) is here achieved by primary means: the effect of the masses themselves. Instead of a stable and rigid compactness of the various parts, Wright *detaches the masses from the whole* and rearranges their composition. . . . In this way Wright has created a new 'plastic' architecture. His masses slide back and forth and left and right; there are plastic effects in all directions. This movement, which one finds in his work, opens up entirely new aesthetic possibilities for architecture."[16]

Van't Hoff's and Oud's views of Wright's importance were similar to

FIGURE **147**

Robert van't Hoff, A. B. Henny villa, Huis ter Heide, Netherlands, 1916–18. Photograph by Frank den Oudsten.

those of architect Jan Wils, also a protégé of Berlage and a contributor to *De stijl*. Wils, who worked in Berlage's office from 1914 to 1916, responded to Wright's work in this period. One of Wils's drawings for a villa of 1916 adapted the graphic motifs of Wright's depiction of Unity Temple in the Wasmuth folio of 1910.[17] In 1916 Wils met Theo van Doesburg, the founder and leader of De Stijl, and Wils contributed to *De stijl* in 1918 and 1919. In these years Wils's work incorporated motifs from Wright's. Wils also lectured and he quoted ideas from Wright's essay of 1908, "In the Cause of Architecture," the same essay that had been cited by van't Hoff.[18]

In 1921 Wils wrote an essay on Wright's work, wherein he claimed that its true modernity lay in Wright's plans. Wils stated that "architecture is not an art of planes but of spaces."[19] For Wils, Wright's works excelled because of their composition of tectonic forms in three-dimensional space. After discussing Wright's principles and residential architecture, Wils concluded with a focus on two works, the Larkin Building and Unity Temple. Of the latter, he wrote:

> How great is the effect, how mighty is the repose of the horizontal parapet between the vertical planes of the stairtowers, how simple and obvious is the support of the slab roof, and how controlled is the detail and grouping of the masses. This is pure architecture; this is true building when each material and each element in the mass relates to the whole, and everything is carefully studied and composed. This construction is as clear as the human body, in which the function of each part is expressed. . . .
>
> As a monolith this monument to our time stands in Oak Park, a true milestone in the history of architecture.[20]

Wright's View of Unity Temple from 1925

Among Wright's early writings, the text most cited by the Dutch was his essay "In the Cause of Architecture" (1908). There Wright developed those canonical ideas explored in his writings from 1894, and it was to these that he would return throughout his life: nature as source of inspiration for architecture, unity of form and function, design in the nature of materials, artistic control of the modern machine, individuality of expression, freedom of imagination, harmony of the built environment with its natural surroundings, and aesthetic consistency of architecture. He maintained that only when an architect develops a project from first concept through its last details "will that unity be secured which is the soul of the individual work of art."[21] When Wright presented these ideas in the spring of 1908, he was about to determine Unity Temple's final form, and he cited the church as an embodiment of the principles he elaborated.

Although this text of 1908 contains a wealth of ideas, it did not engage the idea of architecture as space that was central to Wright's writings after 1925. Wright's buildings before 1910 do display a spatial artistry of a high order. Yet the idea of space is absent from his writings about his own work before 1925. Wright's exploration of the idea of space as an entity to be expressed in architecture coincided with his engagement with Dutch views of his work. This idea he developed in his essay "In the Cause of Architecture: The Third Dimension," which was published in the volume on his architecture edited by the Dutch architect Wijdeveld in 1925 as a compilation of articles on Wright that had appeared in the Amsterdam School's architectural periodical *Wendingen*. Introducing the volume, Wijdeveld said: "The new ornament is architecture itself, it is the shaping of spaces."[22] In his essay for *Wendingen,* Hendrik Berlage, who had long upheld the primacy of spatial form in architecture, wrote of Wright's work from 1910: "Admiration increases for the poet of this poem of space."[23] Such accounts, which continued the new line of critical response to Wright's work found in essays by Oud and Wils, now gave Wright an alternative frame of reference for reassessing his early works.

Wright was notably fond of the *Wendingen* volume, and his own essay in it contained his first reappraisal of Unity Temple since 1910. As a general principle, he now asserted that "a modern building may reasonably be a plastic whole – an integral matter of three dimensions."[24] For him "Unity Temple asserts again the quality and value of the third dimension in asserting the form within to be the essential to find expression. The reinforced concrete slab as a new architectural expression, is here used for its own sake as 'Architecture.' . . . A sense of the third dimension in the use of the 'box' and the 'slab' – and a sense of the room within as the thing to be expressed in arranging them are what made Unity Temple."[25]

In his later talks and writings, Wright stated that he first read of this spatial idea of architecture in the early 1920s, when he claimed to have encountered Kakuzo Okakura's *The Book of Tea,* published in 1906. This cited Lao-tse's idea that "the reality of a room . . . was to be found in the vacant space enclosed by the roof and walls, not in the roof and walls themselves."[26] Wright's claim that he had not read of Lao-tse's ideas until the 1920s is supported by the fact that such a concept of space did not appear in Wright's writings before 1925. Yet Wright's discussions of space in architecture may have also responded to Dutch appraisals of his work. Thus, by the time Wright first articulated a view of his architecture as space, he presumably knew both Taoist formulations of the idea and similar concepts from De Stijl.

Wright's concept of spatial form appears in some ways closer to that of De Stijl than to that of Lao-tse. Okakura cited Lao-tse's claim that, if the reality of a room was to be found in its vacant space defined by its roof and walls, then "only in vacuum lay the true essential."[27] This view of space as negative void or empty vessel shaped by material enclosure differs from De Stijl's idea of space as positive substance. Wright wrote of space as a positive entity.[28] Thus, in a later handwritten note on one of his drawings of the interior of Unity Temple's auditorium (see Fig. 117), he described the design as "sense of space – to be lived in – the REALITY of the building." Lao-tse had written of space as a contained void, whereas De Stijl artists treated space as an infinite continuum. De Stijl's architecture expressed the continuity of space as an openness between interiors and exteriors. In Unity Temple, Wright designed a space that was, on one level, contained within a concrete shell. Yet, on another level, the open clerestories of Unity Temple's auditorium, through which one sees the exterior columns, suggest continuity of space between inside and outside.

Lao-tse wrote of space as a still or static volume, as would be found in the empty vessel of a water pitcher. Yet, in the theory of De Stijl, space was considered as dynamic, associated with movement, and thus unlike the still void of a vacuum. In his retrospective annotation to his drawing of Unity Temple (see Fig. 117), Wright similarly invoked the image of space in architecture as an entity in motion, when he described "the big room coming through – the outside coming in."[29] Finally, Lao-tse's idea of space as void contained by materials differed from both De Stijl's and Wright's idea of the interpenetration of space and materials. Wright's metaphor of architecture as weaving in three dimensions was distinct from Lao-tse's idea of space as like the hollow of a cast vessel. It was this interweaving of material planes through three-dimensional space that Wright had developed throughout Unity Temple.

In Wright's view, this expression of a third dimension distinguished his work from that of certain modernists in Europe. From the mid-1920s, his role as forerunner of a new architecture was closely assessed. Each year from 1925 to 1931 there appeared several European publications on his work, mainly in those journals that were then presenting new European modern architecture. Wright was well aware of what was happening internationally, and of modernism's impact on American regard for his work. In his articles on "Modern Architecture" in the *Architectural Record* of 1928, Henry-Russell Hitchcock termed Wright a "New Traditionalist," in contrast to Le Corbusier as a "New Pioneer."[30] An English translation of Le Corbusier's *Vers une architecture* appeared in that same year, and, in his review of this book, Wright tried to distinguish his position from that of Le Corbusier.

In his text Le Corbusier had reminded architects that "surface and mass" were among the key elements of a renewed art. Yet Wright stated that an emphasis on surface and mass "ignored the essential element that alone can guide either surface or mass to life. That element is depth. Depth: That quality of 'the third dimension,' is all important. Without it there is no great Architecture, Old or New. . . . The 'New' pioneers are without it and so making another kind of picture building by leaving off all the ornament, so called."[31] By contrast Wright emphasized his idea of the third dimension, asserting that "the conception of the room *within,* the interior spaces of the building to be conserved, expressed, and made living as architecture – the architecture of the *within* – that is precisely what we are driving at, all along. And this new quality of thought in architecture, the third dimension, let us say, enters into every move that is made to make it."[32]

Wright subsequently presented this idea as central to his architecture. In 1930 an exhibition of his work began a tour of the United States at Princeton University. The show traveled to The Art Institute of Chicago and other American venues, before going to eight European cities in 1931.[33] In conjunction with this exhibition, Wright's publications were *Modern Architecture, The Kahn Lectures for 1930,* given at Princeton and published in 1931, and *Two Lectures on Architecture,* given at The Art Institute of Chicago, of 1931. In these new writings, Wright developed the idea of space as the conceptual framework within which his pre-1910 buildings had been created. In a first lecture at The Art Institute, entitled "In the Realm of Ideas," he wrote of Unity Temple:

> But, as reward for independent thinking in building, first plainly shown in the constitution and profiles of Unity Temple at Oak Park, more clearly emerging from previous practice, now came clear *an entirely new sense of architecture,* a higher conception of architecture: architecture not alone as form following function, but conceived as space enclosed. The enclosed space itself might now be seen as the reality of the building. The sense of the "within" or the room itself, or the rooms themselves, I now saw as the great thing to be expressed as *architecture.* This sense of interior space made exterior as architecture transcended all that had gone before, made all the previous ideas useful only now as a means to the realization of a far greater ideal. . . . This interior conception took architecture entirely away from sculpture, away from painting and entirely away from architecture as it had been known in the antique. The building now became a creation of interior space in light.[34]

In 1929 Wright had authorized his apprentices to make new drawings of several of his major early works, including Unity Temple (Fig. 148). One apprentice recalled that he suggested to Wright "that we might try to reduce his delicate renderings of his best-known buildings to a two-dimensional black-on-white graphic presentation 'Modern Architects' were addicted to. His answer: '*Do it.*'"[35] Of these drawings of 1929, executed in black ink on window shades, the one of Unity Temple contrasts with the earlier rendering depicting the church's west side along Kenilworth Avenue (see Fig. 81). In their graphic conventions, these images are a generation apart. In the new drawing of 1929 Unity Temple's pictorial context has all but disappeared. Gone are the color, the human figures, and almost all the foliage of the earlier drawing. Unity Temple has lost its specificity of place; nothing of its surroundings is now shown except indications of its ground plane. Also omitted are any rendition of the concrete's texture and the inscription over the entrance.

The shifted viewpoint of the new 1929 rendering (Fig. 148), from the northwest rather than the southwest, permitted severely foreshortened depiction of the building's north front toward Lake Street, now sharply con-

FIGURE **148**

Wright, Unity
Temple, drawing
of 1929 (Frank
Lloyd Wright Ar-
chives, Drawing
No. 0611.007,
© The Frank
Lloyd Wright
Foundation 1959).

trasted to the long west flank. Horizontal lines sweep across this side at many levels. The new drawing gives Unity Temple a dynamic appearance, as if it were less resting on the earth than hovering in space. Representation of light is now stylized. On the building, black indicates unlit planes starkly set against seemingly sunlit surfaces. The 1929 drawing shows the gridded skylit ceiling between the columns inside the auditorium, hinting that exterior walls are screens for interior space. Along the base of the 1929 drawing is a partial plan of Unity Temple. Though the whole plan is axially symmetrical, as Wright had observed of this and his other works in 1908, the partial plan is graphically asymmetrical, as if to resemble the asymmetrical plan of a modernist work. Rather than recalling the pictorial form of Japanese prints or renderings of the Viennese Secession like the drawing of 1906, the graphic style of the 1929 drawing compares with that of European modern architects such as Erich Mendelsohn, who had visited Wright in 1924.[36] Yet Wright's square emblem and Unity Temple's 1906 date mark the 1929 drawing's lower right corner, linking his personal sign to the early date of the design's aesthetic innovation. Thus was Unity Temple made to appear like the forerunner of modernism that Wright now claimed it had been. The 1929 drawing of Unity Temple was included in the exhibitions of Wright's work at both Princeton and The Art Institute of Chicago in 1930.[37]

After this period, Wright himself added the handwritten notes that ap-

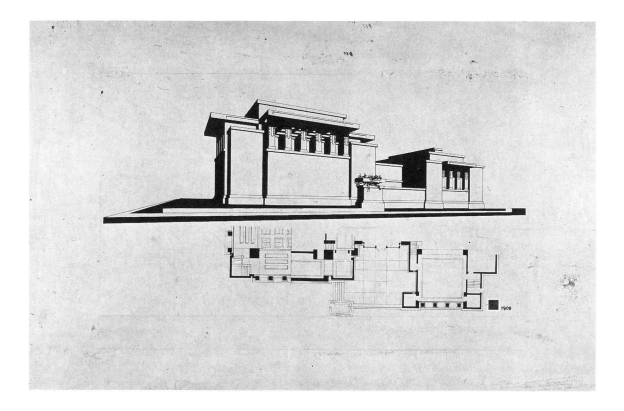

pear on perspective studies of Unity Temple's interior originally drawn early in 1906, before his final revisions in design. As noted, Wright wrote of this idea of space on one interior view (see Fig. 117). On another version of this drawing prepared in 1906 (Fig. 149), Wright later added a caption in its lower left: "The unlimited overhead. Interior space enclosed by screen – fixtures only. Idea later used in Johnson Bldg. Racine Wis." These annotations stressing the expression of space appear intended to reshape historical perception of Unity Temple along the lines that after 1925 Wright deemed to be the most important.

Wright's reappraisal of Unity Temple anticipated his role in the exhibition entitled "Modern Architecture," held at the Museum of Modern Art in New York, from 10 February to 23 March 1932. This was curated by Henry-Russell Hitchcock and Philip Johnson, who also co-authored both its catalogue and the related book, *The International Style,* in that year. Wright was at first reluctant to participate because of the show's emphasis on European modernism, but he later agreed to be included. Of nine architects treated in the catalogue's essays, Wright, the eldest, was treated first and at greatest length. A note prefacing this essay of Hitchcock stated the proofs of Wright's autobiography had been made available before the exhibition "to aid in the preparation of this catalogue."[38] Wright had begun his autobiography as early as 1926 and had completed it by 1931. The first edition was released by its New York publisher, Longmans, Green, on 30 January

FIGURE **149**

Wright, Unity Temple, perspective of preliminary design of auditorium's interior, looking south, corresponding to working drawings of March 1906, with later annotations (Frank Lloyd Wright Archives, Drawing No. 0611.009, © The Frank Lloyd Wright Foundation 1959).

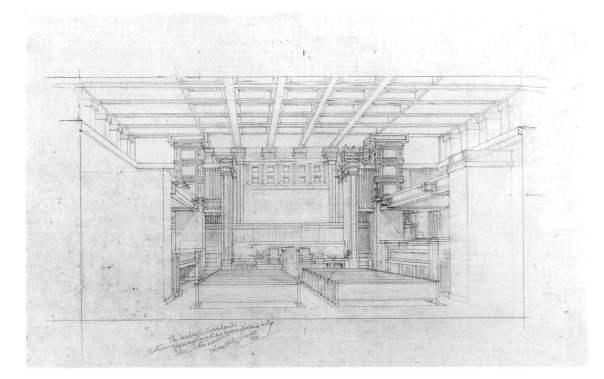

1932, twelve days before the exhibition's opening.[39] In supplying proofs of the text to Hitchcock and Johnson, Wright thus presented, in a direct and timely manner, his revised view of his early work to the critics who would most powerfully shape American perceptions of modernism in architecture.

For Hitchcock and Johnson, a first principle of the new architecture was its emphasis on spatial volume rather than material mass. They credited Wright with this conceptual innovation, declaring that, of modern architects in Europe and the United States, he had been "the first to conceive of architectural design in terms of planes existing freely in three dimensions rather than in terms of enclosed blocks." His European contemporaries "lightened the solid massiveness of traditional architecture; Wright dynamited it."[40] Yet, in spite of Wright's pioneering role, Hitchcock and Johnson perceived a key ideological distinction between his work and that of later modernists. There had developed "a definite breach between Wright and the younger architects who created the contemporary style after the War. Ever since the days when he was Sullivan's disciple, Wright has remained an individualist," whereas "in Europe, and indeed in other parts of the world as well, an increasingly large group of architects work successfully within the disciplines of the new style."[41]

In his reaction to the International Style, Wright was quick to agree that he stood apart. While he had shared the modern idea of architecture as space, he rejected the concept of an encompassing modern style. For Wright, an appropriate direction in modern architecture centered on the organic ideal, which stressed individuality and invention as opposed to what he saw as the reductive and uniform aesthetic of the so-called International Style. Wright's rejection of the International Style's exhibition of 1932 echoed Sullivan's remonstrances against the World's Columbian Exposition in 1893. They viewed these events as importations of European styles that thwarted indigenous American development toward an expressive modern architecture. Wright asked: "Do you think that, as a style, any aesthetic formula forced upon this work of ours in our country can do more than stultify this reasonable hope for a life of the soul? A creative architecture for America can only mean an architecture for the individual."[42]

In his autobiography, Wright had included an extended account of designing Unity Temple to illustrate his approach to the making of a new architecture. His analysis of this building's origins was not simply a recollection of events of twenty-five years before. Instead, it was calculated to address the debate in modern architectural culture in the United States that had crystallized by 1932. Wright's retrospective view of Unity Temple was intended to reveal both his affinity with and distance from other modernists. Wright presented the building as a work of architecture that was conceived as an expression of space; hence its importance as a forerunner of the modern movement. Of the design, he wrote: "The first idea – to keep a noble ROOM in mind, and let the room shape the whole edifice, let the room inside be the architecture outside."[43] Concrete masses were "grouped about an interior space in some such way as to preserve this desired sense of the interior space in the appearance of the whole building."[44]

While Wright claimed that Unity Temple had anticipated the International Style in its expression of space, he also presented the building as a critique of formulaic modernism. Wright maintained that he had not arrived at Unity Temple's design by selecting a style beforehand. Rather, the building had style as a consequence of his analysis of those concerns unique to the project: its function, its context, and its methods of construction. Wright thus presented Unity Temple as the result of rational and independent thought keyed to the individuality of its problem, rather than the adaptation of a preconceived vocabulary of forms. He wrote: "Organic is this matter of style now. . . . We do not choose a style."[45]

Wright made Unity Temple's story serve a larger purpose in the exchanges of the 1930s. Here was an original work of architecture created as a pioneering experiment in response to the specific circumstances of its origin. Wright chose to discuss Unity Temple not as an example of a modern style. Instead, its design was to serve as a case study in arriving at style as individuality of expression. In retrospect, he valued the building not only for its aesthetic innovations, but as an illustration of a method of design. This was what distinguished his architecture from any arbitrary selection of style, whether that style was eclectically historical, as was the practice of the 1890s, or reductively modernistic, as became conventional from the 1930s. In this way, Wright in his autobiographical account of designing Unity Temple was providing a detailed illustration of an attitude that he had first articulated a generation earlier in his address on "The Architect." To his colleagues of 1900 he said: "In the arts every problem carries within itself its own solution and the only way yet discovered to reach it is a very painstaking way – to sympathetically look within the thing itself, to proceed to analyze and sift it, to extract its own consistent and essential beauty, which means its common sense truthfully idealized. That is the heart of the poetry that lives in architecture."[46]

*   *   *

Wright's claims for Unity Temple invite a critical appraisal. If he conceived this building as exterior expression of interior space, then Wright's idea was not historically new. The concept, which could be traced to Lao-tse, had a timeless, universal character. The idea had been explored in church architecture from early Christian times on. It was developed in architectural theory of the Italian Renaissance, and recurred in teachings of the Ecole des Beaux Arts known to Wright's contemporaries.[47] The emphasis on three-dimensional expression that Wright claimed as distinctive in this church was also central to the modern architecture of his younger European contemporaries like Le Corbusier and Mies van der Rohe. In 1932 Wright knew their buildings of the 1920s from photographs like those displayed at the exhibition of the International Style. Yet while he viewed their architecture as constrained by a uniformity of style, key modern works also embody the critical thought and individual expression that Wright valued in Unity Temple.

In 1908 Wright was a nationally known architect (Fig. 150), yet he was not identified with an international modern movement as he was by 1930, when he recalled Unity Temple's story in his autobiography. The building's history reveals much about Wright's creative processes and cultural identity that is not tied to its role as a forerunner of modernism. The church's design marked a convergence of his vision for architecture with the aspirations of liberal religion. The concept that bridged Wright's individual thought and Unitarian Universalist culture was the idea of Unity.

In Wright's architecture, unity meant a consistency and an integration of motifs throughout all scales, from plan to ornament. As he later wrote, building is "taking a motif, a theme and constructing from it an edifice that is all consistent and organic – an organism as a whole."[48] This ideal, too, was not new, but could be inferred from earlier styles of architecture. However, Wright pursued it with a rigor and innovation throughout Unity Temple that gave the traditional principle of aesthetic consistency a new life. Wright limited his vocabulary of forms to the square and the rectangle. He considered such self-imposed limitation to be like constraints of site, function, or materials. They were to be accepted as disciplines for unifying a design. Unity meant congruence of form at all scales. This implied ever further exploration of selected motifs in different details. Unity also implied visual continuity of forms over surfaces, through three-dimensional space, and throughout the exterior architecture. For Wright, such possibilities were resources for expression in which he delighted, and which a commission like Unity Temple enabled him to explore in great depth.

Because of this building's symbolic purpose, Wright had to create a sanctuary that differed in significant ways from his prairie houses of the period. The houses' living spaces are horizontally expansive, whereas the auditorium of Unity Temple is a cubically balanced room for worship. The houses have central fireplaces as the focal points for centrifugal plans of surrounding rooms, while in Unity Temple the plan of the auditorium is inwardly focused on the pulpit. High, solid walls shield the sanctuary from the street, unlike the bands of windows at eye level in the prairie houses. While the prairie houses open into their foliate environs, Unity Temple's clerestories open to surrounding trees well above the worshipers. In his prairie houses, Wright emphasized the relation of dwelling to site as a statement about man's position within nature. Yet Unity Temple was a symbol of an institution's identity within a civic context. The building embodied specific assumptions about the congregation that worshiped within it and how their faith was to be communally perceived. In Unity Temple the novelty of Wright's aesthetic aligned with the modernity of the Unitarian and Universalist tradition.

FIGURE 150

Frank Lloyd
Wright, ca. 1908
(The Frank Lloyd
Wright Archives).

In this way Unity Temple shows an idea that was central to Wright's work: that individual works of architecture are to express the specific character of their clients, whether domestic or institutional. As he stated as early as 1894: "There should be as many types of homes as there are types of people, for it is the individuality of the occupants that should give character and color to the building."[49] He maintained that it was "better to have the courage of your convictions and live in your house, even it if does not win the applause of the gallery, than to live in a borrowed one that does not fit you."[50] Wright developed this idea in 1896 when he wrote of residential architecture as a means of expressing the character of its occupants. At that time he had written that "the opportunity to characterize men and women in enduring building material for their betterment and the edification of their kind is really one of the world's fine opportunities."[51] The architect "may throw himself between the client and the work and shield him, he may reveal him, he may interpret the better side of him that appeals to his imagination and give him something to grow to."[52] Although in this context, Wright was speaking of residential architecture, the same idea presumably underlay his design of Unity Temple as an interpretation of religious ideals that the church espoused and to which it aspired.

In Unity Temple, Wright created a building that helped its congregation define itself. He did much the same for his later religious clients. In his buildings for the First Unitarian Society of Madison, in Shorewood Hills, Wisconsin (1946–51), Beth Shalom Synagogue in Elkins Park, Pennsylvania (1953–59), and the Annunciation Greek Orthodox Church in Wauwatosa, Wisconsin (1956–61), Wright, as at Unity Temple, created symbolic forms that conveyed the ideals of different faiths. In each of these works, as at Unity Temple, Wright selected a distinct geometric figure for the building's basic form as his characterization of the religious life of a congregation. These late works were considered distant from the mainstream of modern architecture, whose theory was less concerned with individuality of character, though the idea had been central to the architectural theory of the Ecole des Beaux Arts. As a former student of the Ecole, Louis Sullivan had advocated buildings that conveyed individual character.[53] Wright, who acknowledged Sullivan as his mentor, sustained the ideal of architecture as individual characterization (of persons or institutions) as a vital principle of his life's work to its end. His theoretical distance from the modern movement on this question helps explain why his late works appear different from each other and from the International Style. At the same time, Wright's pursuit of the idea of character made his work an important point of reference for architects who continued to explore the principle, like Louis Kahn, who had also been educated in the tradition of the Ecole. Kahn focused on this idea in developing his design for the new building for the First Unitarian Church in Rochester, New York (1959–64). From 1889 to 1908 this church's minister had been William Channing Gannett, a central figure among liberal Unitarians in the era of Unity Temple's creation.[54]

In Unity Temple, Wright's artistry served the program of religious ideology that had been pursued by Jenkin Lloyd Jones and sustained by Rodney Johonnot. In the Unitarian tradition, individual character as an ethical and spiritual ideal was an aim of religious life. In his inaugural sermon at Unity Church in 1892, entitled "The Office of the Modern Church," Johonnot had maintained that the first task "is to gather men into brotherhood for the perfecting of individual character. Church members are not saints; they are of common clay with other people, but by coming into a church they announce that they are working for ideal ends; they are striving to develop a character."[55] Thus in Unity Temple, Wright's architectural ideal of expres-

245

**Unity Temple
and Later
Modern
Architecture**

sing institutional character paralleled the Unitarian aim of perfecting individual character.

As an essay in geometric form and a symbol of liberal religion, Unity
Temple exemplifies twin ideals that remained close to the center of Wright's
architectural thinking from his earliest known writings of the mid-1890s to
the end of his career. On one level, Wright maintained that a work of art is
an individual creative construct of forms, or an exercise in imaginative
expression employing the language of a medium. On another level, he
continually emphasized that a work of architecture must have individual or
specific character keyed to its particular function or institutional persona.[56]
In works such as Unity Temple, Wright pursued both of these intentions
simultaneously. The building is both a study in the poetics of three-
dimensional form and a a characterization of the ideals of its worshipers. In
its representation of institutional character, Unity Temple embodied a concept of architectural theory in the nineteenth century, while the building's
engagement with abstraction linked its form to an ideal of modern visual art
in the twentieth century. In the historiography of the modern movement,
Unity Temple, because of its continuity of linear forms over its three-
dimensional surfaces, could be viewed as a forerunner of the concept of
space-time in architecture as discussed by Sigfried Giedion. Yet, if understood as a building meant to serve a particular denominational culture,
Unity Temple also fulfilled Aldo van Eyck's ideal of an architecture of place
and occasion.[57]

Aspirations of liberal leaders like Jones and Johonnot for innovative
design in church architecture provided Wright with a symbolic purpose for
Unity Temple. The building was to crystallize a specific theological movement of its time. On one level, the design conveyed that movement's historical memory. Wright wrote of his auditorium as reviving an older Protestant
type. Thus, if Unity Temple opposed conventions of nearby ecclesiastical
architecture, the building gained expressive clarity from Wright's recourse
to the auditorium as a spatial model with a significant past. Also, Unitarian
belief in the universality of the temple gave him a rationale for Unity Temple's allusive eclecticism.

Multiple references to older Western and non-Western traditions of
religious architecture also appeared in works such as Bernard Maybeck's
slightly later First Church of Christ Scientist in Berkeley, California, of 1909–
11, in which a Beaux-Arts–trained architect characterized another liberal
denominational culture. As Charles De Kay wrote of American church
architecture in 1905: "The various styles belonging to different parts of the
earth are at [the modern architect's] command, and not only those of modern times, but of the remotest past. These are his materials to pick and
choose."[58] Though their churches differ, Wright's and Maybeck's interest in
the architecture of varied peoples was characteristic of American art in its
highly eclectic usage of many pasts. In these buildings, Wright and May-

beck also created visual symbols for religious movements whose modern phase was being shaped mainly in the United States.[59]

Wright's stamp of individuality is on all his works of the period before 1910, yet he stressed to critics that his innovations were rooted in his high regard for the tradition of architecture. Like artists he admired, Wright created an original body of work whose novelty was based not so much on his denial of the past as on his ability to assimilate a large number and wide range of sources into his new language of form. In Unity Temple he brought together not only ideas from his own earlier architecture, such as the designs for the Abraham Lincoln Center, but presumably knowledge of both older and contemporaneous variations on churches with small, centrally focused auditoriums. Wright could simultaneously draw on his experience of Japanese shrines and new American building in concrete. In Unity Temple, his stylistic mode was his own, yet it represented an integration of widely varied types. As a later English critic observed: "Creative work always arises by the synthesis in one man's mind of material from otherwise unrelated sources."[60] Throughout his life, Wright's architecture revealed both his enormous powers of formal invention and an equally great ability to condense multiple precedents. In Unity Temple, the richness of his synthesis depended on the interaction of these different faculties.

If Wright's building encompassed history on one level, it also embodied liberal religion's prophetic aspirations. As Johonnot had described, Wright's church was symbolically distinctive within a well-defined and highly self-conscious suburb of Oak Park in its earliest years of self-government. In this context, the building was intended as a challenging work of architecture, both for its congregation and for its community. Unity Temple provoked a reexamination of belief for the church that chose to build it and a reassessment of that liberal church's role in the civic life of its society. In this way, Unity Temple anticipated Wright's later urban projects, which confronted their surroundings and confounded expectations in order to provoke cultural renewal. Wright's aesthetic in Unity Temple was not only a self-referential world of form, but also a symbolic vehicle for public expression. With this building, Wright's artistic program gave voice to the regional Unitarian convictions that had been central to his own intellectual formation. His architecture's modernity here served as a solution to specific issues of cultural identity. Unity Temple's distinction thus lies not only in its aesthetic complexity and consistency, but in its capacity to signify ideals of a liberal religion.

Appendix:
Care and
Restoration of
Unity Temple from 1909

FROM its completion, Unity Temple's importance prompted concern for the adjacent properties, and the building's heating and ventilation, roofs, exterior and interior finishes, ornament and furnishing, and structural system. In 1913 the Gale family donated the house at 124 Kenilworth Avenue (directly south of Unity House) to the church for use as a parsonage.[1] In 1915 the site itself was given to Unity Church, guarding Unity Temple from other buildings on its south. Another house originally stood to the east of Wright's building, though this lot now serves as a parking lot for the Scoville Manor Apartments farther east on Lake, built in 1926 as the Scoville Park Hotel.[2]

Wright had designed a system of mechanically powered heating and ventilation for the building. Its set of underfloor ducts from a boiler room near the basement's southeast corner fed air into Unity House through its hollow, pierlike registers in front of the central north columns, and into Unity Temple through the hollow cores of its main columns. As vertical ducts for both the supply and return of air, the columns have openings in their outer faces toward the room's corners.[3] In January 1909 this original system of heat and forced-air ventilation was abandoned when a boiler burst.[4] Thus the earliest major modification of the new building was a substitute system of steam heating, entailing the installation of upright cast iron radiators still seen today inside the outer walls of both temple and house.[5]

Wright's complex volumetric design had consequences for the building's maintenance because it meant construction of seventeen separate segments of flat, composition roofing. The original roofing was intended to last for twenty years,[6] and in 1924 it was reported that "during the years [Unity Temple] has stood no cracks have developed."[7] Yet the first composition roofing covering the slabs was not replaced in the period of the

Depression, enabling water to penetrate the slabs. Additionally, the slabs' lighter cinder concrete was exceptionally porous. Thus, a permeable roof and porous concrete combined to permit water to freeze and thaw in many pockets inside the slabs, damaging the concrete's cohesion and rusting its reinforcing.[8] Late in 1938 architect William Drummond, who supervised Unity Temple's construction while in Wright's studio, informed Wright that the church's cantilevers were sagging visibly: "Unity Church needs your most careful attention. I have noticed, of late years, a considerable number of large cracks extending along the fascias of the overhanging eaves of The Temple and some falling off of the outer corners thereof. . . . Rusty steel bars show in the cavities."[9]

Drummond urged Wright to restore the roof himself, and Wright wrote to Ehrman: "I value the building highly as I am sure you do. It is a landmark in the history of American Architecture and of reinforced concrete as well. But the building was erected when we knew much less of reinforced concrete construction than we know now."[10] At this time, Wright had recently built Fallingwater and the Johnson Wax Building, both of which had employed concrete in innovative ways. Early in 1939 Wright assured Drummond that "I have myself agreed with the trustees in charge to fix it all up at my own expense this spring so do not worry about it."[11] However, Wright's archives do not indicate that he directed repair or restoration of Unity Temple between 1909 and his death fifty years later.

The members of Unity Church made major efforts to renew their building in 1961, when the national Universalist and Unitarian churches merged.[12] The congregation, which then changed its name to The Unitarian-Universalist Church in Oak Park, used its own funds to initiate the first major changes in Unity Temple's history. The roofs were repaired, and the classrooms in Unity House's balconies were partitioned.[13] After Wright had died in 1959, it was reported that "the interior, from the beginning, was never very colorful which seemed to disturb Mr. Wright and he mentioned it often on his visits to the church."[14] In the summer and fall of 1961, Unity Temple's interior was painted in shades of yellow, brown, and other earthen colors found in later works of Wright. His associates William Wesley Peters and John Howe helped with this project, which was described as a completion rather than as a transformation of the temple's interior.[15] In that same year, the building's exterior was resurfaced with a stucco-like bonding agent known as Albitol in order to promote adhesion of the pebble aggregate to the outer wall's cement surfaces.[16] This treatment entirely covered the original cement and aggregate with its wood formwork marks and pour lines. In 1966 the coat rooms originally beneath the auditorium were replaced by enclosed classrooms and washrooms.[17]

In 1967 the church initiated a tour program to provide funds for restoration of the building's original elements. In 1968 such funds were first used to restore Unity House's skylights.[18] In the wake of these efforts, an article of 1969 by Henry Wright (no relation to Frank Lloyd Wright) about Unity

Temple's condition and the costs of further restoration prompted Edgar J. Kaufmann Jr. to offer matching funds over three years to enable extensive restoration.[19] This offer was the catalyst for continued efforts, leading to creation of the Unity Temple Restoration Foundation in 1973.[20] Following a fire in Unity House in January 1971, funding had enabled repainting of its interior walls and stripping of its woodwork. One of the consultants for this project was Frank Lloyd Wright's eldest son, the architect Lloyd Wright.[21] In March 1971 Unity Temple was designated a National Historical Landmark.[22]

The restoration foundation funded a second resurfacing of the exterior in 1973–74, for which Lloyd Wright prepared the basic specifications.[23] First, the Albitol coating was sandblasted to reveal the original surfaces. These were recoated with a thin layer of sprayed-on concrete, known as shotcrete or Gunnite. Its cement, sand, and an aggregate of pea gravel were selected to approximate those of the original surface. The Gunnite was troweled by hand while wet, then lightly sandblasted when dry to expose its aggregate.[24] Coats of linseed oil were then applied as a sealant. These efforts resulted in the exterior visible after 1974, whose texture and color approximate the original surface, although without marks of the original formwork and pour lines. Only the ornamental exterior columns and undersides of the roof slabs visible above them were not sprayed with Gunnite after removal of the Albitol coating, so one can here see remnants of the original surface. The concrete flower boxes atop the terrace steps on both sides of the building were also reconstructed, as the originals had been removed earlier.[25] In 1972 the roof was extensively repaired a second time, before the most recent reroofing of the building in 1982.[26]

In 1979 another study of the building's interior walls to discover Wright's original colors provided information for a subsequent repainting of Unity House that is now seen.[27] In 1984 thorough investigation of Unity Temple's colors was the basis for their restoration later in that year, when the room's woodwork was also cleaned and its plaster repaired in time for the dedication's seventy-fifth anniversary in 1984. Then the entrance's original colors were also restored.[28] In 1987 interior surfaces of Unity House were reexamined in order to more precisely identify their original colors.[29] In that year, the foundation commissioned a comprehensive, detailed report on the building's condition and on future priorities for its restoration.[30] Among its recommendations was an analysis of the exterior concrete, particularly the roof slabs, which was undertaken in 1988.[31] At this time, a grant enabled the first efforts at repair and restoration of the art glass in Unity Temple's skylights. The Unitarian-Universalist Church of Oak Park, Illinois, also signed an agreement with the Landmarks Preservation Council of Illinois to maintain the building in its historic appearance. Through this unanimous congregational action, the church became the first in the nation to grant such a preservation easement for a historic building.[32]

While related to cycles of critical and historiographic interest in Wright's architecture, efforts at restoration in Unity Temple's lifetime were sustained by local perceptions of the building's importance, as attested by the unabating stream of visitors to the church from the United States and abroad. This phenomenon dates from the time of the church's opening in 1908. In 1924 it was reported that Unity Temple "is known wherever there are architects and men from foreign parts come frequently to see the structure they consider wonderful."[33] By the mid-1980s visitors to Unity Temple numbered over one thousand per month.[34]

Notes

INTRODUCTION

1. Early accounts of Unity Temple include Rev. Rodney F. Johonnot, *The New Edifice of Unity Church* (Oak Park, Ill.: Unity Church, 1906), partially republished in "Unity Temple and Unity House, Oak Park, Ill.," *Inland Architect and News Record* 52 (December 1908): 77; Wright, "In the Cause of Architecture," *Architectural Record* 23 (March 1908): 212, and *Ausgeführte Bauten und Entwürfe von Frank Lloyd Wright* (1910; reprint, Palos Park, Ill., 1975), description of Plate LXIII.

   Wright's later retrospections on Unity Temple appeared in his "In the Cause of Architecture, IV: Fabrication and Imagination," *Architectural Record* 62 (October 1927): 318–319; "In the Cause of Architecture, I: The Logic of the Plan," ibid., 63 (January 1928): 49–57; "In the Realm of Ideas," *Two Lectures on Architecture* (Chicago: The Art Institute of Chicago, 1931), 25–26; *An Autobiography* (New York: Longmans, Green, 1932), 153–164; "Recollections – The United States, 1893–1920," *Architect's Journal* 84 (16 July–6 August 1936), reprint, Frederick Gutheim, ed., *Frank Lloyd Wright on Architecture: Selected Writings, 1894–1940* (New York: Duell, Sloan and Pearce, 1941), 177–191; *Architectural Forum* 68 (January 1938): 35; and his talk to the Taliesin Fellowship on 13 August 1952, quoted in Bruce Brooks Pfeiffer, ed., *Letters to Architects: Frank Lloyd Wright* (Fresno: California State University Press at Fresno, 1986), 48. On these later accounts, see Conclusion, 234–237.

   Discussions of Unity Temple appeared in Charles R. Ashbee, "Man and the Machine: The Soul of Architecture, II," *House Beautiful* 28 (July 1910): 55–56; Robert van't Hoff, "Architectuur en haar ontwikkeling (bij bijlage VIII)," *De stijl* 2 (no. 4, 1919): 40–43; Jan Wils, "Frank Lloyd Wright," *Elsevier's Geiellustreerd Maandschrift* 61 (1921): 217–227, translated in H. Allen Brooks, ed., *Writings on Wright: Selected Comment on Frank Lloyd Wright* (Cambridge, Mass.: MIT Press, 1981), 139–145. On the Dutch responses, see Conclusion, 230–234. On Unity Temple, see also Henry-Russell Hitchcock, *In the Nature of Materials: The Buildings of Frank Lloyd Wright, 1887–1941* (New York: Duell, Sloan and Pearce, 1942), 53–54; Talbot Hamlin, *Forms and Functions of Twentieth-Century Architecture*, 4 vols. (New York: Columbia University Press, 1952), II, 197; Grant C. Manson, *Frank Lloyd Wright to 1910: The First Golden Age* (New York: Van Nostrand Reinhold, 1958), 156–162; Vincent J. Scully Jr., *Frank Lloyd Wright* (New

York: George Braziller, 1960), 20–21; Peter Blake, *The Master Builders* (New York: W. W. Norton, 1960), 328–332; Donald Drew Egbert, "Religious Expression in American Architecture," in James W. Smith and A. Leland Jamison, eds., *Religious Perspectives in American Culture* (Princeton: Princeton University Press, 1961), 397–398; Henry Wright, "Unity Temple Revisited," *Architectural Forum* 130 (5 June 1969): 28–37; Yukio Futagawa and Martin Pawley, *Frank Lloyd Wright: Public Buildings* (New York: Simon and Schuster, 1970), 12–13; Geoffrey Broadbent, *Design in Architecture: Architecture and the Human Sciences* (New York: John Wiley and Sons, 1973), 40–43; Robert C. Twombly, *Frank Lloyd Wright: His Life and His Architecture* (New York: John Wiley and Sons, 1979), 101–102; Thomas A. Chulak, *A People Moving thru Time* (Oak Park, Ill.: The Unitarian Universalist Church in Oak Park, 1979); George A. Lane, *Chicago Churches and Synagogues* (Chicago: Loyola University Press, 1981), 116–117; Merfyn Davies, "The Embodiment of the Concept of Organic Expression: Frank Lloyd Wright," *Architectural History* 25 (1982): 120–130; and H. Allen Brooks, *The Prairie School: Frank Lloyd Wright and His Midwest Contemporaries* (1972; New York: W. W. Norton, 1976), 39–40.

    Recent analyses of Unity Temple include Otto A. Graf, *Die Kunst des Quadrats: Zum Werk von Frank Lloyd Wright,* 2 vols. (Vienna: Herman Böhlhaus, 1983), I, 124–260; "Drawings and Photographs of Unity Temple," *Perspecta* 22 (1984): 142–187; Narciso G. Menocal, "Frank Lloyd Wright and the Question of Style," *Journal of Decorative and Propaganda Arts* 2 (Summer–Fall 1986): 11; Brendan Gill, *Many Masks: A Life of Frank Lloyd Wright* (New York: G. P. Putnam's Sons, 1987), 173–184; Wiss, Janney, Elstner Associates, Inc., *Unity Temple: Historic Structures Report* (Chicago, 1987); Robert McCarter, "Abstract Essence: Drawing Wright from the Obvious," in Robert McCarter, ed., *Frank Lloyd Wright: A Primer on Architectural Principles* (New York: Princeton Architectural Press, 1991), 17; MacCormac, "Form and Philosophy," in ibid., 106, 123; Kenneth Frampton, "The Text-Tile Tectonic: The Origin and Evolution of Wright's Woven Architecture," in ibid., 135–137; Jonathan Lipman, "Consecrated Space: The Public Buildings of Frank Lloyd Wright," in ibid., 198–201; McCarter, "The Integral Ideal: Ordering Principles in the Architecture of Frank Lloyd Wright," in ibid., 238–289; Joseph Siry, "Unity Temple: Frank Lloyd Wright and Architecture for Liberal Religion in Chicago, 1885–1909," *Art Bulletin* 73 (June 1991): 257–282; Paul Laseau and James Tice, *Frank Lloyd Wright: Between Principle and Form* (New York: Van Nostrand Reinhold, 1992), 117–132, 164–175, 182–187; Meryle Secrest, *Frank Lloyd Wright: A Biography* (New York: Alfred A. Knopf, 1992), 179–181; David Larkin and Bruce Brooks Pfeiffer, eds., *Frank Lloyd Wright: The Masterworks* (New York: Rizzoli and The Frank Lloyd Wright Foundation, 1993), 70–75; Kevin Nute, *Frank Lloyd Wright and Japan: The Role of Traditional Japanese Art and Architecture in the Work of Frank Lloyd Wright* (New York: Van Nostrand Reinhold, 1993), 124–125, 149–150, 167–170; and William A. Storrer, *The Frank Lloyd Wright Companion* (Chicago: University of Chicago Press, 1993), 92–93.

2. Editorial, "Village Hall Site," *Oak Leaves* (8 May 1903): 12. On Unity Temple's site, see Chapter 2, 70–71, and 282 nn. 77–81. On Oak Park's population, see "18,060 Souls Here," *Oak Leaves* (20 June 1908): 4.

3. "Is It Beautiful?" *Oak Leaves* 28 (First Supplement, after December 1909): 3.

4. Graf, *Kunst des Quadrats,* I, 212, 258, similarly notes the contrast between the lowered darkness of the cloisters and the elevated brightness of the auditorium. On passage from darkness to light as a religious idea, see Mircea Eliade, *The Sacred and the Profane: The Nature of Religion,* trans. Willard R. Trask (1957; reprint, New York: Harcourt Brace Jovanovich, 1987), 179–184, and "Sacred Architecture and Symbolism," in Diane Apostolos-Cappadona, ed., *Symbolism, the Sacred, and the Arts* (New York: Crossroad, 1985), 107–109. See also Scully, *Frank Lloyd Wright,* 20.

5. Wright, *Autobiography* (1932), 154.

6. "Unity Plans Unique," *Oak Leaves* (24 February 1906): 7.

CHAPTER 1
RELIGIOUS AND INSTITUTIONAL ARCHITECTURE
OF THE LLOYD JONES FAMILY

1. Wright, quoted in Pfeiffer, ed., *Letters to Architects*, 244. On the family of Wright's father, William C. Wright, see Donald Leslie Johnson, "Notes on Frank Lloyd Wright's Paternal Family," *Frank Lloyd Wright Newsletter* 3 (1980): 5–7. Wright described himself as deeply religious and spoke of Nature as his church in an interview with Mike Wallace, September 1957, in Patrick J. Meehan, ed., *The Master Architect: Conversations with Frank Lloyd Wright* (New York: John Wiley and Sons, 1984). Wright also identified architecture as a kind of religion in "Really to Believe in Something," talk to the Taliesin Fellowship, 7 December 1958, in Bruce Brooks Pfeiffer, ed., *Frank Lloyd Wright: His Living Voice* (Fresno: California State University Press at Fresno, 1987), 206.

2. Wright, *Autobiography* (1932), 14. On Wright's father's ministry in Weymouth, see Twombly, *Frank Lloyd Wright*, 7–9; and Gill, *Many Masks*, 42–46.

3. On the Wrights with the Lloyd Joneses and in Madison, see Mary Jane Hamilton with Anne E. Biebel and John O. Holzhueter, "Frank Lloyd Wright's Madison Networks," and Mary Jane Hamilton, "The Unitarian Meeting House," in Paul E. Sprague, ed., *Frank Lloyd Wright and Madison: Eight Decades of Artistic and Social Interaction* (Madison, Wis.: Elvehjem Museum of Art, 1990), 1–2, 179. Wright's own accounts of his youthful contact with the Lloyd Joneses appear in his *Autobiography* (1932), 3–7, 14–20, 25–28. See also William Cronon, "Inconstant Unity: The Passion of Frank Lloyd Wright," in Terence Riley, ed., *Frank Lloyd Wright: Architect* (New York: The Museum of Modern Art, 1994), 9–12.

4. Jenkin Jones's chapel of 1733 stood within the local Unitarian cemetery, the building certifying Jones's personal ownership of the surrounding plot. In 1834 a second chapel, now identified as the Old Chapel, was built nearby. A third (or new) chapel was constructed not far away in 1879. On these structures, see Chester Lloyd Jones, *Youngest Son* (Madison, Wis., 1938), opp. 16, 91; D. Elwyn Davies, *"They Thought for Themselves": A Brief Look at the Story of Unitarianism and the Liberal Tradition in Wales and beyond Its Borders* (Llyandysul: J. D. Lewis and Sons, 1982), 34–35; Graham and Judy Hague, *The Unitarian Heritage: An Architectural Survey of Chapels and Churches in the Unitarian Tradition in the British Isles* (Sheffield: Unitarian Heritage, 1986), 114–115, 121–122; and Secrest, *Frank Lloyd Wright*, 20–23. See also Anthony Jones, *Welsh Chapels* (Cardiff: National Museum of Wales, 1984), 17, Plate vii; Emyr Humphreys, *The Taliesin Tradition: A Quest for Welsh Identity* (Glamorgan, Wales: Poetry Wales Press, 1983), 101–105; and Jan Morris, *The Matter of Wales* (New York: Oxford University Press, 1984), 297–299.

   Accounts of the Lloyd Joneses' settlement in the United States include "Jenk's Story (Excerpts from Sermons of Jenkin Lloyd Jones)," in Thomas Graham, ed., *Trilogy: Through Their Eyes* (Spring Green, Wis.: Unity Chapel, 1986), 1–23; C. L. Jones, *Youngest Son*, 9–51; Maginel Wright Barney, *The Valley of the God-Almighty Joneses* (1965; reprint, Spring Green, Wis.: Unity Chapel, 1986), 19–42; and Secrest, *Frank Lloyd Wright*, 19–38. See also Alan Conway, "Welsh Emigration to the United States," *Perspectives in American History* 7 (1973): 191–226; and Humphreys, *Taliesin Tradition*, 157–166.

On Wright's Taliesin in relation to Welsh traditions, see Thomas Beeby, "The Song of Taliesin," *Modulus, The University of Virginia School of Architecture Review* (1980–81): 2–11; Neil Levine, "The Story of Taliesin: Wright's First Natural House," and Scott Gartner, "The Shining Brow: Frank Lloyd Wright and the Welsh Bardic Tradition," in Narciso G. Menocal, ed., *Wright Studies, I: Taliesin 1911–1914* (Carbondale and Edwardsville: Southern Illinois University Press, 1992), 2–27, 28–43; and Anthony Alofsin, *Frank Lloyd Wright: The Lost Years, 1910–1922: A Study in Influence* (Chicago: University of Chicago Press, 1993), 123–126. See also Walter L. Creese, *The Crowning of the American Landscape: Eight Great Spaces and Their Buildings* (Princeton: Princeton University Press, 1985), 241–249, 253–265.

5. Jones, *The Ideal Church* (Chicago: Colegrove, 1882), 4, 5, 6. On the founding of All Souls Church, see Charles H. Lyttle, *Freedom Moves West: A History of the Western Unitarian Conference 1852–1952* (Boston: Beacon, 1952), 158–162. All Souls Church's early membership comprised a remnant of the moribund Fourth Unitarian Church in Chicago. The city's three older Unitarian congregations had not yet invited Jones to a pastorate. His views were radically remote from those of Boston's American Unitarian Association, which then financially aided many churches in the Midwest. On the dependence of western Unitarians on the American Unitarian Association, see Lyttle, *Freedom Moves West,* 94–99, 131–136. Jones's position within the national spectrum of Unitarian thought is discussed in Conrad Wright, *A Stream of Light: A Short History of American Unitarianism* (Boston: Skinner House, 1975), 84–94. Chicago's Unitarian churches and their founding dates were the centrally located First Unitarian Society (1836), Unity Unitarian Church (1859) on the North Side, Third Unitarian Church (1868) on the West Side, and Fourth Unitarian Church (1869) on the South Side. See George S. Phillips, *Chicago and Her Churches* (Chicago: E. B. Myers and Chandler, 1868), 271–287, 412–416; Alfred T. Andreas, *History of Chicago,* 3 vols. (Chicago: A. T. Andreas, 1886), III, 824–825; Homer A. Jack, "Unitarian Universalist Co-operation in Chicago," *Unity* 141 (September–October 1955): 48; and Lyttle, *Freedom Moves West,* 46–47, 156–158.

On Jenkin Lloyd Jones's life, see Samuel A. Eliot, ed., *Heralds of a Liberal Faith,* 4 vols. (Boston: American Unitarian Association, 1910–52), IV, 164–173; Lyttle, *Freedom Moves West,* 221–228; Richard H. Thomas, "Jenkin Lloyd Jones: Lincoln's Soldier of Civic Righteousness," Ph.D. diss., Rutgers University, 1967; David Robinson, *Unitarians and Universalists* (Westport, Conn.: Greenwood, 1985), 117–119, 284–285; and Thomas E. Graham, "Jenkin Lloyd Jones and 'The Gospel of the Farm,'" *Wisconsin Magazine of History* 67 (Winter 1983–84): 121–148. Jones's obituaries appeared in the *Chicago Tribune* (13 September 1918): 11, and *Chicago Herald Examiner* (13 September 1918): 1. Testimonies to his life's work appeared in *Unity* 82 (28 November 1918): 135–158.

Jenkin Lloyd Jones's mother tongue was Welsh, and he attended a bilingual elementary school. After the Civil War he studied at the Meadville Theological School in Pennsylvania (1866–70). He served churches in Illinois and Wisconsin, and became secretary of the Western Unitarian Conference, founded in 1852, with headquarters in Chicago. In this and other roles Jones served the conference with great energy from 1878 to 1882, annually traveling thousands of miles to visit scores of nascent churches in remote locales. On his work in this period, see T. E. Graham, "The Making of a Secretary: Jenkin Lloyd Jones at Thirty-One," *Proceedings of the Unitarian Universalist Historical Society* 19 (1982–83): Part II, 36–55. On his service in the Civil War, see Jones, *An Artilleryman's Diary* (Madison, Wis.: Wisconsin History Commission, 1914). On the Meadville Theological School, see Lyttle, *Freedom Moves West,* 55–66.

In 1878 Jones and others initiated publication of the conference's weekly journal, which they titled simply *Unity.* Its editorial program advanced what became the chief goals of the conference: an independence of religious life and thought that knew no doctrinal boundaries, and a commitment to humanitarian social and political causes in Chicago and throughout the world. In 1878 its editors declared: "*Unity* aims to represent a religion that is rational, and a rationalism that is religious. In and for the West, it is nevertheless national and international. Of and with the Unitarians, it yet believes in a world-inclusive religion, and it seeks to use the Unitarian word and serve the Unitarian cause only in so far as they help to break down that sectarian spirit that stands in the way of realizing the central spirit of all true religion – a feeling for and belief in UNITY." *Unity* Subscription Card, n.d., 188? (William C. Gannett Papers, Department of Rare Books and Special Collections, University of Rochester Library).

6. Jones, "The New Problems in Church Architecture," *Unity* 15 (20 June 1885): 202–205. When Jones's church purchased its site, Oakwood Boulevard lay just beyond the south city line of Chicago; thus a new All Souls Church was sited in what was then a suburban district. Oakwood's major streets were tree-lined, hence the image of All Souls Church as akin to a suburban house was contextually plausible. In this way, the new All Souls would contrast with neighboring larger stone churches of other denominations built in the 1880s along Oakwood and on nearby Drexel Boulevard. The city of Chicago finally annexed the district of Oakwood along with Hyde Park in 1889. Earlier Oakwood's development as a preferred residential locale outside of Chicago was attributed to "the natural affection for a rustic retreat from city cares, that made villas in the vicinage of ancient Rome fashionable" (Alfred T. Andreas, *History of Cook County, Illinois, from the Earliest Period to the Present Time* [Chicago: A. T. Andreas, 1884], 522). On the annexation of Hyde Park, see Charles E. Merriam, Spencer D. Paratt, and Albert Lepawsky, *The Government of the Metropolitan Region of Chicago* (Chicago: University of Chicago Press, 1933), 138, 140; Louis P. Cain, "To Annex or Not? A Tale of Two Towns. Evanston and Hyde Park," *Explorations in Economic History* 20 (1983): 58–72; and Ann D. Keating, *Building Chicago: Suburban Developers and the Creation of a Divided Metropolis* (Columbus: Ohio State University Press, 1988), 109–110. On the boulevard system near All Souls Church, see Daniel M. Bluestone, *Constructing Chicago* (New Haven: Yale University Press, 1991), 52–61.

   Church structures near All Souls included the original building of the Church of the Holy Angels (1880) on the south side of Oakwood west of Langley, and the Memorial Baptist Church (acquired 1881) on the south side of Oakwood Boulevard east of Langley. See Andreas, *History of Cook County*, 523–524. Both of these buildings were replaced on their sites in the 1890s, as discussed on pp. 34–35 and 264, n. 77. Also near All Souls Church were the South Park Congregational Church (1885), now the New Testament Memorial Baptist Church, northwest corner of South Drexel Boulevard and East 40th Street (Commission on Chicago Landmarks, Form No. 36-04-13-047); the Oakland Methodist Church (1887), southwest corner of Oakwood Boulevard and Langley Avenue (C.C.L., Form No. 38-04-14-005); and the Forty-First Street Presbyterian Church (1889), designed by Solon S. Beman, now the Metropolitan Community Church, 4100 South Martin Luther King Drive. See Lane, *Chicago Churches and Synagogues*, 58.

7. The son of a Unitarian minister, Rev. William Silsbee, Joseph Silsbee designed the Dutch Reformed Church (1878–81) and Oakwood Cemetery Chapel (1879–80) in Syracuse, N.Y., where he worked before coming to Chicago. These buildings were medievally inspired stone monuments, whereas the church for Jones resembled Silsbee's suburban houses near Chicago from the mid-1880s. On Silsbee, see Manson, *Frank Lloyd Wright*, 14–21; Hitchcock, *Nature of Materials*, 4–7; Susan K. Sorrell, "Silsbee: The Evolution of a Personal Style," and "A Catalog of Work by J. L. Silsbee," *Prairie School Review* 7 (Fourth Quarter 1970): 5–13, 17–21; and Thomas J. McCormick, "The Early Work of Joseph Lyman Silsbee," in Helen Searing, ed., *In Search of Modern Architecture: A Tribute to Henry-Russell Hitchcock* (New York and Cambridge, Mass.: The Architectural History Foundation and MIT Press, 1982), 172–184. Joseph Silsbee's father was a graduate of Harvard Divinity School (1836), where he became a friend of Henry Whitney

Bellows, the prominent minister of All Souls Church in New York City. See Walter D. Kring, *Henry Whitney Bellows* (Boston: Skinner House, 1979), 8. From 1868 Rev. William Silsbee was pastor of the Unitarian church at Trenton, N.Y. On Sunday, 10 October 1886, two days before the dedication of the new All Souls Church, Rev. Silsbee led a prayer from its platform. Jones's *Unity* 17 (16 October 1886): 91, noted that "it is pleasant to think of him worshipping within the walls which his son as architect had so successfully shaped."

8. Gannett, who was related to J. L. Silsbee by marriage, wrote to Jones in February 1885: "I enclose Mr. Silsbee's note. . . . If you care to call on him and interest him in your double-faced church idea, I should not wonder if he could help you well. I've told him that another Chicago architect has already tried his hand at the problem rather successfully." Rev. W. Gannett to Jones, 11 February 1885 (William C. Gannett Papers, Department of Rare Books and Special Collections, University of Rochester Library, Box 8, Folder 1). Before Jones engaged Silsbee, a project for the building designed in a residential Queen Anne style appeared in *All Souls Church Second Annual* in early 1885.

9. "Religious News," *Chicago Tribune* (12 September 1886): 11.

10. Jones, "New Problems in Church Architecture," 202. In the course of his first trip to Europe, in the summer of 1882, Jenkin Lloyd Jones toured the English cathedrals and abbeys of Winchester, Chester, York, Wells, Salisbury, and St. David's. On the Continent, he saw the cathedrals of Antwerp, Cologne, Strasbourg, Paris, and ten to twelve other examples of the type. See Jones, "Home Again," *Unity* 10 (1 October 1882): 310–312. Jones believed that medieval faith emphasized devotional emotion rather than critical thought; thus Gothic cathedrals of that period "provided no seats for listeners, no light for readers, and the human voice was broken into unintelligent [sic] echoes among its arches. It was no place to listen, to work, or to think. It kindled a mystic imagination, but strangled the judgment. It was never meant to be warmed in winter or to be ventilated in summer. Its 'dim religious light' is an offense to the inquirer." Jones, "New Problems in Church Architecture," 203–204.

11. Jones, "New Problems in Church Architecture," 204. In his view of cathedrals, Jones echoed the perceptions of the Boston Unitarian poet, James Russell Lowell, whose poem, "The Cathedral (1870)" was read in All Souls Church (*Unity* 39 [29 July 1897]: 460). Wright knew Lowell's poetry from childhood, as noted in Wright, *Autobiography* (1932), 14.

12. Jones, "New Problems in Church Architecture," 204. In proposing such an alternative ideal for the design of churches, Wright's uncle stressed that he did not thereby "advocate any change that will make the church less a shrine, less an altar, at which the soul confronts the solemnities of life. . . . We need indeed a sanctuary, literally 'a clean place,' 'a pure room.'"

13. Ibid.

14. Ibid.

15. "Church and Parsonage. A Proposed Plan for All Souls Church, Chicago," *Unity* 15 (20 June 1885): 202. Subsequent announcement of Silsbee as the building's architect appeared in *Inland Architect and News Record* 6 (August 1885): 8; and *Building Budget* 1 (October 1885): 66. All Souls Church was discussed in Hitchcock, *Nature of Materials*, 4; and Manson, *Frank Lloyd Wright*, 15–16. On the building's meaning for Jones's ministry, see Lyttle, *Freedom Moves West*, 158–160.

    In plan, All Souls had a semicircular auditorium with a platform against the east interior wall, north and south walls of windows, and a high central skylight. Fireplaces stood toward the rear to either side of the outer ring of pews. A desk stood on the front platform, with no altar. The auditorium's arrangement attests to Jones's interest in lighting and acoustics, whereas the seating may emphasize the fact that the church did not have individual pews rented by parishioners. At the auditorium's rear, the circumference of the space opened directly to a ring of rooms, including a parlor in the center. This arrangement was intended to permit later expansion of the auditorium via removal of the partitions between these smaller rooms, whose functions could be moved to spaces on the second floor. The axial arrangement of the auditorium and parlor in Silsbee's early plan for All Souls Church corresponds to that found in his Unity Chapel, as shown in Fig. 17, designed about the same time. The idea recurred in Wright's Church of the First Unitarian Society of Madison, Wis., built 1947–51.

16. Editorial, "Why Churches Are Nicknamed," *Unity* 17 (1 May 1886): 119. Jones intended his building to contrast with that of All Souls Church in New York City, one of the most well-known Unitarian churches. In 1853, following the building of two earlier structures, All Souls in New York commissioned the English-born architect Jacob Wrey Mould (1825–86) to design its new building on Fourth Avenue at 20th Street, completed in 1855. As an example of Ruskinian polychromy in American architecture, the church had a cruciform plan, yet, unlike Wright's later Unity Temple, the sides were transept-like expansions of the nave with all pews facing front. Its style was based on the basilica of San Giovanni Battista, of A.D. 595, at Monza, north of Milan. This was the earliest Christian edifice ever to serve as a model for a church in the United States. The pre-Gothic prototype for All Souls perhaps signified that its Unitarian teachings represented early periods of Christianity, antedating later creeds associated with Gothic art of the Middle Ages. In this way, the style of All Souls was not only tied to contemporaneous Ruskinian criticism, but also was consistent with Unitarian ideology. However, Mould's striated yellow stone and red brick soon inspired the building's popular name, "The Church of the Holy Zebra." On Mould's All Souls Church in New York, see H.-R. Hitchcock, "Ruskin and American Architecture, or Regeneration Long Delayed," in *Concerning Architecture: Essays on Architectural Writers and Writing Presented to Sir Nikolaus Pevsner* (London: Allen Lane, 1968), 176–179; David T. Van Zanten, "Jacob Wrey Mould: Echoes of Owen Jones and the High Victorian Gothic Styles in New York, 1853–1865," *Journal of the Society of Architectural Historians* 27 (March 1969): 41–43, 47, 54–56; and Kring, *Henry Whitney Bellows,* 124–135, 147–159.

17. "Notes from the Field," *Unity* 17 (3 April 1886): 65. Accounts of the opening and dedication of All Souls Church appeared in "Yesterday's Sermons," *Chicago Tribune* (13 September 1886): 44; "Notes from the Field," *Unity* 18 (18 September 1886): 38; Jones, "The Church of All Souls," ibid. (25 September 1886): 44; "A New Church Dedicated," *Chicago Tribune* (13 October 1886): 3; "Dedication of All Souls Church, Chicago," *Unity* 18 (16 October 1886): 90; "Dedication of a Church," and "Financial Exhibit of All Souls Church," ibid. (23 October 1886): 98–99; and "Scripture Selections," ibid. (30 October 1886): 115–116.

Just over $4,000 of the $10,000 cost of constructing the new All Souls Church, including part of the land's cost, had been donated by the American Unitarian Association in Boston on the condition that the building to go on the site be used as a Unitarian church; the remainder was borne by members and friends of the church. See "'Report of the Auditing Committee on the Building Fund of All Souls Church," *All Souls Church Fourth Annual* (Chicago, 1887), 23–24; Jones, "Never a Unitarian, Always a Unitarian," *Unity* 33 (21 June 1894): 258–259, and "A Church in Search of a Home – A Retrospect," *Unity* 52 (17 and 24 December 1903): 248.

18. Wright, *Autobiography* (1932), 69. A residential appearance without ecclesiastical imagery may have signified that All Souls served its community throughout the entire week. By 1892 the church boasted study clubs, a library, a manual training school, and a kindergarten, which were "maintained for the benefit not only of the church but for the good of the neighborhood" ("All Souls' Church," *Chicago Evening Post* [12 September 1892]: 5). Given his ideal of a communal orientation for All Souls, Wright's uncle hoped that his building, because it did not have the architectural character of surrounding churches, would appear as a nonsectarian meeting place for all nearby residents. The

building's domestic image also signified the fact that it was the residence of Jenkin Lloyd Jones, who broke with convention by putting the apartment of the parsonage on the church's second floor. Jones likened the inclusion of the parsonage in the church building to a residential medieval abbey. Silsbee's arched portico may allude to Romanesque monastic monuments, signifying the importance that Jones gave to resident clergy (Jones, "New Problems in Church Architecture," 205). This porch also corresponds to that on the corner of the Oakland Methodist Church (1886–87) across Langley Avenue from All Souls Church.

19. Eliot, ed., *Heralds of a Liberal Faith,* IV, 169. A later description of the interior of All Souls Church noted that "large fireplaces give it an air of substantial comfort and warm the cockles of the heart of every one that reads the scriptural quotations cut into the wood of the mantels over the fireplaces" ("All Souls' Church," *Chicago Evening Post* [12 September 1892]: 5, reprint, "Eozoic Age of the Lincoln Centre," *Unity* 52 [17 and 24 December 1903]: 256). One such fireplace, whose mantel is carved with the motto, "However things may seem, no good thing is failure, no evil thing success," is illustrated in *All Souls Church Tenth Annual* (Chicago, 1893), 15. The practice of carving ethical and literary sayings in the mantels of this church's fireplaces may have inspired Wright's similar practice in his own home in Oak Park of 1889 and in other later works.

20. *All Souls Church Second Annual* (Chicago, 1885), 7, cited in Wilbert R. Hasbrouck, "The Earliest Work of Frank Lloyd Wright," *Prairie School Review* 7 (Fourth Quarter 1970): 15.

21. *All Souls Church Fourth Annual* (Chicago, 1887), 8, cited in Hasbrouck, "Earliest Work of Frank Lloyd Wright," 15.

22. Wright, *Autobiography* (1932), 69.

23. Hasbrouck, "Earliest Work of Frank Lloyd Wright," 14–16. The drawing of All Souls Church that appeared in its third annual of 1886 matches that published by Hasbrouck (p. 16), which he identified as a drawing done by Silsbee. In addition to Wright's and Silsbee's drawings, Hasbrouck also published another drawing that served as the worksheet from which Wright made his perspective of All Souls Church. Hasbrouck (p. 14) noted that Wright's drawing and worksheet from which Wright made his perspective of All Souls Church were in "the files of Jenkin Lloyd Jones now [1970] held in the collection of the Meadville Theological Seminary." In July 1989 these drawings were not found in this collection.

24. Twombly, *Frank Lloyd Wright,* 16–18; Gill, *Many Masks,* 57–59; and Secrest, *Frank Lloyd Wright,* 82–83, have suggested that Jones's patronage of Silsbee helped Wright find work with him. All Souls is listed as Silsbee's first institutional commission in Chicago in Sorrell, "Catalogue of Work by J. L. Silsbee," 17–21.

25. F. L. Hosmer, letter, *Unity* 9 (16 August 1882): 256–257, discusses Jones's itinerary on his visit and the new chapel at Llwynrhydowen of 1879. On this building, see also Davies, *"They Thought for Themselves,"* 38–40, and photograph opposite p. 96; and Hague, *Unitarian Heritage,* 122.

Before his death in 1885, Richard Lloyd Jones imagined a chapel at his familial homestead that would be a focus for gatherings of his clan. Jenkin Lloyd Jones and his siblings had gathered at the familial homestead at the death of their mother, Mary Lloyd Jones, in 1870. Subsequent annual grove meetings of the local farming community had been held every August at the anniversary of her death near her grave. See Jane Lloyd Jones, "In Memoriam," and Thomas E. Jones, "A Tribute to My Parents," in Graham, ed., *Trilogy,* 37–39, 46–47. The chapel on that site was to be used for Sunday and occasional meetings, as well as memorial services for family members who were interred nearby. See William C. Gannett, "Richard Lloyd Jones," *Unity* 16 (19 December 1885): 199; George and Robert M. Crawford, eds., *Memoirs of Iowa County, Wisconsin,* 2 vols. (Madison: Northwestern Historical Association, 1913), I, 261; Thomas, "Jenkin Lloyd Jones," 24–25; and Secrest, *Frank Lloyd Wright,* 5–6.

26. William C. Gannett, "The Editor's Vacation," *Unity* 15 (22 August 1885): 320. Gannett envisioned the new chapel as "'a three-roomed church, to hold at minimum one hundred, and at maximum, by unfolding audience-room into parlor, two hundred, with a kitchen corner tucked in somewhere, – this cased in a form so simply pretty that it will beautify the hills, not blot them with another stiff church-box, – and all for $1,000 or $1,200, – this is our problem for the architects." In May 1886, at an annual meeting of the Western Unitarian Conference, Jones presented a paper on "The Unity Church That Is Possible in Every Community." Silsbee was scheduled to follow with a talk on "A Practical Reform in Church Architecture" (*Unity* 17 [15 May 1886]: 162. See also editorial, ibid. [8 May 1886]: 131). Earlier Jones had advocated that architecture for liberal religious communities in the western United States should avoid extravagance for both financial and symbolic reasons. New buildings often had to be partly funded by Boston's American Unitarian Association, so reduction in their cost would free congregations from denominational control. In 1881 *Unity* had declared: "Until societies are wealthy enough and generous enough to pay for their own architectural elegancies, it is for them by their earnestness, their intelligence and their zeal, to make radiant with life-giving beauty such plain and simple walls as will give them adequate room within. We put the value of handsome walls, stained glass, and all that . . . at a minimum. We cannot answer the inquiries of the growing mind of this generation with brick and mortar." Editorial, "Beware of Architects," *Unity* 8 (16 September 1881): 262.

27. Letter, *Unity* 16 (7 November 1885): 126. See "Unity Church, Topeka," ibid. (24 October 1885): 3. Recalling the early Protestant meetinghouses in Holland and England, one observer stated: "I think a change in church architecture of more importance than a change in the wording of creeds, for surroundings determine methods largely. What the American people need is not more places to be preached *at* but more religious conference houses, . . . where men and women come to bind themselves to higher things" (Letter, *Unity* 16 [7 November 1885]: 117–18). Wright signed a sketch as architect for a Unitarian Chapel in Sioux City, Iowa, *Inland Architect and News Record* 9 (June 1887). See Hitchcock, *Nature of Materials,* 5; Manson, *Frank Lloyd Wright,* 16–18; Gill, *Many Masks,* 58; and Patrick Pinnell, "Academic Tradition and the Individual Talent: Similarity and Difference in the Formation of Frank Lloyd Wright," in McCarter, ed., *Wright: A Primer,* 23–24. On Unity Church in Sioux City, see *Unity* 16 (12 December 1885): 186; and Lyttle, *Freedom Moves West,* 147.

28. Wright to Jones, 22 August 1885, in B. B. Pfeiffer, ed., *Letters to Clients: Frank Lloyd Wright* (Fresno: California State University Press at Fresno, 1986), 1. Wright wrote this letter on the stationery of his employer in Madison, the engineer Allan D. Conover. Frank Lloyd Wright Memorial Foundation, Microfiche Id. No. J001A01. On this letter, see also Pinnell, "Academic Tradition and the Individual Talent," in McCarter, ed., *Wright: A Primer,* 294, n. 8.

29. Editorial, *Unity* 16 (3 October 1885): 62–63.

30. "Helena Valley Chapel Meeting," [Spring Green, Wis.] *Weekly Home News* (19 August 1886): 2. See "Unity Chapel, for the Unitarian Church in Helena Valley, Wisconsin," *Unity* 16 (26 December 1885): 1.

31. "Unity Chapel, Helena, Wis.," *All Souls Fourth Annual* (Chicago, 1887). This drawing has been reproduced and discussed in Hasbrouck, "Earliest Work of Frank Lloyd Wright," 14–15; Twombly, *Frank Lloyd Wright,* 17; and Gill, *Many Masks,* 59.

32. "Helena Valley Chapel Meeting," 2. Jones wrote that he had been to Wisconsin "to look in upon the little Helena Chapel, which is being built to house my first missionary movement, my home parish which is fast approaching completion." Jones to Samuel Barrows, 3 June 1886 (Charles H. Lyttle Collection, I: 1875–87, William C. Gannett Papers, Department of Rare Books and Special Collections, University of Rochester Library, Box 26, Folder 6).

33. "Helena Valley Chapel Meeting," 2.

34. Jenkin Lloyd Jones, Address, Funeral Services of David Timothy at Hillside, Wis., 9 June 1909, 6. Jane Lloyd Jones Papers, 1899–1940, Box 1, Archives Division, State Historical Society of Wisconsin, Madison. Timothy's stonework for Unity Chapel echoes the varied interlocked patterns of H. H. Richardson's stonework, then at the height of its influence. On Timothy's role in building Wright's Romeo and Juliet windmill for the Hillside Home School, see Wright, *Autobiography* (1932), 134–135. On Timothy, see also Barney, *Valley of the God-Almighty Joneses*, 85–86; and Secrest, *Frank Lloyd Wright*, 38, 140–141. W. C. Gannett, "Christening a Country Church," *Unity* 17 (28 August 1886): 356, compared Unity Chapel to a cottage or a schoolhouse. Chicago architect William Boyington designed a schoolhouse of similar form at Highland Park, Ill., illustrated in *Inland Architect and Builder* 8 (August 1886): 17.

35. "Helena Valley Chapel Meeting," 2.

36. Gannett, "Christening a Country Church," *Unity* 17 (28 August 1886): 357. Secrest, *Frank Lloyd Wright*, 7, notes Wright's claim to have designed the chapel's ceiling as a motif of concentric squares made of oak wood bands. On Unity Chapel, see also Pinnell, "Academic Tradition and the Individual Talent," in McCarter, ed., *Wright: A Primer*, 22; and Storrer, *Wright Companion*, 3.

37. Wright, *Autobiography* (1932), 26. On Unity Chapel's origins and subsequent history, see Elizabeth Wright Ingraham, "The Chapel in the Valley," *Frank Lloyd Wright Newsletter* 3 (Second Quarter 1980): 1–4; and Secrest, *Frank Lloyd Wright*, 3–8.

38. In 1934 Wright designed a chapel for the Newmann family in Cooksville, Wis., which he identified as a "Memorial to the tillers of the ground, making the earth a feature of the monument, or vice versa." On this unrealized work, see Yukio Futagawa, ed., *Frank Lloyd Wright Monograph 1924–1936* (Tokyo: A.D.A. EDITA, 1990), 234–237; Bruce Brooks Pfeiffer, *Frank Lloyd Wright Drawings* (New York: Harry N. Abrams, 1990), 93; and Riley, ed., *Frank Lloyd Wright*, 252.

    This project anticipates Wright's 1956 design for a memorial, to be called Unity Temple, and sited just west of Unity Chapel and its cemetery, to which the new temple would be closely related. A new tower was to align with Richard Lloyd Jones's funerary obelisk. The unbuilt memorial, equal in area to the chapel's main room, was to be a square ring of squared sandstone piers on a four-stepped base of stone. Within this ring of piers was to be a square of glass doors, with glass stepping up and out at the corners. From inside, one would see the landscape all around, as in Unity Chapel. The skylit interior was to have a black marble floor and a fireplace in its southeast corner. Outside to the south was to be a walk along a row of sarcophagi for Wright, his Taliesin family, and his colleagues. Beyond would be a reflecting pool enhancing the sunlit view of the hills in the distance. Wright's drawings show the memorial aligned with the rolling horizon, as Jones's stationery depicted Unity Chapel in this landscape. On this unbuilt Unity Temple, see Yukio Futagawa, ed., *Frank Lloyd Wright Monograph 1951–1959* (Tokyo: A.D.A. EDITA, 1988), 334; and Secrest, *Frank Lloyd Wright*, 13–14. The design resembled Wright's second project for a Christian Science Church in Bolinas, Calif., of 1955, recorded as Frank Lloyd Wright Foundation, Project No. 5527.

    Wright's project for a Unity Temple near Unity Chapel may have been linked to his first and only visit to Wales in 1956. There is no record of his having gone to the Lloyd Joneses' familial chapel or homestead, but Secrest, *Frank Lloyd Wright*, 560–562, notes that he did see the tomb of Lloyd George, made of boulders among old trees and a garden.

39. On the Hillside Home School of 1901–2, see Hitchcock, *Nature of Materials*, 49–50, Plates 81–84; Manson, *Frank Lloyd Wright*, 130–133; Storrer, *Frank Lloyd Wright*, 69; Twombly, *Frank Lloyd Wright*, 97–98; Yukio Futagawa, ed., *Frank Lloyd Wright Monograph 1902–1906* (Tokyo: A.D.A. EDITA, 1987), 1–7; and Storrer, *Wright Companion*, 66.

40. Ellen C. Lloyd Jones to William C. Gannett, 12 December 1886 (William C. Gannett Papers, Department of Rare Books and Special Collections, University of Rochester Library, Box IX, Folder 2). On Welsh Unitarian academies in the eighteenth century, see Davies, *"They Thought for Themselves,"* 35–36, 155–164; and Humphreys, *Taliesin Tradition,* 104.

41. William H. Harper, *In the Valley of the Clan: The Story of a School* (n.d., 1902?), 2. See also Hillside Home School, Announcement, 1914–15 (Rare Books Collection, State Historical Society of Wisconsin, Madison); Wright, *Autobiography* (1932), 130; and Mary Ellen Chase, *A Goodly Fellowship* (New York: Macmillan, 1939), 97–98.

42. On Hillside Home School's origins and program, see Harper, *Valley of the Clan;* Chase, *Goodly Fellowship,* 87–121; Florence F. Bohrer, "The Unitarian Hillside Home School," *Wisconsin Magazine of History* 38 (Spring 1955): 151–155; and Barney, *Valley of the God-Almighty Joneses,* 113–123. See also the school's annual announcements for 1888–89, 1891–93, 1895–97, 1898–1900, 1906–7, 1908–10, 1911–12, and 1913–14, and additional circulars (Rare Book Collection, State Historical Society of Wisconsin, Madison).

     On Silsbee and Wright's Hillside Home School Building of 1887, see Hitchcock, *Nature of Materials,* 12; Manson, *Frank Lloyd Wright,* 18–19; William A. Storrer, *The Architecture of Frank Lloyd Wright,* 2nd ed. (Cambridge, Mass.: MIT Press, 1978), 1; Twombly, *Frank Lloyd Wright,* 19; Gill, *Many Masks,* 58; and Storrer, *Wright Companion,* 3.

43. Jane Lloyd Jones to Mrs. Emmons Blaine, Chicago, 15 October 1901, in Letters, 1901–3, by Jane Lloyd Jones, in Mrs. Anita McCormick Blaine Papers (Archives Division, State Historical Society of Wisconsin, Madison). Spring Green's *Weekly Home News* (17 October 1901): 3, noted that "owing to increased attendance the principals have decided to build a new school house. The plans have been drawn and sent from the studio of Frank Ll. Wright, architect, Chicago, and work upon the construction will begin at once."

44. Wright, talk to Taliesin Fellowship, 13 August 1952, quoted in Futagawa, ed., *Frank Lloyd Wright Monograph 1902–1906,* 3. James F. O'Gorman, *H. H. Richardson: Architectural Forms for an American Society* (Chicago: University of Chicago Press, 1988), 139–141, and *Three American Architects: Richardson, Sullivan, and Wright, 1865–1915* (Chicago: University of Chicago Press, 1991), 150, compares Wright's Hillside Home School to Richardson's rural architecture. Roberts sent his son Chapin to the Hillside Home School for four years until his graduation in 1907. The school listed Roberts as a reference (*The Hillside Home School, Catalogue for 1906–1907,* 33, 34, 35, Rare Book Collection, State Historical Society of Wisconsin, Madison). See also Leonard K. Eaton, *Two Chicago Architects and Their Clients: Frank Lloyd Wright and Howard Van Doren Shaw* (Cambridge, Mass.: MIT Press, 1969), 77. Roberts's support for the school is discussed in Charles E. Buell to Jenkin Lloyd Jones, 20 April 1912; Ellen C. Lloyd Jones to Charles E. Roberts, n.d., ca. 1912/1913; and Charles E. Roberts to Mrs. Andrew Porter (née Jane Lloyd Wright), 5 December 1915. By the time the Lloyd Jones sisters transferred control of the school's assets to Wright in May 1915, other than the Lloyd Jones sisters, only Roberts and Susan Lawrence Dana, also a client of Wright, owned shares of stock in the school issued after it had been incorporated in 1904. See "By-Laws of Hillside Home School, adopted March 1904," and the legal agreement between Ellen C. and Jane Lloyd Jones and Frank Lloyd Wright, dated May 1915 (Jane Lloyd Jones Papers, 1899–1940, Archives Division, State Historical Society of Wisconsin, Madison). On the school's financial demise, see Alofsin, *Wright: Lost Years,* 350, n. 57. On Roberts and Unity Temple, see Chapter 2, 72–73, and 283–284, nn. 90–94.

45. "Hillside," [Spring Green, Wis.] *Weekly Home News* (12 December 1901): 1; "The Field," *Unity* 43 (22 June 1899): 297; ibid. (3 August 1899): 394; ibid., 44 (14 Septem-

ber 1899): 490. Spring Green's *Weekly Home News* (12 December 1901): 1, noted that "the neighbors have kindly contributed men and teams to forward the work on the new school house."

46. "Hillside," *Weekly Home News* (6 November 1902): 5.

47. Barney, *Valley of the God-Almighty Joneses,* 73. Wright, *Autobiography* (1932), 8, recalled that his mother's prenatal wish for him to become an architect was linked to images of cathedrals. He wrote: "Fascinated by buildings, she took ten full-page wood-engravings of the old English Cathedrals from 'Old England,' a pictorial periodical to which father had subscribed, had them framed simply in flat oak and hung upon the walls of the room that was to be her son's." Such engravings, several of which Wright kept all his life, were actually published in *Harper's Weekly* from 1877 to 1881. Wright's early exposure to them may have been inconsistent with his family's Nonconformist beliefs, yet Jenkin Lloyd Jones visited many of the same monuments on his first trip to Europe in 1882. See above p. 256, nn. 10–11, and Edgar J. Kaufmann Jr., "Frank Lloyd Wright's Mementoes of Childhood (1982)," in *Nine Commentaries on Frank Lloyd Wright* (New York and Cambridge, Mass.: The Architectural History Foundation and MIT Press, 1989), 34–35.

   The publication to which Wright referred was presumably Knight's *Old England,* published six times from 1845 to 1872. Presented as the largest collection of engravings on all facets of British history ever published in one work, *Old England* included separate sets of colored engravings, though these were not mainly views of English medieval cathedrals. Knight's images accompanied a copious, detailed text on all manner of English artifacts from pre-Roman times, intended "to open to all ranks of the people, at the cheapest rate, a complete view of the Regal, Ecclesiastical, Baronial, Municipal, and Popular Antiquities of England." See Charles Knight, "Advertisement," *Old England,* 2 vols. (1845; reprint, New York: Arno, 1978), I.

48. Knight, *Old England,* I, 3.

49. Ibid., 6. Following antiquarian consensus of the period, Knight linked Stonehenge to other antiquities of the British Isles, which "have a distinct resemblance to other monuments of the same character scattered over Asia and Europe, and even found in the New World, which appear to have had a common origin." Druid origins were thought to be Phoenician or even Indian. Knight's view of Stonehenge as Druidic countered that of English Renaissance architect Inigo Jones, who thought that Stonehenge was Roman in origin. See Joseph Rykwert, *The First Moderns: The Architects of the Eighteenth Century* (Cambridge, Mass.: MIT Press, 1980), 10–12; and Inigo Jones, *The Most Notable Antiquity of Great Britain, Vulgarly Called Stone-Heng,* 3rd ed. (London, 1725).

50. Ralph Waldo Emerson, "Stonehenge," in *English Traits* (1876), in E. W. Emerson, ed., *Complete Works of Ralph Waldo Emerson,* V, 276–277. On Emerson and Thomas Carlyle's visit to Stonehenge, see John McAleer, *Ralph Waldo Emerson: Days of Encounter* (Boston: Little, Brown, 1984), 434–438.

51. Emerson asserted: "All inquiry into antiquity, all curiosity respecting the Pyramids, the excavated cities, Stonehenge, the Ohio circles, Mexico, Memphis, – is the desire to do away [with] this wild, savage, and preposterous There or Then, and introduce in its place the Here and the Now." Emerson, "History (1841)," in Larzer Ziff, ed., *Ralph Waldo Emerson: Selected Essays* (New York: Penguin, 1982), 154.

52. Jenkin Lloyd Jones, "Home Again," *Unity* 10 (1 October 1882): 311.

53. Ibid.

54. Editorial, *Unity* 49 (24 April 1902): 115.

55. On archaeology and ritual at Stonehenge around 1900, see Christopher Chippindale, *Stonehenge Complete* (Ithaca, N.Y.: Cornell University Press, 1983), 164–174; and Sir William Gowland, "Recent Excavations at Stonehenge," *Archaeologia* 58 (1902): 37–118.

56. On the motto "Truth against the World," see Wright, *Autobiography* (1932), 14–15;

Humphreys, *Taliesin Tradition,* 108, 160; Morris, *Matter of Wales,* 155; and Secrest, *Frank Lloyd Wright,* 79–81.

57. Jones, "The Religion of the Majority," *Unity* 4 (16 October 1879): 246.

58. Jane Lloyd Jones, "'In Memoriam': The Lloyd Jones Family," in Graham, ed., *Trilogy,* 39.

59. Harper, *Valley of the Clan,* 6; and Jane Lloyd Jones, "'In Memoriam,'" 38.

60. The biblical verses are Isaiah 40:1, "Comfort ye, comfort ye my people, saith your God," and Isaiah 40:31, "[But] they that wait upon the Lord shall renew their strength; they shall mount up with wings as eagles; they shall run and not be weary; they shall walk and not faint." Wright, *Autobiography* (1932), 4–5, noted his grandfather's citation of other passages from Isaiah 40. See also Jane Lloyd Jones, "'In Memoriam,'" 33, 39. On recurrence of verses from this biblical chapter in Wright's early design for Unity Temple's auditorium, see Chapter 3, 105–106.

61. Barney, *Valley of the God-Almighty Joneses,* 117; Chase, *Goodly Fellowship,* 113; and Futagawa, ed., *Frank Lloyd Wright Monograph 1902–1906,* 2.

62. "Hillside," *Weekly Home News* (6 November 1902): 5.

63. Barney, *Valley of the God-Almighty Joneses,* 117.

64. Harper, *Valley of the Clan,* 6.

65. On the Roberts Room, see Harper, *Valley of the Clan,* 5; Chase, *Goodly Fellowship,* 112–114; Barney, *Valley of the God-Almighty Joneses,* 116; Jane Lloyd Jones, "'In Memoriam,'" 39.

66. Plans for expansion of Silsbee's building were noted in the Board of Trustees, "Reports for the Year Ending January 1, 1889," *All Souls Church Sixth Annual* (Chicago, 1889), 5. An unrealized design for a new parsonage south of Silsbee's church on this annual's inside back cover is shown in Sorrell, "Catalog of Work by J. L. Silsbee," *Prairie School Review* 7 (Fourth Quarter 1970): 18. Alternative plans for expanding the 1886 church to its east were noted in Charles P. Parish to Jones, 10 July 1890 (Jenkin Lloyd Jones Collection, University of Chicago, Box III, Folder 9).

   On the national movement of which All Souls was a part, see George W. Cooke, "The Institutional Church," *New England Magazine* 14 (August 1896): 645–660; and Editorial, *New Unity* 34 (13 August 1896): 396. On the Abraham Lincoln Center, see George W. James, "Jenkin Lloyd Jones and His Master-Work, the Abraham Lincoln Center," *Arena* 37 (April 1907): 375–386; Hitchcock, *Nature of Materials,* 4, 102; Lyttle, *Freedom Moves West,* 221–224; Manson, *Frank Lloyd Wright,* 156–158; Storrer, *Frank Lloyd Wright,* 95; Stuart E. Cohen, *Chicago Architects* (Chicago: Swallow, 1976), 14, 36; Jack Quinan, *Frank Lloyd Wright's Larkin Building: Myth and Fact* (New York and Cambridge, Mass.: The Architectural History Foundation and MIT Press, 1987), 21, 23–24, 26; Futagawa, ed., *Frank Lloyd Wright Monograph 1887–1901* (Tokyo: A.D.A. EDITA, 1987), 108, 164–169; Jerry D. Wright, "Architecture and Liberal Faith: Three Unitarian Efforts to Build for Inclusiveness," Ph.D. diss., Meadville-Lombard Theological School, Chicago, 1988, Chapter 2; Joseph Siry, "The Abraham Lincoln Center in Chicago," *Journal of the Society of Architectural Historians* 50 (September 1991): 235–265; Secrest, *Frank Lloyd Wright,* 141–143; Ellen Christensen, "A Vision of Urban Social Reform," *Chicago History* 22 (March 1993): 50–61; and Storrer, *Wright Companion,* 90.

67. Report of the Trustees, *All Souls Church Ninth Annual* (Chicago, 1892), 6–7.

68. "All Souls' Church," *Chicago Evening Post* (12 September 1892), 5, reprint, "The Eozoic Age of the Lincoln Centre," *Unity* 52 (17 and 24 December 1903): 256.

69. Ibid. Jones's early program of each floor serving a different class of needs adapted the Boston Unitarian leader Rev. James Freeman Clarke's classification of physical, intellectual, moral, and spiritual needs, as discussed in Clarke, *Self-Culture: Physical, Intellectual, Moral, and Spiritual* (Boston: Houghton Mifflin, 1880). On Clarke, see Chapter 2, 53–55, and 272–273, nn. 16–21.

70. Jones, ed., *A Chorus of Faith* (Chicago: Unity, 1893), 11. See John H. Barrows, *The*

World's Parliament of Religions, 3 vols. (Chicago: Parliament, 1893); Walter R. Houghton, ed., *Neely's History of the Parliament of Religions* (Chicago: Alice B. Stockham, 1893); and Charles C. Bonney and Paul Carus, *The World's Parliament of Religions* (Chicago: Open Court, 1896). On Jones's role in the parliament, see Lyttle, *Freedom Moves West,* 205–211; and T. E. Graham, "Jenkin Lloyd Jones and the World's Columbian Exposition of 1893," in Association for Liberal Religious Studies, *Collegium Proceedings* I (1979), 75–81. On the parliament and non-Western religious architecture, see also Chapter 5, 202–203.

71. Lyttle, *Freedom Moves West,* 163–214; and Conrad Wright, *Stream of Light,* 77–94. See also William H. Pease, "Doctrine and Fellowship: William Channing Gannett and the Unitarian Creedal Issue," *Church History* 25 (September 1966): 210–238.

72. American Congress of Liberal Religious Societies, "Articles of Incorporation," quoted in "The Liberal Congress of Religion," *Unity* 40 (9 September 1897): 608. On the origins of the congress, see Graham, "Jenkin Lloyd Jones," 79–81. On its inaugural meetings at Sinai Temple, see *Unity* 33 (31 May, 7 June, and 14 June 1894).

73. Jones, "The American Congress of Liberal Religious Societies," *Unity* 33 (21 June 1894): 263. On All Souls Church's debt to the American Unitarian Association, see "Report of the Auditing Committee on the Building Fund of All Souls Church," *All Souls Church Fourth Annual* (Chicago, 1887), 23–24; and "A Church in Search of a Home – A Retrospect," *Unity* 52 (17 and 24 December 1903): 248.

74. Jones, "Never a Unitarian, Always a Unitarian," *Unity* 33 (21 June 1894): 258–259. See also "Jenkin Lloyd Jones Withdraws from the Unitarians," *Universalist* 11 (19 May 1894): 4.

75. On his second trip to Europe, from February to April 1897, Jones saw the cathedrals and other major monuments of Naples, Rome, Florence, Venice, Milan, Genoa, Nice, Monaco, Marseilles, and Paris. An itinerary is in Jones's souvenir book of his trip (Jones Collection, University of Chicago, Box VI, Folder 13). See Jones, "Editorial Correspondence," *Unity* 39 (15 April 1897): 118–119. Like Jane Addams, Jones envisioned the modern counterparts of cathedrals as centers of social service "to include all men in fellowship and mutual responsibility even as the older spires and pinnacles indicated communion with God." Addams, *Twenty Years at Hull-House* (New York: Macmillan, 1909), 149, quoted in G. Szuberla, "Three Chicago Settlements; Their Architectural Form and Social Meaning," *Journal of the Illinois State Historical Society* 52 (May 1977): 119.

76. Jones, "The New Cathedral: A Study of the Abraham Lincoln Centre," *Unity* 48 (6 February 1902): 358–359. Jones thought that the church's sectarian fragmentation since medieval times had resulted in the demise of the Gothic cathedral as an architectural type signifying human unity. See Jones, "From Luther to Emerson," *Unity* 64 (7 October 1909): 504–507.

77. J. E. McGavick, *History of Holy Angels Parish 1880–1920* (Chicago, 1920), 18–30; and Lane, *Chicago Churches and Synagogues,* 73. Jones noted his response to this church's architecture in "The Inside Work of the Church," *Unity* 44 (28 September 1899): 515. On the Oakland Methodist Church of 1886–87, see n. 1.6. On the second edifice for the Memorial (now Monumental) Baptist Church, see Commission on Chicago Landmarks, Form No. 38-04-14-004. Its construction was noted in *Economist* 22 (9 September 1899): 313.

78. Jones, "The New Cathedral," 359, 360.

79. Ibid., 360.

80. Ibid. In this way the project pointed a "way to the rehabilitation of the church into the place of relative usefulness which it once held in society" (William Kent, chairman of the Building Committee, introductory note to a reprinting of "The New Cathedral," entitled, "The Cathedral, Past and Prospective," *Unity* 52 [17 and 24 December 1903]: 262). Unlike church buildings open mainly for services, the new All Souls was to "'be

alive with personalities, warmed and lighted as needed seven days a week, fifty-two weeks in the year, and all the working hours of every day.'" Jones, "The New Cathedral," 361.

81. Jones, quoted in Evelyn H. Walker, "Into the Abraham Lincoln Center," *Unity* 55 (27 April 1905): 156. On Jones's rationale for the term "center," see Jones, "The New Cathedral," 361–362. On his proposal to legally distinguish All Souls Church from the new Abraham Lincoln Center, see "Our Next Step in Organization," *Unity* 52 (17 and 24 December 1903): 244. The name "Lincoln Centre" had appeared in 1900, in *All Souls Church Seventeenth Annual,* 73, 75. Jones did not wish to call his project a "social settlement" because he felt that this name implied work of a privileged class in the service of another class and thus conveyed an assumption of social division contrary to the ideal of human unity.

82. *All Souls Church Seventeenth Annual,* 75.

83. To Jones, Lincoln was "the greatest and noblest and dearest of Americans who ever lived . . . a man who would represent national and civic interests, and who has already outgrown all partisanship, who has already won his place in the hearts of the representatives of all creeds" (Jones, quoted in "The Social Dedication of the Abraham Lincoln Centre," 252). Jones's presentation of Lincoln's religious views appears in his sermon, "Abraham Lincoln's Church," *Unity* 55 (16 February 1905): 392–396. On Jones's view of himself as a "Lincoln Soldier," see Thomas, "Jenkin Lloyd Jones," 64–65; and Jones, "The New Cathedral," 362.

Jones's appropriation of Lincoln's reputation was part of a larger cultural process of redefining this president's historical image as a model for the Progressive Movement at the turn of the century. Jane Addams similarly cultivated a view of Lincoln's life as an inspiration for urban social work (Addams, *Twenty Years at Hull-House,* 23–42). On the changes in Lincoln's historic image, see Christopher Thomas, "The Lincoln Memorial and Its Architect, Henry Bacon (1866–1924)," Ph.D. diss., Yale University, 1990, 284–326; and Merrill D. Peterson, *Lincoln in American Memory* (New York: Oxford University Press, 1994), esp. 178–179, 183.

Interpretations of Lincoln were shaped in the period just after his death when Wright was born in 1867. Both the Lloyd Joneses' support for Lincoln during the Civil War and Wright's father's local funeral oration for Lincoln suggest why Wright had originally been named Frank Lincoln Wright, a name recorded as changed to Frank Lloyd Wright by 1887, when he had moved to Chicago and joined All Souls Church. There Wright was first listed as a member in *All Souls Church Fourth Annual,* 32, published in the winter of 1887, wherein his address is given as 3921 Vincennes Avenue. Wright's middle name was noted as abbreviated from Lloyd in the University of Wisconsin's yearbook for 1886–87, as cited in Thomas S. Hines Jr., "Frank Lloyd Wright – the Madison Years: Records versus Recollections," *Wisconsin Magazine of History* 50 (Winter 1967): 116. On Wright's original name, and his family's veneration of Lincoln, see Gill, *Many Masks,* 25; and Secrest, *Frank Lloyd Wright,* 39, 49–50, 79, 81.

84. Wright to Jones, 15 May 1894 (Jones Collection, University of Chicago, Box IV, Folder 4). John Lloyd Wright, *My Father Who Is on Earth,* ed. Narciso Menocal (1946; Carbondale: Southern Illinois University Press, 1994), 20–21, stated that Frank Lloyd Wright began work on the new All Souls building in 1888 while still a draftsman for Adler and Sullivan. Corroborating evidence for such an early date for the project's beginning is not known, and the date may refer to Silsbee's All Souls building of 1886, as noted in Storrer, *Wright Companion,* 90.

85. The church acted on the project at its annual meeting in January 1895, when it was noted that "every Sunday morning shows that All Souls Church has unquestionably outgrown the shell which has housed it so comfortably and so well for more than eight years past." A building committee was then appointed "to take steps toward the erection of a more commodious home for the church and its activities," which it was hoped

would materialize within two years ("Notes from the Field," *Unity* 34 [17 January 1895]: 632). The committee was chaired by William Kent, long a trustee of the church. Initial designs for a new All Souls were noted at the annual meeting of January 1898, by which time the church had repaid its debt to the American Unitarian Association and revised its bylaws to become "un-denominational." See "The Abraham Lincoln Centre," *Unity* 52 (17 and 24 December 1903): 243.

Manson, *Frank Lloyd Wright,* 156, cites 1897 as the probable year of Wright's first involvement with the Abraham Lincoln Center, based on recollections of Perkins. Eric E. Davis, In "Dwight Heald Perkins: Social Consciousness and Prairie School Architecture," an essay in the catalogue of an exhibition of the same title co-curated by Davis and Karen Indek at Gallery 400, University of Illinois at Chicago, April 1989, 7, cites 1896 as the year in which Perkins and Wright were jointly commissioned as associated architects. On Perkins, see also Donna R. Nelson, "School Architecture in Chicago during the Progressive Era: The Career of Dwight H. Perkins," Ph.D. diss., Loyola University of Chicago, 1988; Eleanor E. Perkins, *Perkins of Chicago* (Evanston, Ill.: privately printed, 1966); Thomas E. Tallmadge, "Dwight Heald Perkins," *Brickbuilder* 24 (June 1915): 146; and "Dwight H. Perkins – Father of Today's 'New' School Ideas . . . ," *Architectural Forum* 97 (October 1952): 119–125.

86. On Wright, Perkins, and their colleagues in Steinway Hall, see Brooks, *Prairie School,* 27–31, 37–44; and E. E. Davis, "Dwight Heald Perkins," 4–6. Perkins was listed as a member in *All Souls Church First Annual* (Chicago, 1884), 16. Illustrations of Steinway Hall are in Davis, "Dwight Heald Perkins," 4; and *Inland Architect and News Record* 29 (February 1897). See also E. Fuhrer, "The Cinema Unique," *Western Architect* 39 (November 1930): 175–177; and N. Remisoff, "The Punch and Judy Theatre," ibid., 182–183.

87. Wright, *Genius and the Mobocracy* (New York: Duell, Sloan and Pearce, 1949), 61. On Wright's claims to involvement with design of Adler and Sullivan's commercial buildings, see Quinan, *Larkin Building,* 3–7.

88. Wright to Jones, 25 February 1898, © Frank Lloyd Wright Foundation 1990, Microfiche Id. No. J001B01.

89. Jones to W. C. Gannett, 27 February 1899 (William C. Gannett Papers, Department of Rare Books and Special Collections, University of Rochester Library, Box 15, Folder 4). Wright and Perkins's joint commission for the new All Souls Church building was noted in "Brick and Terra Cotta Work in American Cities," *Brickbuilder* 7 (November 1898): 240; and ibid., 8 (January 1899): 17–18.

90. *Chicago Architectural Club Annual* (1900), 82–84. The exterior perspective of the same project was published in "Lincoln Centre," *All Souls Church Seventeenth Annual,* 73; and Robert C. Spencer Jr., "The Work of Frank Lloyd Wright," *Architectural Review* [Boston] 7 (June 1900): 71–72.

91. Spencer, "Work of Frank Lloyd Wright," 71.

92. Manson, *Frank Lloyd Wright,* 158, and Quinan, *Larkin Building,* 21, compared this version of Wright and Perkins's design for the All Souls Building with Adler and Sullivan's Wainwright Building in St. Louis. Wright assessed this work in "Louis H. Sullivan – His Work," *Architectural Record* 56 (July 1924): 29; and *Genius and the Mobocracy,* 59–60.

93. "Lincoln Centre," *All Souls Church Seventeenth Annual,* 73.

94. Wright, *Genius and the Mobocracy,* 61. On the Meyer Building, see Hugh Morrison, *Louis Sullivan: Prophet of Modern Architecture* (New York: W. W. Norton, 1935), 168–169; and Carl W. Condit, *The Chicago School of Architecture: Commercial and Public Building in the Chicago Area, 1875–1925* (Chicago: University of Chicago Press, 1964), 136–137. Its semi-mill construction is documented in the Historic American Buildings Survey (1963), H.A.B.S. Survey No. ILL-1026, and in an appraisal report of 1952, notes on which are in the Richard Nickel Committee Files, Office of John Vinci, A.I.A.,

Chicago. The projected Meyer Building's structure was noted in the *Economist* 7 (20 February 1892): 275; and ibid., 7 (9 April 1892): 554.

95. Wright and Perkins to Ernest Flagg, 4 March 1901, © Frank Lloyd Wright Foundation 1990, Microfiche Id. No. F001A01. Like Perkins, Flagg advocated an indigenous and innovative American architecture, in such addresses as "The Architectural Society and Its Progressive Influence," quoted in *Architectural Annual* 1 (Philadelphia, 1900), 119.

96. On Flagg's religious architecture, see Mardges Bacon, *Ernest Flagg: Beaux-Arts Architect and Urban Reformer* (New York and Cambridge, Mass.: The Architectural History Foundation and MIT Press, 1986), 107–112.

97. Flagg to Wright and Perkins, 20 March 1901 (Jenkin Lloyd Jones Collection, Meadville-Lombard Theological School, Chicago).

98. Jones to Wright, 8 May 1901, Jones Letter Book, 13 April 1900–25 June 1901, 558 (Jones Collection, Meadville-Lombard).

99. Ibid.

100. Jones to Wright, 2 January 1902, Jones Letter Book, 9 July 1901–18 June 1902, 334–336 (Jones Collection, Meadville-Lombard).

101. "The Abraham Lincoln Centre: A Ground-Breaking Festival," *Unity* 49 (26 June 1902): 261–264. Kent to Jones, 21 July 1902, advocated commencing construction to show good faith to contributors (Jones Collection, Meadville-Lombard).

102. Jones to Wright, 13 January 1902, Jones Letter Book, 9 July 1901–18 June 1902, 360 (Jones Collection, Meadville-Lombard).

103. "The Work of Frank Lloyd Wright," *Chicago Architectural Annual* (Chicago, 1902), 58. In the project of 1902, a pastor's study, Unity Club, library, and offices of the church remained at street level. Above the auditorium, the fourth floor was given over to residential quarters and seminary rooms for students of divinity and social work whom Jones hoped to attract to the center (Jones, "The New Cathedral," 361). The fifth story, linked inside by stairs to a sixth-floor mezzanine, was to be "a club room floor divided into large halls, with [the] mezzanine for gymnasium work." See Spencer, "Work of Frank Lloyd Wright," 58.

104. Materials for ornamental motifs on the exterior of Wright and Perkins's design of 1902 are noted on Frank Lloyd Wright Foundation drawings 0010.030 (north, or alley, elevation) and 0010.031 (west, or Langley Avenue, elevation). On Unity Temple's details and ornament of cast concrete, see Chapter 4, 150–154, and 309 n. 54.

105. Jones to Wright, 13 January 1902, Jones Letter Book, 9 July 1901–18 June 1902, 360 (Jones Collection, Meadville-Lombard).

106. Wright to Jones, n.d. © Frank Lloyd Wright Foundation 1990, Microfiche Id. No. J001C01. Christensen, "Vision of Urban Social Reform," 58, notes that Wright's quote is a reworded line from Gilbert and Sullivan's *Mikado*. On Wright's youthful interest in their music, see Wright, *Autobiography* (1932), 32–33; and Secrest, *Frank Lloyd Wright*, 68, 136.

107. Kent to Wright and Perkins, 21 July 1902 (Jones Collection, Meadville-Lombard). Kent's committee further charged that in the overhauled design, "the loggia must be wiped off, . . . the corner columns must be wiped off," and that all parts of such a new scheme "must pass muster as to light, ventilation and practical workableness for the purposes outlined. Also must be considered as 'good' in its exterior. These points must be decided by one or two disinterested and expert men." Jones wrote to Wright and Perkins: "You see it is really a concession to my desires that your plans and you should have one more fair test. It involves a hopeless delay of time even if you can come within the requirements. As you know, I did my best to avert this overhauling. If your plans fail to go through then the committee will proceed I think to get competitive designs. . . . You ought to know, perhaps contrary to your expectations, that I was the only one who fought for your plans." Jones to Wright and Perkins, 22 July 1902, Jones Letter Book, 18 June 1902–17 June 1903, 40 (Jones Collection, Meadville-Lombard).

108. Jones to Wright and Perkins, 2 August 1902, Jones Letter Book, 18 June 1902–17 June 1903, 66–67, 69 (Jones Collection, Meadville-Lombard). Jones's remarks suggest that Wright may have defended his design with references to the classical tradition of monumental architecture. In his critique of the elevation, Jones may have been urging Wright to go beyond what Wright had thought of as "radical" interpretations of the classical orders in the piers and lintels of his earlier elevations. If so, then it was Jones who sought functional form, while Wright, in this his first tall building, was still working in a style like Sullivan's. On Wright's early apprenticeship with Sullivan, see Wright, *Autobiography* (1932), 88–91, 93–96, 101–107; Hitchcock, *Nature of Materials*, 7–14; Wright, *Genius and the Mobocracy*, 39–67; Manson, *Frank Lloyd Wright*, 21–34, and "Sullivan and Wright: An Uneasy Union of Celts," *Architectural Record* 118 (November 1955): 297–300; Twombly, *Frank Lloyd Wright*, 19–25; Gill, *Many Masks*, 60–86, 94–101; Kaufmann, "Frank Lloyd Wright's 'Lieber Meister,'" in *Nine Commentaries on Frank Lloyd Wright*, 37–62; and Secrest, *Frank Lloyd Wright*, 104–123.

In August 1902 Jones had asked Perkins if he would be designing the next façade, "for after all our discussions it would be interesting to see the work of another hand." Jones to Perkins, 30 August 1902, Jones Letter Book, 18 June 1902–17 June 1903, 120 (Jones Collection, Meadville-Lombard). In September Jones urged Wright that "the matter of the façade must not be delayed. If you cannot present it promptly after the estimates are in, do let Dwight take hold of it. . . . I do not care who does it, only we must have the elevation and I shall expect my wishes respected in that elevation." Jones to Wright, 6 September 1902, Jones Letter Book, 18 June 1902–17 June 1903, 137 (Jones Collection, Meadville-Lombard). Wright wanted the façade's final design to be "put off as late as possible" after specifications and plans were completed toward the end of January 1903. Jones to Wright, 22 December 1902, Jones Letter Book, 18 June 1902–17 June 1903, 338 (Jones Collection, Meadville-Lombard).

109. W. Kent, "Building Committee," *All Souls Church Twentieth Annual* (Chicago, 1903). Drawings for the project of February 1903 are in the collection of the Frank Lloyd Wright Foundation, numbered as 0010.003–.020. They are not labeled with the name of Wright or Perkins. Six of these (drawings no. 0010.004, 0010.006, 0010.013, 0010.015, 0010.011, 0010.012) have been published in Futagawa, ed., *Frank Lloyd Wright Monograph 1887–1901*, 164–169. These are presumably drawings that Wright was finishing in order to submit the design for bidding by 1 February 1903, as noted in Perkins to Jones, 19 December 1902 (Jones Collection, Meadville-Lombard).

110. Kent, "Building Committee." The revised elevation of 1903 still recalled Adler and Sullivan's Wainwright Building, even though the Abraham Lincoln Center housed different functions inside and was to have outer walls of bearing brick piers and not structural steel columns. In Sullivan's view a building's exterior form should express its distinct type and structure. If Wright had adhered to Sullivan's theory of the relation of character to expression, then the unique program of the Abraham Lincoln Center would have suggested that its form be different from that of a tall office building. Perhaps because this was Wright's first attempt to design a monumental public edifice, he fell back on Sullivan's style for buildings of comparable height, rather than fully exploring the implications of Sullivan's concept that form follows function. Sullivan's statement of this principle appeared in "The Tall Office Building Artistically Considered" (1896), in R. Twombly, ed., *Louis Sullivan: The Public Papers* (Chicago: University of Chicago Press, 1988), 103–112. One interpretation of Sullivan's functional theory is in J. Siry, *Carson Pirie Scott: Louis Sullivan and the Chicago Department Store* (Chicago: University of Chicago Press, 1988), 235–237.

On the south elevation of Wright and Perkins's project of 1903, four stout piers with ornamental terra cotta capitals, the lower halves of which appear to be open books, support a concrete lintel above the first floor. What these books were to represent is not shown in the drawing or noted elsewhere. As ornamental motifs, these capitals resemble those at the entrance to Wright's Oak Park studio of 1895. These motifs were first published in Alfred H. Granger, "An Architect's Studio," *House Beautiful* 7 (December 1899): 36; and "Work of Frank Lloyd Wright," *Chicago Architectural Annual* (1902): 47.

111. Barney, *Valley of the God-Almighty Joneses,* 100–101. Need of plans and specifications for bids is noted in Jones to Wright, 19 February 1903, Jones Letter Book, 18 June 1902–17 July 1903, 430–431 (Jones Collection, Meadville-Lombard).

112. Perkins to Jones, 15 August 1903, included a copy of the contract of 8 June 1903 between Perkins and Jones and the building committee for Lincoln Center. Perkins to Jones, 3 March 1903, referred to his role as that of Jones's "constructing architect" (Jones Collection, Meadville-Lombard).

113. Jones dated the start of building in "The Abraham Lincoln Centre," *Unity* 54 (22 December 1904): 258. On the building's opening and dedication in the spring of 1905, see E. H. Walker, "Into the Abraham Lincoln Centre," 155–156; "Lincoln Centre Flag Up," *Chicago Tribune* (28 May 1905): 8; "Church in a New Home," ibid. (29 May 1905): 14; and E. H. Walker, "Dedication of the Abraham Lincoln Centre," *Unity* 55 (1 June 1905): 229–230. Their correspondence indicates that Perkins worked with Jones to the building's completion, as their contract indicated (Jones Collection, Meadville-Lombard).

114. "Our Artist Helper," *Unity* 52 (17 and 24 December 1903): 244. Wright's uncle emphasized that "the severest simplicity has been aimed at; no money will be spent on exterior embellishments, because all will be needed to furnish the interior with the tools and life that will justify the expenditure" ("Abraham Lincoln Centre," 256). Jones admired Adler and Sullivan's Jewish Training School in Chicago of 1889–90 (Siry, "Abraham Lincoln Center," 240–241). Simplicity was typical of other institutional church buildings of this period, like Bosworth and Holden's Bronx Church House, 171st Street and Fulton Avenue, New York City, opened in 1907. This building served as the headquarters of social work for all Episcopal parishes in its borough. See "The Bronx Church House," *Architectural Record* 22 (December 1907): 509–511.

115. "Abraham Lincoln Centre," 256. Jones asserted that the "Lincoln Centre has one front on the avenue and another on the alley, and both are builded [sic] of the same material and carry the same architectural façade. We have not had cut stone, or pressed brick for a front – with common brick, such as are builded into livery stables, for the rear. Our work, like our building, stands four-square to the world, bearing the same front and carrying the same hospitality all around" (Jones, "Thirty Years After," *The Abraham Lincoln Centre / All Souls Church: Reports for 1912* [Chicago, 1913], 122). In such ways Jones hoped that "the building will be emblematic of the hearty, straight-forward ideal of the man for whom it is named," and that, when completed, "'it will have a soul, the light and beauty of which will shine through and beyond its walls'" ("The Abraham Lincoln Centre," 256).

116. Wright to Curtis W. Reese, *Unity* 141 (March–April 1955): 15.

117. Barney, *Valley of the God-Almighty Joneses,* 101.

118. Walker, "Into the Abraham Lincoln Centre," 156.

CHAPTER 2
UNITY CHURCH IN OAK PARK TO 1905

1. Andreas, *History of Cook County,* 785. The rationale for the congregation's name appeared in "Unity Church," *Oak Leaves (Fifth Anniversary Number)* (27 April 1907): 100.

2. On Universalism, see Robinson, *Unitarians and Universalists;* Russell E. Miller, *The Larger Hope,* 2 vols. (Boston: Unitarian Universalist Historical Society, 1979, 1985); and

Ernest Cassara, ed., *Universalism in America: A Documentary History of a Liberal Faith* (Boston: Beacon, 1971).

3. Denominational histories of Unitarians in the United States include George Willis Cooke, *Unitarianism in America* (Boston: American Unitarian Association, 1902); Earl Morse Wilbur, *History of Unitarianism,* 2 vols. (Cambridge, Mass.: Harvard University Press, 1945, 1952); Wright, *Stream of Light;* and Sydney E. Ahlstrom and Jonathan S. Carey, *An American Reformation: A Documentary History of Unitarian Christianity* (Middletown, Conn.: Wesleyan University Press, 1985). See also Ahlstrom, *A Religious History of the American People* (New Haven: Yale University Press, 1972), 388–402. European antecedents of American liberal religions are detailed in Joseph H. Allen and Richard Eddy, *A History of the Unitarians and Universalists in the United States,* American Church History Series, vol. 10 (New York: Christian Literature, 1894), 1–169, 255–371. On American Unitarians and modern thought, see William R. Hutchison, *The Modernist Impulse in American Protestantism* (Cambridge, Mass.: Harvard University Press, 1976), 12–40. On attitudes toward specific creeds among American Unitarians and Universalists, see Robert M. Hemstreet, "Identity and Ideology: Creeds and Creedlessness in Unitarianism and Universalism," Unitarian Universalist Association Advanced Study Paper No. 3, 1977.

4. Quoted in Chulak, *A People Moving thru Time,* 3; and "Unity Church," 100. Unity Church's constitution declared simply that "the object of this society is to promote moral and spiritual improvement and the dissemination and practice of the truths and principles of Christianity," with no other reference to specific points of doctrine.

5. Unity Church's first building was described in "A Suburban Sanctuary," *Chicago Tribune* (12 August 1872): 6. The structure may have been modeled after that of St. Paul's Universalist Church in Chicago, built in 1855–56 by William Boyington on the northwest corner of Wabash and Van Buren Street. See Phillips, *Chicago and Her Churches,* 167–169; "St. Paul's Church Buildings," *Universalist* 9 (17 December 1892): 5; and Bluestone, *Constructing Chicago,* 80, 84. Edwin O. Gale (1832–1913), a founder of Unity Church, gave $5,600 of the almost $14,000 needed to complete its edifice. When the new building had a service of dedication in August 1872, even Oak Park's predominant Congregationalists had yet to begin construction of their new edifice, so Unity Church was the village's earliest prominent church building. See "Unity Church Fire," *Oak Leaves* (10 June 1905): 13; Chulak, *A People Moving thru Time,* 2, 5; "Unity Church," 100–101; and "Death of E. O. Gale," *Oak Leaves* (25 January 1913): 3, 10.

   Edwin O. Gale was one of the sons of Abram Gale (1796–1881), a founding member of the First (later St. Paul's) Universalist Society in Chicago, after Abram Gale came from Boston with his wife. She had been a staunch member of that city's main Universalist church founded by the movement's most influential American thinker, Rev. Hosea Ballou. Abram Gale moved to Oak Park in 1866, where he was remembered as the supportive patriarch of Unity Church until his death. On Abram Gale, see Andreas, *History of Cook County,* 788–789; Edwin O. Gale, *Reminiscences of Early Chicago and Vicinity* (Chicago: Fleming H. Revell, 1902), 19, 68, 363–368; "Universalism in Early Chicago," *Universalist Leader* 6 (16 May 1903): 614–615; "The Early Days in Chicago," ibid. (13 June 1903): 754–755; Jack, "'Unitarian-Universalist Co-operation in Chicago," 48–49; and Henry Ericsson, *Sixty Years a Builder* (1942; reprint, New York: Arno, 1972), 176–177, 197. On the early Universalists around Boston, see Justin Winsor, ed., *Memorial History of Boston,* 4 vols. (Boston: Ticknor, 1886), III, 483–508. On Ballou, see Allen and Eddy, *Unitarians and Universalists,* 427–460.

6. "Unity Church Destroyed by Fire," *Universalist Leader* (17 June 1905): 753. The auditorium's capacity and the church's membership were noted in "A Suburban Sanctuary," 6.

7. Halley, *Pictorial Oak Park,* 46; and "Struck by Lightning," *Oak Park Reporter-Argus* (10 June 1905): 4. The addition of the organ was noted in "Unity Church Fire," 14.

8. "Suburban Sanctuary," 6. Elaborate arrangements of flowers were a noted feature of worship in old Unity Church. See "Church News," *Universalist Leader* 2 (22 April 1899): 14.

9. On auditorium churches in Chicago from the 1860s, see Bluestone, *Constructing Chicago,* 85–86. On auditorium churches in the United States in the late nineteenth century, see Egbert, "Religious Expression in American Architecture," 382–385; James F. White, *Protestant Worship and Church Architecture* (New York: Oxford University Press, 1964), 124; and Jeanne Halgren Kilde, "Spiritual Armories: A Social and Architectural History of Neo-Medieval Churches in the U.S., 1869–1910," Ph.D. diss., University of Minnesota, 1991. American adaptation of auditorium plans corresponded to English Victorian auditorium churches for non-Anglican congregations in suburbs of London and other large cities. These large, centrally planned structures were built from the 1870s. See Martin S. Briggs, *Puritan Architecture and Its Future* (London: Lutterworth, 1946), 39–47. Comparable large, centrally and polygonally planned churches were also built in German cities from the 1880s. See K. E. O. Fritsch, *Der Kirchenbau des Protestantismus, von der Reformation bis zur Gegenwart,* edited by the Berlin Society of Architects (Berlin: Ernst Toeche, 1893), 372–406.

10. Unity Church, "Members Signatures," 2–3, in Unity Church Historical Files. Wright also retained membership in All Souls Church. Decisive growth of Unity Church, and of Oak Park, dated from the economic upswing of the 1880s. In May 1886 Rev. Augusta Chapin (1836–1905) became the church's sixth minister, serving until November 1891. The second woman to be ordained in the Universalist faith, Rev. Chapin later chaired the Women's Committee of the Department of Religion at the Columbian Exposition of 1893, which was linked to the World's Parliament of Religions. There she worked with Rev. Jenkin Lloyd Jones, who earlier may have helped his sister Anna and her children settle with Chapin in Oak Park. On Chapin, see C. F. Hitchings, "Unitarian and Universalist Women Ministers," *Journal of the Universalist Historical Society* 10 (1975): 43–44. On her service at Unity Church, see Chulak, *A People Moving thru Time,* 11–13.

In May 1887 Wright's mother, Anna, wrote from Madison to her son, who was then living near Jones's All Souls Church: "If you will find a place in Chicago where you are likely to stay a year I will rent my house [in Madison], will get Jennie a school in some good place and Maginel and I will come to Chicago" (Anna Lloyd Wright to Frank Lloyd Wright, 28 May 1887; © Frank Lloyd Wright Foundation 1992, Microfiche Id. No. W025C06). In 1887 Anna L. Wright was listed as residing at Rev. Chapin's address at 214 Forest Avenue in Oak Park, where Wright and his sisters also lived until Wright built his first home in 1889. *Oak Park Directory,* Oak Park, Ill., 1887, 30, 54. On Anna Lloyd Wright and her family's residence at the home of Rev. Chapin, see Wright, *Autobiography* (1932), 78; and Barney, *Valley of the God-Almighty Joneses,* 127–128.

11. Chulak, *A People Moving thru Time,* 13, 29; (Chicago) *Universalist* 9 (12 March 1892): 5; ibid. (14 May 1892): 5.

12. Johonnot's Quaker maternal ancestors had emigrated from England to Massachusetts in 1635. His father's Huguenot forebears had left France in 1688 after the revocation of the Edict of Nantes. Two of his great-grandfathers had fought in the War of Independence (one at the Battle of Bunker Hill) and Johonnot was active in the Sons of the American Revolution. His father enlisted in the Union Army in 1861, and died in the service the next year. Raised as a Methodist, Johonnot later referred to memories of the White Mountains of New Hampshire and the granite coast of Maine. Self-supporting from the age of thirteen, he worked his way through Bates College, graduating in 1879 as salutatorian of his class. He taught school and then studied law at Boston University, where he completed a three-year program of study in one, graduating with high honors in 1882. Admitted to the bar the following spring, Johonnot had his own legal practice in Boston from 1883 to 1885, when he also served as the principal of a large night

school. Brief accounts of his life appear in "Dr. Johonnot," *Oak Leaves* (2 May 1902): 3–4, and "Sketch of Dr. Johonnot," *Oak Park Reporter-Argus* (24 February 1906): 3. On the Johonnot family among emigrés in colonial Boston, see Jon Butler, *The Huguenots in America* (Cambridge, Mass.: Harvard University Press, 1983), 79–89; and Charles W. Baird, *History of the Huguenot Emigration to America,* 2 vols. (1885; reprint, Baltimore: Regional, 1966), 212, 268, 281. See also pp. 58–59, and 273, n. 26.

13. Assessments of Rev. Johonnot's ministry at Oak Park appear in "Johonnot Resigns," *Oak Leaves* (5 June 1909): 3; "Dr. Johonnot and Oak Park," ibid. (12 June 1909): 11; "The General Convention," *Universalist Leader* 12 (3 July 1909): 857; "The Testimonial," *Oak Leaves* (9 July 1910): 4; and "Chicago Letter," *Universalist Leader* 13 (16 July 1910): 874–875. Johonnot's Unitarian and Universalist ordinations are noted in *General Catalogue of the Divinity School of Harvard University 1905* (Cambridge, Mass., 1905), 108.

14. "Dr. Rodney F. Johonnot," *Christian Leader* 35 (16 April 1932): 495. Johonnot's pastoral success at Oak Park was a pattern that would repeat in his subsequent ministries elsewhere. He was described as "eminently successful as a pastor, not alone because of his eloquence as a speaker, but also because of his devotion to his church. He always assumed the responsibilities of his parish in large measure; and the business ability necessary for a successful executive was augmented by his legal study and practise."

15. Wright, *Autobiography* (1932), 153.

16. Johonnot's association with Clarke was noted in "Dr. Johonnot," 3–4; and "Dr. Rodney F. Johonnot," *Christian Leader* 35 (16 April 1932): 494–495. On Johonnot's attendance at Clarke's church, see "Dr. R. F. Johonnot," *Lewiston [Maine] Journal* (7 April 1932): 2. On Clarke's work, see Edward Everett Hale, ed., *James Freeman Clarke: Autobiography, Diary, and Correspondence* (Boston and New York: Houghton Mifflin, 1891); and Arthur S. Bolster Jr., *James Freeman Clarke: Disciple to Advancing Truth* (Boston: Beacon, 1954).

17. Bolster, *James Freeman Clarke,* 140–142. On the case for voluntary support of churches, see Clarke, "The Pew System," *Christian World* 1 (23 December 1843); "A Church and Its Methods," *Christian Register* 47 (29 August 1868); and "The Experiment of the Free Church: Its Difficulties and Advantages," *Christian Register* 55 (23 September 1876). On the origins of the Church of the Disciples, see Hale, ed., *James Freeman Clarke,* 144–168.

18. The cornerstone-laying of Samuels's building for the Church of the Disciples was noted in the *Boston Evening Transcript* (9 July 1868): 4. On the church's dedication, see "Church of the Disciples," *Boston Daily Advertiser* (1 March 1869): 1. On the building, see *King's Handbook of Boston,* 7th ed. (Cambridge, Mass.: Moses King, 1885), 177, 191; Hale, ed., *James Freeman Clarke,* 211–212; Charles S. Damrell, *A Half-Century of Boston's Building* (Boston: Louis P. Hager, 1895), 42; and Bolster, *James Freeman Clarke,* 298–300. Concord Baptist Church bought the building in 1947.

19. "Churches of the Disciples," 1.

20. James Freeman Clarke to his sister, 14 March 1869, quoted in Hale, ed., *James Freeman Clarke,* 211. On the cost of the building, see Bolster. 298–299.

21. See Clarke's poem, "To the Old Meeting House, Hingham," *Christian World* 1 (30 September 1843). On this structure, see Chapter 3, 93, and 289–290, n. 52. Atop its polygonal, polychromed slate roof, the Church of the Disciples had an octagonal lantern "surmounted by a Greek cross and an open globe," rather than the convention of a Latin cross atop a solid orb ("Church of the Disciples," 1). Samuels's exterior thus combined references to a square meetinghouse, a neo-Gothic parish church, and a lanterned roof like the Church of San Vitale in Ravenna, which may have been valued for its associations with earlier Christian traditions. Such a reference would antedate the sources of neighboring spired churches, in the same way as All Souls Church in New York. Yet unlike this monument, Clarke's new Church of the Disciples did not stand out in its residential district, as if its architecture signified the institution's identification with

its neighborhood. As Clarke wrote in praise of Boston's older monuments, "a part of the moral education of a community consists of the influence of surrounding objects." Clarke, "The Value and Influence of Historic Landmarks on Education and Character," *Christian Register* 51 (14 December 1872).

22. On King's Chapel, see Henry W. Foote, *Annals of King's Chapel,* 2 vols. (Boston, 1882, 1886), II, 42–127; Carl Bridenbaugh, *Peter Harrison: First American Architect* (Chapel Hill: The University of North Carolina Press, 1949), 54–63; Hugh Morrison, *Early American Architecture* (New York: Oxford University Press, 1952), 450–453; and William H. Pierson Jr., *American Buildings and Their Architects, I: The Colonial and Neoclassical Styles* (1970; reprint, New York: Oxford University Press, 1986), 145–146. Johonnot cited the chapel in a letter, *Universalist Leader* 10 (21 December 1907): 1617. See Chapter 5, 198. For King's Chapel, Harrison planned a spired tower, but it was not built. This motif, like other elements of the design, was inspired by earlier London churches of James Gibbs, notably St. Martin-in-the-Fields. This source is especially evident inside King's Chapel, where rows of coupled Corinthian columns support the galleries and ceiling with plaster groin vaults.

23. Unity Temple's resemblance to granite was noted in Wright, "In the Cause of Architecture (1908)," 212; *Christian Register* 87 (5 November 1908): 26–27; "Opening Service in Unity Temple, Oak Park, Ill.," *Universalist Leader* 11 (7 November 1908): 28–29; and "A Masterpiece in Concrete Work," *Cement World* 2 (15 February 1909): 747. See Chapter 4, 146, and Chapter 5, 199.

24. Clarke, "Dr. Freeman and King's Chapel," *Christian Register* 51 (30 March 1872); "King's Chapel, Boston. How It Became a Unitarian Church," *Independent* 32 (5 February 1880): 6–7; and Hale, ed., *James Freeman Clarke,* 81–82. On Freeman and King's Chapel, see also Foote, ed., *Annals of King's Chapel,* II, 378–406; Allen and Eddy, *Unitarians and Universalists,* 154–159, 185; and Robinson, *Unitarians and Universalists,* 259–261.

25. "Address of Rev. James Freeman Clarke," in "King's Chapel: The Two Hundredth Anniversary Celebration," *Christian Register* 65 (23 December 1886): 812–813. At this time, Clarke wrote: "Among the ancient buildings of Boston which have not yet passed away, besides Faneuil Hall, the Old State House, and the old South Church, the King's Chapel is most conspicuous. Situated in the heart of the city, its old gray walls and its square tower of rough stone give an archaic character to its exterior" (Clarke, "King's Chapel," 6).

26. On the Faneuil family's support for King's Chapel and the Johonnot family's membership, see Butler, *Huguenots in America,* 84–85. On Huguenot affiliation with the chapel, see Foote, *Annals of King's Chapel,* II, 153–154; and Robert M. Kingdon, "Why Did the Huguenot Refugees in the American Colonies Become Episcopalian?" *Historical Magazine of the Protestant Episcopal Church* 49 (1980): 317–335. Earlier, in 1716, the Johonnots were among those who had financed a small stone chapel known as the French Church, home of the city's Huguenot community to the mid-eighteenth century. On this nonextant building, see Percival Merritt, "The French Protestant Church in Boston," *Publications of the Colonial Society of Massachusetts* 26 (1926): 323–337.

27. Notices of Johonnot's trip to Europe appeared in *Universalist Leader* 6 (2 May 1903): 564; "The Johonnots in Europe," *Oak Leaves* (26 June 1903): 10; *Universalist Leader* 6 (18 July 1903): 915; "The Johonnots Return," *Oak Leaves* (18 September 1903): 8; *Universalist Leader* 6 (19 September 1903): 1201. In January and February 1904 Johonnot gave a series of five lectures on his travels, illustrated with his own photographs of sites including Chester, Stratford, Warwick, Oxford, London, and Canterbury in England; Belgium; the Rhine; northern Switzerland and Geneva; Milan, Venice, Florence, and Rome in Italy; and Paris. See "Dr. Johonnot's Subjects," *Oak Leaves* (1 January 1904): 21; "Church Notices," ibid. (8 January 1904): 11; and "The Last 'Travel Talk,'" ibid. (5 February 1904): 13.

Johonnot was in Rome at the time of the coronation of Pius IX. On his return, one account noted that, while Johonnot "recognizes the great value of the treasuries of European art and architecture, which it is impossible to match in the new world," he nonetheless felt that "so far as countries and peoples and natural scenery go, America so far outranks the old world that to an American acquainted with his own country the old countries seem very tame and commonplace" ("The Johonnots Return," 8).

28. Johonnot, letter, *Universalist Leader* 10 (21 December 1907): 1617.

29. "The Johonnots in Europe," *Oak Leaves* (26 June 1903): 10. On English Unitarian thought, see Johonnot, "The Religion of a Great Thinker – James Martineau," *Universalist Leader* 3 (3 March 1900): 270; and ibid. (10 March 1900): 302.

30. On English Unitarian chapels within the tradition of Nonconformist architecture to the early nineteenth century, see Ronald P. Jones, *Nonconformist Church Architecture* (London: Lindsey, 1914), 3–33; John Betjeman, "Nonconformist Architecture," *Architectural Review* 88 (December 1940): 160–174; Briggs, *Puritan Architecture,* 11–37; H. Lismer Short, "The Evolution of Unitarian Church Buildings," *Transactions of the Unitarian Historical Society* (1949): 146–153; and Hague, *Unitarian Heritage.*

31. Formerly an Anglican, Rev. Theophilus Lindsey (1723–1808) began his pioneering Unitarian ministry in 1774. Four years later he built Essex Chapel as a reconstruction of the hall of a seventeenth-century house in Essex Street, between the Strand and the Thames Embankment. See Allen and Eddy, *Unitarians and Universalists,* 149–154; Mortimer Rowe, *The Story of Essex Hall* (London: Lindsey, 1959), 11–25; and Hague, *Unitarian Heritage,* 52, 108–109. In this chapel (see Fig. 48), above the lofty ceiling was a large circular lantern with clerestory windows beneath a dome. The organ and lamps were added later. In front of the pulpit was a table pew for Communion. This table was to a chapel what an altar was to a church. See Andrew L. Drummond, *The Church Architecture of Protestantism* (Edinburgh: T. & T. Clark, 1934), 24, 42–43; and G. W. O. Addleshaw and Frederick Etchells, *The Architectural Setting of Anglican Worship* (London: Faber and Faber, 1948), 25–29.

32. See Chapter 4, 192. Secrest, *Frank Lloyd Wright,* 180, noted that Unity Temple's space was consistent specifically with Welsh Nonconformist chapels in its close disposition of seating around the focal pulpit.

33. "Church News," *Universalist Leader* 4 (13 April 1901): 475.

34. "City of Many Churches," *Oak Park Reporter-Argus* (5 May 1906): 8. On Oak Park's population and churches, see *Oak Park Argus* (14 December 1900): 2, cited in Arthur E. Le Gacy, "Improvers and Preservers: A History of Oak Park, Illinois, 1833–1940," Ph.D. diss., University of Chicago, 1967, 48. In Oak Park of 1900, church affiliation, measured as a percentage of total Sunday school attendance in the community, was Congregationalist (40.5%), Methodist (14.3%), Presbyterian (11.7%), Baptist (9.5%), Episcopal (8.0%), Lutheran (5.0%), Universalist and Unitarian (4.0%), and Roman Catholic (3.5%).

35. On the First Congregational Church's first building of 1873, see Andreas, *History of Cook County,* 785; and Charles Gregersen, *Dankmar Adler: His Theatres and Auditoriums* (Athens, Ohio: Swallow and Ohio University Press, 1990), 10, 43–44. The building stood on a plot of land donated by a founder, James Scoville, whose mansion and grounds to the east later became Scoville Park. In 1884–85 Adler and Sullivan enlarged James W. Scoville's factory building (of 1877, by Burling and Adler) at 619-631 West Washington Street in Chicago. See Robert Twombly, *Louis Sullivan: His Life and Work* (New York: Elizabeth Sifton Books/Viking Penguin, 1986), 128; and Paul E. Sprague, "Sullivan's Scoville Building, A Chronology," *Prairie School Review* 11 (Third Quarter 1974): 16–23. The architecture of First Congregational Church in Oak Park was probably modeled on Chicago's Union Park Congregational Church of 1869–71, by Gurdon Randall. On this building, see Lane, *Chicago Churches and Synagogues,* 30–31; and Bluestone, *Building Chicago,* 85–86.

36. *The First Congregational Church, Souvenir of the Thirty-Eighth Anniversary of Its Organ-*

ization (Oak Park, 1901), 10–11; Rev. William E. Barton, "First Congregational Church," *Oak Leaves (Fifth Anniversary Number)* (27 April 1907): 98; "First Congregational," *Oak Leaves (Forty-Third Anniversary Edition)* (23 February 1924): 191; and "Death of N. S. Patton," *Oak Leaves* (20 March 1915): 3, 7. On Patton, see also "Mr. Normand S. Patton," *Oak Leaves* (25 December 1903): 1, 20; Withey, *American Architects,* 460; and *Journal of the American Institute of Architects* 3 (June 1915): 248. A new church was built on the site after a fire of 1916. See "First Congregational," *Oak Leaves (Forty-Third Anniversary Number)* (23 February 1924): 179; Barton, *The Autobiography of William E. Barton* (Indianapolis: Bobbs-Merrill, 1932), 255–256; and Frank J. Platt, *Century of Promise* (Oak Park, Ill.: First Congregational Church, 1963), 14.

37. *First Congregational Church, Red Book* (Oak Park, 1904), 6. The sanctuary was transformed by the decorators A. W. and S. E. Pebbles, the same Oak Park firm whose store on Lake Street Wright remodeled in 1907. Their repainting of the church created a room where "the prevailing tones are olive and old yellow. The body of the church from the floor up for ten or twelve feet is a rich brown, a little lighter than chocolate in shade, while above that the olive tints are carried well up into the roof, where the yellow prevails. . . . The whole color scheme is in the most delightful harmony with the beautiful windows" ("Redecoration," *Oak Leaves* [9 October 1903]: 10). The naturalistic colors of this scheme compare with those Wright employed for Unity Temple and Unity House designed shortly afterward across Lake Street.

38. Platt, *Century of Promise,* 15.

39. "Redecoration," 10–11. The symbols were: (1) a type of Chrisma (a monogram of Christ, the Greek letters X. P., or Chi Rho) known as the Labarium (a Chrisma with the Greek Alpha and Omega in small letters on each side); (2) the Jerusalem cross of the Crusades; and (3) a circle inscribed with a central X as the common last letter of four Latin words set on all four sides: Rex-Lex-Lux-Dux, meaning Christ as king, law, light, and leader.

40. Union Thanksgiving services were held in the newly renovated sanctuary of the First Congregational Church ("Union Thanksgiving Service," *Oak Leaves* [20 November 1903]: 16). The following year, similar services at the same church drew participants from the First Presbyterian, First Methodist, First Baptist, and Unity churches ("Thanksgiving Day," ibid. [26 November 1904]: 7). Later evangelistic services were held at First Congregational ("The Revival Begins," ibid. [1 January 1910]: 3, 6, 26–27). See also "Union Evening Service," *Oak Leaves* (6 May 1904): 12; "Union Services," *Oak Park Reporter-Argus* (14 May 1904): 5; "Union Sunday Evening Services," ibid. (18 June 1904): 4; "A Union Meeting," ibid. (21 January 1905): 4; "Open-Air Services," ibid. (29 April 1905): 4; "Opposed to Union Service," ibid. (2 September 1905): 8; "Summer Evening Union Services," *Oak Leaves* (16 June 1906): 10; and May Estelle Cook, *Little Old Oak Park 1837–1902* (Oak Park, 1961), 46.

41. "Death of N. S. Patton," 7.

42. *A Brief History of the Organization, Building and Dedication of the Scoville Institute, Oak Park, Cook County, Illinois* (Oak Park, Ill., 1888), 16. This publication noted: "The original inspiration comes from the Romanesque, but it has been adapted to modern American requirements, and at the present time may fairly claim to be the typical American style for public buildings. The Institute building illustrates the capabilities of this style in combining breadth and simplicity of effect with richness of detail whenever an important part needs emphasis."

Later, in 1891, Patton wrote: "The Romanesque of today is truly of American growth. It is not a revival of the ancient nor is it a copy of European work; it is rather a continuation and developing of Romanesque. . . . Now that we have a style that is rational and which we may fairly claim as our own, it is time that our schools of architecture ceased to copy the false methods of the French 'Ecole des Beaux Arts' and become an exponent of a living style." Normand Patton, "Architectural Design," *Inland Architect and News Record* 17 (March 1891): 19–20.

Patton's Scoville Institute was influenced by the works of H. H. Richardson, such as his smaller public libraries. Several of these were individually endowed as gifts to their communities. The Scoville Institute was the first regional work in Richardson's style to appear in Chicago's *Inland Architect and News Record* in February 1885. This was before Richardson himself was commissioned to design his major late buildings in Chicago. M. G. van Rensselaer, *Henry Hobson Richardson* (1888; reprint, New York: Dover, 1969), 140, recorded his late Chicago commissions as: Marshall Field Wholesale Store (April 1885); J. J. Glessner House (May 1885); and the Franklin MacVeagh House (July 1885). Patton's design was contemporaneous with Burnham and Root's Art Institute of Chicago on Michigan Avenue, one of the city's newly founded cultural centers to which the Scoville Institute was compared (*Scoville Institute,* 22). On the Art Institute, see Donald Hoffmann, *The Architecture of John Wellborn Root* (Baltimore: Johns Hopkins University Press, 1973), 49, 53–54, 58–59.

43. "Dedication," *Oak Leaves* (4 April 1902): 3; "Presbyterian," ibid. (11 April 1902): 9–10; and David Grant, "First Presbyterian Church," *Oak Leaves (Fifth Anniversary Number)* (27 April 1907): 114–115. The interior of the new First Presbyterian Church featured elaborate stained glass as part of the decorative program designed and executed by Louis Millet, one of Louis Sullivan's noted collaborators. A large gallery, part of the original design, was added to the sanctuary in 1909 ("350 More Seats," *Oak Leaves* [2 October 1909]: 12). Williamson's design had called for a new building with an image of permanence and monumentality, superseding its predecessor of wood on the same site. The new structure cost $63,000, exclusive of its organ. First Presbyterian Church's membership was noted in "Church Statistics," *Oak Park Reporter-Argus* (28 April 1906): 5.

44. On Grace Episcopal Church, see "Grace Church," *Oak Leaves (Fifth Anniversary Number)* (27 April 1907): 116; "Grace Church Parish," *Oak Leaves (Forty-Third Anniversary Edition)* (23 February 1924): 134; and John Moelmann, ed., *Grace Church, Oak Park, 1879–1939* (Oak Park, 1939). On the church's membership, see "Church Statistics," and "City of Many Churches," ibid. (5 May 1906): 8. Founded in 1879, Grace Church's early home was a small brick building of 1883 on Forest Avenue north of Lake Street. It was taken down in 1901, and was replaced on the site by a home for a vestryman of the church, Frank W. Thomas, whose residence was designed by Wright as his first prairie house in Oak Park. On this house, which still stands at 210 Forest Avenue, see Hitchcock, *Nature of Materials,* 42, 43; Manson, *Wright to 1910,* 110; Storrer, *Frank Lloyd Wright,* 67; and Futagawa, ed., *Frank Lloyd Wright Monograph 1887–1901,* 180–187.

45. "John Sutcliffe Dies," *Oak Leaves* (23 October 1913): 6–7. Sutcliffe's major works included St. Luke's Church, Evanston, St. Paul's Church, Springfield, and Christ Church, Chicago, the last published in *Inland Architect and News Record* 52 (July 1908).

46. "Open Grace Church," *Oak Leaves* (2 December 1905): 7–10; and "Grace Church," *Oak Leaves (Fifth Anniversary Number)* (27 April 1907): 118–119. See also Moelmann, ed., *Grace Church,* 7–21.

47. "Open Grace Church," 8; and Moelmann, ed., *Grace Church,* 17. See also "Real Estate Sales," *Oak Leaves* (11 December 1903): 7. The interior walls were red Roman brick laid in putty. The nave's roof beams were huge timbers of oak, supporting a paneled ceiling of the same material that was intentionally left without oiling or staining so that in time the church's interior wood surfaces would change color, as in old English cathedrals. The design was so costly that in 1901, after Grace Church's walls had risen 12 ft. above ground, they were covered with a temporary flat roof for four years until funds could be raised to complete the work. Construction resumed in 1905. A parish house adjacent to the church included workshops, a gymnasium, a bowling alley, a rectory, and an audience hall seating four hundred. These required more space than was first anticipated, so more property was purchased in 1903 adjacent to the original lot.

In a dedicatory sermon of December 1906, the Episcopal bishop of Chicago said of Sutcliffe's sanctuary: "Its lines are true Gothic, the downward line telling that God comes down to His people in His church; the upward, that man's petitions reach the throne of grace. The whole is cruciform – cross-built, cross-crowned – the symbol of love, the heart of faith and the victory over death." Of the church's plan of a nave, chancel, and altar, the bishop said: "This building represents our convictions and our faith. It is fashioned as God commanded the style of the tabernacle and the temple – in a threefold division – the court of the people, the court of the priests and the Holy of Holies. . . . Its uninterrupted sweep of ceiling from one end to the other portrays the Christian life from the church here to that beyond. Its plain, unvarnished beams and rafters speak for truth." Bishop C. P. Anderson, quoted in "Grace Church Opening," *Oak Park Reporter-Argus* (9 December 1905): 4.

48. To resist "the onslaught of flat builders" was the theme of local ordinances and editorials. One of the latter asserted that "the one thing that has determined conditions in Oak Park more than all else up to the present time is its suburban character – the setting of individual homes amidst grass and trees . . . with each household near enough to the others to give all the advantages of the best forms of human society, but separate enough from the others to give that exclusive family life essential to good health, good morals and high ideals" ("Oak Park Face to Face with Its Doom," *Oak Leaves* [9 January 1909]: 12). A norm of individual home ownership was promoted as the key to preservation of the suburb on the model of its past, for "when a man becomes the owner of a home he becomes vitally interested in the numerous questions affecting the welfare of the town. His interest is keener, his pride is greater, and he becomes a more useful citizen to the community." Editorial, *Oak Park Reporter-Argus* (19 May 1906): 2.

49. John A. Lewis, *Chapters of Oak Park History* (Oak Park, Ill., by the author, 1913), 22.

50. The alignment of Oak Park's churches along Lake Street recalled the clustering of Chicago's early churches along east–west Washington Street, described in Bluestone, *Constructing Chicago*, 64–69. Among these had been the First Universalist Society's original building of 1843, described and illustrated in Gale, *Reminiscences*, 367; and "St. Paul's Church Buildings," 5.

On Oak Park's appropriation of the historical model of the Puritan village, see James F. Bundy, "Fall from Grace: Religion and the Communal Ideal in Two Suburban Villages, 1870–1917," Ph.D. diss., University of Chicago, 1979. On the spatial centrality of church buildings in town greens of colonial New England, see J. Frederick Kelly, *Early Connecticut Meeting Houses* (New York: Columbia University Press, 1948), xxiii–xxvii; Anthony N. B. Garvan, *Architecture and Town Planning in Colonial Connecticut* (New Haven: Yale University Press, 1951), 42, 51, 61–66, 130; Carl Feiss, "Early American Public Squares," in Paul Zucker, ed., *Town and Square from the Agora to the Village Green* (New York: Columbia University Press, 1959), 237–255; and John W. Reps, *Town Planning in Frontier America* (Princeton: Princeton University Press, 1965), 103–114. See also John R. Stilgoe, "The Puritan Townscape: Ideal and Reality," *Landscape* 20 (Spring 1976): 3–7; "Town Common and Village Green in New England: 1620–1981," in Ronald L. Fleming and Lauri A. Halderman, eds., *On Common Ground: Caring for Shared Land from Town Common to Urban Park* (Harvard, Mass.: Harvard Common Press, and Cambridge, Mass.: Townscape Institute, 1982); and *Common Landscape of America, 1580 to 1845* (New Haven: Yale University Press, 1982), 43–58. See also Alice M. Earle, "The New England Meeting House," *Atlantic Monthly* 67 (February 1891): 193.

51. Editorial, "A Message to Church Builders," *Oak Leaves* (16 May 1908): 11. This observer envisioned that if old mansions that then stood along these blocks became sites for apartment buildings, "then instead of being set off and made more effective in appearance by homes and well kept grounds, we shall have the churches sandwiched in among a lot of flat buildings, which would spoil the street anyway, even if the churches were not there to be shut in and obscured and marred by their undesirable surroundings." Another local orator stated in May 1905: "A community may be judged by its

public buildings. . . . Lake Street, like the sacred road of Rome, has already been flanked with substantial and beautiful edifices, the churches, the high school, the library, to which will soon be added the post office and the Colonial Club, making this road the center toward which the whole communal life will flow and from which mighty currents will radiate." Dr. Sydney Strong, address at cornerstone-laying, "Y.M.C.A. Building," *Oak Leaves* (27 November 1903): 10.

52. "Church to Expand," *Oak Leaves* (30 December 1905): 3. See Barton, "First Congregational Church," *Oak Leaves (Fifth Anniversary Number)* (27 April 1907): 98; and Barton, *Autobiography,* 255. The church's action was consistent with local restrictions on the design of apartment houses. These ordinances were "so drawn that it is not possible to erect any more of the dry-goods-box style of apartment buildings." Originally passed shortly after Oak Park achieved municipal independence in 1901, such laws had their intended effect. Early in 1910 it was reported that "in the last few months about forty such projects have been stopped or modified to conform to the artistic lines contemplated by the law." Editorial, "Enforcing the Building Ordinance," *Oak Leaves* (5 February 1910): 26.

Oak Park's restrictions on flat-building encouraged the construction of two-apartment residences, which "give a free access of light and air on all sides, and have all the outward appearance of a high class residence." These residences also provided a higher rate of return on investment in central properties. Two-apartment dwellings were perceived to be "desirable in less aristocratic parts of Oak Park" only if their designs were subject to "the requirements that should be made of all buildings used for residential purposes, that a sufficient space should intervene between them and other buildings." This could mean setting each building at least 10 ft. inside its lot line, so that there would be at least 20 ft. between every two residences. Each residence was to be set well back from its frontal lot line, thus approximating the spacing of individual suburban residences. These laws were interpreted to be politically progressive reforms, thus meriting the support of the village's churches (Editorial, "Improve the Building Ordinance," *Oak Leaves* [16 July 1904]: 16). Wright's siting of Unity Temple on its narrow lot with the auditorium set back from the front and inset from the sides may reflect concerns for separation between buildings throughout Oak Park. See Chapter 3, 81–83, 84–85.

53. Johonnot, quoted in "Annual Sermon," *Oak Leaves* (13 May 1904): 15.

54. Ibid.

55. Johonnot, "The Needs of the West," *Universalist Leader* 2 (4 November 1899): 14.

56. Walter S. Holden, letter, "Fellowship Club Meeting," *Oak Leaves* (3 December 1904): 11. On the club's program, see "Church Hit by Bolts," *Chicago Tribune* (5 June 1905): 4. Events hosted by Unity Church's Fellowship Club prior to the destruction of the old church building in 1905 included a joint meeting of Rev. Johonnot and Oak Park's Methodist, Episcopalian, Congregational, and Baptist ministers on "Religious and Moral Conditions in Oak Park," in "Views of Clergy," *Oak Leaves* (1 May 1903): 3, 19–21; an evening of presentations on the physical, spiritual, and educational needs of children ("The Child's Due," ibid. [11 December 1903]: 7); addresses on conditions and prospects of African-Americans, to which Wright's uncle, Rev. Jenkin Lloyd Jones, was invited ("Southern View," ibid. [22 January 1904]: 3–4); speakers on railroad track elevation or depression ("Discuss Elevation," ibid. [14 January 1905]: 3–5); and an evening of addresses on "What Can Be Done to Beautify Oak Park and Render It More Desirable as a Village of Homes," in "To Beautify Oak Park," ibid. [4 March 1905]: 3–4, 6–7, 13–14.

57. "Children's Home," *Oak Leaves* (29 May 1903): 20–22; "Children's Aid," ibid. [27 May 1904]: 3–4; "Children's Home and Aid Society Organized in Oak Park," *Oak Park Reporter-Argus* (28 May 1904): 4; "Hephzibah Home Election," *Oak Leaves* (25 June 1904): 14; "From Hephzibah Home," ibid. [9 December 1905]: 35; "Aid for Hephzi-

bah," ibid. [17 March 1906]: 12–13; "Hephzibah Annual Meeting," ibid. [5 May 1906]: 2; "Hephzibah's Report," ibid. [26 May 1906]: 16–17; "Thanks for Hephzibah," ibid. [4 August 1906]: 16–17; "Hephzibah Facts," ibid. [9 February 1907]: 8–9; and Johonnot, "Hephzibah's Work," ibid. [20 April 1907]: 9–10. Johonnot to J. L. Jones, 5 January 1893, noted Johonnot's coordination of Oak Park's varied philanthropies (Jones Collection, Meadville-Lombard). By 1906 Johonnot's pastorate of fourteen years had become the second longest in the history of Oak Park, as noted in "Looking Backward," *Oak Leaves* (12 May 1906): 4–5; and "Faithful Services," *Oak Park Reporter-Argus* (19 May 1906): 4.

58. "Unity Church," *Oak Leaves (Fifth Anniversary Number)* (27 April 1907): 101. The suspicion that existed among Oak Park's other churches toward Unity Church derived from perceptions of Unitarian and Universalist thought as being on the edge of the Christian tradition. In 1903 or 1904 Johonnot authored a pamphlet written for local readers and intended "to give a brief statement of the faith, history and form of the organization of the Unitarian and Universalist denominations [and] to state the position of Unity Church." After briefly tracing the history of these twin liberal traditions, Johonnot concluded that Unity Church invited "to its fellowship all persons who believe in a broad and rational interpretation of religion, as set forth in the simple tests of Jesus, consisting in love and service of God and man. It plants itself upon this broad, simple platform of faith as the one thing needful to ennoble human life." Johonnot, *Unity Church, Oak Park, Illinois,* n.d., 1 (Unity Temple Historical Files, Folder 1900–1919). This document bears the handwritten note: "This pamphlet was issued about 1903 or 1904 as I recall. R. F. Johonnot. Nov. 1, 1919." Wright's subsequent design for Unity Temple was interpreted as a symbol of these ideals. See Chapter 5, 198.

59. From its origins in 1857 until its independence in 1901, Oak Park was one of a cluster of over ten villages that constituted Cicero Township, incorporated in 1867. The township as a whole was governed by seven elected trustees. Within the township of Cicero, individual villages like Oak Park were political nonentities with no direct form of self-government. While not in full control of its affairs, Oak Park was an extraordinarily well defined and homogeneous community. Its area of four and one half square miles constituted a single school district governed only by Oak Park's residents. The village's compactness and homogeneity contributed powerfully toward its drive for self-government. This movement began in the late 1880s, when Wright moved to the community. At that time, self-government was promoted to prevent Oak Park's annexation to Chicago, which had doubled its area with the annexation of Hyde Park in 1889. From 1894 to 1927 the city of Chicago attempted twenty-four annexations, only five of which succeeded. Annexation was almost always by referendum within the community to be annexed. However, because Oak Park was only a part of Cicero Township, it could not protect itself against annexation if a majority of the township's residents preferred it. Oak Park also wished to control its own tax revenues and public expenditures. Local political struggles culminated in 1901, when Oak Park broke from Cicero to form a village that elected its own officers, managed its own revenues, and controlled its own ordinances. At this time, Oak Park's model was Brookline, Massachusetts. See Le Gacy, "Improvers and Preservers," 22–25, 53–124. Accounts of Oak Park's political history to 1901 included Jesse A. Baldwin's address at the cornerstone-laying of the municipal building, reprinted in "Corner Stone," *Oak Leaves* (20 November 1903): 19–26, and "Oak Park – Past and Present," *Oak Leaves (Fifth Anniversary Number)* (27 April 1907): 49–52. On the relationship between Oak Park's social and political history, see Kathryn E. Ratcliff, "The Making of a New Middle-Class Culture: Family and Community in a Midwest Suburb, 1890–1920," Ph.D. diss., University of Minnesota, 1990.

Later, local discussion of annexation occurred under the auspices of Unity Church's Fellowship Club, as recorded in "Annex to Chicago," *Oak Leaves* (12 February 1910): 3, 10, 16; "Talk on Annexation," ibid. (19 February 1910): 3, 8–9; and "Against

Annexation," ibid. (26 February 1910): 3, 14. See also Michael P. McCarthy, "The New Metropolis: Chicago, the Annexation Movement, and Progressive Reform," in Michael H. Ebner and Eugene M. Tobin, eds., *The Age of Urban Reform: New Perspectives on the Progressive Era* (Port Washington, N.Y.: Kennikat, 1977), 43–54; and Robert D. Karr, "Brookline and the Making of an Elite Suburb," *Chicago History* 13 (Summer 1984): 36–47.

On John Lewis's contribution to Oak Park's independence, see "Corner Stone," 25; and editorial, "Mr. John Lewis," *Oak Leaves* (20 November 1903): 16. The form of government that Oak Park adopted specified that its president and trustees were to serve without compensation, for it was thought that there were ample numbers of able citizens wealthy enough to hold public office without pay. Lewis, a lawyer, advocated this approach to avert corruption and to foster civic idealism, concluding "that in this way the village will be most likely to secure the services of its best citizens and consequently to enjoy the most economical government and the most efficient administration of its affairs" (*Oak Park Reporter* [21 November 1901]: 1, 8). See also Le Gacy, "Improvers and Preservers," 109–124; and Lewis, *Chapters of Oak Park History,* 39–43. Johonnot, *New Edifice of Unity Church,* 19, noted Lewis's service on the board of trustees from 1905 to 1907.

60. On this building, see "Village Hall," *Oak Leaves* (31 July 1903): 3–5; and "The New Municipal Building of Oak Park," Supplement to *Oak Park Reporter-Argus* (8 October 1904). On Roberts, see Frances Steiner, "E. E. Roberts: Popularizing the Prairie School," *Prairie School Review* 10 (Second Quarter 1973): 5–24. The site chosen for the hall had been offered by James Scoville for only $2,500 as an act of civic philanthropy ("Tempting Offer," *Oak Leaves* [15 May 1903]: 3–4). Early in 1903, before this site had been acquired, it was proposed that the hall be on the southeast corner of Lake Street and Kenilworth Avenue, the same site where Unity Temple would soon be built (Editorial, "The Village Hall Site," *Oak Leaves* [8 May 1903]: 12). Unity Temple's urban position and classical stylistic affinity may have been tied to the civic idealism identified with Lewis.

61. On the creation of Oak Park's central village green, see pp. 308–309, n. 51. The YMCA building, opened in 1904, had its cost of $80,000 met wholly by local residents. See "Gift for Y.M.C.A.," *Oak Leaves* (25 April 1902): 3–4, and Editorial, "As to the Y.M.C.A.," ibid., 12; "New Oak Park Y.M.C.A. Building," ibid. (7 August 1903): 2; "Ready to Build," ibid., 3–6, 8; "Y.M.C.A. Building," ibid. (27 November 1903): 10–13; "Y.M.C.A. Building," ibid. (22 April 1904): 8–9; "Is a Model Building," *Oak Park Reporter-Argus* (19 November 1904): 8; "Y.M.C.A. Is Opened," ibid. (26 November 1904): 4; and "Becomes Great Center," ibid. (12 May 1906): 8. The architects, Allen B. and Irving K. Pond, were well known for their additions to Hull House in Chicago from 1890. See Szuberla, "Three Chicago Settlements," 116–124; and Allen B. Pond, "The Settlement House," *Brickbuilder* 11 (July 1902): 140–145; ibid. (August 1902): 160–164; ibid. (September 1902): 178–185.

Oak Park's post office was begun Saturday, 13 May 1905, the day before Wright and his wife returned from Japan. The building was superseded in 1933 by the new Oak Park post office on the southwest corner of Lake Street and Kenilworth Avenue, across from Unity Temple, designed by Charles E. White Jr., one of Wright's assistants at the time of Unity Temple's design. On the post office of 1905, see "Corner-Stone Is Laid," *Oak Park Reporter-Argus* (20 May 1905): 4, 8. On its design and siting, see "Post Office Plans," *Oak Leaves* (4 June 1904): 3; "U.S. Post Office," ibid. (15 October 1904): 24–25; "New Oak Park Post Office Building," ibid. (18 March 1905): 20–21; "Post Office Ready," ibid. (17 March 1906): 3. Although this building was federally funded and designed, its site was also given at a low cost by Scoville, whose own mansion then stood on the north rise of what became Scoville Park. See "In New Post Office," *Oak Leaves* (24 March 1906): 4.

62. Editorial, "Close of a Remarkable Year," *Oak Leaves* (24 December 1904): 12.

63. Early in 1904 old Unity Church needed new exits and electrical wiring for code compliance (Meetings of the Board of Trustees, 7 and 10 February 1904, *Record,* 88–91, 92, Unity Temple Historical Files). By 1905 rehabilitation of the structure and redecoration of the auditorium were being discussed (Minutes, Ladies Social Union, 27 January and 10 March 1905, Unity Church, Oak Park, Ill., Ladies Social Union, Membership List and Minutes, 28 October 1904 to 11 March 1910, III, 4, 6, Unity Temple Historical Files).

64. Johonnot, *New Edifice of Unity Church,* 3.

65. As one colonial minister had written: "There is not just ground in scripture to apply such a trope as church to a house for public assembly" (quoted in Kelly, *Early Connecticut Meeting Houses,* xxiv). Such a distinction was especially meaningful in a culture of religious dissent, for in Anglican usage a church was a consecrated structure, unlike the colonial Puritan meetinghouses or other buildings created for Nonconformist groups, such as Unitarians.

66. On *temples protestants,* see Chapter 3, 90–92, and 289, nn. 48–50.

67. Johonnot, "The Modern Reformation," *Universalist Leader* 12 (19 June 1909): 779–781. Johonnot's concerns for renewal of religious art and architecture compare with other voices of the period. See, for example, Rev. A. P. Bourne, "The Aesthetic Regeneration of Protestantism," *Christian Art* 1 (April 1907): 27–32.

68. Johonnot, "Modern Reformation," 779. He wrote: "The effect of Puritanism upon the Protestant movement, while nobly fruitful in its emphasis upon personal righteousness and the spiritual life, was distinctly to deprive the Church of that appeal to the emotional nature made by the beauty of form. In its protest against Romanism, it did not sufficiently distinguish between form and essence; and in its endeavor to make the church spiritual and destroy mere formalism, it cut out much that was nobly emotional" (ibid., 780).

69. Ibid. Johonnot maintained that "worship must satisfy the emotions as well as the intellect and the arts, painting, sculpture, architecture, music, and ritual, through which these emotions find proper expression and by which they are also evoked, must have their place. Art will again become the handmaiden of religion in order that the religious feelings may be properly called out, expressed, directed, and restrained."

70. In soliciting donations, the trustees wrote of the original building of 1872: "While a splendid monument to the devotion of the members of that day, it is not adequate for all our present needs nor does it represent present ideas of church architecture. . . . When we remember that one church in this village gives several thousand dollars to its building fund each Easter, may we not expect an offering of at least some hundred dollars." Board of Trustees to the Friends of Unity Church, December 1904 (Unity Temple Historical Files, Folder, 1900–1919). Johonnot's request for this appeal was noted in the Minutes of the Board of Trustees, 4 December 1904, in *Record,* 112–113 (Unity Temple Historical Files).

71. Johonnot maintained that "the best welfare of Oak Park demanded the continuance and growth of a church which stands for the freest and largest interpretation of religion." Johonnot, Anniversary Sermon, paraphrased in "Thirteen Years," *Oak Leaves* (13 May 1905): 10.

72. Special Meeting of the Parish, 24 May 1905, in *Annual Reports 1902 to 1921,* 74 (Unity Temple Historical Files).

73. "Three Churches Struck by Bolts," *Chicago Tribune* (5 June 1905): 5.

74. "Unity Church Fire," *Oak Leaves* (10 June 1905): 12. Thomas J. Skillin, a church trustee who later worked with Wright on Unity Temple, then stated: "We have been planning to build another church. We will hurry the plans now, and Unity congregation will have another and better home soon." Quoted in "Struck by Lightning," *Oak Park Reporter-Argus* (10 June 1905): 4.

75. James Heald Jr., quoted in Chulak, *A People Moving thru Time,* 19.

76. Meetings of the Board of Trustees, 11 June and 3 September 1905, *Record,* 124, 134

(Unity Temple Historical Files). See "Church Will Build," *Oak Leaves* (10 June 1905): 3; "Unity Church Committees," ibid. (24 June 1905): 7; and "About the Village," *Oak Park Reporter-Argus* (17 June 1905): 8.

77. "Church Will Build," *Oak Leaves* (10 June 1905): 3.

78. "Unity Church Committees," *Oak Leaves* (24 June 1905): 7.

79. Ibid.

80. "Unity Church Site," *Oak Leaves* (12 August 1905): 3.

81. Wolfgang Braunfels, *Urban Design in Western Europe,* trans. Kenneth J. Northcott (Chicago: University of Chicago Press, 1988), 32.

82. Special Meeting of the Board of Trustees, 30 August 1905, *Record,* 132–133 (Unity Temple Historical Files). The members of the plans committee that selected the architect were Mrs. A. W. Bryant, representing the Ladies Social Union as a major donor to the project; Mrs. John Lewis, wife of the civic leader Edwin H. Ehrman (an associate of Charles Roberts in the Chicago Screw Company); Dwight Jackson; and Johonnot. As chairman of the committee, Rev. Johonnot told the trustees that he "wished the task might have fallen to someone more competent," requesting "instructions as to the scope and authority of the committee's work; especially as to whether it has the power to decide on an architect and to accept a plan." He added: "Should such authority be given, the committee will, I am sure, determine on a plan only after the fullest consultation with the Board of Trustees and after giving the members of the parish the fullest opportunity to make suggestions and criticism upon the plans proposed." Johonnot to Board of Trustees, 13 June 1905 (Unity Temple Historical Files, 1900–1919).

Of the nine architects mentioned, Emory S. Hall (1869–1939) had recently designed the Tabernacle Baptist Church in Chicago, and had also remodeled a number of the city's theaters. On Hall, see Withey, *American Architects,* 257; and *Illinois Society of Architects Monthly Bulletin* 24 (February–March 1940): 7–8. On the Tabernacle Baptist Church at 3300-3308 West Monroe Street, see Commission on Chicago Landmarks, Form No. 27-27-13-001. On Hall's later work, see Peter B. Wight, "The Y.M.C.A. College in Chicago," *Architectural Record* 39 (May 1916): 394–418; and Commission on Chicago Landmarks, *YMCA College Building* (Chicago, 1988). Williamson had designed the Richardsonian First Presbyterian Church. E. A. Mayer is unidentified, while John Sutcliffe had designed the Neo-Gothic Episcopal Grace Church. Harned (1849–1934) was a church member listed in "Parish Directory," *Year Book and Manual of Unity Church, Oak Park, Illinois 1904–1905* (n.p., n.d.). On Harned, see *Illinois Society of Architects Monthly Bulletin* 18 (February–March 1934): 7.

83. At that time the minister of All Souls Unitarian Church in Evanston was Rev. James Vila Blake, a colleague of Jenkin Lloyd Jones. See David T. Van Zanten, "The Early Work of Marion Mahony Griffin," *Prairie School Review* 3 (Second Quarter 1966): 6–9. In 1902 Perkins had spoken at Unity Church on "The Architectural Future of Chicago," noted in "Fellowship Club," *Oak Leaves* 21 (5 December 1902): 4. Perkins's talk was hosted by Mr. O. W. Nash, whose wife was later a member of the plans committee for Unity Temple.

84. On Otis, see Withey, *American Architects,* 450; and Art Institute of Chicago, *Chicago Architects Design* (New York: Rizzoli, 1982), 44. On the Hull Memorial Chapel, see Lane, *Chicago Churches and Synagogues,* 188.

85. On Patton, see p. 60, and 274–275, n. 36. On the Memorial Baptist Church, see Chapter 1, 34, and 264, n. 77.

86. Johonnot, quoted in "Unity Plans Unique," *Oak Leaves* (24 February 1906): 3.

87. Editorial, *Unity* 55 (29 June 1905): 291.

88. Jones to Johonnot, 14 June 1905, Jones Letter Book, 14 June 1905–28 March 1906 (Jones Collection, Meadville-Lombard). Jones's phrase, that "new occasions teach new duties," referred to a sermon of the same title by Rev. James Freeman Clarke, published in *The Monthly Journal of the American Unitarian Association* 6 (February 1865): 79–

84. Upon coming to Oak Park in 1892, Johonnot wrote to Jones: "I have, of course, known of you and your work for many years, have heard you in Boston, and have long been desirous to meet you" (Johonnot to J. L. Jones, 14 May 1892, Jones Collection, Meadville-Lombard). In December 1902 Johonnot had wished for Jones "that 1903 may see the fruit of your long labors – the erection of the Lincoln Center." Johonnot to J. L. Jones, 26 December 1902 (Jones Collection, Meadville-Lombard).

89. On Wright's George W. Smith House of 1898 at 404 Home Avenue, Oak Park, see Storrer, *Frank Lloyd Wright,* 45. On Wright's houses for Thomas H. Gale, 1019 Chicago Avenue (1892), Walter Gale, 1031 Chicago Avenue (1893), and R. P. Parker, 1027 Chicago Avenue (1893), see Hitchcock, *Nature of Materials,* 18–19; Manson, *Frank Lloyd Wright,* 48, 52–53; Storrer, *Frank Lloyd Wright,* 16, 17, 20; and Futagawa, ed., *Frank Lloyd Wright Monograph 1887–1901,* 21, 34–35. Wright soon remodeled the Pebbles and Balch Shop, 1107 Lake Street (1907), for Frank M. Pebbles, also a member of Unity Church. See also Storrer, *Wright Companion,* 17, 20, 41, 132.

90. Roberts served for twenty-five years (1879–1904) as the superintendent of Unity Church's Sunday school. He "brought to this office not only a great interest but a rare fidelity, often coming home from Detroit, where some of his business interests are located, arriving Sunday morning or Saturday evening, and leaving again for Detroit on Sunday evening, in order that he might be at the session of the school" (Editorial, *Universalist Leader* 7 [9 January 1904]: 38). His work in Sunday schooling was noted in *Universalist Leader* 2 (25 March 1899); and "The Oak Park Sunday School," ibid., 5 (18 January 1902): 77. Roberts served as director of Unity Church's Sunday school again in 1905–6, when he stated that "the Sunday School has labored at a disadvantage during the year on account of the unsuitableness of its temporary quarters" (Minutes of the 36th Annual Meeting of Unity Church Society of Oak Park, 25 March 1906, in *Annual Reports, 1902 to 1921,* 101, Unity Temple Historical Files). Roberts's concern for the school's vitality perhaps underlay Wright's spatial provisions for it in the new Unity House. See Chapter 3, 81–83, and Chapter 4, 158–159.

On Roberts, see "Death of Charles E. Roberts," *Oak Leaves* (29 March 1934): 10; Leonard K. Eaton, *Two Chicago Architects and Their Clients: Frank Lloyd Wright and Howard Van Doren Shaw* (Cambridge, Mass.: MIT Press, 1969), 77–79; and Secrest, *Frank Lloyd Wright,* 179–180. Like several of Wright's other early clients, Roberts was both mechanically inventive and musical. In Chicago in 1873 he had founded his firm, the Charles E. Roberts Company, for manufacture of screws. His family's only photograph of Roberts showed him on an early electric automobile of his own design and assembly ("Pioneer and Early Auto," *Oak Leaves* [19 April 1934]: 62). He reportedly spent his first dollar on a parlor organ that he taught himself to play, and read music, played the piano, and sang as a daily pastime throughout his life, such that "this artistic impulse appeared to be a part also of his mechanical genius" ("Charles E. Roberts," 10).

91. In 1892 Roberts had commissioned Wright to design a house in Oak Park, which was never constructed (Futagawa, ed., *Frank Lloyd Wright Monograph 1887–1901,* 19). In 1896 Wright designed additions, new interiors, and stables for Roberts's own house in Oak Park, near Wright's. On this work see *Oak Park Reporter* (22 May 1896): 4, which noted its completion; Hitchcock, *Nature of Materials,* 109; Storrer, *Frank Lloyd Wright,* 40–41; Futagawa, ed., *Frank Lloyd Wright Monograph 1887–1901,* 90–93; Secrest, *Frank Lloyd Wright,* 180; and Storrer, *Wright Companion,* 37–38. He designed an unbuilt summer cottage for Roberts in 1896 (Futagawa, ed., *Frank Lloyd Wright Monograph 1887–1901,* 233). In 1897 Wright designed his first project for a factory for Roberts's Chicago Screw Company, also unbuilt. This is documented in the Frank Lloyd Wright Foundation, Drawing nos. 9704.001–9704.010, dated 20 July 1897, when Wright noted his office as 1107 Steinway Hall, Chicago.

Like a number of other residents of Oak Park, Roberts invested in suburban real estate and in 1896 Wright designed for him five small gabled and hipped roof houses for lots in "Ridgeland," the railroad suburb just east of Oak Park. This project, too, did not come to fruition. See Futagawa, ed., *Frank Lloyd Wright Monograph 1887–1901*, 94–99; and Frank Lloyd Wright Foundation, Drawing nos. 9608.001–9608.009 (House A, dated 15 January 1896), 9608.010–9608.019 (House B, 20 January 1896), 9608.020–9608.027 (House C), 9608.028–9608.037 (House D), and 9608.038–9608.046 (House E). On Ridgeland's origins, see Andreas, *History of Cook County*, 775–792, 805–808, condensed in "Oak Park – Past and Present," *Oak Leaves (Fifth Anniversary Number)* (27 April 1907): 49–50. In 1897 Wright planned an unbuilt house for Roberts, perhaps as a prototype for twenty-two houses on the block Roberts owned in Oak Park (Futagawa, ed., *Frank Lloyd Wright Monograph 1887–1901*, 109). Another plan of Wright for Roberts for this block is dated to 1903. Also unbuilt, it shows twenty-four small, low, hip roofed prairie houses as a community with gardens (Futagawa, ed., *Frank Lloyd Wright Monograph 1902–1906*, 64–65).

As Wright's largest project for Roberts, this 1903 plan was related to Wright's Quadruple Block Plan of 1901 for a block near Roberts's house. This plan had financial support, presumably from Roberts, who was interested in a variation of it through 1904. As seen atop Figure 110, Wright introduced the plan in his text, "A Home in a Prairie Town," *Ladies Home Journal* 18 (February 1901): 17. See "New Idea for Suburbs," *Oak Park Reporter* (18 July 1901): 4; Hitchcock, *Nature of Materials*, 34, 55; Manson, *Frank Lloyd Wright*, 207; Norris K. Smith, *Frank Lloyd Wright: A Study in Architectural Content* (Englewood Cliffs, N.J.: Prentice-Hall, 1966), 85–89; Twombly, *Frank Lloyd Wright*, 53–54; and Gwendolyn Wright, *Moralism and the Model Home: Domestic Architecture and Cultural Conflict in Chicago 1873–1913* (Chicago: University of Chicago Press, 1980), 138–139. Charles E. White Jr. to Walter Willcox, 19 May 1904, wrote: "Father Roberts has resigned from the Screw Company, and is gradually pulling out some of his interests. He wants to start in some manufacturing business with Owen and Chapin. Is thinking of going ahead with the Wright scheme of twenty houses on his block." Nancy K. Morris Smith, ed., "Letters, 1903–1906, by Charles E. White, Jr., from the Studio of Frank Lloyd Wright," *Journal of Architectural Education* 25 (Fall 1971): 107.

One of Roberts's daughters, Isabel, managed Wright's office and Wright designed her house in River Forest in 1908. On Isabel Roberts, see Charles E. White to Walter Willcox, 13 May 1904, in Smith, ed., "Letters, 1903–1906, by Charles E. White, Jr.," 105; Wright, "In the Cause of Architecture (1908)," 164; Manson, *Frank Lloyd Wright*, 217; and Gill, *Many Masks*, 11–13, 208, 302. On Isabel Roberts's house, see Wright, *Ausgeführte Bauten und Entwürfe* (1910), Plate LI; Hitchcock, *Nature of Materials*, 43–45; Manson, *Frank Lloyd Wright*, 176–177; Storrer, *Frank Lloyd Wright*, 150; and Futagawa, ed., *Frank Lloyd Wright Monograph 1907–1912*, 61. Isabel's sister, Alice Roberts, was the wife of Charles E. White Jr., then one of Wright's assistants ("Charles E. Roberts," 10).

92. Ellen C. Lloyd Jones to Charles E. Roberts, n.d., ca. 1912/1913 (Jane Lloyd Jones Papers, 1899–1940, Box I, Archives Division, State Historical Society of Wisconsin, Madison). On Roberts and the Hillside Home School, see Chapter 1, 25, and 261, n. 44.

93. Wright, *Autobiography* (1932), 153.

94. Wright to [Rev. William] Norman Guthrie, 20 November 1928, © Frank Lloyd Wright Foundation 1992, Microfiche Id. No. G004B10. In 1908 Wright designed an unbuilt residence for Guthrie in Sewanee, Tenn. (*Ausgeführte Bauten und Entwürfe*, 1910, Plate LXI). On Wright and Guthrie's later unrealized project for St. Mark's in the Bouwerie, see Gill, *Many Masks*, 313–315. At the end of his introduction to the Wasmuth folio, Wright named Roberts as the first of three of his most important clients "who have believed and befriended the work when natural opposition from without and inherent faults within threatened to make an end of it. Without their faith and help this work would never have reached its present development" (*Ausgeführte Bauten und Entwürfe*, 8).

95. Special Meeting of the Board of Trustees, 30 August 1905, *Record,* 132–133 (Unity Temple Historical Files). For the construction of Unity Temple, Roberts would later donate $1,350, the single largest individual contribution among the 130 donations to the project. See "Subscribers to Building Fund, September 23, 1908, revised December 28, 1908" (Unity Temple Historical Files). In 1901 Roberts had offered the congregation's largest single donation to the Universalists' national denominational treasury. See "Twentieth Century Fund," *Universalist Leader* 4 (23 February 1901): 228; and "Twentieth Century at Oak Park, Ill.," ibid., 232.

96. Regular Meeting of the Board of Trustees, 3 September 1905, *Record,* 134–135 (Unity Temple Historical Files).

97. "Frank Lloyd Wright Chosen," *Oak Leaves* (16 September 1905): 13.

CHAPTER 3
WRIGHT'S DESIGN FOR UNITY TEMPLE

1. Wright, "The Architect," *Construction News* 10 (23 June 1900): 540.

2. "Chicago and Vicinity; Unity – Oak Park," *Universalist Leader* 8 (23 September 1905): 1202.

3. Regular Meeting of the Board of Trustees, 3 September 1905, *Record,* 134–135 (Unity Temple Historical Files). On the trustees' spatial program for the new church building, see Chulak, *A People Moving thru Time,* 22.

4. Wright, *Autobiography* (1932), 155.

5. Susan T. Perry, "In the Old Meeting House," *Universalist* 11 (25 June 1892): 6.

6. Wright, *Autobiography* (1932), 153–154. In recalling the design of Unity Temple, Wright referred consistently to a single building committee composed of seven men: himself, Roberts, Rev. Johonnot, Thomas J. Skillin, and three others. As noted, shortly before Wright's selection was announced, Johonnot did propose that the plans and building committees collaborate in the formulation of plans. See p. 73. Skillin was trustee president from April 1905 to March 1906, when Wright's designs were under review, as noted in Johonnot, *New Edifice of Unity Church,* 19. See also "Good Citizen Dies," *Oak Leaves* (22 June 1912): 12–13.

    The church trustees, sometimes with committee members, did meet with Wright to discuss the design at least five times from January 1906, after Wright presented plans, to May 1906, when building began. When the trustees approved Wright's design at their meeting of 7 February, the chief responsibility passed from the plans committee to a newly formed special committee consisting of the plans committee, building committee, and the trustees. This group supervised preparation of working drawings and specifications for bids, and was also "given full authority to make such alterations in the plans submitted as it may deem best to finally determine all details and arrangements relating to the plans and the mode of construction of the building." Meetings of the Board of Trustees of Unity Church, 4 January, 18 January, 7 February, 30 April, and 1 May 1906, *Record,* 145, 155, 160–162, 172, 173 (Unity Temple Historical Files).

7. Beatrice Harraden, "The Traveller and the Temple of Knowledge," *Ships That Pass in the Night* (New York: G. P. Putnam's Sons, 1894), 36–41. On Harraden, see Stanley J. Kunitz and Howard Haycraft, eds., *Twentieth Century Authors* (New York: H. H. Wilson, 1942), 618.

8. J. L. Jones, "The American Congress of Liberal Religious Societies," *Unity* 33 (21 June 1894): 263.

9. Ibid.

10. Frank C. Doan, "Unitarian Theology: The Idea of God as Human," *Christian Register* 88 (7 October 1909): 1063. See also Doan, "The Invisible Humanity of God," in *Religion*

and the Modern Mind (Boston: Sherman, French, 1909), 153–161; Robinson, Unitarians and Universalists, 143–150; and Lyttle, Freedom Moves West, 243–249. On James, see John E. Smith, introduction to Henry James, The Varieties of Religious Experience (1902; reprint, Cambridge, Mass.: Harvard University Press, 1985), xi–li.

11. Johonnot, "The Gain of a Continued Pastorate," quoted in "Thirteen Years," Oak Leaves (13 May 1905): 12.

12. Johonnot, The New Edifice of Unity Church, 18.

13. Bluestone, Constructing Chicago, 65–70.

14. Sullivan, quoted in "Church Spires Must Go," Chicago Tribune (30 November 1890): 36. Sullivan cited the towers of Notre-Dame Cathedral in Paris as an example of functional forms that housed the church's sonorous bells.

15. Cook, Little Old Oak Park, 40–41.

16. Editorial, "The Modern Church Construction," Church Economist 10 (May 1905): 180.

17. Ibid.

18. Ibid.

19. Ibid.

20. Quoted in "Two New Influences on Church Architecture," Literary Digest 31 (5 August 1905): 181.

21. McKim, Mead, and White, quoted in "Sky-Pointer vs. Sky-Scraper," Church Economist 10 (May 1905): 168. On the Madison Square Presbyterian Church, see Leland Roth, McKim, Mead & White, Architects (New York: Harper and Row, 1983), 275–279.

22. Wright, Autobiography (1932), 137–138.

23. Wright, "In the Cause of Architecture (1908)," 157.

24. Wright, Ausgeführte Bauten und Entwürfe (1910), 7.

25. Wright, Autobiography (1932), 137.

26. Jones, "The Call of the Twentieth Century, III: To the Artists," Unity 46 (24 January 1901): 326.

27. Jones, "Unity Church-Door Pulpit: The Divine Benediction," Unity 18 (16 October 1886): 85. For this sermon, Jones took as his text Philippians 4:7, wherein is bestowed the Pauline blessing of "the peace of God, which passeth all understanding." Jones proposed that such a divine peace "is something deeper than knowledge, it is not compassed by our reason."

28. "Gives Land to Unity Church," Oak Leaves (9 December 1905): 8. It was noted that there was "general rejoicing among the church people that Mr. Gale's gift will permit their new edifice to stand well back from [Lake] street."

29. "Mr. Gale Is Generous," Oak Park Reporter-Argus (16 December 1905): 2.

30. Special Meeting of the Board of Trustees, 17 December 1905, Record, 142–143 (Unity Temple Historical Files). Wright to Cudworth Beye, 12 December 1905, noted the building committee's acceptance of the church's design. See John O. Holzhueter, "The Yahara River Boathouse," in Sprague, ed., Frank Lloyd Wright and Madison, 40.

31. Wright, Autobiography (1932), 156.

32. The Avery Library: Selected Acquisitions 1960–1980 (New York: Avery Library, Columbia University, 1980), 22. The drawing has also been published in H. Allen Brooks, Frank Lloyd Wright and the Prairie School (New York: George Braziller, 1984), 63; and in Architectural Institute of Japan, Frank Lloyd Wright Retrospective (Tokyo: Mainichi Newspapers, 1991), 125.

Graf, Kunst des Quadrats, I, 127, 257, maintains that the geometry of Unity Temple's plan develops the geometry of Wright's graphic ornamentation for this edition of House Beautiful. The appearance of this decisive sketch at the back of a copy of this book supports the observation of a formal and symbolic connection between this House Beautiful edition and Unity Temple, designed about nine years apart. See also 302–303, n. 175.

33. On Unity Temple's adjacencies, see the Appendix, 247, and 332–333, n. 2. The

church's plan also recalled Wright's small houses of the same period designed for narrower plots. Designed about the same time as Unity Temple, the De Rhodes house at South Bend, Indiana, of 1906, represents a type that Wright explored in several similar dwellings after 1900. It was to be an exemplary solution for a standard small town lot 50 ft. wide and 150–175 ft. deep. The plan was to give light and air to the house's main rooms by placing them almost as one space though the length of the lot. The entry was at the house's center as a raised porch approached along one side of the frontal pavilion of the living room.

Access to the house was thus channeled to its center, leaving the major rooms to the front and rear free on three sides, so that adjacent houses could not deprive them of the advantages of simultaneous exposure and privacy. Only the porches midway through the lot touched its sides. The plan gave an apron of green space surrounding the domestic image of the foursquare hip-roofed front. This domestic plan type with a recessed entrance permitting a handsome architectural volume toward the street corresponds to Unity Temple's plan, yet also differs from it. In the church two entries appear on raised terraces, unlike the house's single entry porch. The church's terraces are set behind each side of the large auditorium, and the doorways into the church on the terraces do not face the frontal street. Unity Temple, of concrete, is also more monumental than the De Rhodes house, of wood.

Wright, *Ausgeführte Bauten und Entwürfe* (1910), Plate XXIX, compared the De Rhodes house to his earlier houses for Warren F. Hickox, Kankakee, Ill., 1900; E. B. Henderson, Elmhurst, Ill., 1901; J. J. Walser, Austin, Ill., 1903; and George Barton, Buffalo, N.Y., 1903. Mrs. Charles E. Roberts was a sister of Warren Hickox. See Mary Jane Hamilton, with Anne E. Biebel and John O. Holzhueter, "Frank Lloyd Wright's Madison Networks," in Sprague, ed., *Frank Lloyd Wright and Madison*, 8. On the De Rhodes house, see Charles E. Percival, "Making the Most of a Narrow Lot: Solving a Difficult Problem," *House Beautiful* 20 (July 1906): 20–21; Storrer, *Frank Lloyd Wright*, 125; Futagawa, ed., *Frank Lloyd Wright Monograph 1902–1906*, 216–219; and Storrer, *Wright Companion*, 123.

34. Charles E. White Jr. to Walter Willcox, 13 May 1904, in Smith, ed., "Letters, 1903–1906, by Charles E. White, Jr.," 105–106.

35. Wright, *Autobiography* (1932), 161.

36. Wright, *Autobiography* (1932), 70, identified the making of exteriors before plans as the method of Silsbee.

37. James F. O'Gorman, response presented at symposium, "Frank Lloyd Wright: The Perspective of a New Generation," at The Temple Hoyne Buell Center for the Study of American Architecture, Columbia University, 19 February 1994.

38. As a late example of Wright's sketch of a plan below the corresponding elevation, O'Gorman cited one of Wright's studies for Annunciation Greek Orthodox Church, Wauwatosa, Wis., 1956–61. This drawing is most recently published in Riley, ed., *Frank Lloyd Wright: Architect,* 312.

39. Wright, "In the Cause of Architecture (1908)," 161. Recalling Unity Temple's design, Wright observed that "it is impossible to present a 'sketch' when working in this method. The building as a whole must all be in order before the 'sketch' not after it" (Wright, *Autobiography* [1932], 161). On plans and perspectives in Wright's design method, see Joseph Connors, *The Robie House of Frank Lloyd Wright* (Chicago: University of Chicago Press, 1984), 40–45, 56–57.

40. The elevation sketched below Unity Temple's plan may relate to one that Wright drew of Jones's All Souls Building (Frank Lloyd Wright Foundation Drawing No. 9702.001). See Y. Futagawa, ed., *Frank Lloyd Wright Monograph 1887–1901,* 108; and Siry, "Abraham Lincoln Center," 244–245.

41. Wright, *Ausgeführte Bauten und Entwürfe* (1910), Plate XLI, Pettit Memorial Chapel,

Belvidere, Ill. On this building, see also Storrer, *Frank Lloyd Wright,* 116; Futagawa, ed., *Frank Lloyd Wright Monograph 1902–1906,* 256–257; and Storrer, *Wright Companion,* 116.

42. Wright, *Ausgeführte Bauten und Entwürfe* (1910), Plate VI, Atelier of Frank Lloyd Wright, Oak Park, Ill.

43. Charles E. White Jr. to Walter Willcox, 4 March 1906, in Smith, ed., "Letters, 1903–1906, by Charles E. White, Jr.," 110. Wright's house and studio were first published in "Successful Houses, III," *House Beautiful* 1 (15 February 1897): 64–69; and Alfred H. Granger, "An Architect's Studio," ibid., 7 (December 1899): 36–45. See also Donald Kalec, *The Home and Studio of Frank Lloyd Wright in Oak Park, Illinois, 1889–1911* (Oak Park: The Frank Lloyd Wright Home and Studio Foundation, 1982); and Ann Abernathy and John Thorpe, *The Oak Park Home and Studio of Frank Lloyd Wright* (Oak Park: The Frank Lloyd Wright Home and Studio Foundation, 1988). On Wright's home and studio as binuclear planning, see Laseau and Tice, *Frank Lloyd Wright,* 120–121.

44. Hitchcock, *Nature of Materials,* 28, wrote of the Heller House's plan: "Now there is an expansion from within. The space of the rooms seems to break out of the long oblong mass into a cross axis at the dining room bay and into a similar subordinate mass, echoing the main mass, at the front living room bay. Henceforth the new plan schemes, based on a new relation of interior volumes, and the exterior mass compositions are the inevitable counterpart of one another." On the Heller House, see Manson, *Frank Lloyd Wright,* 75–76; Storrer, *Frank Lloyd Wright,* 38; Futagawa, ed., *Frank Lloyd Wright Monograph 1887–1901,* 86–89; Gill, *Many Masks,* 124–125; Pinnell, "Academic Tradition and the Individual Talent," in McCarter, ed., *Frank Lloyd Wright,* 42–43; Werner Seligman, "Evolution of the Prairie House," in ibid., 82–83; MacCormac, "Form and Philosophy," in ibid., 111–112; and Storrer, *Wright Companion,* 36.

45. Wright, *Autobiography* (1932), 159. On "pure design," see the editorial, "Study of Pure Design in Architectural Education," *Inland Architect and News Record* 37 (June 1901): 33; Emil Lorch, "Some Considerations upon the Study of Architectural Design," ibid., 34; and Robert C. Spencer Jr., "Should the Study of Architectural Design and the Historic Styles Follow and Be Based upon a Knowledge of Pure Design?" ibid., 34–35. On Wright and "pure design," see Brooks, *Prairie School,* 39–40; and Menocal, "Wright and the Question of Style," 7–8. On pure design and Arthur Dow's teachings on Japanese art, see Nute, *Wright and Japan,* 86–98.

On Wright and Froebel, see Robert C. Spencer Jr., "The Work of Frank Lloyd Wright," *Architectural Review* (Boston) 7 (June 1900): 69; Wright, *Autobiography* (1932), 11; Manson, "Wright in the Nursery: The Influence of Froebel Education on His Work," *Architectural Review* 113 (February 1953): 349–351, and *Frank Lloyd Wright,* 5–10; Richard MacCormac, "The Anatomy of Wright's Aesthetic," *Architectural Review* 143 (February 1968): 143–146, and "Form and Philosophy: Froebel's Kindergarten Training and the Early Work of Frank Lloyd Wright (1974)," in McCarter, ed., *Wright: A Primer,* 99–109; Edgar J. Kaufmann Jr., "'*Form* Became *Feeling*': A New View of Froebel and Wright" (1981), and "Frank Lloyd Wright: Mementoes of Childhood" (1982), in *Nine Commentaries on Frank Lloyd Wright* (New York and Cambridge, Mass.: The Architectural History Foundation and MIT Press, 1989), 1–18, 19–35; and Jeanne S. Rubin, "The Froebel-Wright Kindergarten Connection, A New Perspective," *Journal of the Society of Architectural Historians* 48 (March 1989): 24–37. Jenkin Lloyd Jones also praised Froebel's achievements. See "The Immortal Froebel," *Unity* 34 (16 April 1896): 119–120.

46. Nute, *Wright and Japan,* 148–150, 167–170. See also Nute, "Frank Lloyd Wright and the Arts of Japan: A Study in How to Borrow Properly," *Architecture and Urbanism* 233 (February 1990): 26–33. On the Taiyu-in and the earlier Tosho-gu mausolea, see Naomi Okawa, *Edo Architecture: Katsura and Nikko* (New York and Tokyo: John Weatherhill,

and Heibonsha, 1964), 28–60. On Wright and Japanese models, Nute, *Wright and Japan,* 7, cites Wright's late talk, "Japanese Culture," at Taliesin: "I found in Japan, not the inspiration which everybody thinks I found. . . . What happened to me was a great confirmation of the feeling I had and work I had done myself before I got there." Tape transcript, 5 February 1956. © The Frank Lloyd Wright Foundation.

47. Wright, "In the Cause of Architecture (1908)," 212.

48. On early Protestant usage of pre-Reformation church buildings, and the origins of the *temple protestant,* see Fritsch, *Der Kirchenbau des Protestantismus,* 19–28, 31–72; Drummond, *Church Architecture of Protestantism,* 19–26, 29–33; Addleshaw and Etchells, *Architectural Setting of Anglican Worship,* 15–45; Georg Germann, *Der protestantische Kirchenbau in der Schweiz von der Reformation bis zur Romantik* (Zurich: Orell Fuessli, 1963), 17–24, 25–31, 35–39, 55–73, 107–144; and Nigel Yates, *Buildings, Faith, and Worship: The Liturgical Arrangement of Anglican Churches, 1600–1900* (Oxford: Oxford University Press, 1991), 23–43. On the centrally planned Protestant church with the Renaissance tradition of central churches, see Paul Frankl, *Principles of Architectural History: The Four Phases of Architectural Style* (1914), trans. James F. O'Gorman (Cambridge, Mass.: MIT Press, 1968), 55–60, 70–74.

    Sir Christopher Wren's London City churches were also a well known group of experiments in Protestant sanctuaries as what Wren termed "'auditories," or rooms that enabled hearing of the liturgy and the sermon as spoken by the clergy. This goal demanded rooms of limited size, unlike churches not intended for lay participation, which could therefore be unlimited in size like medieval cathedrals. Wren set forth his ideas in a letter of 1708, wherein he wrote: "I hardly think it practicable to make a single room so spacious, with pews and galleries, as to hold above 2,000 persons, and all to hear the service, and both to hear distinctly, and see the preacher." Wren to London City Commissioners, 1708, in Stephen Wren, *Parentalia: or, Memoirs of the Family of the Wrens* (London, 1750), 320. On the liturgical rationale of Wren's city churches, see Drummond, *Church Architecture of Protestantism,* 35–37; Briggs, *Puritan Architecture,* 29–32; Addleshaw and Etchells, *Architectural Setting for Anglican Worship,* 52–58, 247–250; and Eduard F. Sekler, *Wren and His Place in European Architecture* (New York: Macmillan, 1956), 71–80.

49. Jacques Perret, *Des fortifications et artifices. Architecture et perspective* (Paris, ca. 1601). See Germann, *Der protestantische Kirchenbau,* 31–35. Patricia M. O'Grady gave an analysis of Perret's text as "A Huguenot Statement in Architectural Terms, ca. 1601," a paper in the session on French Art of the 17th and 18th Centuries, College Art Association Annual Meeting, New York City, 18 February 1994.

50. Fritsch, *Der Kirchenbau des Protestantismus,* quoted in "The Design of Protestant Churches I," *American Architect and Building News* 53 (26 September 1896): 100–101.

51. Wright, *Autobiography* (1932), 154.

52. On the renovation of the Old Ship Meeting House, see Murray P. Corse, "The Old Ship Meeting-House in Hingham, Massachusetts," *Old Time New England* 21 (July 1930): 19–30. See also A. R. Willard, "The New England Meeting-House and the Wren Church," *New England Magazine,* n.s., 1 (September 1889–February 1890): 500; Aymar Embury II, *Early American Churches* (Garden City: Doubleday, Page, 1914), 35–39; Rev. Charles A. Place, "From Meeting House to Church in New England, I: The Meeting House in the First Hundred Years," *Old Time New England* 13 (October 1922): 74–76; Morrison, *Early American Architecture,* 80–81; John Coolidge, "Hingham Builds a Meetinghouse," *New England Quarterly* 24 (December 1961): 435–461; and Marian C. Donnelly, *The New England Meeting House of the Seventeenth Century* (Middletown, Conn.: Wesleyan University Press, 1968), 72–78.

    Architect William Ralph Emerson perhaps undertook an earlier restoration of the Hingham Building in about 1869, shortly before Wright's family moved to nearby Weymouth. See William D. Austin, "A History of the Boston Society of Architects in the

Nineteenth Century," 1942 (unpublished typescript in the Boston Athenaeum), Chapter 5, p. 15, cited in Cynthia Zaitzevsky, *The Architecture of William Ralph Emerson 1833–1917* (Cambridge, Mass.: Fogg Art Museum, 1969), 3.

53. On the architecture of the First Unitarian Church in Philadelphia, see J. Thomas Scharf and Thompson Westcott, *History of Philadelphia 1609–1884,* 3 vols. (Philadelphia: L. H. Everts, 1884), II, 1404–1406; Helen M. P. Gallagher, *Robert Mills: Architect of the Washington Monument 1781–1855* (New York: Columbia University Press, 1935), 78; Talbot Hamlin, *Greek Revival Architecture in America* (1944; reprint, New York: Dover, 1964), 50–53; Elizabeth Geffen, *Philadelphia Unitarianism 1796–1861* (Philadelphia: University of Pennsylvania Press, 1961), 78–79; Pierson, *American Buildings and Their Architects,* I, 375–377; and Rhodri W. Liscombe, *The Church Architecture of Robert Mills* (Eastley, S.C.: Southern Historical Press, 1985), 11, and *Altogether American: Robert Mills, Architect and Engineer, 1781–1855* (New York: Oxford University Press, 1994), 50–51.

54. On Baltimore's First Unitarian Church, see Robert L. Alexander, *The Architecture of Maximilien Godefroy* (Baltimore: Johns Hopkins University Press, 1974), 132–157; and Rebecca Funk, *A Heritage to Hold in Fee 1817–1917: First Unitarian Church of Baltimore* (Baltimore: Garamond, 1962), 9–16, 29–37.

55. "Church Spires Must Go," *Chicago Tribune* (30 November 1890): 36. See also "St. Paul's Church Buildings," *Universalist* 9 (17 December 1892): 5.

56. On Adler and Sullivan's building for Kehilath Anshe Ma'ariv, see Hyman L. Meites, ed., *History of the Jews of Chicago* (Chicago: Jewish Historical Society of Illinois, 1924), 171; Morrison, *Louis Sullivan,* 124; Wright, *Genius and the Mobocracy,* 63; Morris A. Gutstein, *A Priceless Heritage: The Epic Growth of Nineteenth Century Chicago Jewry* (New York: Bloch, 1953), 78–80; Lauren Weingarden Rader, "Synagogue Architecture in Illinois," in Spertus Museum of Judaica, *Faith and Form* (Chicago: Spertus College Press, 1976), 40–43; Lane, *Chicago Churches and Synagogues,* 64–65; Robert Twombly, *Louis Sullivan: His Life and Work* (New York: Viking Penguin, 1986), 248–249; Gregersen, *Dankmar Adler,* 74–75; and Sarah R. Nazimova, "The Evolution of a Congregation's Identity: Adler and Sullivan's Kehilath Anshe Ma'ariv Synagogue," Honors Thesis, History of Art, Wesleyan University, 1986.

On Adler and Sullivan's earlier Sinai Temple of 1875–76, and renovations of this building in 1891–92 that also coincided with the period of Wright's employment, see Weingarden Rader, "Synagogue Architecture in Illinois," 39–40; Twombly, *Louis Sullivan,* 70–71, 85–92, 269–271; and Gregersen, *Dankmar Adler,* 45–46.

57. On Adler and Sullivan's building for K.A.M., one observer wrote that "there seems to be nothing except the inscription over the entrance that would suggest that this building is a religious edifice much less a Jewish edifice. There is hardly a molding or ornament that indicates ecclesiasticism" (*Reform Advocate* 1 [12 June 1891]: 285–286, quoted in Weingarden Rader, "Synagogue Architecture in Illinois," 40). Sullivan said of the design: "It is the nineteenth century school. That is all I can say for it. It has no historical style. It is the present" (Sullivan, quoted in "Church Spires Must Go," 36, partially reprinted in Twombly, ed., *Sullivan: Public Papers,* 72–73).

Hip roofs recur in synagogues of the eighteenth century in Berlin, Franconia, Bavaria (the region of Germany from which K.A.M.'s founders had emigrated), and Saxony, whence Adler's family had come to the United States. Adler visited Saxony on his travels in the summer of 1888, shortly before the first plans for K.A.M. were drawn in the spring of 1889. His father, Liebman Adler, was the synagogue's longtime rabbi (Nazimova, "Evolution of a Congregation's Identity," 86–87, 93–94). See also Helen Rosenau, "German Synagogues in the Early Period of Emancipation," in Joseph Gutmann, comp., *The Synagogue: Studies in Origins, Archaeology, and Architecture* (New York: Ktav, 1975), 314–332; and Harold Hammer-Schenk, *Synagogen in Deutschland,* 2 vols. (Hamburg: Hans Christians Verlag, 1981), I, 17–37.

Nazimova, "Evolution of a Congregation's Identity," 89, noted that K.A.M.'s tiered roofs recall those crowning the wooden synagogues of rural Poland built in the seventeenth through the nineteenth centuries. On these structures, see Carol Krinsky, *Synagogues of Europe: Architecture, History, Meaning* (New York and Cambridge, Mass.: The Architectural History Foundation and MIT Press, 1985), 53–55, 225–230; and Maria Piechotka and Kazimiera Piechotka, *Wooden Synagogues* (Warsaw: Arkady, 1959), 44, who note the influence of Polish wood synagogues on those of Bavaria and Saxony before 1800.

58. On Unity Temple's signification of the antiquity of liberal beliefs, see Chapter 5, 208.

59. On Isaiah Temple's building, see Gutstein, *Priceless Heritage*, 85–87; Weingarden Rader, "Synagogue Architecture in Illinois," 48; Lane, *Chicago Churches and Synagogues*, 78–79; and Gregersen, *Dankmar Adler*, 89–90. Adler's original drawings for the building were published in Sarah C. Mollman, ed., *Louis Sullivan in the Art Institute of Chicago: The Illustrated Catalogue of Collections* (New York: Garland, 1989), 105–117. Descriptions of Isaiah Temple's design appeared in *Reform Advocate* 16 (10 September 1898): 53; "Dedication of Isaiah Temple," ibid., 17 (18 March 1899): 140; and ibid. (25 March 1899): 163–165. On the congregation's origins, see Meites, ed., *History of the Jews of Chicago*, 187–188, 518–522; Gutstein, *Priceless Heritage*, 46; and Temple Isaiah Israel, *Our First Century 1852–1952* (Chicago, 1952), 28–32.

   Unity Temple's plan may be compared to that of Shearith Israel Synagogue, built in New York City in 1897 and illustrated in Russell Sturgis, *A Dictionary of Architecture and Building*, 3 vols. (New York: Macmillan, 1902), III, 707–708.

60. "Dedication of Isaiah Temple," *Unity* 43 (23 March 1899): 75. See also "Jewish Joy and Prophecy," ibid., 65–66; and "A Welcome to Isaiah Temple," *The New Unity* 39 (16 January 1896): 727; "Isaiah Temple," ibid., 737. At Isaiah Temple's dedication, Rabbi Stolz claimed that the building embodied historical continuity. He told the congregation that "this house does not stand alone. It is the last link in that long chain of Jewish sanctuaries belting the earth since the tabernacle was erected in the wilderness and King Solomon dedicated his temple on Mount Zion. The spiritual eye here discerns the accretion of centuries." Yet he also implied that the new building's relative stylistic modernity signified a reverence for the future, observing that "the rising sun is our emblem, not the risen sun. The bright windows [are] our symbol, not the gloomy wall." He then compared the new temple to a cheerful house, a bright home, and a happy school, concluding that "we should be telescopes expectantly searching through present darkness for coming light, and in the light of the new knowledge welcome the restatement of any of the old doctrines, symbols or duties. That is the idea of the departure from the old lines of Moorish architecture and that is the idea of these big windows and hundreds of electric lights – progress. This is the home of progressive Judaism, not the mausoleum of antiquated ideas" (Rabbi Joseph Stolz, "Introductory Address," *Reform Advocate* 17 [25 March 1899]: 163).

61. "Will Share Unity," *Oak Leaves* (21 August 1909): 3. On Hugh Garden's Third Church of Christ, Scientist (now the Metropolitan Missionary Baptist Church), see Lane, *Chicago Churches and Synagogues*, 80; and Commission on Chicago Landmarks, *Third Church of Christ, Scientist* (Chicago, 1988). The design was first published in "A Church Built of Enamel Brick," *Brickbuilder* 10 (November 1901): 241. On the church's dedication, see *Chicago Inter Ocean* (14 July 1901) and *Christian Science Journal* 19 (August 1901). Garden's functional rationale for his church anticipated ideas in his address, "The Influence of the New Thought in Design on Architecture," *Inland Architect and News Record* 62 (December 1903): 35–36. Gill, *Many Masks*, 182, compared the church to Austrian Secessionist architecture, to which Garden referred in this address. On Garden's relationship with Wright, see Bernard C. Greengard, "Hugh M. G. Garden," *Prairie School Review* 3 (First Quarter 1966): 6.

   On Beman and his Christian Science churches, see his "The Architecture of the

Christian Science Church," *The World To-day* 12 (June 1907): 582–590; and Thomas J. Schlereth, "Solon Spencer Beman: The Social History of a Midwest Architect," *Chicago Architectural Journal* 5 (1985): 8–31. Beman's works in Chicago included the First Church of Christ, Scientist, now Grant Memorial A. M. E. Church, 4017 South Drexel Boulevard, 1897 (Lane, *Chicago Churches and Synagogues,* 75; Commission on Chicago Landmarks, Form No. 30-04-13-058); Second Church of Christ, Scientist, 2700 North Pine Grove Avenue, 1899; Fourth Church of Christ, Scientist, northeast corner of Harvard Avenue and Marquette Road, 1904; Fifth Church of Christ, Scientist, 4840 South Dorchester Avenue; Seventh Church of Christ, Scientist, 5318 North Kenmore Avenue, 1907; Sixth Church of Christ Scientist, 11321 South Prairie Avenue, 1910–11. Beman's drawings for these buildings, all of which are extant, survive in the Architecture Department, The Art Institute of Chicago. See also L. M. Holt, *Christian Science Church Architecture* (Los Angeles, 1908), 78–81, 84–89.

    Dana's involvement with Christian Science was noted by Professor Alice Friedman, "Frank Lloyd Wright and Feminism," paper presented at the symposium, "Frank Lloyd Wright: The Perspective of a New Generation," at The Temple Hoyne Buell Center for the Study of American Architecture, Columbia University, 19 February 1994. On Martin's involvement with Christian Science, see Marjorie L. Quinlan, *Rescue of a Landmark: Frank Lloyd Wright's Darwin D. Martin House* (Buffalo: Western New York Wares, 1990), 22, 75–76. See also Theodore Turak, "Mr. Wright and Mrs. Coonley: An Interview with Elizabeth Coonley Faulkner," in Richard Guy Wilson and Sidney K. Robinson, eds., *Modern Architecture in America: Visions and Revisions* (Ames: Iowa State University Press, 1991), 144–163.

62. William Pierson, "Richardson's Trinity Church and the New England Meeting House," in Craig Zabel and Susan Scott Munshower, eds., *American Public Architecture: European Roots and Native Expressions* (University Park: The Pennsylvania State University Press, 1989), 12–56.

63. Wright, *Autobiography* (1932), 156.

64. Wright, *Autobiography* (1943), 155.

65. "Unity Plans Unique," *Oak Leaves* (24 February 1906): 6.

66. On Scheme B's possible relation to the Taiyu-in mausoleum's plan, see also Nute, *Wright and Japan,* 169.

67. Thirty-seventh Annual Meeting of Unity Church, 9 March 1909, *Annual Reports 1902–1921,* 137–138 (Unity Temple Historical Files).

68. Charles E. White Jr. to Walter Willcox, 4 March 1906, in Smith, ed., "Letters, 1903–1906, by Charles E. White, Jr.," 110. On membership in local churches, see "Church Statistics," *Oak Park Reporter-Argus* (28 April 1906): 5.

69. See "Fellowship Club Resumes Meetings," *Oak Leaves* (9 November 1907): 2; "Discuss Waterway," ibid. (16 November 1907): 3; "First Fellowship Club Meeting," ibid. (3 October 1908): 12; "Neighbors Meet," ibid. (31 October 1908): 23; "Laymen's League," ibid. (2 January 1909): 12; "Fellowship Club Program," ibid. (13 February 1909): 18; "City – Annexation," ibid. (12 February 1910): 16; "Talk on Annexation," ibid. (19 February 1910): 3, 8–9; and "Against Annexation," ibid. (26 February 1910): 3, 14.

70. "Unity Plans Unique," 6.

71. Edgar Tafel, *Apprentice to Genius: Years with Frank Lloyd Wright* (New York: McGraw-Hill, 1979), 71–72.

72. Views of Unity Temple's west and north fronts, like Figs. 81 and 88 (top), were first published in "Unity Plans Unique," *Oak Leaves* (24 February 1906): 4, 5. Wright wrote in his autobiography that a perspective view, presumably an exterior, was made from the plan prior to the design's first presentation to the "building committee," indicating that the first such drawing of Unity Temple was made before the committee's acceptance of the design by 12 December 1905.

73. Charles E. White Jr. to Walter Willcox, 4 March 1906, in Smith, ed., "Letters, 1903–1906, by Charles E. White, Jr.," 110. See also H. Allen Brooks, "Frank Lloyd Wright and the Wasmuth Drawings," *Art Bulletin* 48 (June 1966): 194–195, who attributed the drawings of Unity Temple to Mahony. Barry Byrne, in a review of Arthur Drexler, *The Drawings of Frank Lloyd Wright, Journal of the Society of Architectural Historians* 22 (May 1963): 108–109, stated that the exterior perspective of Unity Temple's west front had the graphic style of an imitator of Mahony, suggesting that the related interior perspective may not have been by her.

74. Wright, *Autobiography* (1932), 157–158.

75. On Wright's final changes in the auditorium, see Chapter 4, 171–189.

76. Wright, *Autobiography* (1932), 4.

77. Ibid., 159.

78. Wright, "In the Cause of Architecture, I: The Logic of the Plan," *Architectural Record* 63 (January 1928): 50.

79. Wright, *Autobiography* (1932), 154.

80. Ibid., 105.

81. *Construction News* 20 (23 September 1905): 235. The same description of the building accompanied solicitation of bids (ibid., 21 [3 March 1906]: 167). See 303, n. 4. Graf, *Kunst des Quadrats*, I, 134, also notes an early scheme in brick and stone, similar in form to Unity Temple as built in concrete.

82. Wright, *Autobiography* (1932), 154–155.

83. Charles E. White Jr. to Walter Willcox, 4 March 1906, in Smith, ed., "Letters, 1903–1906, by Charles E. White, Jr.," 110.

84. Johonnot, *New Edifice of Unity Church,* 13.

85. Ibid.

86. "A Village Church, Cost Fifty Thousand Dollars; Program," *Brickbuilder* 8 (July 1899): 135; R. C. Sturgis, "Contribution," ibid., 135–136; Ernest Coxhead, "Village Church," ibid. (August 1899): 156–158; Allen B. Pond, "Village Church," ibid. (September 1899): 173–176; and T. H. Randall, "Village Church," ibid. (October 1899): 195–196.

87. Johonnot, *New Edifice of Unity Church,* 13. On Unity Temple's costs, see Chapter 4, 193, and 309–310, n. 65.

88. James P. Beck, Universal Portland Cement Company, "'King Portland' and the Great Central Market," *Cement Era* 6 (April 1908): 93.

89. "Growth of Reinforced Concrete," *American Contractor* 27 (6 October 1906): 56. See "The Production of Portland Cement in the United States in 1897–98," *Brickbuilder* 8 (February 1899): 36; and Carl W. Condit, *American Building* (Chicago: University of Chicago Press, 1968), 155–159. In 1905, the most nationally prominent builder in concrete was Ernest Ransome, who developed the "Daylight Factory" as a multistory frame with large windows into a standard type of modern industrial architecture. Ransome was then presenting his ideas in lectures to architects and engineers all over the country. His most influential buildings were the second phase of the Pacific Coast Borax works in Bayonne, N.J., and the United Shoe Machinery Plant at Beverly, Mass., both begun in 1903 and completed by 1906. See Reyner Banham, *A Concrete Atlantis: U.S. Industrial Building and European Modern Architecture* (Cambridge, Mass., MIT Press, 1986), 31–38, 56–82, 104–107; and Ernest Ransome and Alex Saurbrey, *Reinforced Concrete Buildings* (New York: McGraw-Hill, 1912). Amy Slayton of the University of Pennsylvania is currently pursuing research on American factories of reinforced concrete from 1900 to 1920.

The American Concrete Institute was founded in 1905 and published proceedings of its annual conventions from that year. Trade journals devoted to concrete flowered during this period: *Cement and Engineering News* (Chicago, 1896–1924), *Cement* (New York, 1900–1913), *Cement Era* (Chicago, 1903–17), *Concrete* (Detroit and Chicago, 1904–12), *Cement Age* (New York, 1904–12), *Cement Age* (Philadelphia, 1905–

8), *Concrete Age* (Atlanta, 1905–23), *Concrete Review* (Philadelphia, 1905–11), *Cement World* (Chicago, 1907–17), and *Concrete Engineering* (Cleveland, 1907–10). Like their counterparts in the eastern United States, Chicago's architectural periodicals, *Inland Architect and News Record* and *American Contractor,* regularly included articles on recent feats in concrete building.

By 1906 seven handbooks on reinforced concrete design had appeared in English, following an earlier tradition of such engineering publications in France and Germany. See "The Literature of Reinforced Concrete," *American Architect* 89 (12 May 1906): 159–160. English books were L. J. Mensch, *Architects' and Engineers' Hand-book of Reinforced Concrete Constructions* (Chicago: Cement Engineering News, 1904); Albert W. Buel and Charles S. Hill, *Reinforced Concrete* (New York: Engineering News, 1904); Charles F. Marsh, *Reinforced Concrete* (New York: D. Van Nostrand, 1904); Frederick Winslow Taylor and Sanford E. Thompson, *A Treatise on Concrete, Plain and Reinforced* (New York: John Wiley and Sons, 1905); Louis C. Sabin, *Cement and Concrete* (New York: McGraw, 1905); Walter N. Twelvetrees, *Concrete-Steel: A Treatise on the Theory and Practice of Reinforced Concrete Construction* (London and New York: Whittaker, 1905); and Frank D. Warren, *A Handbook on Reinforced Concrete, for Architects, Engineers, and Contractors* (New York: D. Van Nostrand, 1906).

90. Beck, "King Portland," 94.

91. On Montgomery Ward's warehouse, see "The Contractor's Plant Used in Constructing the Montgomery Ward Building," *Engineering Record* 55 (11 May 1907): 571–573; *Architectural Record* 22 (1907): 115–120; P. B. Wight, "Utilitarian Architecture in Chicago – I," ibid., 27 (February 1910): 196–197; and Condit, *Chicago School of Architecture,* 192–193.

On the concrete pavilions of Schmidt, Garden, and Martin, see "Concrete Adds Beauty to Chicago Park," *Cement Era* 6 (October 1908): 225. Those of D. H. Burnham and Company of 1904–6 for the South Park system were noted in Nancy Austin, "Traditions of Exposed Concrete in American Architecture: An Essay on New Materials, History, and Change," lecture given to the Society of Architectural Historians, Latrobe Chapter, National Building Museum, Washington, D.C., 24 May 1994. On these structures, Austin cites a pamphlet published by the Vulcanite Portland Cement Company in June 1905. A list of D. H. Burnham and Company's eighteen buildings and other projects for Chicago's South Park Commissioners, dated from 1903 to 1912, including parks and addresses, is in Charles Moore, *Daniel H. Burnham: Architect, Planner of Cities,* 2 vols. (Boston: Houghton Mifflin, 1921), II, 211.

In Chicago after 1900 the efforts to promote innovative exploration of concrete's versatility included competitions sponsored by cement manufacturers for architectural designs for houses in the new material. In 1908 Universal Portland Cement Company sponsored a competition for a suburban residence ("Architectural Prize Competition," *American Contractor* 29 [7 November 1908]: 76), which elicited an elegant design in concrete block by Marion Mahony. This appeared in *Plans for Concrete Houses* (Chicago: Universal Portland Cement Company, 1909), Figures 50–53. On houses entirely of concrete, see Charles De Kay, "Villas All Concrete," *Architectural Record* 17 (February 1905): 85–100; and "Concrete in Its Modern Forms and Uses," *Craftsman* 8 (September 1905): 760–765.

In 1906 Wright designed his first project for a house all of concrete block, for Harry E. Brown in Genesco, Ill. See Frampton, "The Text-Tile Tectonic," in McCarter, ed., *Wright: A Primer,* 136–138. During this period, Wright was also known for his use of cement plaster as an exterior finish for wood frame houses. In 1910 Universal Portland Cement Company published his Evans house in Longwood, near Chicago, Gilmore house in Madison, and Stockman house in Mason City, Iowa, all of 1908. The company also supplied materials for Wright's first executed house of reinforced concrete, for Edmund D. Brigham on Sheridan Road in Glencoe. Designed in 1908, this house was reported to be in construction in the winter of 1908–9, making it Wright's next building after Unity Temple made of monolithic concrete. The house appears in *Representative Cement Houses* (Chicago: Universal Portland Cement Company, 1910). Olgivanna L. Wright, *Frank Lloyd Wright: His Life, His Work, His Words* (New York: Horizon, 1965), 211; Hitchcock, *Nature of Materials*, 121; Storrer, *Frank Lloyd Wright*, 184; and Pfeiffer, "Lists of Project Numbers," in Anthony Alofsin, ed., *Frank Lloyd Wright: An Index to the Taliesin Correspondence*, 5 vols. (New York: Garland, 1988), I, xxviii, date the Brigham house to 1915. Storrer, *Wright Companion*, 186, notes that the house was designed in 1908. On Wright's prairie houses of cement over wood frame, see Sanford E. Thompson, "The Coming of the Concrete Age," *Suburban Life* 7 (1908): 116; Charles E. White Jr., "Insurgent Architecture in the Middle West," *Country Life in America* 22 (1912): 15–18, and "The Best Way to Use Cement," *House Beautiful* 34 (1913): 130–134. See also David Handlin, *The American Home: Architecture and Society, 1815–1915* (Boston: Little, Brown, 1979), 299–302.

92. Irving K. Pond, "Concrete Architecture," *Inland Architect and News Record* 50 (November 1907): 50–51, also published in *Cement Era* 5 (December 1907): 352–353. See also C. Howard Walker, "The Artistic Use of Steel and Reinforced Concrete," *American Architect* 93 (11 January 1908): 17; ibid. (18 January 1908): 25–26, also published in *Inland Architect and News Record* 50 (November 1907): 56–57; ibid. (December 1907): 76–77.

93. A. O. Elzner, "The Artistic Expression of Concrete," *Inland Architect and News Record* 50 (November 1907): 54. This paper was also published in *Cement Era* 6 (March 1908): 69–71. See also Elzner, "The Artistic Treatment of Concrete," *American Contractor* 28 (2 February 1907): 62.

94. Elzner, "Artistic Expression of Concrete," 56, where Carrere and Hastings's St. Augustine church was also noted. Exterior photographs of St. David's, Rolland Park, appeared in *Inland Architect and News Record* 51 (March 1908): 47–48. On Our Lady of Loreto in East New York, see "Fine Concrete Church," *American Contractor* 29 (4 July 1908): 86. On Temple Adath Israel in Boston, see Taylor and Thompson, *Treatise on Concrete*, 626–627. See also "Churches Built of Concrete Blocks," *Craftsman* 16 (April 1909): 96–99.

Historically styled concrete churches with stone facing included Cram, Goodhue, and Ferguson's Second Presbyterian Church, Springfield, Ill., 1908. The associated Chicago architect for this building was Herman von Holst, to whom Wright entrusted his practice upon leaving Oak Park in 1909. On this church, see *Inland Architect and News Record* 51 (May 1908): 47–48; and *American Contractor* 29 (13 June 1908): 52. On Cram's view of technical innovations in neo-Gothic architecture, see Douglas S. Tucci, *Church Building in Boston 1720–1970* (Concord, Mass.: Rumford, 1974), 57–59.

95. Jones to Wright, 23 September 1902, Jones Letter Book, 18 June 1902–17 June 1903, 193 (Jones Collection, Meadville-Lombard).

96. Wright, "The Architect," paper read before the second annual conference of the Architectural League of America, Chicago, June 7–9, 1900, and published in Bruce Brooks Pfeiffer, ed., *Frank Lloyd Wright: Collected Writings, Vol. I: 1894–1930* (New York: Rizzoli, 1992), 52. Wright's paper resonated with Louis Sullivan's briefer statement to the league's inaugural meeting the year before, entitled "The Modern Phase of Architecture," published in *Inland Architect and News Record* 33 (June 1899): 40, and reprinted in Twombly, ed., *Sullivan: Public Papers*, 123–125. Wright's position also recalled that of Dankmar Adler in his "The Influence of Steel Construction and Plate Glass upon the Development of Modern Style," *Inland Architect and News Record* 28 (November 1896): 34–36. Wright, *Genius and the Mobocracy*, 43, wrote that "[Adler's] ideas throughout were advanced far beyond his time . . . . Reading (or rereading) some of the papers he prepared and read to the A.I.A. at that time, for instance, the paper, 'Modifying Buildings by the Use of Steel,' would astonish most modernites."

97. Wright, "The Art and Craft of the Machine," first published in *Catalogue of the Fourteenth Annual Exhibition of the Chicago Architectural Club* (1901), 14, reprinted in Pfeiffer, ed., *Wright: Collected Writings*, I, 65. On this address, see David A. Hanks, *The Decorative Designs of Frank Lloyd Wright* (New York: E. P. Dutton, 1979), 63–67; idem, "Frank Lloyd Wright's 'Art and Craft of the Machine,'" *Frank Lloyd Wright Newsletter* 2 (1979): 6–9; idem, "Frank Lloyd Wright's 'Art and Craft of the Machine,'" in Kenneth L. Ames, ed., *Victorian Furniture: Essays from a Victorian Society Autumn Symposium*, published as *Nineteenth Century* 8 (1982): 205–211; Joseph Connors, "Wright on Nature and the Machine," in Carol R. Bolon, Robert S. Nelson, and Linda Seidel, eds., *The Nature of Frank Lloyd Wright* (Chicago: University of Chicago Press, 1988), 9–12; Narciso G. Menocal, "Frank Lloyd Wright as the Anti-Victor Hugo," in Zabel and Munshower, eds., *American Public Architecture*, 138–150; and Joseph Siry, "Frank Lloyd Wright's 'The Art and Craft of the Machine': Text and Context," in Martha Pollak, ed., *The Education of the Architect: Historiography, Urbanism, and the Growth of Architectural Knowledge*, festschrift for Stanford Anderson (Cambridge, Mass.: MIT Press), forthcoming.

98. Wright, "In the Cause of Architecture (1908)," 157. Wright's view of materials informed his other investigations of concrete during the period. Among those most closely related to Unity Temple were two unbuilt designs, one for a concrete apartment house for Warren MacArthur Sr., dated to either 1905 or 1906, to be built in the Kenwood district in the South Side of Chicago, and "A Fireproof House for $5,000," of 1906 and published in the *Ladies' Home Journal* of April 1907. Both designs observed principles of concrete as it is cast in wooden molds or formwork. These were, first, the repetition of forms to enable many castings of concrete to be made from the same mold, and, second, the planar and rectilinear simplicity of detail to facilitate casting the concrete in its wooden molds.

For the MacArthur Apartment House, Wright proposed a building in which all elements would be rectilinear. Base, walls, mullions, moldings, and roof were to be simple shapes that could readily be cast in wooden boxes. Windows repeat in size across and up the walls, suggesting that the whole plan conforms to a single grid of modular dimensions. This plan also divides the building into projecting and receding blocks that could be cast sequentially to reuse formwork. See Wright, *Ausgeführte Bauten und Entwürfe* (1910), Plate LIV. Concrete flat-building at Kenwood for Warren McArthur; Hitchcock, *Nature of Materials*, 54–55, Plates 131–132; and Futagawa, ed., *Frank Lloyd Wright Monograph 1902–1906*, 196.

Wright applied the same principles to his project for a Fireproof House, of which he wrote: "Changing industrial conditions have brought reinforced concrete construction within the reach of the average home-maker. The maximum strength peculiar to the nature of both concrete and steel is in this system utilized with great economy." Wright then characterized the house's plan as "the result of a process of elimination due to much experience in planning the inexpensive house," yielding a type "which is trimmed to the last ounce of the superfluous." Wright's square plan of 30 ft. on a side within the house facilitated casting with wood formwork as "the house has been designed all four sides alike in order to simplify the making of these forms, and so that, if necessary, forms made for one side may serve for all four" (Wright, "A Fireproof House for $5000," *Ladies Home Journal* 24 [April 1907]: 24). On its exterior, the house from base to chimney exhibits the same attention to simplicity of the casting process evident in the MacArthur Apartment House. In both projects, the main architectural effect derives from the shadowed overhang of the flat roof slab capping simple cubic masses, not unlike Unity Temple. On the project for a Fireproof House, see Wright, *Ausgeführte Bauten und Entwürfe* (1910), Plate XIV. Concrete house originally designed for *Ladies' Home Journal*; Hitchcock, *Nature of Materials*, 44–45, Plates 128–129; Manson, *Frank Lloyd*

Wright, 181–183; Brooks, *Prairie School,* 124–126; and Futagawa, ed., *Frank Lloyd Wright Monograph 1902–1906,* 246–247.

Wright's unbuilt projects of the period included other designs for concrete that might also have been carried out in traditional materials. In 1901 *Brickbuilder* published Wright's design for "A Village Bank," which he described as a building designed to be "constructed entirely in brick." An unpublished version of this same text described the design as "cast as a monolith in cement." When the same drawing appeared in the exhibit of Wright's work at the Chicago Architectural Club in the following spring of 1902, Wright labeled it as "a study for a village bank . . . designed to be cast in concrete entire." The project was so labeled in the Wasmuth folio of 1910 for an international audience. See Wright, "The 'Village Bank' Series, V," *Brickbuilder* 10 (August 1901): 161; "The Work of Frank Lloyd Wright," *Chicago Architectural Annual* (1902): 52–53; and Wright, *Ausgeführte Bauten und Entwürfe* (1910), Plate XIII: Village Bank in cast concrete. See also Hitchcock, *Nature of Materials,* 35, Plate 65; Manson, *Frank Lloyd Wright,* 86–88; Brooks, *Prairie School,* 135; Futagawa, ed., *Frank Lloyd Wright Monograph 1887–1901,* 63; and Pfeiffer, ed., *Wright: Collected Writings,* I, 70. Manson and Pfeiffer note that Wright labeled another drawing for this project (Frank Lloyd Wright Foundation, Drawing No. 9408.001) as a "Study for Concrete Monolithic Bank, 1894."

In July 1906 Wright had prepared a set of working drawings for the house and studio of sculptor Richard Bock, intended for a site in suburban Maywood Village, Ill., but not built. The drawings, such as the front elevation, reveal that the project was conceived here as a wood frame building, with planes of cement plaster edged in wide bands of lumber along the building's base and along the fascia of the roof above (Frank Lloyd Wright Foundation, Drawing No. 0612.009). As published in the Wasmuth folio four years later, in 1910, the Bock project was labeled as an "atelier in concrete." The revised accompanying perspective of the design accordingly omitted the rendering of plaster and wood found in the working drawings. Instead, the view presents a dwelling whose base, walls, and roof slabs appear to be of reinforced concrete. This atelier for Richard Bock was the penultimate project in the Wasmuth folio, placed just before the drawings of Unity Temple. See Wright, *Ausgeführte Bauten und Entwürfe* (1910), Plate LXII. On Bock's studio, see Manson, *Frank Lloyd Wright,* 124–126; Donald P. Hallmark, "Richard W. Bock, Sculptor, II: The Mature Collaborations," *Prairie School Review* 8 (Second Quarter 1971): 20–21; Futagawa, ed., *Frank Lloyd Wright Monograph 1902–1906,* 242–245; and Bock, *Memoirs of an American Artist,* 92.

Wright's one large built structure in concrete prior to Unity Temple's design was the E-Z Polish Factory for Darwin and William Martin at 3005-3017 West Carroll Avenue, built in 1905 on the Galena line of the Chicago and Northwestern Railroad that ran west from Chicago to Oak Park. Charles E. White Jr. to Walter Willcox, 19 May 1904, noted that Wright and his assistants had "recently designed the stove polish factory" for the Martin brothers (Smith, ed., "'Letters, 1903–1906, by Charles E. White, Jr.," 106). On this building, see Hitchcock, *Nature of Materials,* 52; Manson, *Frank Lloyd Wright,* 163–165; Storrer, *Frank Lloyd Wright,* 114; Banham, *Concrete Atlantis,* 89; Futagawa, ed., *Frank Lloyd Wright Monograph 1902–1906,* 186–187; Gill, *Many Masks,* 156–161; and Storrer, *Wright Companion,* 113, who notes that it was originally only two stories with the upper floors added after a fire of 1913. Although this factory is described as a reinforced concrete frame, its brick-faced walls contrast with Ransome's daylight factories, whose frames were exposed and whose bays were filled with glass. Wright's design thus recalled earlier factories with structural piers of brick. Prevalent in Chicago and Buffalo, these earlier factories would have been known to the Martins as clients. On such factories, see Banham, *Concrete Atlantis,* 43–45; and Wight, "Utilitarian Architecture in Chicago – I," 193–196.

99. Wright, *Autobiography* (1932), 155. Wright wrote in 1927: "Concrete is a plastic mate-

rial but sets so slowly as yet that moulds or so called 'forms' are used to give it shape. . . . The materials from which the moulds are made, will, therefore, modify the shape the concrete naturally takes" (Wright, "Fabrication and Imagination," 318–319).

100. Wright, "In the Cause of Architecture, Second Paper," *Architectural Record* 34 (May 1914): 406.

101. Wright, "Logic of the Plan," 49.

102. Ibid.

103. Wright, "In the Cause of Architecture (1908)," 160–161.

104. Wright, talk to Taliesin Fellowship, 13 August 1952, quoted in Pfeiffer, ed., *Letters to Architects,* 48, and in Pfeiffer, ed., *Wright: Living Voice,* 26–27. On Wright's development of the Larkin Building's corners as architecturally distinct forms, see Quinan, *Larkin Building,* 27–30. See also Chapter 4, 189–192, and 315–316, nn. 157–159.

105. Wright, *Autobiography* (1932), 160.

106. Ibid. Bruce Brooks Pfeiffer, introduction to Yukio Futagawa, ed., *Frank Lloyd Wright Monograph 1951–1959* (Tokyo: A.D.A. EDITA, 1988), ix, wrote that Wright had stated that it had taken forty sketches to get to his final design for Unity Temple in 1905, and that not one of them remained.

107. Editorial, "Temple or Social Workshop," *Church Economist* 10 (August 1905): 286–287.

108. Ibid., 287. Architect Allen B. Pond studied this issue in a design for "A Village Church, Cost Fifty Thousand Dollars," in *Brickbuilder* 8 (September 1899): 173–175, the year he rented an office in Steinway Hall, where Wright then had his (Brooks, *Prairie School,* 30–31). Pond had designed the expanded buildings of Chicago's Hull House, whose mission was distinctly social and nonsectarian. Yet he stated: "The vital and permanent function for the church [is] to foster the life of the spirit. . . . Our task is to design a building which shall be a fit 'house of worship,' a place beautiful as befits the life of the spirit, a place instilling by its aspect calmness of mind, a place in harmony with feelings of reverence and of faith, and calculated by subtle suggestion to stimulate these emotions." Pond maintained that the church's social functions supplemented its role as a place of worship; hence a parish house with provision for social activities should be adjacent to and ideally united to the building for worship. Like Wright with his humanistic view of Unity Temple, Pond wished for the parish house to express and upbuild social unity, complementing "the church as house of God with the church as house of man." Thus, "the type of our parish house will be ecclesiastical, because it is still the church, though in its social aspect." In Pond's design, a basilican church stands at right angles to the parish hall at its rear. Both have low roofs that respond to a suburban residential context. As Pond wrote: "We . . . connect our house of God with our house of Man, emphasizing thus the necessity of an intimate connection between the life of the spirit and the activities of men."

109. Johonnot, quoted in "Unity Plans Unique," 5. In 1910 Johonnot wrote: "Everywhere and in all time [religion] has reared altars and built temples for public worship. It has found such worship to be its main reliance in appealing to men and the main purpose for which it is organized. . . . Social gatherings play their part. But it yet remains that an ordered service of public worship and preaching are the most important functions of the church and the methods by which alone it can succeed" (Johonnot, "The Paragraph Pulpit," *Universalist Leader* 13 [26 March 1910]: 394).

110. Johonnot, *New Edifice of Unity Church,* 2–3. Unlike James F. Clarke and Jenkin Lloyd Jones, Johonnot advocated the auditorium's differentiation from other functions of a church, as did more conservative Unitarians. In 1884, while Johonnot was living in Boston, architect Robert S. Peabody, himself a Unitarian, wrote that in the design of Unitarian church buildings, "the church should be a church from bottom to top, sacred to devotion from foundation to spire. . . . I believe that the social meetings, the sewing circles, the parish parties should be held in an adjoining structure. It is sometimes

cheaper to have them in the basement, but it does not save so very much. On the other hand, the grouping of church and parish building will be attractive outside and the sentiment of keeping the church sacred to the worship of God certainly is worth something" (Robert S. Peabody, "Unitarian Church Building," *American Architect and Building News* 16 [22 November 1884]: 248).

111. Wright, *Ausgeführte Bauten und Entwürfe* (1910), 7.

112. Byrne, Review of Drexler, *Drawings of Frank Lloyd Wright,* 109.

113. Charles E. White Jr. to Walter Willcox, 13 May 1904, in Smith, ed., "Letters, 1903–1906, by Charles E. White, Jr.," 105–106.

114. Wright, "In the Cause of Architecture (1908)," 160. On Wright's unit system as a method of design, see Wright's remarks at University of California at Berkeley, 24 April 1957, transcribed in Meehan, ed., *Master Architect: Conversations with Wright,* 217; and Wright, "The Unit System," talk to Taliesin Fellowship, 30 July 1952, in Pfeiffer, ed., *Wright: Living Voice,* 182–184. See also MacCormac, "Anatomy of Wright's Aesthetic," 143–146, and "Form and Philosophy," in McCarter, ed., *Frank Lloyd Wright,* 99–123; McCarter, "The Integrated Ideal: Ordering Principles in the Architecture of Frank Lloyd Wright," in ibid., 255–258; Menocal, "Frank Lloyd Wright and the Question of Style," 15–19; David Van Zanten, "Schooling the Prairie School: Wright's Early Style as a Communicable System," in Bolon et al., eds., *Nature of Frank Lloyd Wright,* 70–73; Laseau and Tice, *Frank Lloyd Wright,* 16–19, 43, 99, 110; Menocal, "Taliesin, the Gilmore House, and the 'Flower in the Crannied Wall,' " in *Taliesin 1911–1914,* 84–90; and Storrer, *Wright Companion,* 55, 98.

115. E.-E. Viollet-le-Duc, *Lectures on Architecture* (1863, 1872), 2 vols., trans. Benjamin Bucknall (1877, 1881; reprint, New York: Dover, 1987), I, 466. See also Donald Hoffmann, "Frank Lloyd Wright and Viollet-le-Duc," *Journal of the Society of Architectural Historians* 28 (October 1969): 173–183; and Cronon, "Inconstant Unity," in Riley, ed., *Frank Lloyd Wright: Architect,* 17.

116. Adler, "The Tall Business Building," *Cassier's Magazine* 12 (November 1897): 197.

117. Wright, "Logic of the Plan (1928)," 50. In one edition of *An Autobiography* (London: Faber and Faber, 1945), 201, Wright wrote that "music and architecture blossom on the same stem; sublimated mathematics. Mathematics as presented by geometry. Instead of the musician's systematic staff and intervals, the architect has a modular system as the framework of design." Quoted in Eaton, *Two Chicago Architects,* 46; and Menocal, "Frank Lloyd Wright and the Question of Style," 15.

118. Wright, "Logic of the Plan," 51.

119. Ibid., 57.

120. Charles E. White Jr. to Walter Willcox, 4 March 1906, in Smith, ed., "Letters, 1903–1906, by Charles E. White, Jr.," 110, wrote that then "all hands are working on the working drawings" for Unity Church. Barry Byrne, review of Drexler, *Drawings of Frank Lloyd Wright,* 109, recalled making drawings for Unity House under Wright's supervision. The working drawings, dated March 1906, and specifications were approved by trustees at their meeting of 28 April. See Chapter 4, 138–139, and 304, n. 11.

121. Spencer, "Work of Frank Lloyd Wright," 69.

122. Wright, *Autobiography* (1932), 155, wrote of Unity Temple's form: "Geometric shapes through human sensibility have thus acquired human significance as, say, the cube or square, integrity; the circle or sphere, infinity; the straight line, rectitude; if long drawn out . . . repose." This concept may be traced to Froebel, as discussed in Cronon, "Inconstant Unity," in Riley, ed., *Frank Lloyd Wright: Architect,* 15. Emerson also linked ethics and aesthetics. See Robert McCarter, "Abstract Essence: Drawing Wright from the Obvious," in McCarter, ed., *Wright: A Primer,* 12.

123. Special Meeting of the Board of Trustees, 2 January 1906, *Record,* 140–141 (Unity Temple Historical Files).

124. Ibid.

125. Special Meeting of the Board of Trustees, 4 January 1906, *Record,* 145 (Unity Temple Historical Files).

126. Ibid.

127. Wright, *Autobiography* (1932), 162.

128. Special Joint Meeting of the Board of Trustees of Unity Church of Oak Park with the Plans and Building Committees, 14 January 1906, *Record,* 149–150 (Unity Temple Historical Files).

129. Special Meeting of the Board of Trustees of Unity Church with the Plans, Building, and Finance Committees, 18 January 1906, *Record,* 156 (Unity Temple Historical Files).

130. Meeting of the Board of Trustees of Unity Church with the Finance Committee, 21 January 1906, *Record,* 157 (Unity Temple Historical Files).

131. Ibid., 158.

132. Wright, *Autobiography* (1932), 161–162.

133. Ibid., 162.

134. "Unity Church Men See Plans," *Oak Leaves* (3 February 1906): 12.

135. "Annual Report of the Secretary for the Year Ending March 23rd, 1906," in Unity Church, Oak Park, Ill., Ladies Social Union, Membership List [and] Minutes, III, October 28, 1904 to March 11, 1910, 33 (Unity Temple Historical Files).

136. This notation, in Wright's hand, appears on a print of this photograph of the plaster model for Unity Temple (Frank Lloyd Wright Foundation 0611.80). The ornamentation on the temple's columns shows a foliate motif that appeared on the interior perspective (Fig. 80) and two exterior views (Figs. 81 and 88, top) like those published in February 1906. These motifs were changed to a geometric design on working drawings of March 1906, indicating that this was the model made by January's end.

137. Wright, *Autobiography* (1932), 158.

138. Meeting of the Board of Trustees, 7 February 1906, *Record,* 160 (Unity Temple Historical Files). This account may refer to the alternative sets of plans for Unity Temple, labeled Scheme A, with the pulpit on the south side, and Scheme B, with pulpit on the north side. See pp. 101–103.

139. Ibid., 161.

140. Wright, *Autobiography* (1932), 162.

141. Charles E. White Jr. to Walter Willcox, 4 March 1906, Smith, ed., "Letters, 1903–1906, by Charles E. White, Jr.," 110.

142. The same text appeared in both "Unity Plans Unique," *Oak Leaves* (24 February 1906): 3, 5–7, and "Description of the New Edifice . . . ," *Oak Park Reporter-Argus* (24 February 1906): 3. The text begins with a section of about five hundred words that gives a theological and contextual rationale for the new church's unusual form. This introduction prefaces a description of about one thousand words devoted to the building. Rev. Johonnot was probably the author of the theological introduction, as it contains ideas that recurred in his later statements on the project. These appear in *The New Edifice of Unity Church* (1906), and a letter, *Universalist Leader* 10 (21 December 1907). On these texts, see Chapter 5, 195–198, and 316, n. 1. Physical description of the design may have been written by Wright, as its architectural detail is comparable to that found in his essay on his other main nonresidential work of the period, the Larkin Building in Buffalo. See Wright, "The New Larkin Administration Building," *The Larkin Idea* 6 (November 1906): 2–9, reprinted in *Prairie School Review* 7 (First Quarter 1970): 15–19; and Quinan, *Larkin Building,* 140–144.

143. "Church Notices," *Oak Leaves* (24 February 1906): 29; and "Churches," *Oak Park Reporter-Argus* (24 February 1906): 7.

144. Bock, *Memoirs of an American Artist,* 90.

145. "Unity Plans Unique," 3.

146. Johonnot, quoted in "Unity Plans Unique," 3.

147. Charles De Kay, "What Do Our Church Buildings Express?" *Review of Reviews* 32 (December 1905): 689–698.

148. Ibid., 689.

149. Ibid.

150. Ibid., 691.

151. Ibid., 693. As an alternative to conventional ecclesiastical types, De Kay advised that the "origin of temple, church, and synagogue in a subterranean tomb or cave should not be forgotten when examining the religious edifices of ancient and modern peoples; it will often give a clew [sic] to things which otherwise seem a puzzle" (ibid., 694).

152. Johonnot, quoted in "Unity Plans Unique," 3.

153. Graf, *Kunst des Quadrats,* I, 134, proposes that Wright's depiction of Unity Temple as isolated amid trees helped negate the character of the surrounding environs.

154. Johonnot, *New Edifice of Unity Church,* 19. Reports of meetings of Oak Park's Improvement Association include: "Improvement Association," *Oak Leaves* (8 May 1903): 13; ibid. (12 June 1903): 15; "Plan a Boycott," ibid. (17 July 1903): 11–12; "Annual Meeting," ibid. (11 March 1904): 25–27; "Civic Beauty," ibid. (25 March 1904): 6, 24–25; "Improvement Association," ibid. (15 April 1904): 8–9; ibid. (29 April 1904): 17; "Improvement Association," *Oak Park Reporter-Argus* (6 May 1905): 1, 8; ibid. (28 October 1905): 8; "New Officers Elected," ibid. (10 February 1906): 6; "Improvement Association," ibid. (31 March 1906): 3; ibid. (14 April 1906): 8; ibid. (28 April 1906): 6; "Oak Park Improvement Association," ibid. (12 May 1906): 8; "Improve Oak Park," ibid. (9 June 1906): 5; "Association Met," ibid. (11 August 1906): 1; and "Improvement Club Meeting," *Oak Leaves* (15 December 1906): 37.

155. Editorial, "Trees by Special Assessment," *Oak Leaves* (29 October 1904): 16. Shade trees lining streets of Oak Park's oldest central residential section (north of Madison Street and south of Chicago Avenue) were first planted by Henry W. Austin (1828–89), who had built his own house in 1859 on his grounds north of Lake Street and west of Forest Avenue. A founder of First Congregational Church, Austin had bought Oak Park's saloons to close them, and, as a member of the Illinois state legislature, he made it illegal to publicly sell alcohol in Oak Park, giving it a unique distinction among surrounding villages. Wright referred to Austin as one of his first acquaintances in the community, and Austin sold to Wright the lot on which Wright built his own house on the southeast corner of Forest and Chicago avenues in 1889. On Austin, see Andreas, *History of Cook County,* 787; Le Gacy, "Improvers and Preservers," 48–49, 66–67; and *Oak Leaves* (14 April 1935): 60, 77. His funding of shade trees was recognized in Wright, "'An Unpatriotic Ordinance," *Oak Park Reporter* (23 August 1900): 3. See also Wright, *Autobiography* (1932), 79–83, 103.

156. Editorial, "More Shade Trees Wanted," *Oak Leaves* (23 July 1904): 4. The local forester observed: "What is there more refreshing to the eye than to gaze upon the healthy green foliage of trees after a day of toil in the busy, noisy city?" ("Save the Trees," *Oak Leaves* [24 July 1909]: 10). See also E. D. Philbrick, letter, "About the Trees," ibid. (7 August 1909): 4; "Arts Forester," ibid., 28; E. D. Philbrick, "Urban Forestry," ibid. (21 August 1909): 20–21; and Winthrop R. Kendall, letter, "Halt, Axman! Halt," ibid. (6 November 1909): 10.

157. Wright, "'Why Tinker the Shape of the Tree?" *Oak Park Reporter* (23 August 1900): 1. See also his address to Unity Church's Fellowship Club of 1900, "Concerning Landscape Architecture," in Pfeiffer, ed., *Wright: Collected Writings,* I, 54–57.

158. Wright, *Ausgeführte Bauten und Entwürfe* (1910), 6.

159. Charles E. White Jr. to Walter Willcox, 16 November 1903, in Smith, "Letters, 1903–1906, by Charles E. White, Jr.," 104.

160. Wright, "In the Cause of Architecture (1908)," 155–156.

161. Ibid., 156.

162. Wright, *Ausgeführte Bauten und Entwürfe* (1910), 8. On the influence of Japanese

prints on Wright's renderings, see Arthur Drexler, ed., *The Drawings of Frank Lloyd Wright* (New York: Horizon, 1962), 7–16; Julia Meech and Gabriel Weisberg, *Japonisme Comes to America: The Japanese Impact on the Graphic Arts 1876–1925* (New York: Harry N. Abrams and The Jane Voorhees Zimmerli Art Museum, Rutgers University, 1990), 191–200; and Nute, *Wright and Japan,* 108–114.

163. On Wright's connoisseurship of Japanese prints, see Julia Meech-Pekarik, "Frank Lloyd Wright and Japanese Prints," *The Metropolitan Museum of Art Bulletin* 40 (Fall 1982): 49–56; *Frank Lloyd Wright and Japanese Prints: The Collection of Mrs. Avery Coonley* (Washington, D.C.: The American Institute of Architects Foundation, The Octagon, 1983); and "Frank Lloyd Wright's Other Passion," in Bolon et al., eds., *Nature of Frank Lloyd Wright,* 125–153. On the exhibitions of 1906 and 1908, see Nute, *Wright and Japan,* 151.

164. Wright, *The Japanese Print: An Interpretation* (Chicago: Ralph Fletcher Seymour, 1912), reprinted in Pfeiffer, ed., *Wright: Collected Writings,* I, 122.

165. Ibid.

166. Wright, *In the Cause of Architecture* (Buffalo, 1909), reprinted in Quinan, *Larkin Building,* 167.

167. Wright, "The Architect and the Machine (1894)," in Pfeiffer, ed., *Wright: Collected Writings,* I, 23. Wright's aesthetic ideal of simplicity may have been related to the theological ideals of Jenkin Lloyd Jones. Preaching in 1902 on "The Gospel of Simplicity," Wright's uncle had said: "In religion simplicity is an escape from the complexities of form and perplexities of creeds and formulas to the simple trusts, the far-reaching hopes, the love-hunger and the thirst for beauty which characterizes all faiths at their highest, inspires all progress, directs all pilgrimages and is the fundamental consecration of all shrines" (Jones, "The Simplicity of the Gospel and the Gospel of Simplicity," *Unity* 50 [25 September 1902]: 56).

168. Wright, "A Philosophy of Fine Art," paper prepared for the Architectural League of The Art Institute of Chicago, 1900, in Pfeiffer, ed., *Wright: Collected Writings,* I, 42. Wright, *Japanese Print,* in Pfeiffer, ed., *Wright: Collected Writings,* I, 119, wrote that "to conventionalize is, in a sense, to simplify."

169. Wright, "A Philosophy of Fine Art," in Pfeiffer, ed., *Wright: Collected Writings,* I, 43. Other accounts of Wright's concept of conventionalization include Hanks, *Decorative Designs of Wright,* 9–16; Graf, *Kunst des Quadrats,* I, 31–32; Nute, *Wright and Japan,* 107–108; Alofsin, *Wright: Lost Years,* 120–123; and Cronon, "Inconstant Unity," in Riley, ed., *Frank Lloyd Wright: Architect,* 17–18. On Sullivan's ornament as conventionalization of natural forms, see Siry, *Carson Pirie Scott,* 153–154. On the meaning of this idea in English ornamental theory, see Sarah Bradford Landau, *P. B. Wight: Architect, Contractor, and Critic, 1838–1925* (Chicago: The Art Institute of Chicago, 1981), 25.

170. Wright, *Japanese Print,* in Pfeiffer, ed., *Wright: Collected Writings,* I, 119–120, 123–124. On Wright's response to the aesthetic of the Japanese print, see Nute, *Wright and Japan,* 100–119.

171. Wright, *Ausgeführte Bauten und Entwürfe* (1910), 6.

172. Wright, "In the Cause of Architecture (1908)," 162.

173. Ibid., 158.

174. Wright, *Japanese Print,* in Pfeiffer, ed., *Wright: Collected Writings,* I, 125.

175. Ibid. If conventionalization implied architecture as a setting for the life within, this idea perhaps underlay Wright's printing of William Channing Gannett's sermon, *The House Beautiful,* in 1896–97. Wright recalled that the sermon was "an essay which I admired very much and which had been delivered in All Souls' Church. It was a charming thing, and it charmed me" (Wright, quoted in Futagawa, ed., *Frank Lloyd Wright Monograph 1902–1906,* 102–103). Gannett wrote mainly on the human tone and character of familial living as the essential beauty of the home, while saying little about the appropri-

ate or specific architectural form for such a life. Wright perhaps saw his role as designing environments that enabled realization of Gannett's vision of domesticity. He may have conceived prairie houses as conventionalizations of such ideas for living. On Wright and Gannett's text, see N. K. Smith, *Frank Lloyd Wright,* 68–72; Twombly, *Frank Lloyd Wright,* 37–39; and Gill, *Many Masks,* 111.

CHAPTER 4
CONSTRUCTION OF UNITY TEMPLE

1. Wright, "Logic of the Plan," 49.
2. Wright, *Autobiography* (1932), 162.
3. Ibid., 162–163.
4. F. D. Warren, "Reinforced Concrete Work," *Inland Architect and News Record* 49 (February 1907): 25. After the trustees accepted Wright's preliminary plans on 7 February 1906, *Construction News* 21 (3 March 1906): 167, announced that Wright was taking figures on Unity Church's building, yet there was no mention of its design in concrete. Instead the project was described in the same way as it had been in its announcement of September 1905 (Chapter 3, 108, and 293, n. 81): a one-story building of brick and stone with a slate roof to cost $35,000. Perhaps Wright's call for bids indicated a conventional construction in order to interest builders, who might have been put off if concrete was noted.
5. Wright, *Autobiography* (1932), 150. See also Wright, "In the Cause of Architecture (1908)," 158–159. By April 1906 only two contractors had submitted bids. One proposed "to furnish all labor and material to erect and complete the concrete work, carpenter work, sheet metal, plastering, painting, roofing, structural iron and monolithic floors" for $62,841 (J. H. Johnson to Wright, 25 April 1906), while the other bid for this work was $51,459 (H. Eilenberger and Company to Wright, 21 April 1906, Unity Temple Collection, Oak Park Public Library). Unity Temple and Unity House cost about $60,000 ("Cost of Unity Church," n.d., Unity Temple Collection, Oak Park Public Library). The initial estimate of $36,000 was noted in a trustees' meeting of 7 February 1906 (*Record,* 160, Unity Temple Historical Files). See also p. 316, n. 167.
6. W. W. Kimball Company to E. H. Ehrman, 8 August 1907. This organ company later wrote that "the plans were of such a peculiar character that it is almost impossible to make any results that are satisfactory out of them. Therefore we have waited until your building was nearer completion before we thought it advisable to draw you up a specification." W. W. Kimball Company to E. H. Ehrman, 7 September 1907 (Unity Temple Collection, Oak Park Public Library).
7. Heillgreen, Lane and Company to R. F. Johonnot, 14 November 1907 (Unity Temple Collection, Oak Park Public Library).
8. Special Meeting of the Board of Trustees of Unity Church, 18 January 1906, *Record,* 155 (Unity Temple Historical Files). Paul Mueller (1864?–1934) was born in Neuenkirchen in western Germany's Saar Basin, one of the foremost regions for iron production in Europe. He had graduated from the government school of mining and civil engineering in Stuttgart, and had come to the United States at age seventeen, arriving in Chicago in 1881. His earliest work and expertise was in superintending erection of iron and steel buildings. Mueller later recalled that Dankmar Adler first engaged him for a time in 1883. He was then an engineer in Silsbee's office for three years until 1886, when he returned to Adler and Sullivan's as an engineer for the Auditorium, whose construction he supervised as foreman of the office. Mueller retained this position until about 1892, supervising construction of many of the firm's major steel-framed buildings. His years with Adler and Sullivan coincided with Wright's, who was employed there in 1887–93.

Mueller then left to become a partner and engineer with the Probst Construction Company, for whom he supervised the construction of thirty-eight buildings at the Columbian Exposition of 1893. After that time Mueller worked as an independent contractor and builder. His collaborations with Wright included building the Imperial Hotel in Tokyo from 1915 to 1923, and designing the winter resort of San Marcos-in-the-Desert in Arizona, from 1927, which was never built. On Mueller, see "Paul F. P. Mueller, Contractor for Many Years, Dies," *Chicago Tribune* (12 March 1934): 14; Morrison, *Louis Sullivan*, 84–85; Wright, *Autobiography* (1932), 89–90, 94–96, and *Genius and the Mobocracy*, 47, 53; and Edgar Kaufmann Jr., "Frank Lloyd Wright's 'Lieber Meister,'" *Nine Commentaries on Frank Lloyd Wright*, 36–62. Reference to Wright's contact with Mueller about Unity Temple appeared in minutes of the special meeting of Unity Church's trustees, 18 January 1906 (*Record*, 155, Unity Temple Historical Files).

9. Wright, *Autobiography* (1932), 151, and Quinan, *Larkin Building*, 30, noted Mueller as the contractor for the Larkin Building. On his work at the E-Z Polish Factory, see Gill, *Many Masks*, 156–161.

10. Wright, *Autobiography* (1932), 163.

11. Special Meeting of the Board of Trustees, 28 April 1906, *Record*, 169–171.

12. Contract, Paul F. P. Mueller with Unity Church of Oak Park, 28 April 1906, 2 (Unity Temple Collection, Oak Park Public Library). Mueller's premature guarantee of the cost and schedule of construction was decisive for the project's approval. On 30 April Wright and Mueller met with the board at Wright's studio, by which time Mueller had still "had no opportunity to go over the estimates of his engineer," an unnamed collaborator who was credited with calculating the steel reinforcing for Unity Temple's concrete walls, floors, pillars, and beams (Special Meeting of the Board of Trustees, 30 April 1906, *Record*, 172, Unity Temple Historical Files).

13. The start of building was noted in "Unity Church," *Oak Leaves (Fifth Anniversary Number)* (27 April 1907): 102. On Saturday, 12 May, stakes were set to begin construction and "Mr. Wright in detail went over all matters relating to starting the building with Mr. Mueller, at this time" (Arthur C. Tobin to William G. Adams, 15 May 1906, Unity Temple Collection, Oak Park Public Library).

On 20 May the trustees resolved that "it shall be the duty of the building committee to exercise a general supervision over the construction of the new church building and the execution of the contracts therefor" (Special Meeting of the Board of Trustees, 20 May 1906, *Record*, 177, Unity Temple Historical Files). This committee's chair was to certify that all certificates issued by the architect for payment by Unity Church to all contractors were consistent with the plans, specifications, and contract with Mueller. On Sunday, 3 June, one year after the fire that destroyed old Unity Church, and the day before the first concrete was to be poured, Charles Roberts resigned this chairmanship, yet stayed on the committee. His successor as chairman was Edwin Ehrman, Roberts's former associate in the Chicago Screw Company, who worked closely with Wright, Mueller, and others throughout the building process of 1906–9 (Regular Monthly Meeting of the Board of Trustees, 3 June 1906, *Record*, 180, Unity Temple Historical Files). See "E. H. Ehrman Dies: Pioneer, Designer and Inventor," *Oak Leaves* (20 June 1946): 48.

14. "Pushing Church Work," *Daily Reporter-Argus* (29 June 1906): 1.

15. After consultation with Charles Roberts, the trustees resolved that "the church edifice be so placed on the lot that there be a space of three (3) feet between the south foundation at grade and the south line of the lot" (Meeting of the Board of Trustees, 6 May 1906, *Record*, 176, Unity Temple Historical Files).

16. Mueller did considerable extra work on foundations, expanding the bases of the walls and piers beyond what Wright's drawings indicated. Such changes are documented in Paul F. P. Mueller to Unity Church, Oak Park, Ill., "[Additions] To Original Contract for

the Erection of the Unity Church & Unity House buildings," 29 March 1909, Bill No. 2 (Unity Temple Collection, Oak Park Public Library). At first Wright had specified that rubble from foundations of old Unity Church be used as aggregate for the foundations of Unity Temple, yet this was not done (Unity Church, Oak Park, Ill., Specifications, 7, 8, Unity Temple Collection, Oak Park Public Library).

17. Unity Church, Specifications, 8.

18. Unity Church, Specifications, 10. See Wiss, Janney, Elstner, *Unity Temple*, 63.

19. A. M. Ferry, "A Reinforced Concrete Church," *Concrete Engineering* 2 (1 September 1907): 98.

20. Wright, "Logic of the Plan," 51. Wright's selection of a unit system for Unity Temple's formwork to economize on the cost of its carpentry was consistent with practice of the period. F. D. Warren, "Reinforced Concrete Work," *Inland Architect and News Record* 49 (March 1907): 41, wrote that, in order to eliminate excessive cost, an architect must make "the design of the form work conform to systematic units which contain only a sufficient amount of lumber, which may be made with the least expense, and especially which may be erected, removed and re-erected over and over again with the least amount of labor and repair."

21. Warren, "Reinforced Concrete Work," *Inland Architect and News Record* 49 (February 1907): 25. Excerpts from the Boston architect Frank Warren's *Handbook on Reinforced Concrete* appeared in *Inland Architect and News Record* 49 (February 1907): 25–26; (March 1907): 41–42; (April 1907): 56; (May 1907): 60; (June 1907): 75; ibid., 50 (July 1907): 5; (August 1907): 16–17; (September 1907): 30; (October 1907): 45; (December 1907): 74–75; ibid., 51 (February 1908): 5; (April 1908): 34; (June 1908): 55–56.

    Desired economy in preparing liquid mixes of concrete may also have influenced Unity Temple's forms. In 1907, in order to take advantage of new machines as the optimal method for mixing concrete, the material, if economical, had to be mixed in large quantities that could then be poured without serious interruption. In that era, the need to mix and pour the material by machine favored its disposition in large, unbroken walls or masses. This idea underlay usage of the term "monolithic concrete," which often recurred in accounts of Unity Temple's structure. As one of Wright's contemporaries observed, if economic use of concrete required mixture of large quantities by machine, then "it follows naturally that such a structure is more or less perfectly monolithic, and at once this characteristic becomes the dominant note of the situation. Monolithic, i.e., freedom from joints or even semblance of joints. This is the fundamental idea which should be impressed on our concrete design" (A. O. Elzner, "Artistic Expression of Concrete," 54). See also "Something New and Effective in Monolithic Concrete Construction," *Concrete* 7 (August 1907): 22–24; and J. H. Sullivan, "Monolithic Concrete Construction and Its Possibilities," ibid. (November 1907): 23–27. Rev. Johonnot, quoted in "Unity Plans Unique," *Oak Leaves* (24 February 1906): 3, noted that the concrete was to be "poured and stamped in forms, making a structural monolith of the whole." Wright, "In the Cause of Architecture (1908)," 212, similarly described Unity Temple as "a concrete monolith cast in wooden molds or 'forms.'"

22. Wright, "Fabrication and Imagination (1927)," 319.

23. This photograph was published in Ira S. Griffith, "First Monolithic Church in Illinois," *Cement World* 1 (15 May 1907): 78–81, and subsequently republished in "A Masterpiece in Concrete Work," ibid., 2 (15 February 1909): 750. Wright had originally specified that the outer walls of Unity Temple above grade would be unreinforced masses of the same stone concrete used for their foundation. Yet he ultimately directed that the outer walls be reinforced. This meant that steel reinforcing bars had to be placed and braced inside the forms before the concrete was poured. As shown in Figures 97a and 97b, to keep the outer and inner sides of formwork from being pushed apart as the concrete was poured in, wire loops were tied across the void between them, joining the 2 × 4 posts. These wires would remain embedded in the poured concrete, and, once

the forms were removed, the wires were cut off close to the surface of the finished wall so as to be invisible. These wires running across the void of the formwork between its outer and inner sides also became the means of securing the horizontal and vertical reinforcing bars, which were tied to these wires with smaller wires. To keep the form-work's inner and outer sides separated by a uniform distance, temporary wooden braces were set between the sides of the form before the wires were tightened. These temporary braces were then removed as fast as concrete was poured in and tamped (Ferry, "Rein-forced Concrete Church," 98). These methods of bracing formwork and setting reinforc-ing in concrete followed the recommended practice of the period. See Sanford Thompson, "Forms for Concrete Construction," *Concrete* 7 (February 1907): 19–21, 51a; and Ernest McCullough, "Reinforced Concrete: Some Simple Formulas and Ta-bles," *Cement Era* 6 (January 1908): 8–11.

While the design, fabrication, and placement of formwork were painstaking, time-consuming operations, building Unity Temple in concrete had its economic advantages. Johonnot, *New Edifice of Unity Church*, 13, wrote that concrete was much less expen-sive than stone in a building wherein "walls, floors and roof will be built out of it, thus involving little skilled labor and the employment mainly of but one set of workmen." Because this was an early era of concrete construction, the roles of different workers on the job were not as distinguished as they became later in this century, when separate trades were responsible for building formwork, setting reinforcing, or pouring concrete. When the building of Unity Temple began, Mueller employed only carpenters to erect the wooden formwork and laborers to pour the concrete. However, in July 1906, two months after work had begun, the carpenters walked out "when some of the concrete workers on the job were ordered to put in the wires that brace the opposite sides of the framing." The carpenters claimed that "the laborers were usurping their side of the work." Yet Mueller's foreman declared that "the work over which the trouble arose is not carpenter's work, but belongs to the other men" ("Unity Trouble," *Oak Park Reporter-Argus* [25 July 1906]: 3).

24. Mueller to Unity Church, "[Additions] To Original Contract," Bill No. 7.

25. Ibid., Bill No. 14.

26. F. D. Warren, "Reinforced Concrete Work," *Inland Architect and News Record* 50 (July 1907): 5, wrote that "'at the present time, architects are in general not specifying plastered or skimmed coats for exterior walls in order to obliterate the unsightly form marks, but, on the other hand, are removing such blemishes by scraping away the skin from the surface before the concrete has attained hard set or by hammering afterwards. In this way the beautiful texture of the aggregate is brought to the surface and the first triumph in its success has been accomplished."

27. Wright, "Fabrication and Imagination (1927)," 318. Wright repeatedly invoked the con-cept of exposing aggregate to express the composite nature of concrete as a material. In 1910 he designed the Universal Portland Cement Company's principal exhibit at the New York Cement Show, in Stanford White's ornate older Madison Square Garden, where "a display of ornamental concrete will be made, illustrating the possibilities in the decoration of concrete surfaces by means of inlaid colored glass and tile. . . . Mr. Wright has given much study to the subject of reinforced concrete design, with special refer-ence to residence architecture and decoration" (Universal Portland Cement Company, Monthly Bulletin No. 79, December 1910, 3. See also "Universal Exhibits at the Cement Show," Universal Portland Cement Company, Monthly Bulletin No. 80, January 1911, 11–12). Wright's design in tiles and cement was published in *Frank Lloyd Wright: Ausgeführte Bauten* (1911; reprint, New York: Dover, 1982), 111, and documented in Frank Lloyd Wright Foundation, Drawing Nos. 1004.001–1004.005. On this and Wright's 1901 exhibit for the same company at the Pan Pacific Exhibition in Buffalo, N.Y., see Hitchcock, *Nature of Materials*, 49, 118; Storrer, *Frank Lloyd Wright*, 63, 163; and Alofsin, *Wright: Lost Years*, 67–68.

28. "A Masterpiece in Concrete Work," *Cement World* 2 (15 February 1909): 751.

29. Unity Church, Specifications, 7.

30. Ibid., 10.

31. Ibid., 9.

32. Ibid., 10.

33. Ibid., 8.

34. Ibid., 10.

35. M. M. Sloan, "The Architectural Treatment of Concrete Structures; Part II," *Architectural Record* 30 (August 1911): 170. See also Taylor and Thompson, *Treatise on Concrete*, excerpted in "Facing Concrete Walls," *American Architect* 87 (1 April 1905): 103–104.

36. Wright to Trustees of Unity Church, 10 July 1906 (Unity Temple Collection, Oak Park Public Library).

37. Mueller to Unity Church, "[Additions] To Original Contract," Bill No. 20.

38. Wright to Trustees of Unity Church, 10 July 1906.

39. Wright described such a technique in "A Fireproof House for $5000," *Ladies' Home Journal* 24 (April 1907): 24.

40. Sloan, "Architectural Treatment of Concrete Structures; Part II," 168.

41. Wright to Trustees of Unity Church, 10 July 1906.

42. E. H. Ehrman to W. G. Adams, 13 July 1906 (Unity Temple Collection, Oak Park Public Library).

43. "Church Progressing," *Oak Park Reporter-Argus* (14 August 1906): 3.

44. Mueller to Unity Church, "[Additions] To Original Contract," Bill Nos. 7, 8, 9, 10, 11.

45. Figure 99 shows no flower box atop the pedestal flanking the steps to the east entrance terrace. These flower boxes appeared in a photograph of Unity Temple's west side on Kenilworth Avenue (like Fig. 1) which was published in the booklet, *Dedication of the New Unity Church, Oak Park, Illinois, Sunday, September 16th, 1909* (Unity Temple Historical Files). The same photograph appeared on the title page of *Universalist Leader* 12 (16 October 1909).

46. Unity Church, Specifications, 7, 8. See also Wiss, Janney, Elstner, *Unity Temple*, 63.

47. Wright, "In the Cause of Architecture (1908)," 212.

48. Unity Church, Specifications, 10.

49. Ferry, "Reinforced Concrete Church," 98.

50. Wright's preference for simpler molded detail in his walls of concrete recalls that of a contemporary, who wrote: "As concrete has nothing of the fine texture of marble and as it is seldom cut or polished, the mouldings and cornices, when constructed of this material, should be such as can readily be made in wood or metal forms, and, because of its coarse texture and lustreless surface, they should never be fine" (M. M. Sloan, "Architectural Treatment of Concrete Structures; Part I," *Architectural Record* 9 [May 1911]: 402).

Sloan concluded that "while the classical orders have been extensively employed for motifs in the construction of cornices for buildings, in copper, terra cotta, and stone . . . it is probably fortunate that it would be almost impossible to construct such cornice details in concrete; and, where the building is of reinforced or monolithic construction, the cornice must be divided up into simple elements that can readily be moulded in forms with reasonable despatch and removed without danger of destroying the moulded work" (Sloan, "Architectural Treatment of Concrete Structures; Part III," *Architectural Record* 30 [November 1911]: 491).

51. Graf, *Kunst des Quadrats*, I, 124, 135–137, 139–140, 203–205, argues that the flower boxes are a key to Wright's formal logic throughout Unity Temple and Unity House, providing an initial presentation of motifs developed in these structures. Graf also notes that the flower boxes recall Wright's fountain outside the dwelling hall of the Dana house. Wiss, Janney, Elstner, *Unity Temple*, 109, note that the original flower boxes of 1909 were replaced during the shotcrete restoration of the building's exterior in 1973.

See Appendix, 249, and 333, nn. 23–25. The boxes may relate to Wright's unbuilt project of 1909 for a concrete flower box and light for a park. See Futagawa, ed., *Frank Lloyd Wright Monograph 1907–1913*, 127. Unity Temple's flower boxes resemble the concrete fountain of 1909 sited in Scoville Park one block to the east. On this small monument, see "Fountain Unveiled," *Oak Leaves* (31 July 1906): 1, 3–6; Universal Portland Cement Company, Monthly Bulletin No. 67 (December 1909): 1–2; Hallmark, "Richard W. Bock, Sculptor; Part II," 19–20; Storrer, *Frank Lloyd Wright*, 94; Futagawa, ed., *Frank Lloyd Wright Monograph 1902–1906*, 154; and Bock, *Memoirs of an American Artist*, 90.

This fountain was created for the Oak Park Horse Show Commission by one of its leading members, Charles Woodard. This commission, headed by another member of Unity Church, Daniel Trench, held its annual show to raise funds for the Hephzibah Children's Home, which Rev. Johonnot supported. See "Equine Exhibition," *Oak Leaves* (6 August 1904): 5–6; "Horse Show Preparations," ibid. (13 August 1904): 4; ibid., "The Outdoor Horse Show," 9; Editorial, "Merchants and the Horse Show," ibid. (3 September 1904): 16; "Daniel G. Trench," ibid. (17 September 1904): 1; "Boxes Bring Money," ibid. (26 August 1905): 2, 6–7; "Mrs. Trench on Horse," ibid. (2 September 1905): 2; "Red, Yellow and Black," *Oak Park Reporter-Argus* (2 September 1905): 1; "All Things Are Ready," ibid. (9 September 1905): 1; "Hephzibah Is a Gainer," ibid. (16 September 1905); "Show Is for Charity," ibid. (6 September 1906): 1; "Show Attracts Many," ibid. (8 September 1906): 1–2; "Horse Show Ends in Gala Attire," ibid. (10 September 1906): 1; "Show a Success," ibid. (11 September 1906): 2; "Prominent People at the Oak Park Horse Show," ibid., 5; "Appeal for Home," *Oak Leaves* (3 November 1906): 20; ibid., "Permanent Home" (24 November 1906): 8; "Trench Is Chosen," ibid. (9 February 1907): 10–11; "Horse Show Next," ibid. (31 August 1907): 3; "A High Standard," ibid. (5 September 1908): 4–5; "Altruism and the Horse Show," ibid., 17; "Fifth Horse Show," ibid. (12 September 1908): 3, 10–11, 19; "Horse Show Parade," ibid. (14 August 1909): 3; "Horse Show Beneficiaries," ibid. (4 September 1909): 1; "Horse Show Much Advertised," ibid., 2; "Boxes Bring $1,600," ibid., 3, 11; and "The Horse Show," ibid. (11 September 1909): 3.

A trustee of Unity Church, Woodard had commissioned the fountain from sculptor Richard Bock while he was working on modeling Unity Temple's ornamental exterior columns. Bock, *Memoirs of an American Artist*, 90, recalled that Woodard, who helped raise funds for Wright's building as a member of the ways and means committee, "had the ability to see this strange structure [of Unity Temple] come to life." Johonnot, *New Edifice of Unity Church*, 19, noted Woodard's service with Johonnot and Wright on the committee for this booklet's publication. On Woodard's service as head of Oak Park's Improvement Association, see Chapter 3, 132, and 301, n. 154. See also "Charles S. Woodard," *Oak Leaves* (10 December 1904): 13.

Of the fountain, Bock, *Memoirs of an American Artist*, 90, recalled that "I showed my design to Mr. Wright to see how he liked it. He looked at it at length with approval, but he once made a suggestion, took a pencil and poked a square hole right through the shaft, changing it from one shaft into two, with sculptured panels on the inside of each. These shafts supported a flower box." The fountain was a work of Bock, yet, as noted at its dedication, "Frank Lloyd Wright touched the design with his masterful hand and the lines became still more effective" (Charles Woodard, quoted in "Fountain Unveiled," 4). Constructed of the same Universal Portland Cement selected for Unity Temple, Bock's fountain's basic form of piers framing a void below a level cantilevered block is Bock's essay in the artistic potential of cast concrete.

The fountain marked the then private estate of Scoville Place, which residents hoped soon to transform into a central public park. Sited between the Scoville Institute and the new YMCA, the fountain together with these monuments was to mark the bounds of the village square, or Scoville Park. Both Bock's fountain and its position were keyed to the civic goals then being pursued by certain members of Unity Church. Among these, Wright's former assistant, architect Charles E. White, served as president of Oak Park's Fine Arts Society. On the proposed transformation of private Scoville Place to what became Scoville Park, see Editorial, "Scoville Place," *Oak Leaves* (12 December 1902): 12; A. T. Hemingway, letter, in "Park Question," ibid. (11 December 1903): 3–4; Editorial, "An Oak Park Park," ibid., 16; "Park Promoter," ibid. (18 December 1903): 9–10; Editorial, "Another Park Opportunity," ibid. (12 August 1905): 12; Editorial, "Chance for a Park," ibid. (24 February 1906): 18; Editorial, "One More Park Opportunity," ibid. (21 July 1906): 18; Editorial, "Organize Park Propaganda Now," ibid. (1 December 1906): 18; Editorial, "The Park Site Question, and Other Questions" (15 December 1906): 42; "Tracks and Park," ibid. (22 December 1906): 9; "Debate on Parks," ibid. (12 January 1907): 28; "Park in Campaign," ibid. (16 February 1907): 20; "Discuss Parks," ibid. (11 May 1907): 16; "Park Question," ibid. (8 August 1908): 18–19; "How to Get a Park," ibid. (22 August 1908): 20–21.

52. Kazuo Nishi and Kazuo Huzumi, *What Is Japanese Architecture?*, trans. H. Mack Horton (New York: Kodansha International, 1985), 48.

53. On Wright's adaptation of Japanese lanterns in his designs for lighting, and his photograph of a Shinto shrine with outer stone lanterns, see Margaret W. Norton, "Japanese Themes and the Early Work of Frank Lloyd Wright," *Frank Lloyd Wright Newsletter* 4 (Second Quarter 1981): 4–5. Graf, *Kunst des Quadrats*, I, 162–163, argues that the main square face of Unity Temple's exterior lamps anticipates in miniature the geometry of the auditorium's skylit ceiling, while the lamp's narrow rectangular front presages the form of Unity House's skylights.

54. Bock, *Memoirs of an American Artist*, 90; and Hallmark, "Richard W. Bock, Sculptor; Part II," 19. Graf, *Kunst des Quadrats*, I, 140–144, analyzes the ornamental columnar shafts, partly as an abstraction of laurel leaves. He maintains that these are "the most ingenious columns of the century." Graf sees their bases as abstracted versions of Ionic bases, and their tops as abstractions comparable to Corinthian motifs. He also emphasizes the integration of the columnar ornament with that of the window band behind.

55. Wright, "On Ornamentation," *Oak Leaves* (16 January 1909): 20, reprint, "Ethics of Ornament," *Prairie School Review* 4 (First Quarter 1967): 16–17.

56. Wright, *Autobiography* (1932), 159–160.

57. Wright, "Fabrication and Imagination," 319.

58. Ferry, "Reinforced Concrete Church," 99.

59. Wright, *Autobiography* (1932), 163.

60. Ibid., 155.

61. Johonnot, *New Edifice of Unity Church*, 13.

62. Wright, "In the Cause of Architecture (1908)," 159. In this text Wright refers to different types of roofs (low-pitched roofs with simple gabled pediments, low-pitched hip roofs, and simple flat slabs) that he employed in his works.

63. Wright, *Autobiography* (1932), 161.

64. "Oak Park," *Universalist Leader* 9 (15 September 1906): 1169. The trustees had hoped that problems with the novel techniques of concrete could be discovered and solved in Unity House before constructing Unity Temple's auditorium facing Lake Street (Special Joint Meeting of the Board of Trustees with the "Plans" and "Building" Committees, 14 January 1906, *Record*, 150–151, Unity Temple Historical Files).

65. E. H. Ehrman to Paul Mueller, 30 January 1907 (Unity Temple Collection, Oak Park Public Library). At the annual meeting on 25 March, William Adams, then president of the board, explained to Unity Church's congregation that "the delay in the work of building the new church had been due to no fault on the part of the contractor but to unavoidable obstacles and the desire to do the work in a thorough manner" ("The New Church Building," *Universalist Leader* 10 [6 April 1907]: 433). In his report, Rev. Johonnot expressed concern, stating that many in the congregation were "waiting for the new

church to awake in them the spirit which should be in their hearts first out of which to create a new church home" (Minutes of the Thirty-Seventh Annual Meeting of Unity Church Society of Oak Park, 25 March and 1 April 1907, in *Annual Reports 1902–1921*, 112, 114–115, 117, Unity Temple Historical Files). The trustees were soon authorized to borrow such "sums of money as may be necessary to complete the new church edifice," with confidence that new pledges would cover its costs. Meetings of the Board of Trustees, 28 March, 2 June, 6 October, and 11 October 1907, *Record*, 195, 210–212, 213–214 (Unity Temple Historical Files).

66. Wright to Ehrman, 18 March 1907 (Unity Temple Collection, Oak Park Public Library).
67. "Open 'Unity House,'" *Oak Leaves* (21 September 1907): 16.
68. Johonnot to "Dear Friends of Unity Church," 4 September 1907 (Unity Temple Historical Files).
69. "Open 'Unity House,'" 16.
70. Wright, *Autobiography* (1932), 158.
71. Ibid., 156.
72. Unity Church, Specifications, 22, noted that glass folding screens were originally intended to serve as spatial partitions for upper and lower side rooms of Unity House.
73. Wright, "A Home in a Prairie Town," *Ladies' Home Journal* 18 (February 1901): 17. On this project, see also Hitchcock, *Nature of Materials*, 33–34, Plates 58–59; Manson, *Frank Lloyd Wright*, 103–105; Twombly, *Frank Lloyd Wright*, 52–53; Gwendolyn Wright, *Moralism and the Model Home*, 136–138; and Futagawa, ed., *Frank Lloyd Wright Monograph 1887–1901*, 156.
74. Wright, *Autobiography* (1932), 158.
75. On the reciprocity of religion and domesticity in Wright's work, see N. K. Smith, *Frank Lloyd Wright*, 20–21.
76. "Open 'Unity House,'" *Oak Leaves* (21 September 1907): 16.
77. The small columns on Unity House's balcony fronts appeared as mullions for glass folding screens in Figure 91, a longitudinal section through Unity Temple and Unity House. Graf, *Kunst des Quadrats*, I, 190–191, observes that the beams beneath Unity House's balconies and the small columns set in the balconies constitute a system of elements that has its culmination in the lamps hanging from the arms cantilevered out from the small columns. Overall, he concludes that the inner construction of Unity House is independent from the building's outer shell.
78. Wright, "In the Cause of Architecture (1908)," 162, wrote of his work: "The present industrial condition is constantly studied in the practical application of these architectural ideals and the treatment simplified and arranged to fit modern processes and to utilize to the best advantage the work of the machine." Wright first presented these ideas in his earliest known statement, "The Architect and the Machine (1894)," in Pfeiffer, ed., *Wright: Collected Writings*, I, 20–26. Wright disagreed with Chicago advocates of the Arts and Crafts Movement like Oscar L. Triggs, who valued handwork over machines. See H. A. Brooks, "Chicago Architecture: Its Debts to the Arts and Crafts," *Journal of the Society of Architectural Historians* 30 (December 1971): 312–317; Richard G. Wilson, "Chicago and the International Arts and Crafts Movements: Progressive and Conservative Tendencies," in John Zukowsky, ed., *Chicago: Birth of a Metropolis 1872–1922* (Munich: Prestel-Verlag, 1987), 208–227; and Siry, "Wright's 'Art and Craft of the Machine.'" See n. 3.97. Wright's position was perhaps related to that of Jane Addams's address of 1897 on "Education," where she envisioned machine work as a means of self-realization for the modern individual. See Roger Cranshawe, "Frank Lloyd Wright's Progressive Utopia," *Architectural Association Quarterly* 10 (1978): 4.
79. Wright, "Art and Craft of the Machine," 13.
80. "A Masterpiece in Concrete Work," 751.
81. Unity Church, Specifications, 9.
82. Ibid., 112. In 1971 all the woodwork in Unity House was stripped and bleached.

Originally it had been stained a dark brown, like the wood in Unity Temple. See Appendix, 249, and 333, n. 21; and Robert A. Furhoff, "Site Investigation for Color Identification, Unity Church, Unity House Interior (1987)," 4, in Wiss, Janney, Elstner, *Unity Temple*, Appendix.

83. Wright, *A Testament* (New York: Bramhall House, 1957), 66.

84. Wright, *Autobiography* (1932), 141.

85. Mueller to Unity Church, "[Additions] to Original Contract," Bill No. 54.

86. Robert A. Furhoff to author, 4 August 1994.

87. Unity Temple, Specifications, 18.

88. Wiss, Janney, Elstner, *Unity Temple*, 95–96.

89. On this technique, see Wright, "A Fireproof House for $5000," 24.

90. Furhoff, "Unity House Interior," 4.

91. Unity Church, Specifications, 24.

92. Furhoff, "Unity House Interior," 4. By 1994 Unity House's interior surfaces showed approximately the eleventh coat of paint applied in the room's lifetime. Later coats were more opaque than the water-based paints used in 1907. Except for certain details, the surfaces of 1994 approximate but do not match Wright's original colors (Furhoff, "Unity House Interior," 1, 8; and Wiss, Janney, Elstner, *Unity Temple*, 96).

93. Furhoff, "Unity House Interior," 7.

94. Ibid., 5.

95. "Open 'Unity House,'" 16.

96. Wright, "In the Cause of Architecture, IV: The Meaning of Materials – Wood," *Architectural Record* 63 (May 1928): 485.

97. Ibid., 487.

98. Wiss, Janney, Elstner, *Unity Temple*, 101–102. Unity Church, Specifications, 25, noted that, other than in the ceiling lights of Unity Temple and of Unity House, "all pattern glass otherwise shown shall be worked in metal sash bar of weight and construction as detailed and furnished and set by the Contractor."

99. Hanks, *Decorative Designs of Frank Lloyd Wright*, 221, notes that the Temple Art Glass Company made the art glass for Wright's Harvey P. Sutton house in McCook, Nebr. (1907), and his Francis W. Little house in Wayzata, Minn. (1913), whose living room was rebuilt at the Metropolitan Museum of Art in New York in 1982. On the art glass in this room, see Edgar Kaufmann Jr., "Frank Lloyd Wright at the Metropolitan Museum of Art," *Metropolitan Museum of Art Bulletin* 40 (Fall 1982): 34.

100. Kirk D. Henry, "American Art Industries – III: Stained Glass Work," *Brush and Pencil* 7 (December 1900): 153–154. On the processes of fabricating Wright's stained glass, see Hanks, *Decorative Designs of Frank Lloyd Wright*, 56–58.

101. Henry, "Stained Glass Work," 162.

102. Ibid. See also Sharon S. Darling, *Chicago Ceramics and Glass: An Illustrated History from 1871 to 1933* (Chicago: Chicago Historical Society, 1979), 120–128.

103. Wright, "Art and Craft of the Machine," 15.

104. Erne R. and Florence Frueh, "Ecclesiastical Stained Glass in Chicago," in Lane, *Chicago Churches and Synagogues*, 98.

105. Wright, "In the Cause of Architecture (1908)," 161.

106. Ibid.

107. George R. Dean, "A New Movement in American Architecture, II: Glass," *Brush and Pencil* 6 (April 1900): 33.

108. Wright, "In the Cause of Architecture (1908)," 163. See T. Donham Wray, "The Stained Glass of Frank Lloyd Wright and His Theory of Ornament," *Glass* 6 (1978): 8–23.

109. Thomas H. Beeby, "The Grammar of Ornament / Ornament as Grammar," in Stephen Kieran, ed., *Via III: Ornament* (Cambridge, Mass.: MIT Press, 1977), 18–22. See also Jean Castex, *Frank Lloyd Wright: Le Printemps de la Prairie House* (Brussels: Pierre Mardaga, 1985), 107–121; and Nute, *Wright and Japan*, 85–98. Graf, *Kunst des Quad-*

rats, I, 202, observes that the art glass motifs in Unity House's skylights display geometric patterns like the quadruples of squares framing the exterior inscription over the building's entrances.

110. John Vinci, *The Trading Room: Louis Sullivan and the Chicago Stock Exchange* (Chicago: The Art Institute of Chicago, 1989), 25–47.

111. "Artists at Fellowship Club," *Oak Leaves* (8 February 1908): 3; "Fellowship Club Notice," ibid. (15 February 1908): 3; "Fellowship Club Session Postponed," ibid. (22 February 1908): 32; "Fellowship Club," ibid. (29 February 1908): 3, 6–7.

112. "Fellowship Club," 3.

113. "Fellowship Club Session Postponed," 32.

114. Wright chose to vary the flooring, perhaps to distinguish between Unity Temple and the entrance foyer and Unity House. He specified that floors of Unity Temple be of monolithic concrete "laid perfectly smooth to a dead level, troweled perfectly smooth and hard with a 2″ cove at adjoining vertical surfaces" (Unity Church, Specifications, 14). The central floors of Unity House and the foyer are of magnesite, a concrete product with wood shavings that has a brownish tone (Wiss, Janney, Elstner, *Unity Temple*, 38; and Unity Church, Specifications, 7, 13–14). On Wright's experiments with magnesite, see Quinan, *Larkin Building*, 56, 176; Wright, "The New Larkin Administration Building (1906)," and George Twitmyer, "A Model Administration Building (1907)," reprinted in Quinan, *Larkin Building*, 142–143, 150–151.

Wright specified that all floors be horizontal as laid, for there would be no materials atop the poured concrete to cover unevenness in their surfaces. He also preferred that there be a continuous level from the exterior terraces in to the foyer's floor. Yet, as the terraces were being poured, Ehrman called Wright's attention to "the fact that the floor of the vestibule is apparently on the same level with the terrace floors," as if Ehrman was concerned that such evenness of level would subject the foyer to flooding from accumulations of rain or snow on the terraces (Ehrman to Wright, 7 November 1907, Unity Temple Collection, Oak Park Public Library). Mueller added drain pipes under the outer terraces (Mueller to Unity Church, "[Additions] To Original Contract," Bill No. 38).

115. The original coat rooms were enclosed as classrooms and washrooms in 1966. See Appendix 248, and 333, n. 17.

116. While the foyer's central ceiling is just over 9 ft. high, the segments of the ceiling just inside its doors are only 7 ft. 3 in., a dimension that fixes the impression of lower height at entrance, thus accentuating by contrast the greater height of Unity Temple and Unity House. Wright made similar low ceilings at entrances to his prairie houses of the period, as in the ground floor's foyer of the Robie house in Chicago of 1908–10. On Wright's sensitivity to such a device, see Pfeiffer, ed., *Wright: Living Voice*, 151.

117. Furhoff, "Unity House Interior," 1.

118. E. H. Ehrman to Mueller, 20 November 1907. After Unity Temple was completed, Mueller declared bankruptcy and sought additional compensation from the church to alleviate his situation (D. Buell to Unity Church, 3 March 1910, and Ehrman to W. G. Adams, 21 March 1910, Unity Temple Collection, Oak Park Public Library).

119. Wright to Trustees of Unity Church, 20 March 1908 (Unity Temple Collection, Oak Park Public Library).

120. Ehrman to Wright, 19 March and 7 April 1908; W. G. Adams to Mueller, 16 and 20 November 1907; 7 April and 20 May 1908 (Unity Temple Collection, Oak Park Public Library).

121. Johonnot, for Committee on Plans, to Trustees of Unity Church, 14 March 1908. On pews, see also W. G. Adams to Mueller, 30 March 1908; Mueller to Adams, 4 April 1908; Adams to Mueller, 20 May 1908; and Adams to Wright, 20 May 1908 (Unity Temple Collection, Oak Park Public Library). Placing of art glass in Unity Temple was noted in Joseph J. Vogel, President, The Temple Art Glass Company, to Ehrman, 23

September 1908; Vogel to W. G. Adams, 12 October 1908; and Vogel to C. E. Roberts, 17 November 1908 (Unity Temple Collection, Oak Park Public Library).

122. E. H. Ehrman to Wright, 7 April 1908 (Unity Temple Collection, Oak Park Public Library).

123. Unity Church Board of Trustees, Resolution, 5 July 1908 (Unity Temple Collection, Oak Park Public Library).

124. Ehrman to American Monolith Company, 16 July 1908. See also Adams to Mueller, 1 and 7 July 1908; and Adams to Roberts, 7 July 1908 (Unity Temple Collection, Oak Park Public Library). At this time, the monolithic flooring in the entrance foyer and in Unity Temple's cloisters had yet to be laid (Ehrman to American Monolith Company, 16 July 1908; Adams to Mueller, 1 and 7 July 1908; and Adams to Roberts, 7 July 1908, Unity Temple Collection, Oak Park Public Library).

125. Ehrman to American Seating Company, 16 September 1908; and American Seating Company to Adams, 21 September 1908 (Unity Temple Collection, Oak Park Public Library).

126. Wright, *Autobiography* (1932), 161.

127. Drexler, ed., *Drawings of Frank Lloyd Wright*, 12, 293 (Fig. 33). See also Conclusion, 238–239, and Figure 149.

128. See p. 164, and 311, n. 83.

129. Kenneth Frampton, "The Text-Tile Tectonic," in McCarter, ed., *Frank Lloyd Wright*, 124–149. Graf, *Kunst des Quadrats*, I, 126–127, 136, 140, argues that the metaphor of weaving is central to Wright's concept of architecture. In discussing the auditorium, Graf (pp. 248–257) offers other interpretations of the art glass panels in Unity Temple's skylights, arguing, for example, that their interwoven pattern represents the idea of congregational interaction across the auditorium (east–west) and between pulpit and congregation (north–south). Of Wright's details in this room, Graf concludes (p. 249) that "the sacramental character of the abstract rhythms and the ornamentation must not be overlooked."

130. Wright, "In the Cause of Architecture (1908)," 163.

131. Mueller to Unity Church, "[Additions] to Original Contract," Bill Nos. 26, 35. Wright's steps and bases for balcony pews appear on Frank Lloyd Wright Foundation, Drawings No. 0611.036 ("Corrected Plan of Balcony") and 0611.084 ("Unity Church, Seating Arrangement").

132. Editorial, *[The New] Unity* 39 (20 May 1897): 224.

133. Committee on Plans to Board of Trustees, 14 March 1908, 1 (Unity Temple Collection, Oak Park Public Library).

134. Ibid., 1–2.

135. Wright, "In the Cause of Architecture (1908)," 157. Graf, *Kunst des Quadrats*, I, 218, observes that the dark horizontal planes of the pews in the upper and lower galleries continue the visual logic of the horizontal wood bands on the faces of the galleries' railings.

136. Mueller to Unity Church, "[Additions] To Original Contract," Bill No. 51 (Unity Temple Collection, Oak Park Public Library). Mueller, Bill No. 47, also recorded that Wright altered wood bands on faces of the main columns after motifs shown on working drawings had been partially placed.

137. H. Taylor Booraem, "Architectural Expression in a New Material," *Architectural Record* 33 (April 1908): 252. Graf, *Kunst des Quadrats*, I, 227–228, also considers the main columns' ornamental details as crucial distinctions between the built auditorium and earlier designs, concluding that without these framing motifs, "Unity Temple would not be that which it is."

138. Wright, *Autobiography* (1932), 146.

139. In 1951 Wright said of the Gale house: "There is the progenitor of Fallingwater." Quoted in Futagawa, ed., *Frank Lloyd Wright Monograph 1907–1913* (Tokyo: A.D.A. EDITA,

1987), 102. On the Gale house, see Hitchcock, *Nature of Materials* 45; Brooks, *Prairie School*, 87; Storrer, *Frank Lloyd Wright*, 98; and Storrer, *Wright Companion*, 94–95.

140. The drawing of the Gale house with the handwritten date 1904 was published in Drexler, ed., *Drawings of Frank Lloyd Wright*, 293; and Futagawa, ed., *Frank Lloyd Wright in His Renderings 1887–1959* (Tokyo: A.D.A. EDITA, 1984), Figure 48.

141. Before Wright built Mrs. Thomas Gale's house, she owned another dwelling on an adjoining property ("Building on Elizabeth Court," *Oak Leaves* [12 June 1909]: 12). Mrs. Gale and her children occupied their Wright house late in 1909 (ibid. [11 December 1909]:8). In 1909 Mrs. Gale also commissioned Wright to design three cottages for rental in summer at Whitehall, Mich., as noted in Storrer, *Frank Lloyd Wright*, 88; Futagawa, ed., *Frank Lloyd Wright Monograph 1902–1906*, 70; and Storrer, *Wright Companion*, 84.

Thomas Gale, one of the prominent sons of Edwin Gale, was a local lawyer and realtor ("Thomas H. Gale Dead," *Oak Leaves* [23 March 1907]: 3). In 1892 he had commissioned Wright to design his earlier house at 1019 Chicago Avenue, as noted in Chapter 2, 72, and 283, n. 89. In 1897 Gale commissioned Wright to design a summer cottage in Whitehall, Mich. (Storrer, *Wright Companion*, 83). Shortly before he died, Gale and his family had moved into a new residence at 109 North Kenilworth Avenue, across Kenilworth and south of Unity Temple. This address was noted in *Unity Church Year Book and Manual, 1904–1905* (Unity Temple Historical Files); "Mrs. Gale's Japanese Afternoons," *Oak Leaves* (6 May 1905): 10; and Johonnot, Funeral Remarks for Thomas H. Gale, in *Oak Leaves* (23 March 1907): 6. This suggests that Mrs. Gale then commissioned Wright to design the house on Elizabeth Court for herself and her children after her husband's death.

142. Wright, *Autobiography* (1932), 146. In this period, Wright designed motifs of wood bands on plaster exteriors of the Stephen M. B. Hunt house in LaGrange, Ill., of 1907, the G. C. Stockman house in Mason City, Iowa, of 1908, and the Robert W. Evans house in Longwood, near Chicago, also 1908. On these works, see Hitchcock, *Nature of Materials*, 43, 44; Storrer, *Frank Lloyd Wright*, 138–140; Futagawa, ed., *Frank Lloyd Wright Monograph 1907–1913*, 26, 54–57, 70–71; and Storrer, *Wright Companion*, 138, 139, 141. The Hunt house's plan was based on that of "A Fireproof House for $5000," published in *Ladies' Home Journal* in April 1907. Yet, as built, the Hunt house was a wood frame with plaster exterior surfaces onto which were set wood bands marking the house's corners with long vertical rectangles. These motifs made the corners appear like large square piers framing the central banks of windows in the front wall beneath the broad hip roof. There may be a relationship to Joseph Olbrich's works around 1900. Similar vertical panel motifs appeared on his Exhibition Building at Darmstadt of 1900–1906 (Ian Latham, *Joseph Maria Olbrich* [New York: Rizzoli, 1980], 100–111) and on Olbrich's Joseph Feinhals house at Cologne of 1908 (Robert J. Clark, "J. M. Olbrich 1867–1908," *Architectural Design* 37 [December 1967]: 571). On Wright's visit to Olbrich's works at Darmstadt in 1910, see Alofsin, *Wright: Lost Years*, 35–40.

The plan of the Evans house, which was built in 1908, developed the square form of the Hunt house in several ways, notably at its corners, whose semidetached articulation may have been an echo of Unity Temple's corner stair towers. On its plastered exterior, the Evans house originally featured wood bands. However, unlike the Hunt house of the previous year, the Evans house had a motif of horizontal bands that flowed around its frontal corners to join vertical bands along each face. The corners thus read less like piers upholding the roof and more like planes folded at right angles. These corners were thus less like foursquare masses and more like light screens, a term that Wright often used to describe his work to 1909. (See Wright, *Autobiography* [1932], 139, 161.) In his Evans house front, corner wood bands align visually with the outward-flaring overhangs of its hip roof above. The same motif appeared on the Stockman house, also of 1908. Storrer, *Wright Companion,* 139, notes that Wright called the motif "back-band trim." It had appeared in several of his earlier works, such as the Hills house of 1900, in Oak Park, the Charles A. Brown house of 1905, in Evanston, and the P. D. Hoyt house of 1906, in Geneva, Ill.

143. Mueller to Unity Church, "[Additions] To Original Contract," Bill No. 4. The organ screen as built, and final wood details for adjacent piers and columns, is shown in Frank Lloyd Wright Foundation, Drawing No. 0611.045 ("Unity Temple, Elevation of South End of Temple").

144. "Oak Park," *Universalist Leader* 12 (27 March 1909): 14–15.

145. Jones, "The Sermon of the Organ," *Unity* 55 (20 July 1905): 342.

146. George A. Audsley, "The Organ Architecturally Considered," *Inland Architect and News Record* 51 (April 1908): 31.

147. Audsley, "Organ Architecturally Considered," ibid. (May 1908): 44.

148. Mueller to Unity Church, "[Additions] To Original Contract," Bill No. 23.

149. Charles E. White Jr. to Walter Willcox, 13 May 1904, in Smith, ed., "Letters, 1903–1906, by Charles E. White, Jr.," 106. Graf, *Kunst des Quadrats,* I, 224, 229, observes that the ratio of vertical slots in the central organ screen (33) to slots in each side section of the screen (5) matches the ratio of the distance between main columns (about 33 ft.) to the breadth of these columns (5 ft.), as another example of the correspondence between elements that gives Wright's design its aesthetic unity.

150. Mueller to Unity Church, "[Additions] To Original Contract," Bill No. 24.

151. Ehrman to H. Gensch, 23 October 1908, 1–2 (Unity Temple Collection, Oak Park Public Library).

152. Barry Bryne, "Frank Lloyd Wright and His Atelier," *Journal of the American Institute of Architects* 39 (June 1963): 110. Alofsin, *Wright: Lost Years,* 13–15, noted a similarity between Wright's cubic lamps for Unity Temple and those designed by Peter Behrens for the reading room of the State Library in Dusseldorf, reconstructed as part of the German exhibit at the Louisiana Purchase Exposition of 1904 at St. Louis, which Wright saw and admired. His cubic lamps also compare with those of C. R. Mackintosh, as in his Hill house of 1904 at Helensburgh, Scotland. Earlier examples of Mackintosh's cubic lamps appeared in Charles Holme, ed., *Modern British Domestic Architecture and Decoration* (London, 1901), 113, 115, published as a special number of *The Studio.* Wright knew this periodical. See Chapter 5, 221, and 325, n. 120.

153. On fixed stone altars in early Protestant churches, see Addleshaw and Etchells, *Architectural Setting for Anglican Worship,* 25–29.

154. Mueller to Unity Church, "[Additions] To Original Contract," Bill No. 5. Earlier studies for Unity Temple's pulpit include Frank Lloyd Wright Foundation, Drawing Nos. 0611.033 and 0611.023, which approximated the final design. Graf, *Kunst des Quadrats,* I, 219–221, analyzes the built pulpit's form in part as a miniature analog to the whole building's north elevation, as shown in Figure 87, where the high central temple corresponds to the pulpit's raised central reading desk, so that similar formal compositions recur at different scales.

155. See Chapter 3, 132. In the Winslow house's dining room of 1893–94, Wright's art glass patterns blend visually with foliage outside the windows as seen from inside the room. This idea is also suggested in the drawing of the living room of the B. H. Bradley house, Kankakee, Ill., 1900, in *Ausgeführte Bauten und Entwürfe* (1910), Plate XXII.

156. Specification of a Two Manual Organ proposed by Coburn and Taylor of Chicago, Ill., for Unity Church, Oak Park, Ill. (Unity Temple Collection, Oak Park Public Library).

157. On Unity Temple's comparability to the Larkin Building, see Hendrik P. Berlage, "The New American Architecture (1912)," reprinted in Brooks, ed., *Writings on Wright,* 133; Wils, "Frank Lloyd Wright (1921)," in ibid., 142–145; Wright, *Autobiography* (1932) 152; Hitchcock, *Nature of Materials,* 49–54; Manson, *Frank Lloyd Wright,* 156, 158; Blake, *Master Builders,* 333–335; Scully, *Frank Lloyd Wright,* 19–21; Twombly, *Frank*

Lloyd Wright, 98–101; Graf, *Kunst des Quadrats*, I, 136, 237; Gill, *Many Masks*, 164–184; Lipman, "Consecrated Space," in McCarter, ed., *Wright: A Primer*, 196–201; and Laseau and Tice, *Frank Lloyd Wright*, 124–133.

158. Berlage, "New American Architecture," in Brooks, ed., *Writings on Wright*, 33.

159. On the Larkin Building's capitals, see Quinan, *Larkin Building*, 56, 60, 108.

160. Wright, *Autobiography* (1932), 163.

161. "Temple and Faith," *Oak Leaves* (31 October 1908): 3.

162. Ibid.

163. "Oak Park," *Universalist Leader* 11 (5 December 1908): 1551.

164. *Inland Architect and News Record* 52 (December 1908): 77.

165. "On Ornamentation," *Oak Leaves* (16 January 1909): 20.

166. "Our New Church at Oak Park, Ill.," *Universalist Leader* 12 (24 April 1909): 543.

167. Agreement, Unity Church of Oak Park and Paul F. P. Mueller, 28 April 1906, noted contracted amount of $32,661. "Cost of Unity Church," n.d., also Unity Temple Collection, Oak Park Public Library, noted total construction costs of $60,344.55. Cost of the lot, and amounts from the building fund, insurance, and sale of the old lot were noted in the minutes of a Special Joint Meeting of the Board of Trustees, 14 January 1906, *Record*, 148–149 (Unity Temple Historical Files). Cost of Unity Temple's organ was noted in Agreement, Coburn and Taylor and Unity Church of Oak Park, 23 September 1908 (Unity Temple Collection, Oak Park Public Library) and in *Christian Register* 87 (5 November 1908): 26. The cost of heating, ventilating, plumbing, and electric wiring appeared in Agreement, Unity Church of Oak Park and Foster and Glidden Company, Oak Park, 24 September 1906 (Unity Temple Collection, Oak Park Public Library). Wright's fee was noted in minutes of the Regular Monthly Meeting of the Board of Trustees, 6 May 1906, *Record*, 178 (Unity Temple Historical Files).

168. "Subscription to Building Fund," 23 September 1908, revised 28 December 1908 (Unity Temple Historical Files). Oak Park Trust and Savings Bank to James H. Heald Jr., 13 May 1908, noted a loan of $6,500. That of $8,000 was noted in Trust Deed, Unity Church of Oak Park to Oak Park Trust and Savings Bank, 4 February 1910 (Unity Temple Collection, Oak Park Public Library).

169. Minutes of the Thirty-Seventh Annual Meeting of the Unity Church Society of Oak Park, 9 March 1909, in *Annual Reports 1902 to 1921*, 143–144 (Unity Temple Historical Files).

CHAPTER 5
RELIGIOUS AND ARCHITECTURAL INTERPRETATIONS
OF UNITY TEMPLE

1. Unity Church's trustees authorized production of the brochure just after their initial acceptance of Wright's design and its local publication. The committee charged with the brochure's preparation included Charles S. Woodard, Johonnot, and Wright (Regular Monthly Meeting of the Board of Trustees, 4 March 1906, *Record*, 155, Unity Temple Historical Files).

2. "Print Brochure," *Oak Park Reporter-Argus* (3 July 1906): 1; and "Brochure of Unity Church," *Oak Leaves* (14 July 1906): 8.

3. Johonnot, *New Edifice of Unity Church*, 15.

4. Ibid., 3.

5. Ibid., 15–16. Johonnot's closing quoted St. Paul's address to the Athenians in the Areopagus, as recorded in Acts 17:24–28.

6. "New Church at Watertown, N.Y.," *Universalist Leader* 10 (19 October 1907): 1327.

7. All Souls Church in Watertown was Hobart Upjohn's first ecclesiastical commission,

after which he went on to build over one hundred churches in New York State and over 250 nationwide. See "H. B. Upjohn Dies," *New York Times* (24 August 1949): 26; *Architectural Record* 106 (October 1949): 158; and Withey, *American Architects*, 610.

8. H. B. Upjohn, quoted in "New Church at Watertown, N.Y.," 1327. Hobart Upjohn's description of his Watertown church recalls his grandfather Richard Upjohn's description of 1848 for his design for the Church of the Ascension in Philadelphia, wherein he stated: "The object is not to surprise with novelties in church Architecture, but to make what is to be made truly ecclesiastical." Quoted in Everard M. Upjohn, *Richard Upjohn: Architect and Churchman* (New York: Columbia University Press, 1939), 97.

9. "Editorials," *Universalist Leader* 10 (19 October 1907): 1317.

10. Johonnot, letter, *Universalist Leader* 10 (21 December 1907): 1617.

11. Ibid.

12. Ibid.

13. The new edifice for Boston's Church of the Disciples was illustrated in *Laying the Corner-Stone; Church of the Disciples; October 14, 1904* (Boston: George H. Ellis, 1904). See also "The Church of the Disciples," *Church Economist* 11 (May 1906): 146–147.

14. Johonnot, letter, *Universalist Leader* 10 (21 December 1907): 1617.

15. "Temple and Faith," *Oak Leaves* (31 October 1908): 8.

16. *Christian Register* 87 (5 November 1908): 26–27. See also "Opening Service in Unity Temple, Oak Park, Ill.," *Universalist Leader* 11 (7 November 1908): 28–29. Rev. Johonnot also emphasized an elemental religion in his first sermon preached in Wright's auditorium at its opening in October 1908, entitled "Unity Church: Its History, Faith and Aims." There he stated that this church had been organized in 1871 "to give a larger liberty of thought, to preach a simple and rational gospel, to foster a reverent search for new truth." Its sole article of faith asserted "belief in God as the Maker of all things." Johonnot concluded that "If God is our Father, man as his child must partake in the nature of God, must be divine. He is created imperfect but called to be perfect. This destiny under the laws of God he must fulfill" ("Temple and Faith," 8–10).

17. Special Meeting of the Board of Trustees, 20 May 1906, *Record*, 178–179 (Unity Temple Historical Files). In April 1907, when the entrance foyer was built, the trustees directed Wright to "order metal letters and squares to be used over the entrance of the new church." Meeting of the Board of Trustees, 7 April 1907, *Record*, 197 (Unity Temple Historical Files).

18. Rev. William C. Gannett, "Things Commonly Believed among Us," first presented at the annual meeting of the Western Unitarian Conference, All Souls Church, Chicago, 1887, quoted in Lyttle, *Freedom Moves West*, 189–190. In 1904 the phrase "For the Worship of God and the Service of Man" had also been used in the dedication of the new Church of the Disciples in Boston. George W. Thatcher, Chairman of the Building Committee, Address, in *Laying the Corner-Stone; Church of the Disciples*, 8. Local opinion on Unity Temple's severity was cited in Charles E. White Jr., "Criticises Critic," *Oak Leaves* (27 November 1909): 24, and "Is It Beautiful?" ibid., 28, First Supplement after December 1909, II–IV.

Graf, *Kunst des Quadrats*, I, 125, 131, 164–165, 187, notes that the quadruplets of squares flanking the bronze lettering over Unity Temple's entrance are recurrent motifs inside the building, as they are in Wright's other works.

19. "Unity Church, Oak Park, Ill.," *Christian Register* 88 (14 October 1909): 1107. Unity Temple's dedication in September 1909 marked a break in the lives of both Wright and Rev. Johonnot. After twenty-two years in Oak Park, Wright left his family and practice there to begin his first journey to Europe on Thursday, 23 September, three days before the dedication (*Oak Leaves* [25 September 1909]: 32). Maintaining that his pastorate had fulfilled its mission, Johonnot had resigned from Unity Church in May 1909, though he later agreed to stay until July 1910, while the church searched for a new minister. See

"Johonnot Resigns," *Oak Leaves* (5 June 1909): 3; "Ask Pastor to Stay," ibid. (12 June 1909): 3; Editorial, "Dr. Johonnot and Oak Park," ibid. (12 June 1909): 11; Johonnot to the Members and Board of Trustees of Unity Church, 15 June 1909 (Unity Temple Historical Files); "Johonnot Remains," *Oak Leaves* (26 June 1909): 3.

20. "Unity Dedicated," *Oak Leaves* (2 October 1909): 4.

21. Editorial, *Unity* 64 (30 September 1909): 4.

22. C. H. Fitch, "Interprets Unity," *Oak Leaves* (22 January 1910): 22. As a source for the metaphor of the rock of Abraham, Fitch cited Isaiah 51:1–2: "Hearken to me, you who pursue deliverance, you who seek the Lord; look to the rock from which you were hewn, and to the quarry from which you were digged. Look to Abraham your Father and to Sarah who bore you; for when he was but one I called him, and I blessed him and made him many." As a basis for comparison of Lincoln to the biblical Abraham, Fitch cited Galatians 3:6: "Thus Abraham 'believed God, and it was reckoned to him as righteousness.'".

23. "Masterpiece in Concrete Work," *Cement World* 2 (15 February 1909): 747.

24. Jones, "Ralph Waldo Emerson," *Unity* 3 (16 July 1879): 145. Before 1905 Wright cited Emerson in "Architect, Architecture, and the Client (1896)" and "A Philosophy of Fine Art (1900)," in Pfeiffer, ed., *Wright: Collected Writings*, I, 28, 43. On Emerson's importance for Wright, see John Lloyd Wright, *My Father Who Is on Earth* (1946), 33; Richard P. Adams, "Emerson and the Organic Metaphor," *Publications of the Modern Language Association* 69 (March 1954): 117–138, and idem, "Architecture and the Romantic Tradition: Coleridge to Wright," *American Quarterly* 9 (Spring 1957): 46–62; Donald D. Egbert, "The Idea of Organic Expression in American Architecture," in Stow Persons, ed., *Evolutionary Thought in America* (New York: George Braziller, 1956), 336–396; Barney, *Valley of the God-Almighty Joneses*, 59–60; Raymond H. Geselbracht, "Transcendental Renaissance in the Arts, 1890–1920," *New England Quarterly* 48 (December 1975): 463–486; Betty E. Chmaj, "The Journey and the Mirror: Emerson and the American Arts," *Prospects* 10 (1986): 353–408; Quinan, *Larkin Building*, 102–108, and idem, "Frank Lloyd Wright's Guggenheim Museum: A Historian's Report," *Journal of the Society of Architectural Historians* 52 (December 1993): 470–471; David M. Hertz, *Angels of Reality: Emersonian Unfoldings in Wright, Stevens and Ives* (Carbondale: Southern Illinois University Press, 1993); and Cronon, "Inconstant Unity," in Riley, ed., *Frank Lloyd Wright: Architect*, 12–14.

25. Jones, "Ralph Waldo Emerson," 146.

26. Jones, "From Luther to Emerson," *Unity* 64 (7 October 1909): 504.

27. Gannett, "Emerson's Vision of Unity," *Unity* 51 (25 June 1903): 262. See also Sherman Paul, *Emerson's Angle of Vision* (Cambridge, Mass.: Harvard University Press, 1952), 35–37. For Emerson's centennial, his son, Edward W. Emerson, edited *The Complete Works of Ralph Waldo Emerson*, 12 vols. (Boston: Houghton Mifflin, 1903–4). To mark Emerson's centennial, the following articles also appeared in *Unity* 51: "Emerson: An Appreciation" (2 July 1903): 288–289; "Emerson in Germany," ibid., 289–291; "Emerson's Religion" (9 July 1903): 306–7; "Emerson: A Tribute" (23 July 1903): 333–335; "Emerson's Essays" (30 July 1903): 352–353; "Emerson" (6 August 1903): 365–366; "Recollections of Emerson" (20 August 1903): 400–401; "Emerson's Divinity School Address" (27 August 1903): 410; and Edward E. Hale, "The Gospel of Emerson" (10 September 1903): 28–30.

28. Wright, *Autobiography* (1932), 14.

29. Barney, *Valley of the God-Almighty Joneses*, 66.

30. Wright, *Autobiography* (1932), 15.

31. Unity Church, Oak Park, Ill., Ladies Social Union, Membership List [and] Minutes, 3 vols., October 28, 1904 to March 11, 1910, Meeting of 24 January 1908, 75. On Anna Lloyd Wright and Emerson, see also Secrest, *Frank Lloyd Wright*, 225.

32. Emerson, "The Over-Soul (1841)," in Ziff, ed., *Emerson: Selected Essays*, 206–207. On study of Emerson at the newly dedicated Unity Temple, see "Emerson-Whitman," *Oak Leaves* (1 January 1910): 28.

33. Charles C. Everett, *Theism and the Christian Faith*, ed. Edward Hale (New York: Macmillan, 1909), 336–337. On Everett, see Robinson, *Unitarians and Universalists*, 254–255.

34. Johonnot, "Oak Leaves," *Unity* 60 (3 October 1907): 135–136. On his citation of Paul's text, see p. 196.

35. See Chapter 1, 27, and 262, nn. 50–51.

36. Goodrich's *Religious Ceremonies and Customs* is noted in the Frank Lloyd Wright Foundation's records (Location No. 1152.031) of Wright's library, as having been in his father's library. James's *Varieties of Religious Experience* is noted in "Books of Anna Lloyd Wright," a list (Location No. 1033.106) at the Archives of the Frank Lloyd Wright Foundation.

37. Earlier Unitarian studies of comparative religions included Frederick D. Maurice, *Religions of the World in Their Relations to Christianity* (1854), and Samuel Johnson, *Oriental Religions* (1872–77). On Unitarian investigations of non-Western faiths, see Hutchison, *Modernist Impulse in American Protestantism*, 24–29.

38. Barrows, ed., *World's Parliament of Religions*, I, vii.

39. Clarke, *Ten Great Religions: An Essay in Comparative Theology*, 2 vols. (Boston: Houghton Mifflin, 1871, 1883), II, 269. In this account of Buddhist architecture in Asia, Clarke was following James Fergusson's *History of Indian and Eastern Architecture*, 2 vols. (London: J. Murray, 1876).

40. Rev. Eugene Kincaid, "Magnificent Temple," *Christian World* 4 (10 January 1846): 4, described the Buddhist temple at Ava in Burma, built in the style of the classic Ananda Temple in Pagan, Burma, in the twelfth century. The temple at Ava was a stepped pyramid of solid masonry whose square base was 2,000 ft. on a side, with lower walls 8 ft. thick and 70 ft. high. Above this base were three higher stepped levels, each with spires at their four corners, culminating in a throne crowning the top. The whole temple was overlaid with some five thousand images, and hung with two hundred bells that rang in the passing wind. The temple was a continual focus for thousands of pilgrims. It took two years to build, engaging thousands of workers, who donated their time as well as funds. Kincaid wrote of this edifice: "What an example to those who have the means requisite for building temples to [divine] glory throughout the earth, to be filled with intelligent and devout worshippers."

41. The earliest major American account of Japanese art in building was Edward S. Morse, *Japanese Homes and Their Surroundings* (Boston: Ticknor, 1886). Studies that were contemporaneous with Unity Temple include Ralph Adams Cram, *Impressions of Japanese Architecture and the Allied Arts* (New York: Baker and Taylor, 1905); and Katherine C. Budd, "Japanese Houses," *Architectural Record* 19 (January 1906): 1–26. See Clay Lancaster, *The Japanese Influence in America* (New York: Walton W. Rawls, 1963), 64–75. Nute, *Wright and Japan*, 36–46, compares Morse's analysis of the Japanese dwelling and Wright's vision of the American house.

42. Carl Seaburg, *Dojin Means All People: The Universalist Mission to Japan, 1890–1942* (Boston: Universalist Historical Society, 1978). See also Miller, *Larger Hope*, II, 412–459.

43. Notices of Rev. Chapin's support for missionary work in Japan appeared in *Universalist* 7 (11 January 1890): 4; and "Our Japan Sunday," ibid. (1 February 1890): 4.

44. Grant Manson, "Frank Lloyd Wright and the Fair of '93," *Art Quarterly* 16 (Summer 1953): 114–123; David Gebhard, "Note on the Chicago Fair of 1893 and Frank Lloyd Wright," *Journal of the Society of Architectural Historians* 18 (May 1959): 63–65; Scully, *Frank Lloyd Wright*, 12, 17; Lancaster, *Japanese Influence in America*, 76–94; Norton, "Japanese Themes and the Early Work of Frank Lloyd Wright," 1–5; Nute, *Wright and*

Japan, 48–72; and Cronon, "Inconstant Unity," in Riley, ed., *Frank Lloyd Wright: Architect*, 21–23. Nute, *Wright and Japan*, Appendix F, 194–197, reprints Peter B. Wight, "Japanese Architecture at Chicago," from *Inland Architect and News Record* 20 (December 1892): 49–50; ibid. (January 1893): 41.

45. Jones, *Chorus of Faith*, 14.

46. Ibid., 18.

47. On Wright and Fenollosa, see Nute, *Wright and Japan*, 73–84, and idem, "Frank Lloyd Wright and Japanese Art: Fenollosa, The Missing Link," *Architectural History* 34 (1991): 224–230. Wright acknowledged Fenollosa in "The Print and the Renaissance (1917)," in Pfeiffer, ed., *Wright: Collected Writings*, I, 149. On Fenollosa's studies at Harvard, see also Lawrence Chisholm, *Fenollosa: The Far East and American Culture* (New Haven: Yale University Press, 1963), 20–30.

48. Nute, "Wright and Japanese Art," 227. On Okakura, see Nute, *Wright and Japan*, 121–137.

49. Fenollosa, "The Coming Fusion of East and West," *Harper's Monthly* 98 (December 1898): 116.

50. Ibid.

51. D. B. Baldwin, "Thoughts in a Buddhist Temple," *Unity* 45 (8 March 1900): 25–26.

52. Ibid., 25.

53. Wright's departure for Japan was noted in *Oak Leaves* (25 February 1905): 22. Charles E. White Jr. to Walter Willcox, 13 February 1905, wrote that "Wright and wife are to go abroad to Japan on Tuesday next (tomorrow) for four months" (Smith, ed., "Letters, 1903–1906, by Charles E. White, Jr.," 109). The Wrights' return from Japan was noted in *Oak Leaves* (20 May 1905): 4. On the chronology of their journey, see Kathryn Smith, "Frank Lloyd Wright and the Imperial Hotel: A Postscript," *Art Bulletin* 67 (June 1985): 298.

54. Wright, *Hiroshige: An Exhibition of Colour Prints from the Collection of Frank Lloyd Wright* (Chicago: The Art Institute of Chicago, 1906). Wright's talk to the River Forest Women's Club was noted in *Oak Leaves* (10 February 1906): 7. On Wright and Japanese prints, see Chapter 3, 133–136, and 301–302, nn. 162–163, 170.

55. "Unity Club of Unity Church," *Oak Leaves* (24 March 1906): 12.

56. "Fifteenth Annual," *Oak Leaves* (28 April 1906): 12.

57. On the temple of Higashi Hongan-ji Betsuin in Nagoya, see Alexander C. Soper, *The Evolution of Buddhist Architecture in Japan* (1942; reprint, New York: Hacker Art Books, 1978), 276, and Figure 198. On Wright's response to this building, see Nute, *Wright and Japan*, 145.

58. Johonnot, quoted in "Unity Plans Unique," 5.

59. Act of Dedication, Unity Church, Oak Park, Ill., September 26, 1909 (Unity Temple Historical Files). William Gannett's authorship of this dedicatory reading was noted in "Unity Dedicated," *Oak Leaves* (2 October 1909): 5.

60. After the World's Parliament of Religions in 1893, this idea revived with the American Unitarian Association's founding of the International Council of Religious Liberals, whose inaugural meetings were held at Boston in 1900. This council held congresses in London (1901), Amsterdam (1903), and Geneva (1905), before reconvening in September 1907 in Boston. Over two thousand representatives of twenty-four religions came from almost every European country, as well as India and Japan. Meetings took place at Tremont Temple, a major institutional church, and at the nearby King's Chapel. See "The Boston Meetings," *Unity* 60 (3 October 1907): 68–69; "The Boston Conference – A Glowing Prophecy," ibid. (17 October 1907): 100–101; "Boston Congress Notes," ibid. (10 October 1907): 94–95; ibid. (17 October 1907): 109–110; ibid. (24 October 1907): 125–126; ibid. (31 October 1907): 141; and ibid. (7 November 1907): 157–158. Jenkin Lloyd Jones attended, and concluded that the Boston meeting was "clearly the greatest event that has occurred in the history of religion in America since the great parliament of

1893. This body is the legitimate inheritor of the message of that Parliament, the logical successor" ("The Boston Meetings," 69). A "postscript" meeting of Boston delegates was held at Chicago's Lincoln Center, where Jones asserted: "There are two great words that are moving the religious heart of this age, – one is Fraternity, the other is Universality. . . . And this ever widening circle of brotherhood rests more and more securely upon the ever deepening sense of the universal elements that are found in all forms of faith and ritual. The universalities of religion break upon the devout heart like a psalm of thanksgiving when we find how superficial are the labels, how accidental are the doctrines and the dogmas that divide, how absolute and eternal are the universalities that unite" (Jones, quoted in "The Sunday Evening Congress Meeting," *Unity* 60 [10 October 1907]: 85).

61. Johonnot, "Oak Leaves," *Unity* 60 (31 October 1907): 134–136. An account of the sermon appeared in "Universal Faith," *Oak Leaves* (19 October 1907): 15–17.

62. Johonnot, "Oak Leaves," 134.

63. Ibid., 135.

64. Johonnot, *Unity Church, Oak Park, Illinois*, n.d., 3, 4 (Unity Temple Historical Files). This document bears the handwritten note: "This pamphlet was issued about 1903 or 1904 as I recall. R. F. Johonnot Nov. 1, 1919."

65. Johonnot, *New Edifice of Unity Church*, 3.

66. Ibid., 15.

67. Clarke, *Ten Great Religions*, II, 270–271.

68. Johonnot, *New Edifice of Unity Church*, 18. The first scriptural passage is from Habakkuk 2:20, the second from Psalm 96:9. Graf, *Kunst des Quadrats*, I, 136, also compares Unity Temple to Solomon's temple. On the religious significance of Solomon's temple for the English Puritan tradition, see John Bunyan, *Solomon's Temple Spiritualized, or Gospel-Light Fetched Out of the Temple of Jerusalem* (London, 1688). In his library, Wright's father, William C. Wright, possessed Bunyan's *The Holy War* (London, 1682), which Wright kept in his library.

Alternatively there were many fictive reconstructions of Solomon's temple through the late nineteenth century that Wright may have known. These included that of Charles Chipiez, *Temple de Jérusalém* (Paris, 1888–89), whose version of the temple showed massive, archaicizing, blocklike walls of stone. See David Van Zanten, "Sullivan to 1890," in Wim de Wit, ed., *Louis Sullivan: The Function of Ornament* (New York: W. W. Norton, 1986), 19, 22.

69. Clarke, "Introductory Sentences for Morning Prayer," in *Book of Worship: For the Congregation and the Home*, 5th ed. (Boston: Crosby, Nichols, 1856), 3.

70. Johonnot in "Unity Church Unique," *Oak Leaves* (24 February 1906): 5, and *New Edifice of Unity Church*, 7. On Unity Temple's relation to centrally planned churches, see Graf, *Kunst des Quadrats*, I, 136; Castex, *Printemps de la Prairie House*, 143–144; Robert McCarter, "Abstract Essence," in McCarter, ed., *Frank Lloyd Wright*, 15; Laseau and Tice, *Frank Lloyd Wright*, 128; and Joseph Masheck, "Kahn: The Anxious Classicist," in *Building-Art: Modern Architecture under Cultural Construction* (New York: Cambridge University Press, 1993), 132–133. On the centrally planned church as a symbolic form in the Italian Renaissance, see Rudolf Wittkower, *Architectural Principles in the Age of Humanism* (1952; New York: W. W. Norton, 1971), 27–32.

71. Rossiter Johnson, *A History of the World's Columbian Exposition*, 2 vols. (New York: D. Appleton, 1897), II, 327. See Gabriel Weisberg, "Frank Lloyd Wright and Pre-Columbian Art – The Background for His Architecture," *Art Quarterly* 30 (1967): 40–51. As monumental replicas exhibited outside the Anthropological Building, such casts were "more imposing and complete than anything inside," where there were exhibits of smaller artifacts from Japan, China, Korea, the South Pacific, Greece, the Near East, Africa, Latin America, and North America. Hubert H. Bancroft, *The Book of the Fair: An Historical and Descriptive Presentation of the World's Science, Art, and Industry, as*

Viewed through the Columbian Exposition at Chicago 1893, 2 vols. (Chicago: Bancroft, 1895), II, 635–636.

72. On Holmes, see George Kubler, *Aesthetic Recognition of Ancient Amerindian Art* (New Haven: Yale University Press, 1991), 117–126. See also David J. Meltzer and Robert C. Dunnell, introduction to *The Archaeology of William Henry Holmes* (Washington, D.C.: Smithsonian Institution Press, 1992), vii–l.

73. On Holmes as a topographic artist with the United States Geological Survey, see Kubler, "Geology as Panoramic Vision: William Henry Holmes (1846–1933)," *Res* 15 (Spring 1988): 156–162; and C. M. Nelson, "William Henry Holmes: Beginning a Career in Art and Science," *Records of the Columbia Historical Society* 50 (1980): 252–278.

74. William H. Holmes, *Archaeological Studies among the Ancient Cities of Mexico*, 2 vols. (Chicago: Field Columbian Museum, 1895, 1897), I, 20.

75. Dimitri Tselos, "Frank Lloyd Wright and World Architecture," *Journal of the Society of Architectural Historians* 28 (March 1969): 58–59. See also Tselos, "Exotic Influences in the Architecture of Frank Lloyd Wright," *Magazine of Art* 47 (April 1953): 160. On Wright's responses to pre-Columbian architectures in his work after 1910, see Alofsin, *Wright: Lost Years*, 221–260.

76. Wright, *Testament*, 111.

77. Wright(?) to Professor Robert J. Goldwater, Editor, *Magazine of Art*, n.d. (1953?), published in Tselos, "Frank Lloyd Wright and World Architecture," 72.

78. On Wright's relationship to classical architectural culture of his time, see Henry-Russell Hitchcock, "Frank Lloyd Wright and the 'Academic Tradition' of the Eighteen Nineties," *Journal of the Warburg and Courtald Institutes* 7 (1944): 46–63; Neil Levine, "Frank Lloyd Wright's Diagonal Planning," in Searing, ed., *In Search of Modern Architecture*, 247–249, and "Frank Lloyd Wright's Own Houses and His Changing Concept of Representation," in Bolon et al., eds., *Nature of Frank Lloyd Wright*, 20–69; David T. Van Zanten, "Form and Frank Lloyd Wright's Prairie Architecture," paper presented at the symposium, "Wright; The Reality and Myth of Frank Lloyd Wright," 27 July 1989, University of Michigan, Ann Arbor, Mich.; and Secrest, *Frank Lloyd Wright*, 119–123.

79. Frank Lloyd Wright and Baker Brownell, *Architecture and Modern Life* (New York: Harper Brothers, 1938), 17. On primitivism as a central theme in Wright's work after 1910, see Alofsin, *Wright: Lost Years*, 101–104, 258–260, 288–290, 304. See also Frances S. Connelly, *The Sleep of Reason: Primitivism in Modern European Art and Aesthetics, 1725–1907* (College Park, Pa.: Pennsylvania State University Press, 1995).

80. Bancroft, *Book of the Fair*, II, 633.

81. Wright, "Philosophy of Fine Art (1900)," in Pfeiffer, ed., *Wright: Collected Writings*, I, 124. In Wright's *Ausgeführte Bauten* (Berlin: Wasmuth, 1911), replicas of the *Winged Victory of Samothrace* appear in interior photographs of his remodeling of Browne's Bookstore in Chicago of 1908 (p. 104) and the Larkin Building's atrium (132). The *Venus de Milo* appears in the Martin house (53), and Michelangelo's *David* is posed in the Dana house (41), where there were other comparable pieces (37, 43). Similar sculptures were posed in the Coonley house (121, 124, 125) and in Wright's own studio and library in Oak Park (99, 106). For the Hillside Home School, Wright had given "several beautiful pieces of statuary for the assembly hall" ("Hillside," *Weekly Home News* [6 November 1902]: 5). Figures 27 and 28 show the *Venus de Milo*, the *Apollo Belvedere*, and Praxiteles's *Hermes* in the room. See Elaine Harrington, "Classical Sculpture in the Work of Frank Lloyd Wright," *Wright Angles* (Newsletter of the Frank Lloyd Wright Home and Studio Foundation) 16 (Fall 1990), n.p.; and Alofsin, *Wright: Lost Years*, 136–137.

82. On recovery of the *Winged Victory of Samothrace*, see Francis Haskell and Nicholas Penny, *Taste and the Antique: The Lure of Classical Sculpture* (New Haven: Yale University Press, 1981), 333–335; and Karl Lehmann, "The Ship Fountain from the *Victory of Samothrace* to the *Galera*," in Phyllis W. and Karl Lehmann, *Samothracian Reflections: Aspects of the Revival of the Antique* (Princeton: Princeton University Press, 1973),

323

**Notes
to Pages
214–215**

180–190. On Wright's use of the Nike figure, see Patrick Pinnell, "Academic Tradition and the Individual Talent," in McCarter, ed., *Wright: A Primer*, 58.

83. Jones repeatedly visited the Palace of Fine Arts in the summer of 1893, interpreting its display of modern painting and sculpture as proof that the fair as a whole had a spiritual significance apart from vast material display. See Graham, "Jenkin Lloyd Jones and the World's Columbian Exposition," 68. Atwood's building was steel and brick inside in order to insure exhibits. Its exterior of staff (a plaster mixed with straw) was like that of other fair buildings. In 1932 the building was rebuilt to become the Museum of Science and Industry. See Bancroft, *Book of the Fair*, II, 664–674; Bessie L. Pierce, *A History of Chicago*, 3 vols. (Chicago: University of Chicago Press, 1957), III, 504; and Condit, *Chicago School*, 96, n. 2; On Wright's design for Milwaukee's Public Library and Museum, see Hitchcock, "Frank Lloyd Wright and the 'Academic Tradition,'" 61; Pinnell, "Academic Tradition and the Individual Talent," in McCarter, ed., *Wright: A Primer*, 35–37; and Secrest, *Frank Lloyd Wright*, 116–118.

84. Jones, "On to Nashville," *Unity* 38 (4 February 1897): 361; Editorial, ibid., 39 (18 March 1897): 35.

85. Editorial, *The New Unity* 39 (18 March 1897): 35. See "Observations by the Way," ibid. (12 August 1897): 503.

86. Jones, "Sokrates: The Prophet of Reason," *Religions of the World*, 7 vols. (Chicago: Unity, 1893), V, 6.

87. Ibid.

88. A. W. Gould, "Liberal Religion at the World's Fair," *Unitarian* 7 (May 1893): 224–225.

89. Wright, "In the Cause of Architecture (1908)," 159. In 1900 Spencer, "Work of Frank Lloyd Wright," 69, had written: "A careful study of his work as represented upon these pages will show that . . . whether the scheme of wall treatment be horizontal or vertical there is almost invariably a base or stylobate of sufficient size to unify his masses and support the spring of the building from the ground with which it seems firmly and broadly associated. This simple matter of the size and scale of this stylobate, even on a small house, as compared to the weak and puny base of the average building, is a very pleasing departure from precedent and gives to these buildings a touch of the quiet dignity of old Greek temples."

90. Clarke, *Ten Great Religions*, II, 270–271. On Hellenism and Hebraism as polarities in Wright's thought, see N. K. Smith, *Frank Lloyd Wright*, 36–44.

91. H. P. Berlage, "Frank Lloyd Wright," in H. T. Wijdeveld, ed., *The Life-Work of the American Architect Frank Lloyd Wright* (1925: reprint, New York: Horizon, 1965), 83–84.

92. Charles E. White Jr. to Walter Willcox, 4 March 1906, in Smith, ed., "Letters, 1903–1906, by Charles E. White, Jr.," 110.

93. Wright wrote of his response to Hugo's "Ceci Tuera Cela" in "Architect, Architecture, and the Client" (1894), "The Art and Craft of the Machine" (1901), and "The Print and the Renaissance" (1917), in Pfeiffer, ed., *Wright: Collected Writings*, I, 28, 60–61, 149–152. See his "Modern Architecture, III: The Passing of the Cornice" (1930), in *The Future of Architecture* (New York: Horizon, 1953), 112; *Autobiography* (1932), 7, 77; and *Testament*, 17. On Wright's reading of Hugo, see Neil Levine, "The Book and the Building," in Robin Middleton, ed., *The Beaux-Arts and Nineteenth Century French Architecture* (Cambridge, Mass.: MIT Press, 1982), 140–141; Sidney K. Robinson, "Frank Lloyd Wright and Victor Hugo," in Wilson and Robinson, eds., *Modern Architecture in America*, 106–111; and Menocal, "Wright as the Anti-Victor Hugo," in Zabel and Munshower, eds., *American Public Architecture*, 138–150.

94. Victor Hugo, *Nôtre-Dame de Paris 1482* (1831; reprint, Paris: Garnier Frères, 1961), 217. Hugo wrote: "que l'architecture a été jusqu'au quinzième siècle le registre principal de l'humanité . . . que le genre humain enfin n'a rien pensé d'important qu'il ne l'ait écrit en pierre."

95. Wright, *Autobiography* (1932), 7, 77.

96. Jones to William C. Gannett, 18 December 1886, 5 (William C. Gannett Papers, Department of Rare Books and Special Collections, University of Rochester Library, Box 9, Folder 2). Jones wrote of his evening classes: "Both the Emerson and Victor Hugo sections are attended regularly, by from seventy to ninety people." Wright, *Autobiography* (1932), 75–77, recalled attending Jones's classes on Hugo's *Les Misérables*, and a costume party based on the novel.

97. Wright, "Passing of the Cornice," in *Future of Architecture*, 122.

98. Ibid.

99. Hugo, *Nôtre-Dame de Paris*, 222, wrote: "Mais l'architecture ne sera plus l'art social, l'art collectif, l'art dominant."

100. Hugo, *Nôtre-Dame de Paris*, 211–212, wrote: "L'idée mère, le verbe, n'était pas seulement au fond de tous ces édifices, mais encore dans la forme. Le temple de Salomon, par exemple, n'était point simplement le reliure du livre saint, il était le livre saint lui-même. . . . Ainsi le verbe était enfermé dans l'édifice, mais son image était sur son enveloppe." On Quatrèmere de Quincy's response to ancient Egyptian architecture, see Sylvia Lavin, *Quatrèmere de Quincy and the Invention of a Modern Language of Architecture* (Cambridge, Mass.: MIT Press, 1992), 2–61. Secrest, *Frank Lloyd Wright*, 55, noted Wright's father's interest in Egypt.

101. "Why W[illiam] C[hanning] G[annett] Gives 'Our Best Words' God-Speed," *Our Best Words* 6 (January 1885): 6–7, quoted in Pease, "Doctrine and Fellowship," 210.

102. Lyttle, *Freedom Moves West*, 189–190. See Gannett, "A Declaration Concerning Unitarian Fellowship and Doctrine," *Unity* 19 (16 April 1887): 94–95.

103. Gannett, "Things Most Commonly Believed To-day among Us," quoted in Lyttle, *Freedom Moves West*, 189.

104. Ibid.

105. Jones, *Chorus of Faith*, 16.

106. Johonnot, "Unity Church, Its History, Faith, and Aims," in "Temple and Faith," *Oak Leaves* (31 October 1908): 8.

107. Johonnot, quoted in "Unity Plans Unique," 5.

108. An account of the inaugural convention of the Architectural League of America appeared in *Inland Architect and News Record* 33 (June 1899): 41–43. See the league's *Architectural Annual* from 1900. See also George R. Dean, "A New Movement in American Architecture," *Brush and Pencil* 5 (March 1900): 254–259. On Louis Sullivan's relation to the league, see Narciso G. Menocal, *Architecture as Nature: The Transcendentalist Idea of Louis Sullivan* (Madison, Wis.: University of Wisconsin Press, 1981), 82–86; and Twombly, *Louis Sullivan*, 354–356, 364–369. See also Wright, "The Architect (1900)," in Pfeiffer, ed., *Wright: Collected Writings*, I, 45–53.

109. Wright, *Testament*, 105. Wright had criticized the league's motto in "In the Cause of Architecture, II," *Architectural Record* 34 (May 1914): 406.

110. Wright, "In the Cause of Architecture (1908)," 158.

111. Wright, *Autobiography* (1932), 163. Wright claimed that Unity Temple had been based on logical and sympathetic arrangement of its functions, in accord with construction: "Organic is this matter of style now. The concrete forms of Unity Temple will take the character of all we have so far done, if all we have so far done is harmonious with the principle we are waking to work" (ibid., 159). On ideas of style in Unity Temple, see also Conclusion, 240–241.

112. Harriet Monroe, "In the Galleries," *Chicago Examiner* (13 April 1907), in Brooks, *Writings on Wright*, 112.

113. Ibid. The "huge, square nameless structure" to which Monroe referred was Wright and Perkins's 1902 design for the Abraham Lincoln Center, visible toward the rear center in Figure 140. In this view, one also sees a small-scale plaster model of one of the cast concrete columns for Unity Temple's exterior.

114. Charles E. White Jr. to Walter Willcox, 4 March 1906, in Smith, ed., "Letters, 1903–1906, by Charles E. White, Jr.," 110, and in Brooks, ed., *Writings on Wright*, 91.

115. Wright to Harriet Monroe, 18 April 1907 (*Poetry* Magazine Papers, Regenstein Library, Department of Special Collections, University of Chicago), published in Connors, *Robie House*, 68.

116. Ibid.

117. Ibid.

118. Ibid., 69.

119. Wright, "In the Cause of Architecture" (1908), 155. For another interpretation of Wright's "cause conservative," see N. K. Smith, *Frank Lloyd Wright*, 7–34.

120. Wagner, "Modern Architecture," trans. N. Clifford Ricker, *Brickbuilder* 10 (June 1901): 121–128; (July 1901): 143–147; (August 1901): 165–171, reprinted as Wagner, *Modern Architecture* (Boston: Rogers and Manson, 1902). Wright's "The Architect" had appeared in *Brickbuilder* 9 (June 1900): 124–128. See also Roula Geraniotas, "The University of Illinois and German Architectural Education," *Journal of Architectural Education* 38 (Summer 1985): 15–21. On Wagner's possible relation to Wright, see Menocal, "Wright and the Question of Style," 7–8; and Alofsin, *Wright: Lost Years*, 58. Barry Byrne, "Wright and His Atelier," 109, stated that when he arrived in Wright's studio in Oak Park in the late spring of 1902, one of Wright's apprentices then there had spent a year under Otto Wagner in Vienna. If so, it is not known to which apprentice Byrne may have been referring (Lisa D. Schrenk to author, 22 January 1993; Schrenk is continuing research on Wright's studio in Oak Park). On Wright's regard for Wagner, see also p. 329, n. 30.

On Unity Temple and the Secession Building, see James Birrell, *Walter Burley Griffin* (Brisbane: University of Queensland Press, 1964), 29; Scully, Introduction, Bolon et al., eds., *Nature of Frank Lloyd Wright*, xix, xx; Menocal, "Frank Lloyd Wright and the Question of Style," 10–12; Gill, *Many Masks*, 178–184; and Alofsin, *Wright: Lost Years*, 58. Wright's familiarity with *The Studio* around 1900 was noted in David Gebhard and Harriette von Breton, *Lloyd Wright, Architect: 20th Century Architecture in an Organic Exhibition* (Santa Barbara: University of California, Santa Barbara, 1971), 15. Images of the Secession Building appeared in Wilhelm Schölermann, "Modern Fine and Applied Art in Vienna," *The Studio* 16 (1899): 30–38; and "Vienna," ibid., 32 (1904): 348–354. After he left Vienna, Olbrich's early work in Germany was featured in W. Fred, "The Work of Prof. J. M. Olbrich at the Darmstadt Artists' Colony," *The Studio* 24 (1901): 91–100. On Wright and Olbrich, see also Alofsin, *Wright: Lost Years*, 35–40, 56–58. Stylistic similarities between Wright's houses and those by Olbrich and other German architects in the Darmstadt Artists' Colony around 1900 were noted in "Work of Frank Lloyd Wright – Its Influence," *Architectural Record* 18 (July 1905): 64.

121. Robert J. Clark, "Stylistic Interplay between Central Europe and America," in *The Shaping of Art and Architecture in Nineteenth-Century America* (New York: Metropolitan Museum of Art, 1972), 72–73, cited the German architect Alois Ludwig's possession of the *Chicago Architectural Club Annual* of 1902, which documented an early exhibition of Wright's work, as an example of Wright's possible influence in Europe before publication of the Wasmuth folio of 1910.

On Wright's response to the German exhibits at the Louisiana Purchase Exhibition, see Alofsin, *Wright: Lost Years*, 12–16. Brooks, *Prairie School*, 91, recorded that Wright's assistant Barry Byrne recalled that Wright was so impressed by the German installation that he gave train fare to Byrne so that he could see it too. Charles E. White to Walter Willcox, 13 May 1904, wrote that Bruno Möhring, the Berlin architect who designed parts of the German exhibit, visited Wright's studio. White to Willcox, 25 May 1904, wrote of the St. Louis Exposition: "Mr. Wright has been down and says we cannot miss going. . . . [Wright] says it is a liberal education" (Smith, ed., "Letters, 1903–1906, by Charles E. White, Jr.," 105, 107). American accounts of the exhibit include Gustav

Stickley, "The German Exhibit at the Louisiana Purchase Exhibition," *Craftsman* 6 (August 1904): 488-506; and Irving K. Pond, "The German Exhibit of Arts and Crafts," *Architectural Record* 17 (February 1905): 118–125.

122. "'L'architettura' riceve F. Ll. Wright," *L'architettura* 2 (1956): 398, cited in Alofsin, *Wright: Lost Years*, 35. Around 1900 Wasmuth published monographs on Alfred Messel, Joseph Hoffmann, Wilhelm Kreis, and others. See *Hundert Jahre Verlag Ernst Wasmuth* (Berlin, 1972), V.

123. Wright, *Testament*, 84.

124. Wright, *Autobiography* (1932), 164.

125. "Studien fur ein Austellungsgebaude der Vereinigung bildener Kunstler Osterreichs," *Der Architekt* 4 (January 1898): 1, Plate 1; and J. M. Olbrich, "Das Haus der Secession," ibid., 5 (January 1899): 5, 8, Plate 1.

126. Olbrich, "Das Haus der Secession," *Ver Sacrum* 1 (1899): 6–7. The pragmatic design of the Secession Building was detailed in Hermann Bahr, *Die Zeit* (15 October 1898): 42, reprint, "Meister Olbrich," in Bahr, *Secession* (Vienna: Weiner Verlag, 1900), 60–65. See also Ian Latham, *Joseph Maria Olbrich* (New York: Rizzoli, 1980), 24–25, 31.

127. "Art in Society," *Oak Leaves* (21 November 1908): 3, 19.

128. Ibid., 3. Following the lecture in Unity Temple, "the audience moved to Unity House, the numerous passageways and doors and interesting turns permitting the many to move without crowding."

129. "Art in Society," *Oak Leaves* (9 October 1909): 20–23. This second exhibit was devoted mainly to work of local artists. By this time the purposes of the Fine Arts Society had broadened to include support of parks and playgrounds, the advocacy of a state art commission for the design of public monuments, care of local trees, and cleaner streets and properties throughout Oak Park. The 1909 opening was thus a major communal event, with a musical performance in Unity Temple by a chorus including Grace Hall Hemingway, mother of Ernest, who worshiped at First Congregational Church. See "Fine Arts Function," ibid. (18 September 1909): 3, 6; and "The Arts Social," ibid. (25 September 1909): 14. On Oak Park in this period, see Kenneth S. Lynn, *Hemingway* (New York: Simon and Schuster, 1987), 15–27.

130. Wiss, Janney, Elstner, *Unity Temple*, 32, note that Unity House's skylights were later raised in an attempt to counter leakage in its roof; hence their current visibility.

131. Berlage, "Neurere Amerikanische Architektur," in *Schweizerische Bauzeitung* 60 (21 September 1912): 165, as translated by Lily Boecher in Don Gifford, ed., *The Literature of Architecture* (New York: E. P. Dutton, 1966), 611.

132. Ibid.

133. Ibid., 614. See Conclusion, 231.

CONCLUSION
UNITY TEMPLE AND LATER MODERN ARCHITECTURE

1. On this church, see Drummond, "The Work of Guenzel and Drummond," *Western Architect* 21 (February 1915): 11–15, Plate 6; Suzanne Ganschinietz, "William Drummond, I: Talent and Sensitivity," *Prairie School Review* 6 (First Quarter 1969): 11–12; Brooks, *Prairie School*, 125–129; and Lane, *Chicago Churches and Synagogues*, 118–119.

2. Charles E. White Jr. to Walter Willcox, 4 March 1906, noted that Drummond had "designed a Congregational Church in Austin, that will be very fine" (Smith, ed., "Letters, 1903–1906, by Charles E. White, Jr.," 110). Drummond established his own practice in 1909, as noted in "Architect Makes Home Here," *Oak Leaves* (18 September 1909): 22.

3. For later ecclesiastical clients, Drummond designed buildings in more literally historical styles. They include his River Forest Methodist Church (1912) and his Maywood Methodist Episcopal Church (1912). See Ganschinietz, "William Drummond II: Partnership and Obscurity," *Prairie School Review* 6 (Second Quarter 1969): 5–19; Brooks, *Prairie School*, 269; and Jeanette S. Fields, *A Guidebook to the Architecture of River Forest*, 2nd ed. (1990), 26.

Among architects of the Prairie School, William Purcell (1880–1964) and George Feick (1881–1945) designed the Stewart Memorial Church in Minneapolis (1907–9), whose interior details and exterior massing were based in part on Unity Temple. Purcell, Feick, and George Elmslie (1871–1952), sometimes a collaborator of Wright, submitted an unbuilt design for St. Paul's Methodist Episcopal Church in Cedar Rapids, Iowa, 1910, in which the auditorium's volume recalls Unity Temple. See *Western Architect* 19 (January 1913): 6, 9; David Gebhard, *Purcell and Elmslie, Architects*, exhibition catalogue (Minneapolis: The Walker Art Center, 1953); Brooks, *Prairie School*, 132–134, 188–190; Richard Guy Wilson and Sidney K. Robinson, *The Prairie School in Iowa* (Ames: Iowa State University Press, 1977), 18–20; and Brian A. Spencer, *The Prairie School Tradition* (New York: Whitney Library of Design, Watson-Guptill Publications, 1979), 122–123, 125.

Louis Sullivan's accepted design of 1910 for St. Paul's Methodist Episcopal Church in Cedar Rapids was greatly altered in construction. Its expression of its auditorium, although different in form, compares conceptually to Unity Temple. See "Unique Church Building," *American Contractor* 32 (4 November 1911): 92–93; "A Sullivan Design That Is Not Sullivan's," *Western Architect* 20 (August 1914): 85, 87; Morrison, *Louis Sullivan*, 213–216; Willard Connely, *Louis Sullivan* (New York: Horizon, 1960), 256–259; Gerald Mansheim, "Louis Sullivan in Iowa," *Palimpsest* 61 (March–April 1980): 56–64; Twombly, *Louis Sullivan*, 412–413; and Berlage, "Neurere Amerikanische Architektur (1912)," in Gifford, ed., *Literature of Architecture*, 609.

Wright included a drawing for a communal church in his noncompetitive plan for a semiurban section near Chicago, of 1913, an unbuilt design for the City Club of Chicago, published in Alfred B. Yoemans, ed., *City Residential Land Development* (Chicago: University of Chicago Press, 1916), 95–102. In its graphic format, the bird's-eye view of this project recalls that of Oak Park of 1873 (see Fig. 49). The view shows a single church building like Unity Temple. Unlike the multiple spired churches for varied denominations in Oak Park, in this envisioned community, Wright wrote that there would be "but one temple for worship" with "sectarian clubrooms opening on courts at the sides and rear and in connection with it." See Twombly, *Frank Lloyd Wright*, 225–227; Cranshawe, "Wright's Progressive Utopia," 5; and Riley, ed., *Frank Lloyd Wright: Architect*, 328.

4. Berlage, "Neurere Amerikanische Architektur (1912)," in Gifford, ed., *Literature of Architecture*, 607. Berlage also maintained that "Frank Lloyd Wright has an 'aversion to tradition, detests all imitation of style, all formality and convention, and traditional attachment to one type or another,' and . . . [has] achieved the image of his own character, the character of his people, his country, of the situations with which he was confronted in his art." Quoted in "Moderne Bouwkunst in Amerika," *Architectura* 20 (1912): 106, and cited in Sjarel Ex and Els Hoek, "Jan Wils," in *De Stijl: The Formative Years, 1917–1922* (Cambridge, Mass.: MIT Press, 1986), 188.

5. Berlage, *L'Art et la Société* (1913–14; Brussels: Editions Tekhné, 1921), following p. 40, wrote that works such as Wright's Larkin Building and Sullivan's National Farmers' Bank in Owatonna, Minn., "remind us that strength is the essential quality of all works of art. This quality, in which the monuments of the nineteenth century were completely lacking, expresses itself not in the absolute size of the edifice, but in the judicious grouping of the masses." Professor Richard Etlin of the University of Maryland kindly alerted me to this work of Berlage, which is discussed in Richard A. Etlin, *Frank Lloyd Wright and Le*

Corbusier: The Romantic Legacy (Manchester and New York: Manchester University Press, 1994), 189–192.

6. Berlage, "Neurere Amerikanische Architektur (1912)," in Gifford, ed., *Literature of Architecture*, 614.

7. Ibid.

8. On Van't Hoff and Ashbee, see Eveline Vermeulen, "Robert van't Hoff," in *De Stijl: Formative Years*, 206–210. On Ashbee and Wright, see Alan Crawford, *C. R. Ashbee: Architect, Designer, and Romantic Socialist* (New Haven: Yale University Press, 1985), 96–98, 151–155; and Alofsin, *Wright: Lost Years*, 23–24, 61–62.

9. C. R. Ashbee, "Man and the Machine: The Soul of Architecture II," *House Beautiful* 28 (July 1910): 56.

10. Ibid.

11. Ibid.

12. On the Henny villa, see Vermeulen, "Robert van't Hoff," in *De Stijl: Formative Years*, 212–214. See also Reyner Banham, *Theory and Design in the First Machine Age*, 2nd ed. (Cambridge, Mass.: MIT Press, 1980), 154. Unity Temple apparently influenced Bernard Bijvouet's and Johannes Duiker's unbuilt competitive project of 1918 for the Dutch Rijksakademie voor Beeldene Kunsten (Royal Academy of Fine Arts), as discussed in Robert Vickery, "The Architecture of Bijvoet and Duiker," *Perspecta* 13/14 (1971): 133–134.

13. Van't Hoff, "Architectuur en haar ontwikkeling," *De stijl* 2 (no. 4, 1919): 40.

14. Wright, *Ausgeführte Bauten und Entwürfe* (1910), description of Plate LXIII.

15. Vermeulen, "Robert van't Hoff," in *De Stijl: Formative Years*, 214, citing Banham, *Theory and Design*, 154.

16. Johannes J. P. Oud, "Architectonische beschouwing, bij bijlage VIII," *De stijl* 1 (no. 4, 1918): 40–41, in Brooks, ed., *Writings on Wright*, 135–136.

17. Auke van der Woud, "Variatas op een thema," in *Americana, Nederlandse achitectuur 1880–1930* (Otterlo: Rijksmuseum Kroeller-Muller, 1975), cited in Ex and Hoek, "Jan Wils," in *De Stijl: Formative Years*, 189.

18. Wils, "De nieuwe bouwkunst. Bij het werk van Frank Lloyd Wright," *Levende kunst* (1918): 113–119. See Ex and Hoek, "Jan Wils," in *De Stijl: Formative Years*, 190–191.

19. Jan Wils, "Frank Lloyd Wright," *Elsevier's Geillustreerd Maandschrift* 61 (1921): 222, in Brooks, ed., *Writings on Wright*, 141. On Wright and Wils, see Bruno Zevi, *Poetica dell'architettura neoplastica* (Turin: Giulio Einaudi, 1974), and Ezio Godoli, *Jan Wils, Frank Lloyd Wright e De Stijl* (Calenzano: Modulo, 1980).

20. Wils, "Frank Lloyd Wright (1921)," 226, in Brooks, ed., *Writings on Wright*, 143–144.

21. Wright, "In the Cause of Architecture (1908)," 164.

22. H. T. Wijdeveld, "Some Flowers for Architect Frank Lloyd Wright," in Wijdeveld, ed., *Life-Work of Frank Lloyd Wright* (1925; reprint, New York: Horizon, 1965), 3.

23. H. P. Berlage, "Frank Lloyd Wright," in Wijdeveld, ed., *Life-Work of Frank Lloyd Wright*, 83.

24. Wright, "In the Cause of Architecture: The Third Dimension (1925)," in Pfeiffer, ed., *Wright: Collected Writings*, I, 210. Olgivanna L. Wright, Introduction, in Wijdeveld, ed., *Life-Work of Frank Lloyd Wright*, noted Wright's attachment to the Wendingen volume. Wright, "The New Imperial Hotel, Tokio, (1923)," in Pfeiffer, ed., *Wright: Collected Writings*, I, 178, similarly advocated this "three-dimension conception of Architecture" as a distinguishing intention of his own work.

25. Wright, "The Third Dimension (1925)," in Pfeiffer, ed., *Wright: Collected Writings*, I, 212.

26. Kakuzo Okakura, *The Book of Tea*, ed. Everett F. Bleiler (1906; reprint, New York: Dover, 1964), 24. On Wright's response to Okakura, see Levine, "Frank Lloyd Wright's Own Houses," in Bolon et al., eds., *Nature of Frank Lloyd Wright*, 64–66; and Nute,

Wright and Japan, 122–127. In the 1938 issue of *Architectural Forum* on his life's work, Wright introduced Unity Temple, the first building featured, by paraphrasing Lao-tse: "The reality of the building is not in the four walls and roof but in the space enclosed by them to be lived in. Earlier than this I had been trying to bring the room through. But in Unity Temple 1904–5 to bring the room through was consciously a main objective" (Wright, *Architectural Forum* 68 [January 1938]: 35).

27. Okakura, *Book of Tea*, 24.

28. Nute, *Wright and Japan*, 124.

29. Bruce Brooks Pfeiffer, *Frank Lloyd Wright: Drawings from 1883–1959*, exhibition catalogue from the Max Protech Gallery (Chicago: The Frank Lloyd Wright Foundation, 1983), 28, notes that Wright probably annotated his drawings in the 1950s. Pfeiffer, *Frank Lloyd Wright Drawings* (New York: Harry N. Abrams, 1990), 89, notes that Wright annotated many drawings during the summer and fall of 1950 in preparation for the retrospective exhibition of his work entitled "Sixty Years of Living Architecture," which toured from 1950 to 1954.

30. Henry-Russell Hitchcock, "Modern Architecture, Part I: The Traditionalists and the New Traditionalists," *Architectural Record* 63 (April 1928): 337–349, and "Modern Architecture, Part II: The New Pioneers," ibid. (May 1928): 453–460. In this period, Wright also responded to the less central historical position assigned to his work in Thomas E. Tallmadge, *The Story of Architecture in America* (New York: W. W. Norton, 1927) and Fiske Kimball, *American Architecture* (Indianapolis and New York: Bobbs-Merrill, 1928). See Wright, "Fiske Kimball's New Book: A Review," *Architectural Record* 64 (August 1928): 172–173, in Pfeiffer, ed., *Wright: Collected Writings*, I, 319–320. On views of Wright's relation to modern architecture in the late 1920s, see Donald L. Johnson, *Frank Lloyd Wright versus America: The 1930's* (Cambridge, Mass.: MIT Press, 1990), 33–35.

In 1929 Wright suggested that his client Alice Millard visit the works of the three leading French modernists of the period: Le Corbusier, Robert Mallet-Stevens, and André Lurçat (Wright to Alice Millard, 10 July 1929, cited in Anthony Alofsin, "Frank Lloyd Wright as a Man of Letters," in Alofsin, ed., *Wright: Index to Taliesin Correspondence*, I, ix–x). Robert Mallet-Stevens contributed one of the essays, "Frank Lloyd Wright et L'Architecture Nouvelle," in Wijdeveld, ed., *Life-Work of Frank Lloyd Wright*, 92–96. Though Wright had not been to Europe since his two journeys of 1909–11, he would have known their buildings as published in modernist journals like *L'Architecture vivante*, where his own work was profiled in 1924, and where Alice Millard's own house, "La Miniatura," had been published in the winter 1927 issue, Plate 31. See Jean Badovici, "Entretiens sur l'architecture vivante: l'art de Frank Lloyd Wright," *L'Architecture vivante* 2 (Winter 1924): 26–27; and "Frank Lloyd Wright," *Cahiers d'Art* 1 (no. 2, 1926): 30–33.

Wright's review of Le Corbusier appeared as "Towards a New Architecture," *World Unity* 2 (September 1928): 393–395, in Pfeiffer, ed., *Wright: Collected Writings*, I, 317–318. In response to Le Corbusier's reminder to architects that "surface and mass" were among the key elements of the art to be freshly studied as a source of its renewal, Wright wrote that these two elements "were the skeleton products of the ideas that built the Larkin Building in 1904, Unity Temple in 1906, and the Coonley House in 1907." Of his relation to European modernists, he maintained: "I respect and admire Otto Wagner, Berlage, Gropius, Olbrich, Oud, Wijdeveld, Dudok, Mendelsohn, Mallet-Stevens, Perret, Le Corbusier, and a score of their peers and compeers – all fine earnest men at work. We are one family in a great cause. I welcome their advent here in this country. . . . But I am not *of* them. Such as I am, I am myself" (Wright, "In the Cause of Architecture: Purely Personal [1928]," in Pfeiffer, ed., *Wright: Collected Writings*, I, 257).

31. Wright, "In the Cause of Architecture: Purely Personal (1928)," in Pfeiffer, ed., *Wright: Collected Writings*, I, 257.

32. Wright, "In the Cause of Architecture, IX: The Terms," *Architectural Record* 64 (December 1928), in Pfeiffer, ed., *Wright: Collected Writings*, I, 315.

33. Donald L. Johnson, *Wright versus America*, 29, 100, 157–161, 170–171. Earlier, in 1930, Wright's work was shown with that of the Bauhaus at the Museum of Modern Art in New York. This was the first time that his architecture had been exhibited with that of European modernists.

34. Wright, "In the Realm of Ideas," *Two Lectures on Architecture* (Chicago: The Art Institute of Chicago, 1931), 25–26, in Pfeiffer, ed., *Wright: Collected Writings*, II, 89. On Wright's adaptation of spatial form as a concept for presentation of his architecture, see Levine, "Frank Lloyd Wright's Own Houses," in Bolon et al., eds., *Nature of Frank Lloyd Wright*, 43–56, 62.

35. Henry Klumb to Donald Hoffmann, 5 September 1980, quoted in Hoffmann, *Frank Lloyd Wright's Robie House* (New York: Dover, 1984), 27, n. 4; and in Johnson, *Wright versus America*, 101.

36. Brooks, "Frank Lloyd Wright and the Wasmuth Drawings," 197, n. 20. On Mendelsohn's visit to Wright, see Arnold Whittick, *Erich Mendelsohn* (New York: F. W. Dodge, 1956), 69–70; Esther McCoy, *Vienna to Los Angeles: Two Journeys* (Santa Monica, Calif.: Arts and Architecture Press, 1979), 48–49; Thomas S. Hines, *Richard Neutra and the Search for a Modern Architecture* (New York: Oxford University Press, 1982), 5; Dione Neutra, *Richard Neutra: Promise and Fulfillment 1919–1932* (Carbondale: Southern Illinois University Press, 1982), 130; and Kathleen A. James, "Erich Mendelsohn: The Berlin Years, 1918–1933," Ph.D. diss., University of Pennsylvania, 1990, 185–187.

37. Henry Klumb, quoted in Edgar Tafel, ed., *About Wright* (New York: John Wiley and Sons, 1993), 102.

38. Hitchcock, "Frank Lloyd Wright," *Modern Architecture: International Exhibition* (New York: Museum of Modern Art, 1932), 29. On Wright's relationship to this exhibition, see Johnson, *Wright versus America*, 101–105; and Terence Riley, *The International Style: Exhibition 15 and the Museum of Modern Art* (New York: Rizzoli, 1992), 41, 48, 61–62, 71–72, 87–88.

39. On Wright's autobiography, see Gill, *Many Masks*, 323–324; Johnson, *Wright versus America*, 28–32; and Secrest, *Frank Lloyd Wright*, 382–385. Pfeiffer, ed., *Wright: Collected Writings*, II, 11, notes that Wright had completed the manuscript by December 1930.

40. Hitchcock and Johnson, *The International Style: Architecture since 1922* (New York: W. W. Norton, 1932), 41.

41. Ibid., 26–27.

42. Wright, "Of Thee I Sing," *Shelter* 2 (April 1932): 11. After the exhibition opened in New York, Wright asked that his work be removed from the show as it traveled around the country. Yet Lewis Mumford persuaded him to reconsider, and Wright agreed to remain part of the exhibition on the condition that its curators publish and distribute his essay "Of Thee I Sing" (Riley, *International Style*, 87–88). Wright gave his views on the International Style in "Opinion in American Architecture I – Architecture of Individualism," *Trend* 2 (March–April 1934): 59, where he acknowledged that a period's architecture "might be referred to as a style. But I still believe that this mass product would only be seen as 'creative' were the effect of a style subordinate and subsequent to the individual perceptions that gave each building composing the whole its own great individuality; good building in itself unconscious of itself as a feature of any style whatsoever. Style should be the architect's aim, not a style."

    Louis Sullivan's view of the World's Columbian Exposition appeared in his *The Autobiography of an Idea* (1924; reprint; New York: Dover, 1956), 317–326.

43. Wright, *Autobiography* (1932), 154.

44. Ibid., 155.

45. Ibid., 159.

46. Wright, "The Architect," *Construction News* 10 (23 June 1900): 540. Wright's view that "every problem carries within itself its own solution" echoed Sullivan, "The Tall Office Building Artistically Considered (1896)," in Twombly, ed., *Sullivan: Public Papers*, 105.

47. Graf, *Kunst des Quadrats*, I, 136, specifically compares Unity Temple's spatial form to both the Early Christian church of San Lorenzo and the Renaissance church of Santa Maria delle Grazie, both in Milan. On expression of interior space in exterior mass, see Arnaldo Bruschi, *Bramante* (London: Thames and Hudson, 1977), 43–57. See also Wolfgang Lotz, "The Rendering of the Interior in Architectural Drawings of the Renaissance (1956)," in *Studies in Italian Renaissance Architecture* (Cambridge, Mass.: MIT Press, 1977), 1–41. On Beaux-Arts architect Ernest Flagg's advice to Wright about exterior expression of interior space, see Chapter 1, 40. Among historic styles, Wright, when young, much admired the Byzantine, wherein exterior expression of interior space is notably characteristic. See Wright, *Testament*, 205.

48. Wright, talk to Taliesin Fellowship, 30 January 1955, in Pfeiffer, ed., *Wright: Living Voice*, 69–70, cited in Cronon, "Inconstant Unity," in Riley, ed., *Frank Lloyd Wright: Architect*, 10. Graf, *Kunst des Quadrats*, I, 124, 132, describes the recurrence and integration of formal motifs at different scales (plan, structure, and ornament) as "the shipwreck of categories" characteristic of Wright's method of design. Elsewhere Graf (p. 175) concludes that, better than all other architects, "Wright always built a world, a comprehensive ordering, whenever he built. Whoever would construct a true interior, must construct a cosmos. . . . That is called architecture."

49. Wright, "The Architect and the Machine (1894)," in Pfeiffer, ed., *Wright: Collected Writings*, I, 23.

50. Ibid.

51. Wright, "Architect, Architecture, and the Client (1896)," in Pfeiffer, ed., *Wright: Collected Writings*, I, 29.

52. Ibid., 29–30.

53. Sullivan had characterized Henry Hobson Richardson's Marshall Field Wholesale Store of 1885–87 in Chicago as an expression of both its patron's and its architect's individuality. See Sullivan, Kindergarten Chat VI: "An Oasis," *Kindergarten Chats and Other Writings*, ed. Isabella Athey (New York: George Wittenborn, 1947), 30. Sullivan's view of individuality of expression may recall the Ecole des Beaux Arts' theory of specific character in architecture, as discussed in Donald D. Egbert, *The Beaux Arts Tradition in French Architecture* (Princeton: Princeton University Press, 1980), 122–124. See also Siry, "Louis Sullivan's Building for John D. Van Allen and Son," *Journal of the Society of Architectural Historians* 49 (March 1990): 88–89.

On Wright's later religious architecture, see Mary Jane Hamilton, *The Meeting House: Heritage and Vision* (Madison: Friends of the Meeting House, 1991); Patricia Talbot Davis, *Together They Built a Mountain* (Lititz, Pa.: Sutter House, 1974); and John Gurda, *New World Odyssey: Annunciation Greek Orthodox Church and Frank Lloyd Wright* (Milwaukee, Wis.: The Milwaukee Hellenic Community, 1986).

54. Eliot, ed., *Heralds of a Liberal Faith*, IV, 142–147. On Kahn's First Unitarian Church and School in Rochester, of 1959–69, see David B. Brownlee and David G. De Long, *Louis I. Kahn: In the Realm of Architecture* (New York: Rizzoli, 1991), 340–345. On this building's relation to Wright's Unity Temple, see Masheck, "Kahn: Anxious Classicist," in *Building-Art*, 132–133.

55. Johonnot, "Office of the Modern Church," reported in *Universalist* 9 (14 May 1892): 5. The following year, Wright's sister, Jennie Lloyd Wright, wrote and read these thoughts for the Young People's Society of Unity Church: "The force of example exercises great influence upon the formation of character. The examples of noble men and women, the representatives of humanity in its best types, give us an ideal toward which we may shape our own characters. . . . In every human being there is some of the nobility found

in the character of a Whittier or an Emerson" (Jenny Lloyd Wright, "Nobility," *Universalist* 10 [18 March 1993]: 3).

56. Wright, "Philosophy of Fine Art," in Pfeiffer, ed., *Wright: Collected Writings*, I, 41–42, associated both the artist's interpretation of a subject and the creation of a language of form with his concept of conventionalization.

57. On Unity Temple's importance for a spatial aesthetic of the modern movement, see Blake, *Master Builders*, 330–332. On the idea of space-time, see Sigfried Giedion, *Space, Time and Architecture*, 5th ed. (Cambridge, Mass.: Harvard University Press, 1982), 430–443. This may be contrasted with Aldo van Eyck's position in his "Place and Occasion," *Progressive Architecture* 43 (September 1962): 154–161. The influence of Wright on van Eyck was discussed by Maristella Casciato, "When Architecture Meets Human Beings: Frank Lloyd Wright's Anthropocentric Model and the Dutch Reception," a paper presented at the symposium, "Frank Lloyd Wright: Beyond Conventional Boundaries," Society of Architectural Historians and The Museum of Modern Art, New York, 27 April 1994.

58. Charles De Kay, "What Do Our Church Buildings Express?" *Review of Reviews* 32 (December 1905): 698.

59. Jenkin Lloyd Jones identified a liberal Unitarian program with the destiny of the United States after the Civil War. Rev. Johonnot believed that Universalist thought had begun its modern phase in America in the 1770s during the War of Independence. In his view, both the sect and the war arose from a time of intellectual ferment centered on democratic ideals. He concluded: "As the Revolution was its political expression, so the Universalist church was in part its religious result" (Johonnot, "The Contribution to Religion and Life Made by the Universalist Church," *Universalist Leader* 9 [6 January 1906] 11).

In his translator's introduction to Viollet-le-Duc's *Discourses on Architecture*, which was perhaps the edition known to Wright, Henry Van Brunt wrote in 1875 that American architects, being free of any one earlier foreign tradition, were the inheritors of architecture's past in its entirety. Hence they "occupy a position of judicious impartiality. All the past is ours. . . . The question is not whether we shall use [it] but how we shall choose . . . and to what extent shall such choice be allowed to influence our modern practice." See *Architecture and Society: Selected Essays of Henry Van Brunt*, ed. William Coles (Cambridge, Mass.: Harvard University Press, 1969), 103, cited in Mary N. Woods, "Henry Van Brunt: 'The Historic Styles, Modern Architecture,'" in Zabel and Munshower, eds., *American Public Architecture*, 82.

On Maybeck's First Church of Christ Scientist, Berkeley, see William Jordy, *American Buildings and Their Architects, IV: Progressive and Academic Ideals at the Turn of the Twentieth Century* (1972; reprint, New York: Oxford University Press, 1986), 275–285, 300–312; Kenneth H. Cardwell, *Bernard Maybeck: Artisan, Architect, Artist* (Santa Barbara, Calif.: Peregrine Smith, 1977), 118–133; and Sally Woodbridge, *Bernard Maybeck: Visionary Architect* (New York: Abbeville, 1992), 88–98.

60. James F. Osborn, preface to Ebenezer Howard, *Garden Cities of To-morrow* (Cambridge, Mass.: MIT Press, 1965), 20. On this issue in Wright studies, see Vincent J. Scully Jr., introduction, in Bolon et al., eds., *Nature of Frank Lloyd Wright*, xiv, xviii.

APPENDIX
CARE AND RESTORATION OF UNITY TEMPLE FROM 1909

1. Chulak, *A People Moving thru Time*, 30–31.
2. The house originally to Unity Temple's east, owned by Luther Conant, stood on the plot adjoining Edwin Gale's frontage of 105 ft. on Lake Street. In 1905, when Gale had sold

100 ft. of this frontage to Unity Church, he proposed to sell the adjacent strip of 5 ft. to Conant, who would promise to keep the space open, thereby helping insure that Unity Church's new building would be spatially separated from adjacent buildings on its east side. See "Unity Church Site," *Oak Leaves* (12 August 1905): 3.

3. Wiss, Janney, Elstner, *Unity Temple*, 44–45, 55–58.

4. "No Heat at Unity Church," *Oak Leaves* (16 January 1909): 21; "Church Closed for Repairs," ibid. (23 January 1909): 24; and "Oak Park," *Universalist Leader* 12 (February 1909): 240.

5. Wiss, Janney, Elstner, *Unity Temple*, 45–47.

6. Wright to William Drummond, 25 November 1938, © Frank Lloyd Wright Foundation 1992, Microfiche Id. No. D032D03. See Wiss, Janney, Elstner, *Unity Temple*, 32, 87–90.

7. "Unity Temple," *Oak Leaves (Forty-Third Anniversary Number)* (23 February 1924): 222.

8. Wright to Drummond, 25 November 1938, © Frank Lloyd Wright Foundation 1992, Microfiche Id. No. D032D03. See Wiss, Janney, Elstner, *Unity Temple*, 74–79.

9. Drummond to Wright, 1 December 1938, © Frank Lloyd Wright Foundation 1992, Microfiche Id. No. D032D08.

10. Wright to Edwin H. Ehrman, 13 December 1938, © Frank Lloyd Wright Foundation 1992, Microfiche Id. No. E022A06.

11. Wright to Drummond, 20 February 1939, © Frank Lloyd Wright Foundation 1992, Microfiche Id. No. D033C07.

12. Chulak, *A People Moving thru Time*, 44–48.

13. Ibid., 48.

14. William T. Herzog, "Unity Church and Frank Lloyd Wright," *The [North Shore] Art League News* 10 (December 1962): 8. See also Storrer, *Wright Companion*, 92.

15. Unity Temple (The Unitarian Universalist Church), Historic American Buildings Survey (1967), No. ILL-1093, 3.

16. Wiss, Janney, Elstner, *Unity Temple*, 66–67.

17. Unity Temple, H.A.B.S. Survey No. ILL-1093, 4.

18. "Restoration of Unity Temple," *Oak Leaves* (8 August 1972): 4, 8; and Randy Cypret, "Unity Temple Restoration Incomplete," *Oak Park World* (3 August 1975): 6.

19. "Unity Temple Restoration," *Prairie School Review* 7 (Third Quarter 1970): 13–17. The article detailing the building's needs was Henry Wright, "Unity Temple Revisited," *Architectural Forum* 130 (June 1969): 28–37.

20. Chulak, *A People Moving thru Time*, 51; and Randy Cypret, "Unity Temple: Struggle to Save a Landmark," *Oak Park World* (23 July 1975).

21. "Restoration with the Wright Touch," *Oak Leaves-Forest Leaves* (8 August 1971): 55.

22. Chulak, *A People Moving thru Time*, 51.

23. Robert A. Bell, "Shotcrete Restoration of a Historic Landmark," *Concrete Construction* 19 (April 1974): 161–163. See also R. W. Steiger, "Unity Temple: The Cube That Made Concrete History," *Concrete Construction* 31 (September 1986): 807–813.

24. Wiss, Janney, Elstner, *Unity Temple*, 68–72.

25. "Unity Temple Is Getting a Face Lift," *Oak Leaves* (17 October 1973); and Wiss, Janney, Elstner, *Unity Temple*, 108–109.

26. Randy Cypret, "Unity Temple Restoration Incomplete," *Oak Park World* (3 August 1975): 6; and Jeanette Fields, "Architectural Angles, *[Oak Park] Wednesday Journal* (6 October 1982): 29.

27. Furhoff, "Site Investigation, Unity House Interior," in Wiss, Janney, Elstner, *Unity Temple*, Appendix.

28. Furhoff, "Site Investigation, Unity Temple Interior," in Wiss, Janney, Elstner, *Unity Temple*, Appendix; Jeannette Fields, "Architectural Angles; Unity Temple Back to the Original Again," *[Oak Park] Wednesday Journal* (19 September 1984): 11–12; M. W. Newman, "Unity Temple Finally Gets Its Wright Colors," *Chicago Sun-Times* (25 September

————. *History of Cook County, Illinois, from the Earliest Period to the Present Time.* Chicago: A. T. Andreas, 1884.

Architectural Institute of Japan. *Frank Lloyd Wright Retrospective.* Tokyo: Mainichi Newspapers, 1991.

Atlas Portland Cement Company. *Concrete Country Residences.* New York, 1906.

The Avery Library: Selected Acquisitions 1960–1980. New York: Avery Library, Columbia University Press, 1980.

Bacon, Mardges. *Ernest Flagg: Beaux-Arts Architect and Urban Reformer.* New York and Cambridge, Mass.: Architectural History Foundation and MIT Press, 1986.

Baird, Charles W. *History of the Huguenot Emigration to America.* 2 vols. 1885. Reprint. Baltimore: Regional, 1966.

Bancroft, Hubert H. *The Book of the Fair: An Historical and Descriptive Presentation of the World's Science, Art, and Industry, as Viewed through the Columbian Exposition at Chicago 1893.* 2 vols. Chicago: Bancroft, 1895.

Banham, Reyner. *A Concrete Atlantis: U.S. Industrial Building and European Modern Architecture.* Cambridge, Mass.: MIT Press, 1986.

Barney, Maginel Wright. *The Valley of the God-Almighty Joneses.* 1965. Reprint. Spring Green, Wis.: Unity Chapel, 1986.

Barrows, John H. *The World's Parliament of Religions.* 3 vols. Chicago: Parliament, 1893.

Berlage, Hendrik P. *L'Art et la societé.* 1913–14. Reprint. Brussels: Tekhné, 1921.

Blake, Peter. *The Master Builders.* New York: W. W. Norton, 1960.

Blotkamp, Carel, et al. *De Stijl: The Formative Years, 1917–1922.* Cambridge, Mass.: MIT Press, 1986.

Bluestone, Daniel M. *Constructing Chicago.* New Haven: Yale University Press, 1991.

Bock, Richard W. *Memoirs of an American Artist: Sculptor Richard W. Bock.* Edited by Dorothai Bock Pierre. Los Angeles: C. C. Publishing, 1989.

Bolon, Carol R., Robert S. Nelson, and Linda Seidel, eds. *The Nature of Frank Lloyd Wright.* Chicago: University of Chicago Press, 1988.

Bolster, Arthur S. *James Freeman Clarke: Disciple to Advancing Truth.* Boston: Beacon, 1964.

Bonney, Charles C. and Paul Carus. *The World's Parliament of Religions.* Chicago: Open Court, 1896.

A Brief History of the Organization, Building and Dedication of the Scoville Institute, Oak Park, Cook County, Illinois. Oak Park, Ill., 1888.

Briggs, Martin S. *Puritan Architecture and Its Future.* London: Lutterworth, 1946.

Broadbent, Geoffrey. *Design in Architecture: Architecture and the Human Sciences.* New York: John Wiley and Sons, 1973.

Brooks, H. Allen. *Frank Lloyd Wright and the Prairie School.* New York: George Braziller, 1984.

————. *The Prairie School: Frank Lloyd Wright and His Midwest Contemporaries.* 1972. Reprint. New York: W. W. Norton, 1976.

————, ed. *Writings on Wright: Selected Comment on Frank Lloyd Wright.* Cambridge, Mass.: MIT Press, 1981.

Bundy, James F. "Fall from Grace: Religion and the Communal Ideal in Two Suburban Villages, 1870–1917." Ph.D. diss., University of Chicago, 1979.

Butler, Jon. *The Huguenots in America.* Cambridge, Mass.: Harvard University Press, 1983.

Cassara, Ernest, ed. *Universalism in America: A Documentary History of a Liberal Faith.* Boston: Beacon, 1971.

Castex, Jean. *Frank Lloyd Wright: Le Printemps de la Prairie House.* Brussels: Pierre Mardaga, 1985.

Chase, Mary Ellen. *A Goodly Fellowship.* New York: Macmillan, 1939.

Chisholm, Lawrence. *Fenollosa: The Far East and American Culture.* New Haven: Yale University Press, 1963.

Chulak, Thomas. *A People Moving thru Time: The History of the Unitarian-Universalist Church in Oak Park*. Oak Park, Ill., 1979.

Clarke, James Freeman. *Self-Culture: Physical, Intellectual, Moral, and Spiritual*. Boston: Houghton Mifflin, 1880.

———. *Ten Great Religions: An Essay in Comparative Theology*. 2 vols. Boston: Houghton Mifflin, 1871, 1883.

Cohen, Stuart E. *Chicago Architects* Chicago: Swallow, 1976.

Condit, Carl W. *American Building: Materials and Techniques from the First Colonial Settlements to the Present*. Chicago: University of Chicago Press, 1968.

———. *The Chicago School of Architecture: Commercial and Public Building in the Chicago Area, 1875–1925*. Chicago: University of Chicago Press, 1964.

Connors, Joseph. *The Robie House of Frank Lloyd Wright*. Chicago: University of Chicago Press, 1984.

Cook, May Estelle. *Little Old Oak Park 1837–1902*. Oak Park, Ill., 1961.

Cooke, George W. *Unitarianism in America*. Boston: American Unitarian Association, 1902.

Crawford, Alan. *C. R. Ashbee: Architect, Designer, and Romantic Socialist*. New Haven: Yale University Press, 1985.

Darling, Sharon S. *Chicago Ceramics and Glass: An Illustrated History from 1871 to 1933*. Chicago: Chicago Historical Society, 1979.

Davies, D. Elwyn. *"They Thought for Themselves": A Brief Look at the Story of Unitarianism and the Liberal Tradition in Wales and beyond Its Borders*. Llyandysul: J. D. Lewis and Sons, 1982.

Davis, Eric E. and Karen Indek. *Dwight Heald Perkins: Social Consciousness and Prairie School Architecture*. Chicago: Gallery 400, The University of Illinois at Chicago, 1989.

Doan, Frank C. *Religion and the Modern Mind*. Boston: Sherman, French, 1909.

Donnelly, Marian C. *The New England Meeting House of the Seventeenth Century*. Middletown, Conn.: Wesleyan University Press, 1968.

Drexler, Arthur C. *The Drawings of Frank Lloyd Wright*. New York: The Museum of Modern Art, 1962.

Drummond, Andrew L. *The Church Architecture of Protestantism*. Edinburgh: T. & T. Clark, 1934.

Eaton, Leonard K. *Two Chicago Architects and Their Clients: Frank Lloyd Wright and Howard Van Doren Shaw*. Cambridge, Mass.: MIT Press, 1969.

Eliade, Mircea. *The Sacred and the Profane: The Nature of Religion* Translated by Willard R. Trask. 1957. Reprint. New York: Harcourt Brace Jovanovich, 1987.

Eliot, Samuel A., ed. *Heralds of a Liberal Faith*. 4 vols. Boston: American Unitarian Association, 1910–52.

Elliott, Cecil D. *Technics and Architecture: The Development of Materials and Systems for Buildings*. Cambridge, Mass.: MIT Press, 1992.

Emerson, Ralph Waldo. *The Complete Works of Ralph Waldo Emerson*. 12 vols. Edited by Edward W. Emerson. Boston: Houghton Mifflin, 1903–4.

———. *Selected Essays*. Edited by Larzer Ziff. New York: Penguin, 1982.

Etlin, Richard A. *Frank Lloyd Wright and Le Corbusier: The Romantic Legacy*. New York: St. Martin's, 1994.

Everett, Charles C. *Theism and the Christian Faith*. Edited by Edward Everett Hale. New York: Macmillan, 1909.

Foote, Henry W. *Annals of King's Chapel from the Puritan Age of New England to the Present Day*. 2 vols. Boston: Little, Brown, 1882, 1886.

Frankl, Paul. *Principles of Architectural History: The Four Phases of Architectural Style*. Translated by James F. O'Gorman. Cambridge, Mass.: MIT Press, 1968.

Fritsch, K. E. O. *Der Kirchenbau des Protestantismus, von der Reformation bis zur Gegenwart*. Edited by the Berlin Society of Architects. Berlin: Ernst Toeche, 1893.

Funk, Rebecca. *A Heritage to Hold in Fee 1817–1917: First Unitarian Church of Baltimore.* Baltimore: Garamond, 1962.

Futagawa, Yukio, ed. *Frank Lloyd Wright in His Renderings 1887–1959.* Tokyo: A.D.A. EDITA, 1984.

———, ed. *Frank Lloyd Wright Monograph 1887–1901.* Tokyo: A.D.A. EDITA, 1987.

———, ed. *Frank Lloyd Wright Monograph 1902–1906.* Tokyo: A.D.A. EDITA, 1987.

———, ed. *Frank Lloyd Wright Monograph 1907–1913.* Tokyo: A.D.A. EDITA, 1987.

———, ed. *Frank Lloyd Wright Monograph 1924–1936.* Tokyo: A.D.A. EDITA, 1990.

———, ed. *Frank Lloyd Wright Monograph 1951–1959.* Tokyo: A.D.A. EDITA, 1988.

——— and Martin Pawley. *Frank Lloyd Wright: Public Buildings.* New York: Simon and Schuster, 1970.

Gannett, William C. *The House Beautiful.* River Forest, Ill.: Auvergne, 1896–97.

Geffen, Elizabeth. *Philadelphia Unitarianism 1796–1861.* Philadelphia: University of Pennsylvania Press, 1961.

Germann, Georg. *Der protestantische Kirchenbau in der Schweiz von der Reformation bis zur Romantik.* Zurich: Orell Fuessli, 1963.

Gill, Brendan. *Many Masks: A Life of Frank Lloyd Wright.* New York: G. P. Putnam's Sons, 1987.

Godoli, Ezio. *Jan Wils, Frank Lloyd Wright e De Stijl.* Calenzano: Modulo, 1980.

Goodrich, Charles A. *Religious Ceremonies and Customs, or the Forms of Worship Practised by the Several Nations of the Known World.* Hartford: Hutchison and Dwier, 1834.

Graf, Otto A. *Die Kunst des Quadrats: Zum Werk von Frank Lloyd Wright.* 2 vols. Vienna: Herman Böhlhaus, 1983.

Graham, Thomas, ed. *Trilogy: Through Their Eyes.* Spring Green, Wis.: Unity Chapel, 1986.

Gregersen, Charles. *Dankmar Adler: His Theatres and Auditoriums.* Athens, Ohio: Swallow and Ohio University Press, 1990.

Gutheim, Frederick, ed. *Frank Lloyd Wright on Architecture: Selected Writings, 1894–1940.* New York: Duell, Sloan and Pearce, 1941.

Hague, Graham and Judy. *The Unitarian Heritage: An Architectural Survey of Chapels and Churches in the Unitarian Tradition in the British Isles.* Sheffield: Unitarian Heritage, 1986.

Hale, Edward E., ed. *James Freeman Clarke: Autobiography, Diary, and Correspondence.* Boston: Houghton Mifflin, 1891.

Hamlin, Talbot. *Forms and Functions of Twentieth-Century Architecture.* 4 vols. New York: Columbia University Press, 1952.

———. *Greek Revival Architecture in America.* 1944. Reprint. New York: Dover, 1964.

Handlin, David. *The American Home: Architecture and Society, 1815–1915.* Boston: Little, Brown, 1979.

Hanks, David A. *The Decorative Designs of Frank Lloyd Wright.* New York: E. P. Dutton, 1979.

Harper, William H. *In the Valley of the Clan: The Story of a School* (1902?).

Harraden, Beatrice. *Ships That Pass in the Night.* New York: G. P. Putnam's Sons, 1894.

Hertz, David M. *Angels of Reality: Emersonian Unfoldings in Wright, Stevens and Ives.* Carbondale: Southern Illinois University Press, 1993.

Hitchcock, Henry-Russell. *In the Nature of Materials: The Buildings of Frank Lloyd Wright, 1887–1941.* New York: Duell, Sloan and Pearce, 1942.

Holmes, William H. *Archaeological Studies among the Ancient Cities of Mexico.* 2 vols. Chicago: Field Columbian Museum, 1895, 1897.

Holt, L. M. *Christian Science Church Architecture.* Los Angeles, 1908.

Houghton, Walter R., ed. *Neely's History of the Parliament of Religions.* Chicago: Alice B. Stockman, 1893.

Hugo, Victor. *Nôtre-Dame de Paris 1482.* 1831. Reprint. Paris: Garnier Frères, 1961.

Humphreys, Emyr. *The Taliesin Tradition: A Quest for Welsh Identity.* Glamorgan, Wales: Poetry Wales Press, 1983.

Hundert Jahre Verlag Ernst Wasmuth. Berlin: Ernst Wasmuth, 1972.

Hutchison, William R. *The Modernist Impulse in American Protestantism.* Cambridge, Mass.: Harvard University Press, 1976.

James, William. *The Varieties of Religious Experience.* 1902. Reprint. Cambridge, Mass.: Harvard University Press, 1985.

Johnson, Donald L. *Frank Lloyd Wright versus America: The 1930's.* Cambridge, Mass.: MIT Press, 1990.

Johonnot, Rodney F. *The New Edifice of Unity Church.* Oak Park, Ill., 1906.

Jones, Anthony. *Welsh Chapels.* Cardiff: National Museum of Wales, 1984.

Jones, Chester Lloyd. *Youngest Son.* Madison, Wis., 1938.

Jones, Jenkin Lloyd. *An Artilleryman's Diary.* Madison, Wis.: Wisconsin History Commission, 1914.

————, ed. *A Chorus of Faith.* Chicago: Unity, 1893.

————. *The Ideal Church.* Chicago: Colgrove, 1882.

————. *Religions of the World.* 7 vols. Chicago: Unity, 1893.

Jones, Reginald P. *Nonconformist Church Architecture.* London: Lindsey, 1914.

Kaufmann, Edgar, Jr. *Nine Commentaries on Frank Lloyd Wright.* New York and Cambridge, Mass.: The Architectural History Foundation and MIT Press, 1989.

Keating, Ann D. *Building Chicago: Suburban Developers and the Creation of a Divided Metropolis.* Columbus: Ohio State University Press, 1988.

Kelly, J. Frederick. *Early Connecticut Meeting Houses.* New York: Columbia University Press, 1948.

Kilde, Jeanne H. "Spiritual Armories: A Social and Architectural History of Neo-Medieval Churches in the United States, 1869–1910." Ph.D. diss., University of Minnesota, 1991.

Knight, Charles. *Old England: A Pictorial Museum of Regal, Ecclesiastical, Baronial, Munici-pal, and Popular Antiquities.* 2 vols. 1845. Reprint. New York: Arno, 1978.

Kring, Walter D. *Henry Whitney Bellows.* Boston: Skinner House, 1979.

Krinsky, Carol H. *Synagogues of Europe: Architecture, History, Meaning.* New York and Cambridge, Mass.: The Architectural History Foundation and MIT Press, 1985.

Kubler, George. *Aesthetic Recognition of Ancient Amerindian Art.* New Haven: Yale University Press, 1991.

Lane, George A. *Chicago Churches and Synagogues.* Chicago: Loyola University Press, 1981.

Larkin, David and Bruce Brooks Pfeiffer, eds. *Frank Lloyd Wright: The Masterworks.* New York: Rizzoli and The Frank Lloyd Wright Foundation, 1993.

Laseau, Paul and James Tice. *Frank Lloyd Wright: Between Principle and Form.* New York: Van Nostrand Reinhold, 1992.

Latham, Ian. *Joseph Maria Olbrich.* New York: Rizzoli, 1980.

Laying the Corner-Stone; Church of the Disciples; October 14, 1904. Boston: George H. Ellis, 1904.

Le Gacy, Arthur E. "Improvers and Preservers: A History of Oak Park, Illinois, 1833–1940." Ph.D. diss., University of Chicago, 1967.

Lewis, John A. *Chapters of Oak Park History.* Oak Park, Ill., 1913.

Lyttle, Charles H. *Freedom Moves West: A History of the Western Unitarian Conference 1852–1952.* Boston: Beacon, 1952.

Manson, Grant C. *Frank Lloyd Wright to 1910.* New York: Van Nostrand Reinhold, 1958.

McAleer, John. *Ralph Waldo Emerson: Days of Encounter.* Boston: Little, Brown, 1984.

McCarter, Robert, ed. *Frank Lloyd Wright: A Primer on Architectural Principles.* New York: Princeton Architectural Press, 1991.

Masheck, Joseph. *Building-Art: Modern Architecture under Cultural Construction.* New York: Cambridge University Press, 1993.

Meehan, Patrick J., ed. *The Master Architect: Conversations with Frank Lloyd Wright.* New York: John Wiley and Sons, 1990.

Meites, Hyman L., ed. *History of the Jews of Chicago.* Chicago: Jewish Historical Society of Illinois, 1924.

Menocal, Narciso G., ed. *Wright Studies, I: Taliesin, 1911–1914.* Carbondale and Edwardsville: Southern Illinois University Press, 1992.

Miller, Russell E. *The Larger Hope.* 2 vols. Boston: Unitarian-Universalist Historical Society, 1979, 1985.

Moelmann, John, ed. *Grace Church, Oak Park, 1879–1939.* Oak Park, Ill., 1939.

Mollmann, Sarah C., ed. *Louis Sullivan in The Art Institute of Chicago: The Illustrated Catalogue of Collections.* New York: Garland, 1989.

Morris, Jan. *The Matter of Wales.* New York: Oxford University Press, 1984.

Morrison, Hugh. *Louis Sullivan, Prophet of Modern Architecture.* 1935. Reprint. New York: W. W. Norton, 1962.

Nazimova, Sarah R. "The Evolution of a Congregation's Identity: Adler and Sullivan's Kehilath Anshe Ma'ariv Synagogue." Honors Thesis, History of Art, Wesleyan University, 1986.

Nishi, Kazuo and Kazuo Huzumi. *What Is Japanese Architecture?* Translated by H. Mack Horton. New York: Kodansha International, 1985.

Nute, Kevin H. *Frank Lloyd Wright and Japan: The Role of Traditional Japanese Art and Architecture in the Work of Frank Lloyd Wright.* New York: Van Nostrand Reinhold, 1993.

Okawa, Naomi. *Edo Architecture: Katsura and Nikko.* New York and Tokyo: John Weatherhill and Heibonsha, 1964.

Perret, Jacques. *Des fortifications et artifices. Architecture et perspective.* Paris, ca. 1601.

Pfeiffer, Bruce Brooks, *Frank Lloyd Wright Drawings.* New York: Harry N. Abrams, 1990.

———. *Frank Lloyd Wright: Drawings from 1893–1959.* Exhibition catalogue for the Max Protech Gallery. Chicago: The Frank Lloyd Wright Foundation, 1983.

———. *Frank Lloyd Wright: His Living Voice.* Fresno: California State University Press at Fresno, 1987.

———, ed. *Letters to Architects: Frank Lloyd Wright.* Fresno: California State University Press at Fresno, 1986.

———, ed. *Letters to Clients: Frank Lloyd Wright.* Fresno: California State University Press at Fresno, 1986.

——— and Gerald Norland, eds. *Frank Lloyd Wright: In the Realm of Ideas.* Carbondale: Southern Illinois University Press, 1988.

Phillips, George S. *Chicago and Her Churches.* Chicago: E. B. Myers and Chandler, 1868.

Pierson, William H., Jr. *American Buildings and Their Architects, I: The Colonial and Neoclassical Styles.* 1970. Reprint. New York: Oxford University Press, 1986.

Platt, Frank J. *Century of Promise: One Hundred Years of Christian Service.* Oak Park, Ill.: First Congregational Church, 1963.

Quinan, Jack. *Frank Lloyd Wright's Larkin Building: Myth and Fact.* New York and Cambridge, Mass.: The Architectural History Foundation and MIT Press, 1987.

Quinlan, Marjorie L. *Rescue of a Landmark: Frank Lloyd Wright's Darwin D. Martin House.* Buffalo: Western New York Wares, 1990.

Ratcliff, Kathryn E. "The Making of a New Middle-Class Culture: Family and Community in a Midwest Suburb, 1890–1920." Ph.D. diss., University of Minnesota, 1991.

Riley, Terence, ed. *Frank Lloyd Wright: Architect.* New York: The Museum of Modern Art, 1994.

———. *The International Style: Exhibition 15 and the Museum of Modern Art.* New York: Rizzoli, 1989.

Robinson, David. *The Unitarians and the Universalists.* Westport, Conn.: Greenwood, 1985.

Roth, Leland. *McKim, Mead & White, Architects.* New York: Harper and Row, 1983.

Rowe, Mortimer. *The Story of Essex Hall*. London: Lindsey, 1959.

Seaburg, Carl. *Dojin Means All People: The Universalist Mission to Japan, 1890–1942*. Boston: Universalist Historical Society, 1978.

Searing, Helen M., ed. *In Search of Modern Architecture: A Tribute to Henry-Russell Hitchcock*. New York and Cambridge, Mass.: The Architectural History Foundation and MIT Press, 1982.

Secrest, Meryle. *Frank Lloyd Wright: A Biography*. New York: Alfred A. Knopf, 1992.

Sekler, Eduard F. *Wren and His Place in European Architecture*. New York: Macmillan, 1956.

Scully, Vincent J., Jr. *Frank Lloyd Wright*. New York: George Braziller, 1960.

Siry, Joseph M. *Carson Pirie Scott: Louis Sullivan and the Chicago Department Store*. Chicago: University of Chicago Press, 1988.

Smith, Norris K. *Frank Lloyd Wright: A Study in Architectural Content*. Englewood Cliffs, N.J.: Prentice-Hall, 1966.

Soper, Alexander C. *The Evolution of Buddhist Architecture in Japan*. 1942. Reprint. New York: Hacker Art Books, 1978.

Spencer, Brian A. *The Prairie School Tradition*. New York: Whitney Library of Design, Watson-Guptill Publications, 1979.

Storrer, William A. *The Architecture of Frank Lloyd Wright*. 2nd ed. Cambridge, Mass.: MIT Press, 1978.

———. *The Frank Lloyd Wright Companion*. Chicago: University of Chicago Press, 1993.

Sweeney, Robert. *Frank Lloyd Wright: An Annotated Bibliography*. Los Angeles: Hennessey and Ingalls, 1978.

Tafel, Edgar. *About Wright*. New York: John Wiley and Sons, 1993.

———. *Apprentice to Genius: Years with Frank Lloyd Wright*. New York: McGraw-Hill, 1979.

Taylor, Frederick W. and Sanford E. Thompson. *A Treatise on Concrete, Plain and Reinforced*. New York: John Wiley and Sons, 1905.

Thomas, Richard H. "Jenkin Lloyd Jones: Lincoln's Soldier of Civic Righteousness." Ph.D. diss., Rutgers University, 1967.

Twombly, Robert C. *Frank Lloyd Wright: His Life and Architecture*. New York: John Wiley and Sons, 1979.

———. *Louis Sullivan: His Life and Work*. New York: Viking Penguin, 1986.

———, ed. *Louis Sullivan: The Public Papers*. Chicago: University of Chicago Press, 1988.

Universal Portland Cement Company. *Representative Cement Houses*. Chicago, 1910.

Vinci, John. *The Trading Room: Louis Sullivan and the Chicago Stock Exchange*. Chicago: The Art Institute of Chicago, 1989.

Warren, Frank D. *A Handbook on Reinforced Concrete for Architects, Engineers, and Contractors*. New York: D. Van Nostrand, 1906.

White, James F. *Protestant Worship and Church Architecture*. New York: Oxford University Press, 1964.

Wijdeveld, H. Th., ed. *The Life-Work of the American Architect Frank Lloyd Wright*. 1925. Reprint. New York: Horizon, 1965.

Wilbur, Earl M. *History of Unitarianism*. 2 vols. Cambridge, Mass.: Harvard University Press, 1945, 1952.

Wilson, Richard Guy and Sidney K. Robinson, eds. *Modern Architecture in America: Visions and Revisions*. Ames: Iowa State University Press, 1991.

Wiss, Janney, Elstner Associates, Inc. *Unity Temple: Historic Structures Report*. Chicago, 1987.

Wright, Conrad. *A Stream of Light: A Short History of American Unitarianism*. Boston: Skinner House, 1975.

Wright, Frank Lloyd. *An Autobiography*. New York: Longmans, Green, 1932.

———. *An Autobiography*. New York: Duell, Sloan and Pearce, 1943.

———. *An Autobiography*. London: Faber and Faber, and Hyperion Press, 1945.

———. *Frank Lloyd Wright: Ausgeführte Bauten*. 1911. Reprint. New York: Dover, 1982.

————. *Ausgeführte Bauten und Entwürfe von Frank Lloyd Wright.* 1910. Reprint. Palos Park, Ill.: Prairie School, 1975.

————. *Frank Lloyd Wright: Collected Writings, I: 1894–1930.* Edited by Bruce Brooks Pfeiffer. New York: Rizzoli, 1992.

————. *Frank Lloyd Wright: Collected Writings, II: 1930–1932.* Edited by Bruce Brooks Pfeiffer. New York: Rizzoli, 1992.

————. *The Future of Architecture.* New York: Horizon, 1953.

————. *Genius and the Mobocracy.* New York: Duell, Sloan and Pearce, 1949.

————. *The Japanese Print: An Interpretation.* Chicago: Ralph Fletcher Seymour, 1910.

————. *A Testament.* New York: Bramhall House, 1957.

Wright, Gwendolyn. *Moralism and the Model Home: Domestic Architecture and Cultural Conflict in Chicago 1873–1913.* Chicago: University of Chicago Press, 1980.

Wright, Jerry D. "Architecture and Liberal Faith: Three Unitarian Efforts to Build for Inclusiveness." Ph.D. diss., Meadville-Lombard Theological School, Chicago, 1988.

Wright, John Lloyd. *My Father Who Is on Earth.* Edited by Narciso Menocal. Carbondale: Southern Illinois University Press, 1994.

Yates, Nigel. *Buildings, Faith, and Worship: The Liturgical Arrangement of Anglican Churches, 1600–1900.* Oxford: Oxford University Press, 1991.

Yoemans, Alfred B., ed. *City Residential Land Development.* Chicago: University of Chicago Press, 1916.

Zabel, Craig and Susan Scott Munshower, eds. *American Public Architecture: European Roots and Native Expressions.* University Park: The Pennsylvania State University Press, 1989.

Zukowsky, John, ed. *Chicago: Birth of a Metropolis 1872–1922.* Munich: Prestel, 1987.

PUBLISHED ARTICLES

Adams, Richard P. "Emerson and the Organic Metaphor." *Publications of the Modern Language Association* 69 (March 1954): 117–138.

Adler, Dankmar. "The Influence of Steel Construction and Plate Glass upon the Development of Modern Style." *Inland Architect and News Record* 28 (November 1896): 34–36.

————. "The Tall Business Building." *Cassirer's Magazine* 12 (November 1897): 193–210.

"All Souls Church." *Chicago Evening Post* (12 September 1892): 5.

Ashbee, Charles R. "Man and the Machine: The Soul of Architecture, II." *House Beautiful* 28 (July 1910): 53–56.

Audsley, George A. "The Organ Architecturally Considered." *Inland Architect and News Record* 51 (February 1908): 3; (March 1908): 22; (April 1908): 31; (May 1908): 44–45; (June 1908): 52; 52 (July 1908): 8; (August 1908): 17.

Baldwin, D. B. "Thoughts in a Buddhist Temple." *Unity* 45 (8 March 1900): 25–26.

Beeby, Thomas. "The Song of Taliesin." *Modulus, The University of Virginia School of Architecture Review.* (1980–81): 2–11.

————. "The Grammar of Ornament / Ornament as Grammar." In *Via III: Ornament,* edited by Stephen Kieran, 11–29. Cambridge, Mass.: MIT Press, 1977.

Beman, Solon S. "The Architecture of the Christian Science Church." *The World To-day* 1 (June 1907): 582–590.

Berlage, Hendrik P. "Neurere Amerikanische Architektur." *Schweizerische Bauzeitung* 60 (14 September 1912): 148–150; (21 September 1912): 165–167, translated in *The Literature of Architecture: The Evolution of Architectural Theory and Practice in Nineteenth-Century America,* edited by Don Gifford, 606–616. New York: E. P. Dutton, 1966.

Bohrer, Florence F. "The Unitarian Hillside Home School." *Wisconsin Magazine of History* 38 (Spring 1955): 151–155.

Booraem, H. Taylor. "Architectural Expression in a New Material." *Architectural Record* 33 (April 1908): 248–268.

Brooks, H. Allen. "Frank Lloyd Wright and the Wasmuth Drawings." *Art Bulletin* 48 (June 1966): 193–202.

Bull, Robert A. "Shotcrete Restoration of a Historic Landmark." *Concrete Construction* 19 (April 1974): 161–163.

Byrne, Barry. "Frank Lloyd Wright and His Atelier." *Journal of the American Institute of Architects* 39 (June 1963): 109–112.

———. Review of *The Architectural Drawings of Frank Lloyd Wright*, by Arthur Drexler. *Society of Architectural Historians Journal* 22 (May 1963): 108–109.

Christiansen, Ellen. "A Vision of Urban Social Reform." *Chicago History* 22 (March 1993): 50–61.

"Church Spires Must Go." *Chicago Tribune* (30 November 1890): 36.

"Churches Built of Concrete Blocks." *Craftsman* 16 (April 1909): 96–99.

"City of Many Churches." *Oak Park-Reporter Argus* (5 May 1906): 8.

Clark, Robert J. "J. M. Olbrich 1867–1908." *Architectural Design* 37 (December 1967): 565–572.

———. "Olbrich and Vienna." *Kunst im Hessen und am Mittelrhein* 7 (1967): 27–51.

———. "Stylistic Interplay between Central Europe and America: Architecture and Painting from 1860 to 1914." In *The Shaping of Art and Architecture in Nineteenth Century America*, 68–81. New York: The Metropolitan Museum of Art, 1972.

Conway, Alan. "Welsh Emigration to the United States." *Perspectives in American History* 7 (1973): 191–226.

Cooke, George W. "The Institutional Church." *New England Magazine* 14 (August 1986): 645–660.

Corse, Murray P. "The Old Ship Meeting-house in Hingham, Mass." *Old Time New England* 21 (July 1930): 19–30.

Cranshawe, Roger. "Frank Lloyd Wright's Progressive Utopia." *Architectural Association Quarterly* 10 (1978): 3–9.

Creese, Walter L. "Wright's Taliesin and Beyond." In *The Crowning of the American Landscape: Eight Great Spaces and Their Buildings*, 241–278. Princeton: Princeton University Press, 1985.

Cronon, William J. "Inconstant Unity: The Passion of Frank Lloyd Wright." In Riley, ed., *Frank Lloyd Wright: Architect*, 8–31.

Davies, Merfyn. "The Embodiment of the Concept of Organic Expression: Frank Lloyd Wright." *Architectural History* 25 (1982): 120–130.

Dean, George R. "A New Movement in American Architecture, II: Glass." *Brush and Pencil* 6 (April 1900): 31–34.

"Death of Charles E. Roberts." *Oak Leaves* (29 March 1934): 10.

De Kay, Charles. "What Do Our Church Buildings Express?" *Review of Reviews* 32 (December 1905): 689–698.

"Design of Protestant Churches." *American Architect and Building News* 53 (26 September 1896): 100–101.

"Dr. Rodney F. Johonnot." *Christian Leader* 35 (16 April 1932): 494–495.

"Drawings and Photographs of Unity Temple." *Perspecta 22: The Yale School of Architecture Journal* (1984): 142–187.

Egbert, Donald D. "The Idea of Organic Expression and American Architecture." In *Evolutionary Thought in America*, edited by Stow Persons, 336–396. New Haven: Yale University Press, 1956.

———. "Religious Expression in American Architecture." In *Religious Perspectives in American Culture*, edited by James W. Smith and A. Leland Jamison, 361–411. Princeton: Princeton University Press, 1961.

Elzner, E. O. "The Artistic Expression of Concrete." *Inland Architect and News Record* 50 (November 1907): 54–56.

———. "The Artistic Treatment of Concrete." *American Contractor* 28 (2 February 1907): 62.

Fenollosa, Ernest. "The Coming Fusion of East and West." *Harper's Monthly* 98 (December 1898): 114–122.

Ferry, A. M. "A Reinforced Concrete Church." *Concrete Engineering* [Cleveland] 2 (1 September 1907): 97–99.

Fitch, C. H. "Interprets Unity." *Oak Leaves* (22 January 1910): 22.

Frampton, Kenneth. "The Text-Tile Tectonic: The Origin and Evolution of Wright's Woven Architecture." In McCarter, ed., *Wright: A Primer*, 124–149.

Gannett, William C. "Christening a Country Church." *Unity* 17 (28 August 1886): 356–357.

———. "A Declaration Concerning Unitarian Fellowship and Doctrine." *Unity* 19 (16 April 1887): 94–95.

———. "Emerson's Vision of Unity." *Unity* 51 (25 June 1903): 262–264.

———. "Richard Lloyd Jones." *Unity* 16 (19 December 1885): 199.

———. "The Things Most Commonly Believed To-day among Us." *Unity* 19 (9 April 1887): 77–79.

Garden, Hugh M. "The Influence of the New Thought in Design on Architecture." *Inland Architect and News Record* 62 (December 1903): 35–36.

Graham, Thomas E. "Jenkin Lloyd Jones and 'The Gospel of the Farm.'" *Wisconsin Magazine of History* 67 (Winter 1983–84): 121–148.

———. "Jenkin Lloyd Jones and the World's Columbian Exposition of 1893." In Association for Liberal Religious Studies, *Collegium Proceedings* I (1979): 75–81.

———. "The Making of a Secretary: Jenkin Lloyd Jones at Thirty-One." *Proceedings of the Unitarian Universalist Historical Society* 19 (1982–83): Part II, 36–55.

Griffith, Ira S. "First Monolithic Church in Illinois." *Cement World* I (15 May 1907): 78–81.

Hallmark, Donald P. "Richard W. Bock, Sculptor, II: The Mature Collaborations." *Prairie School Review* 8 (Second Quarter 1971): 5–29.

Harrington, Elaine. "Classical Sculpture in the Work of Frank Lloyd Wright." *Wright Angles* [Newsletter of the Frank Lloyd Wright Home and Studio Foundation] 16 (Fall 1990).

Hasbrouck, Wilbert R. "The Earliest Work of Frank Lloyd Wright." *Prairie School Review* 7 (Fourth Quarter 1970): 14–16.

Henry, Kirk D. "American Art Industries – III: Stained Glass Work." *Brush and Pencil* 7 (December 1900): 149–162.

Hines, Thomas S., Jr. "Frank Lloyd Wright – The Madison Years: Records versus Recollections." *Wisconsin Magazine of History* 50 (Winter 1967): 109–119.

Hitchcock, Henry-Russell. "Frank Lloyd Wright and the 'Academic Tradition' of the Eighteen Nineties." *Journal of the Warburg and Courtauld Institutes* 7 (1944): 46–63.

———. "Ruskin and American Architecture, or Regeneration Long Delayed." In *Concerning Architecture: Essays on Architectural Writers and Writing Presented to Sir Nikolaus Pevsner*, 166–208. London: Allen Lane, 1968.

Hoffmann, Donald. "Frank Lloyd Wright and Viollet-le-Duc." *Society of Architectural Historians Journal* 28 (October 1969): 173–183.

Ingraham, Elizabeth Wright. "The Chapel in the Valley." *Frank Lloyd Wright Newsletter* 3 (Second Quarter 1980): 1–4.

Jack, Homer A. "Unitarian Universalist Co-operation in Chicago." *Unity* 141 (September–October 1955): 48–49.

James, George W. "Jenkin Lloyd Jones and His Master-Work, the Abraham Lincoln Center." *Arena* 37 (April 1907): 375–386.

Johnson, Donald L. "Notes on Frank Lloyd Wright's Paternal Family." *Frank Lloyd Wright Newsletter* 3 (1980): 5–7.

Johonnot, Rodney F. "The Contribution to Religion and Life Made by the Universalist Church." *Universalist Leader* 9 (6 January 1906): 11–13.

———. Letter, in "It Looks Like a Church." *Universalist Leader* 10 (21 December 1907): 1617.

———. "The Modern Reformation." *Universalist Leader* 12 (19 June 1909): 779–781.

———. "The Movement toward a Universal Religion." In "Universal Faith." *Oak Leaves* (19 October 1907): 15–17.

———. "The Outlook in the Universalist Church." *Unity* 33 (29 March 1894): 55–56.

———. "Rational Enthusiasm." *Universalist Leader* 8 (4 March 1905): 269–270.

———. "Unity Church, Its History, Faith, and Aims." In "Temple and Faith." *Oak Leaves* (31 October 1908): 3, 8–10.

Jones, Jenkin L. "The American Congress of Liberal Religious Societies." *Unity* 33 (21 June 1894): 260–263.

———. "The Call of the Twentieth Century, III: To the Artists." *Unity* 46 (24 January 1901): 326–328.

———. "From Luther to Emerson." *Unity* 64 (7 October 1908): 504–507.

———. "Never a Unitarian, Always a Unitarian." *Unity* 33 (21 June 1894): 258–259.

———. "The New Cathedral: A Study of the Abraham Lincoln Center." *Unity* 48 (6 February 1902): 358–362. Reprint. "The Cathedral, Past and Prospective." *Unity* 52 (17 and 24 December 1903): 259–263.

———. "The New Problems in Church Architecture." *Unity* 15 (20 June 1885): 202–205.

———. "Ralph Waldo Emerson." *Unity* 3 (16 July 1879): 145–149.

———. "The Religion of the Majority." *Unity* 4 (16 October 1879): 244–247.

———. "The Sermon of the Organ." *Unity* 55 (20 July 1905): 342–345.

———. "The Simplicity of the Gospel and the Gospel of Simplicity." *Unity* 50 (25 September 1902): 56–59.

———. "Unity Church-Door Pulpit: The Divine Benediction." *Unity* 18 (16 October 1886): 85–89.

Levine, Neil A. "Frank Lloyd Wright's Diagonal Planning." In Searing, ed., *In Search of Modern Architecture*, 245–277.

———. "Frank Lloyd Wright's Own Houses and His Changing Concept of Representation." In Bolon et al., eds., *Nature of Frank Lloyd Wright*, 20–69.

Lipman, Jonathan. "Consecrated Space: The Public Buildings of Frank Lloyd Wright." In McCarter, ed., *Wright: A Primer*, 193–217.

Lorch, Emil. "Some Considerations upon the Study of Architectural Design." *Inland Architect and News Record* 37 (June 1901): 34.

McCarter, Robert. "Abstract Essence: Drawing Wright from the Obvious." In McCarter, ed., *Wright: A Primer*. 4–17.

———. "The Integrating Ideal: Ordering Principles in the Architecture of Frank Lloyd Wright." In McCarter, ed., *Wright: A Primer*, 238–289.

McCarthy, Michael P. "The New Metropolis: Chicago, the Annexation Movement, and Progressive Reform." In *The Age of Urban Reform: New Perspectives on the Progressive Era*, edited by Michael H. Ebner and Eugene M. Tobin, 43–54. Port Washington, N.Y.: Kennikat, 1977.

MacCormac, Richard. "The Anatomy of Wright's Aesthetic." *Architectural Review* 143 (February 1968): 143–146.

McCormick, Thomas J. "The Early Work of Joseph Lyman Silsbee." In Searing, ed., *In Search of Modern Architecture*, 172–184.

Manson, Grant C. "Frank Lloyd Wright and the Fair of '93." *Art Quarterly* 16 (Summer 1953): 114–123.

———. "Wright in the Nursery: The Influence of Froebel Education on the Work of Frank Lloyd Wright." *Architectural Review* 113 (February 1953): 349–351.

"A Masterpiece in Concrete Work," *Cement World* 2 (15 February 1909): 746–751.

Meech-Pekarik, Julia. "Frank Lloyd Wright and Japanese Prints." *The Metropolitan Museum of Art Bulletin* 40 (Fall 1982): 49–56.

Menocal, Narciso G. "Frank Lloyd Wright and the Question of Style." *Journal of Decorative and Propaganda Arts* 2 (Summer–Fall 1986): 4–19.

———. "Frank Lloyd Wright as the Anti-Victor Hugo." In Zabel and Munshower, eds., *American Public Architecture*, 138–150.

———. "Taliesin, the Gilmore House, and the 'Flower in the Crannied Wall.'" In Menocal, ed., *Wright Studies, I: Taliesin*, 66–97.

"The Modern Church Construction." *Church Economist* 10 (May 1905): 180.

Norton, Margaret W. "Japanese Themes and the Early Work of Frank Lloyd Wright." *Frank Lloyd Wright Newsletter* 4 (Second Quarter 1981): 1–5.

Nute, Kevin H. "Frank Lloyd Wright and the Arts of Japan: A Study in How to Borrow Properly." *Architecture and Urbanism* 233 (February 1990): 26–33.

———. "Frank Lloyd Wright and Japanese Art: Fenollosa, The Missing Link." *Architectural History* 34 (1991): 224–230.

Olbrich, Joseph M. "Das Haus der Secession." *Der Architekt* 5 (January 1899): 5, 8.

———. "Das Haus der Secession." *Ver Sacrum* 1 (1899): 6–7.

"Open 'Unity House.'" *Oak Leaves* (21 September 1907): 16.

"Opening Service in Unity Temple, Oak Park, Il." *Universalist Leader* 11 (7 November 1908): 28–29.

Oud, Johannes J. P. "Architectonische beschouwing, bij bijlage VIII." *De stijl* 1 (no. 4, 1918): 40–41.

———. "The Influence of Frank Lloyd Wright on European Architecture." In Wijdeveld, ed., *Frank Lloyd Wright*, 79–84.

Patton, Normand. "Architectural Design." *Inland Architect and News Record* 17 (March 1891): 19–20; (April 1891): 31–33.

"Paul F. P. Mueller, Contractor for Many Years, Dies." *Chicago Tribune* (12 March 1934): 12.

Peabody, Robert S. "Unitarian Church Building." *American Architect and Building News* 16 (22 November 1884): 248–249.

Pease, William H. "Doctrine and Fellowship: William Channing Gannett and the Unitarian Creedal Issue." *Church History* 25 (1966): 210–238.

Percival, Charles E. "Making the Most of a Narrow Lot: Solving a Difficult Problem." *House Beautiful* 20 (July 1906): 20–21.

Perry, Susan T. "In the Old Meeting House." *Universalist* 11 (25 June 1892): 6.

Pinnell, Patrick. "Academic Tradition and the Individual Talent: Similarity and Difference in the Formation of Frank Lloyd Wright." In McCarter, ed., *Wright: A Primer*, 18–58.

Pond, Allen B. "A Village Church, Cost Fifty Thousand Dollars." *Brickbuilder* 8 (September 1899): 173–176.

Pond, Irving K. "Concrete Architecture." *Inland Architect and News Record* 50 (November 1907): 50–51.

Quinan, John. "Frank Lloyd Wright, Darwin D. Martin and the Creation of the Martin House." Supplement to *Prairie House Journal* (1987): 5–12.

———. "Frank Lloyd Wright's Guggenheim Museum: A Historian's Report." *Society of Architectural Historians Journal* 52 (December 1993): 466–482.

Robinson, Sidney K. "Frank Lloyd Wright and Victor Hugo." In Wilson and Robinson, eds., *Modern Architecture in America*, 106–111.

Rubin, Jeanne S. "The Froebel-Wright Kindergarten Connection: A New Perspective." *Society of Architectural Historians Journal* 48 (March 1989): 24–37.

Short, H. Lismer. "The Evolution of Unitarian Church Buildings." *Transactions of the Unitarian Historical Society* (1949): 146–153.

Siry, Joseph M. "The Abraham Lincoln Center in Chicago." *Society of Architectural Historians Journal* 50 (September 1991): 235–265.

———. "Frank Lloyd Wright's 'The Art and Craft of the Machine': Text and Context." In *The Education of the Architect: Historiography, Urbanism, and the Growth of Architectural Knowledge*, edited by Martha Pollak. Cambridge, Mass.: MIT Press, forthcoming.

———. "Frank Lloyd Wright's Unity Temple and Architecture for Liberal Religion in Chicago, 1885–1909." *Art Bulletin* 73 (June 1991): 257–282.

———. "Louis Sullivan's Building for John D. Van Allen & Son." *Society of Architectural Historians Journal* 49 (March 1990): 67–89.

"Sketch of Dr. Johonnot." *Oak Park Reporter-Argus* (24 February 1906): 3.

"Sky-Pointer vs. Sky-Scraper." *Church Economist* 10 (May 1905): 168–169.

Sloan, M. M. "The Architectural Treatment of Concrete Structures." *Architectural Record* 30

(May 1911): 401–406; (August 1911): 165–174; (November 1911): 487–494; 31 (January 1912): 69–78.

Smith, Kathryn. "Frank Lloyd Wright and the Imperial Hotel: A Postscript." *Art Bulletin* 67 (June 1985): 296–310.

Smith, Nancy K. Morris, ed. "Letters, 1903–1906, by Charles E. White, Jr., from the Studio of Frank Lloyd Wright." *Journal of Architectural Education* 25 (Fall 1971): 104–112.

Sorrell, Susan K. "Silsbee: The Evolution of a Personal Style," and "A Catalog of Work by J. L. Silsbee." *Prairie School Review* 7 (Fourth Quarter 1970): 5–13, 17–21.

Spencer, Robert C., Jr. "Should the Study of Architectural Design and the Historic Styles Follow and Be Based upon a Knowledge of Pure Design?" *Inland Architect and News Record* 37 (June 1901): 34–35.

———. "The Work of Frank Lloyd Wright." *Architectural Review* [Boston] 7 (June 1900): 61–72.

"A Suburban Sanctuary." *Chicago Tribune* (12 August 1872): 6.

Sullivan, Louis. "The Modern Phase of Architecture." *Inland Architect and News Record* 33 (June 1899): 40.

Szuberla, Guy. "Three Chicago Settlements: Their Architectural Form and Social Meaning." *Journal of the Illinois State Historical Society* 52 (May 1977): 116–124.

"Temple or Social Workshop." *Church Economist* 10 (August 1905): 286–287.

Tselos, Dimitri. "Exotic Influences in the Architecture of Frank Lloyd Wright." *Magazine of Art* 47 (April 1953): 160–169, 184.

———. "Frank Lloyd Wright and World Architecture." *Society of Architectural Historians Journal* 28 (March 1969): 58–72.

"Unity Chapel, for the Unitarian Church in Helena Valley, Wisconsin." *Unity* 16 (26 December 1885): 1.

"Unity Church." *Oak Leaves [Fifth Anniversary Number]* (27 April 1907): 100–102.

"Unity Church Fire." *Oak Leaves* (10 June 1905): 12–14.

"Unity Dedicated." *Oak Leaves* (2 October 1909): 3–5.

"Unity Plans Unique: New Church Edifice Will Be Great Departure from Traditional Church Architecture." *Oak Leaves* (24 February 1906): 3, 5–7.

"Unity Temple and Unity House, Oak Park, Ill." *Inland Architect and News Record* 52 (December 1908): 77.

"Universal Exhibits at the Cement Show." *Universal Portland Cement Co. Monthly Bulletin* (no. 80, January 1911): 11–12.

Van't Hoff, Robert. "Architectuur en haar ontwikkeling, bij bijlage VIII." *De stijl* 2 (no. 4, 1919): 40–43.

Van Zanten, David. "The Early Work of Marion Mahony Griffin." *Prairie School Review* 3 (Second Quarter 1966): 6–9.

———. "Jacob Wrey Mould: Echoes of Owen Jones and the High Victorian Gothic Styles in New York, 1853–1865." *Society of Architectural Historians Journal* 28 (March 1969): 41–57.

———. "Schooling the Prairie School: Wright's Early Style as a Communicable System." In Bolon et al., eds., *Nature of Frank Lloyd Wright*, 70–84.

Walker, C. Howard. "The Artistic Expression of Steel and Reinforced Concrete." *Inland Architect and News Record* 50 (November 1907): 56–57; (December 1907): 76–77.

Walker, Evelyn H. "Dedication of the Abraham Lincoln Centre." *Unity* 55 (1 June 1905): 229–230.

———. "Into the Abraham Lincoln Center." *Unity* 55 (27 April 1905): 155–156.

Weingarden Rader, Lauren. "Synagogue Architecture in Illinois." In Spertus Museum of Judaica, *Faith and Form*, 37–81. Chicago: Spertus College Press, 1976.

Weisberg, Gabriel. "Frank Lloyd Wright and Pre-Columbian Art – The Background for His Architecture." *Art Quarterly* 30 (Spring 1967): 40–51.

White, Charles E., Jr. "The Best Way to Use Cement." *House Beautiful* 34 (1913): 130–134.

————. "Insurgent Architecture in the Middle West." *Country Life in America* 22 (1912): 15–18.

Wils, Jan. "Frank Lloyd Wright." *Elsevier's Geiellustreerd Maandschrift* 61 (1921): 217–227.

Wilson, Richard G. "Chicago and the International Arts and Crafts Movements: Progressive and Conservative Tendencies." In Zukowsky, ed., *Birth of a Metropolis*, 208–227.

Woods, Mary N. "Henry Van Brunt: 'The Historic Styles, Modern Architecture.'" In Zabel and Munshower, eds., *American Public Architecture*, 82–113.

"The Work of Frank Lloyd Wright – Its Influence." *Architectural Record* 18 (July 1905): 60–65.

Wright, Frank Lloyd. "The Architect." *Construction News* 10 (16 June 1900): 518–519; (23 June 1900): 538–540.

————. "Architect, Architecture, and the Client (1896)." In Pfeiffer, ed., *Wright: Collected Writings*, I, 27–38.

————. "The Architect and the Machine (1894)." In Pfeiffer, ed., *Wright: Collected Writings*, I, 20–26.

————. "The Art and Craft of the Machine." In *Catalogue of the Fourteenth Annual Exhibition of the Chicago Architectural Club.* Chicago, 1901.

————. "In the Cause of Architecture." *Architectural Record* 23 (March 1908): 155–221.

————. "In the Cause of Architecture, IV: Fabrication and Imagination." *Architectural Record* 62 (October 1927): 318–324.

————. "In the Cause of Architecture, I: The Logic of the Plan." *Architectural Record* 63 (January 1928): 49–57.

————. "In the Cause of Architecture, IV: The Meaning of Materials – Wood." *Architectural Record* 63 (May 1928): 481–488.

————. "In the Cause of Architecture: Purely Personal (1928)." In Pfeiffer, ed., *Wright: Collected Writings*, I, 255–258.

————. "In the Cause of Architecture: Second Paper." *Architectural Record* 34 (May 1914): 405–413.

————. "In the Cause of Architecture: The Third Dimension." In Wijdeveld, ed., *Frank Lloyd Wright*, 48–65.

————. "Concerning Landscape Architecture (1900)." In Pfeiffer, ed., *Wright: Collected Writings*, I, 54–57.

————. "A Fireproof House for $5000." *Ladies Home Journal* 24 (April 1907): 24.

————. "A Home in a Prairie Town." *Ladies Home Journal* 18 (February 1901): 17.

————. "Opinion in American Architecture, I – Architecture of Individualism." *Trend* 2 (March–April 1934): 55–60.

————. "On Ornamentation." *Oak Leaves* (16 January 1909): 20. Reprint.

————. "The Ethics of Ornament." *Prairie School Review* 4 (First Quarter 1967): 16–17.

————. "A Philosophy of Fine Art (1900)." In Pfeiffer, ed., *Wright, Collected Writings*, I, 39–44.

————. "In the Realm of Ideas." In *Two Lectures on Architecture*, 5–31. Chicago: The Art Institute of Chicago, 1931.

————. "Of Thee I Sing." *Shelter* 2 (April 1932): 10–12.

————. "An Unpatriotic Ordinance." *Oak Park Reporter* (23 August 1900): 3.

————. "The 'Village Bank' Series, V." *Brickbuilder* 10 (August 1901): 160–161.

————. "Why Tinker the Shape of the Tree?" *Oak Park Reporter* (23 August 1900): 1.

Wright, Henry. "Unity Temple Revisited." *Architectural Forum* 130 (5 June 1969): 28–37.

Index

Abraham Lincoln Center (Chicago): auditorium of, 36, 40, 47–50, 90, 99–101; brick of, 38, 46; as built, 46–50; concrete for, 111; dedication of, 72; as institutional church, 32, 34, 35–36; and International Council of Religious Liberals, 320–21 n60; Jenkin Lloyd Jones and, 12, 34–37, 39–49, 182–83, 186, 265 nn81 and 83; and Larkin Building, 114–15; and medieval cathedrals, 34–36, 49, 264 n76; model of, 219, 324 n113; naming of, 36, 265 nn81 and 83, 269 n115; and National Unitarian Conference, 76; opening of, 51; organ screen of, 182–83; program for, 32–33, 264–65 n80; project of 1897, 287 n40; project of 1900, 37–40, 96–97; project of 1902, 41–42, 219, 267 n103, 324 n113; project of 1903, 43–46, 99–101, 268–69 n110; pulpit of, 186; rational design of, 131; and religious unity, 39, 200; and Unity Temple, 46–47, 49–50, 67, 99–101, 117, 182–83, 199, 246, 287 n40; and Wainwright Building, 37–40, 268 n110; Wright and Perkins as architects of, 36–37, 41–49, 72, 182–83, 266 nn85 and 86, 267 nn107 and 108, 287 n40

Adams, William (Unity Church trustee), 309 n65

Addams, Jane, 264 n75, 265 n83, 310 n78

Adler, Dankmar (architect), 59; Isaiah Temple, 95; Kehilath Anshe Ma'ariv Synagogue, 290–91 n57; and Paul Mueller, 303 n8; trip to Europe (1888), 290 n57; and unit system, 120–21; and Wright, 120–21, 295 n96

Adler, Rabbi Liebman (father of Dankmar), 290 n57

Adler and Sullivan (architects), 77, 96; Auditorium, 107–08, 303 n8; Chicago Stock Exchange Trading Room, 168; Jewish Training School, 269 n114; Kehilath Anshe Ma'ariv Synagogue, 94–95, 290–91 n57; Meyer Building, 38; Schiller Building, 36; Scoville Building, 274 n35; Sinai Temple, 34, 290 n56; Wainwright Building, 37–40; Wright and, 265 n84, 290 n56, 303 n8

All Souls Church (Chicago): costs of, 257 n17; covenant of, 198–99; dedication of, 15, 80; design of, 13–15; drawings of, 258 n23; enlargement of, 32, 263 n66, 265–66 n85; as institutional church, 32, 257–58 n18; Jenkin Lloyd

349

287 n33, 296 n98, 297–98 n99,
304 n12, 305 n21, 305–06 n23,
306 n26, 309 n64, 324 n111; construction of, 74–75, 128, 137–47,
150, 152–54, 157, 163–65, 171,
227–28, 304 n13, 305–06 n23,
309 n64, 309–10 n65; construction (or building) committee for, 8,
71, 73, 127, 157, 171, 285 n6,
304 n13; contractor for, 138, 163–
64, 303 nn4 and 5; and conventionalization, 134–36, 152, 167,
188, 225; cost of, 74–75, 108–09,
127–28, 130, 138–39, 157, 171,
193, 303 nn4 and 5, 310 n65,
316 nn167 and 168; and De
Rhodes House, 286–87 n33; dedication of (1909), 199, 207, 223;
design of, 80–90, 97–109, 111–
13, 115–30, 134, 172–92, 212,
240–42, 245–46, 287 n39,
298 n106; drawings of, 81–87,
101–05, 115–20, 131–34, 149–
52, 171–79, 209, 237–39,
287 nn39 and 40, 292 n72,
293 n73, 298 n106, 299 n120,
329 n29; egress from, 8, 98–99;
elevations of, 83–84, 117–20,
124–25, 131–32, 287 n40,
315 n154; engineer for, 304 n12;
entrance into, 3, 5–7, 83–85, 98–
99, 102, 208, 223–24, 229,
252 n4; and Essex Chapel, 58–59;
exterior columns of, 41, 195, 105,
106, 118, 121, 142, 150–56, 188,
209, 212, 215, 225, 230, 236,
300 n136, 308 n51, 309 n54,
324 n113; finance committee, 71,
126, 128, 132; and First Congregational Church (Austin, Ill.), 227–
30; and First Congregational
Church (Oak Park), 60–61, 64–65,
71, 204–05, 226, 275 n37; and
First Presbyterian Church (Oak
Park), 71, 204–05; flooring of,
312 n114, 313 n124; flower boxes
of, 3, 143, 148–50, 249, 307–
08 n51; foliage and, 106, 131–32,
135, 149, 162, 188, 237, 242,
301 n153; formwork for, 140–42,
144, 146, 148, 152, 224,
305 nn20 and 21, 305–06 n23;
foundations of, 139, 156, 199,

304–05 n16; foyer, 3, 8–9, 124,
169–71, 312 nn114 and 116,
317 n17; funds for, 59, 69–70,
157, 193, 220, 281 n70, 285 n95,
309–10 n65; and Grace Episcopal
Church, 62–63, 71, 204–05; and
Greek temples, 214–15; heating
and ventilating of, 105, 247; and
Heller House, 87–88; and Hillside
Home School, 32, 88; influence
of, 227–34, 327 n3, 328 n12; interior columns of, 49–50, 105–06,
122, 123, 128, 140, 176, 178–81,
188, 189, 223, 313 nn136 and
137; and Japanese temples, 88–
90, 102, 204, 206; and King's
Chapel, 55–56; lanterns on, 118,
149–50, 309 n53; and Larkin
Building, 113–14, 189–92; lettering on, 3, 118, 198–99, 218, 225–
26, 311–12 n109, 317 nn17 and
18; lighting of, 50, 127, 129, 164,
175, 177, 185–86, 188, 192,
315 n152; and Mayan architecture, 212; and meetinghouses, 8,
75, 92–93, 177, 191, 245,
281 n65; model of, 128–29, 215,
219, 300 n136; naming of, 196,
208, 281 n65; opening of (1908),
171, 192, 198, 222, 317 n16; organ and organ screen of, 8, 52,
138, 176, 182–83, 186, 189, 191,
303 n6, 315 nn143 and 149; as
organic form, 112–13, 115, 121,
242, 324 n111; ornament of, 106,
129, 152, 172–76, 188, 209, 212,
225, 300 n136, 309 n54,
313 n137, 331 n48; and Pettit
Chapel, 85, 87; photographs of,
132; plans of, 3–9, 18, 80–90,
98–103, 108, 111–13, 121–24,
129, 137, 138, 257 n16, 286 n32,
286–87 n33, 291 n59, 300 n138,
303 n6, 326 n128; plans committee for, 71, 73, 80–81, 99, 101,
127–28, 171, 177, 282 n82,
285 n6; plastering and coloring of,
7, 170–71, 179–80, 187–88, 192,
248, 249; program for, 66, 74–75;
pulpit of, 89, 98, 99, 102, 106,
112, 160, 186–87, 199, 202, 229,
242, 300 n138, 315 n154; rationality of, 131, 137, 198; refacing of